The Organization of Firms
in a Global Economy

The Organization of Firms
in a Global Economy

Edited by

Elhanan Helpman
Dalia Marin
Thierry Verdier

Harvard University Press

Cambridge, Massachusetts

London, England

2008

Library of Congress Cataloging-in-Publication Data

The organization of firms in a global economy / edited by Elhanan
Helpman, Dalia Marin, Thierry Verdier.
p.   cm.
Includes bibliographical references and index.
ISBN 978-0-674-03081-7 (cloth : alk. paper)
1. International business enterprises.   2. International trade.
3. Globalization.
I. Helpman, Elhanan.   II. Marin, Dalia.   III. Verdier, Thierry, 1961–
HD2755.5.O745 2008
338.8′8—dc22
2008019196

Contents

Preface

This book was conceived by the Centre for Economic Policy Research (CEPR) in its International Trade program. The editors invited chapters from individual scholars in order to present a canvas of modern research on international trade. Financial support was provided by the Volkswagen Foundation, both for the preparation of the chapters and for a conference in which they were presented, which took place in Munich in February 2007. We are grateful to the CEPR and the Volkswagen Foundation for making this project possible.

We thank Jane Trahan for supervising the production of this book from beginning to end.

The Organization of Firms
in a Global Economy

Introduction

International trade has been an integral part of economics from the beginning. The subject has changed dramatically over the years, however. While the Ricardian doctrine of comparative advantage dominated the field in the nineteenth century and the beginning of the twentieth, the Heckscher-Ohlin approach—which focuses on differences across countries in factor endowments rather than differences in technology—dominated the field in the twentieth century until the late 1970s. The field was transformed in the 1980s with the introduction of what was dubbed the "new" trade theory, which incorporated monopolistic competition and product differentiation, as well as economies of scale and other forms of imperfect competition, into trade theory. These efforts were aimed at developing a theory that would better fit some of the stylized facts that were unveiled at that time. Importantly, the core of the new trade theory was incorporated into a Heckscher-Ohlin framework, producing a rich model in which trade is driven by factor endowments together with product differentiation and monopolistic competition.

Since the development of the new trade theory, scholars have made major advances in understanding trade flows. Most research had concentrated on sectoral trade flows and the factor content of trade. However, in the 1990s, new firm-level datasets became available, which provide a magnified view of trade structure within industries. What emerged from studying these datasets is a new appreciation of the importance of heterogeneity across firms within industries, such as the relationship between firm characteristics and participation in foreign trade and investment. The new trade theory could not explain these patterns. Neither could it explain the growing internationalization of production nor the changing forms of the organization of production and distribution around the globe. It therefore became evident that a new approach was needed. This need triggered an exciting research program that again revolutionized trade theory, better aligning it with the data.

1

The new new trade theory evolved along two distinct lines, which have since been integrated: it can handle differences in productivity across firms within industries and it allows firms to choose their organizational form. In combination, these extensions yield rich models that predict which firms choose to serve only the domestic market, which export, which engage in horizontal foreign direct investment, which integrate, which outsource, and which—within each of these categories—choose to offshore.

The collection of chapters in this volume consists of original studies in the spirit of this new approach to international trade and foreign direct investment. It is highly representative of the modern work in this field.

In Chapter 1, Antràs and Helpman study the impact of contractual frictions on the organization of firms and their sourcing strategies. Novel features of their theoretical model are the varying degrees of contractibility of headquarter services and intermediate inputs and the varying degrees of contractibility across countries. As in their previous work, firms form in North but they can source intermediate inputs in North or South. Final-good producers and their suppliers make relationship-specific investments that are only partially contractible. Firms differ by productivity and therefore have different incentives to choose organizational forms, described by ownership structure and supplier location. The authors analyze the impact of the quality of the contracting institutions on the prevalence of four organizational forms: integration in North, outsourcing in North, FDI in South, and outsourcing in South. Importantly, they find that the impact of an improvement in the contractibility of an input on the choice between integration and outsourcing depends on the input; better contractibility of headquarter services encourages outsourcing, while better contractibility of intermediate inputs encourages integration. As a result, an improvement in South's contracting institutions increases offshoring, but whether the expansion of offshoring is biased toward FDI or toward outsourcing depends on whether the easing of contractual frictions disproportionately affects headquarter services or intermediate inputs.

In Chapter 2, Nunn and Trefler examine empirically some of the implications of the Antràs-Helpman model, as well as the implications of earlier work along similar lines. Using detailed U.S. data on imports from 210 countries, they show that, consistent with the theory, the share of intrafirm trade is higher in sectors with higher headquarter intensity, as measured by either physical or human capital intensity. They also find that a larger dispersion in the productivity of firms leads to higher shares of intrafirm trade, and that this effect is stronger in more headquarter-intensive sectors.

The evidence on these issues is very strong. Nunn and Trefler also find evidence for the impact of contractibility on the share of intrafirm trade. They construct an index of the interaction between the relationship-specificity of industries and the overall contracting environment of the countries from which the United States imports and they estimate its impact on the share of intrafirm trade. According to the theory, this impact should be positive in high headquarter-intensive sectors. Indeed, this is what they find in the data, except that the relevant coefficients are not very precisely estimated. In summary, this chapter provides evidence in support of the new view of the international organization of production.

In Chapter 3, Ottaviano studies a two-country, North-South dynamic model of innovation and growth that combines endogenous quality ladders à la Taylor with hold-up problems à la Grossman and Helpman. In this model there are two activities, innovation and production; and two organizational decisions, the location of activities and an ownership structure. The location decision is driven by comparative advantage and wage differentials between North and South, while the ownership decision trades off diseconomies of scope from vertical integration, and hold-up frictions from outsourcing. These frictions vary across regions due to differences in the quality of enforcement institutions, and they vary across industries as a result of differences in their potential for technological improvements. The quality of enforcement institutions affects the ownership decision and consequently the return to innovation, R&D intensities, and growth. Ottaviano's analysis identifies a general equilibrium channel through which ownership structure affects the pattern of specialization and trade. Indeed, as long as innovation and production take place in different regions, there will be international payments of royalties, and the extent of these payments will depend on the ownership structure. A change in ownership impacts relative wages through these items in the balance of payments and consequently affects the location decision and the pattern of specialization and trade. The model illustrates a new mechanism through which comparative advantages and growth are jointly determined by international differences in contract enforcement institutions.

In Chapter 4, Costantini and Melitz build a model of firm-level adjustment to trade liberalization that jointly addresses firms' decisions to innovate and to enter the export market. The model reconciles conflicting results in the empirical literature concerning the direction of causation between export participation and productivity. They show how the pace and anticipation of trade liberalization can affect the perceived causal link between export status and productivity. Anticipated trade liberalization brings forward the decision to innovate relative to exporting, and a more abrupt pace of liberalization amplifies this effect. The authors build a model that features idiosyncratic firm uncertainty with respect to future productivity, and forward-looking decisions subject to sunk costs. The benefit of an innovation is a one-time jump in productivity, which leads to a sorting of firms into innovators and noninnovators, similar to the sorting of firms into exporters and nonexporters. As a result, exporting and innovation overlap across the productivity distribution with high-productivity firms doing both. The authors analyze the equilibrium transition from a stationary state with high trade costs to an environment with liberalized trade, and they examine scenarios that differ in the extent to which trade liberalization is anticipated and the speed at which trade costs decline. To perform this analysis, they develop a computational algorithm for solving dynamic models of the evolution of industries with a large number of firms.

In Chapter 5, Marin and Verdier develop a theory in which organizational choices determine productivity differences across business firms. Rather than employing the customary assumption of an exogenous distribution of productivity (e.g., in Chapter 1), their model features heterogeneity in productivity arising as a result of the endogenous allocation of power inside the corporation. The allocation of power depends in turn on a firm's organizational choice as well as on the amount of information collected by headquarters and middle managers. The authors show that in an equilibrium in which all firms adopt an organization that assigns "formal" power to the headquarters, there are firms in which middle managers end up having the "real" power. The latter arises when the headquarters are unsuccessful in identifying new projects and they decide, as a result, to follow the suggestions of their informed middle managers. The model has several novel features. First, the intensity of competition depends on whether headquarters or middle managers have power inside the corporation. In particular, competition is less intense when the headquarters delegate power to middle managers. Second, the model delivers new margins of trade adjustment: the monitoring margin and the organizational margin. Depending on which of these margins dominates, trade liberalization may lead to higher or lower productivity. In particular, trade liberalization may induce firms to adopt organizations that encourage the creation of new ideas that are less suitable for price and cost competition.

In Chapter 6, Feenstra and Ma study the impact of trade on entry and product availability in economies with multiproduct firms that vary by productivity level. Unlike most models of monopolistic competition, they assume that firms are "atoms," so that a firm does not face a constant demand elasticity despite the fact that the differentiated product comes in a continuum of varieties, and preferences for these varieties exhibit a constant elasticity of substitution. Because every firm produces a multiple of these varieties, it perceives a varying elasticity of demand. As a result, markups are endogenous and a firm that chooses the range of its brands endogenously trades off marginal profits from a new brand against the cannibalization of profits from inframarginal brands. In the resulting equilibrium, entry drives expected profits down to zero or close to zero. Naturally, after entry, only firms with high enough productivity stay in the industry. Interestingly, this environment exhibits an inverted U-shaped relationship between productivity and the number of brands a firm chooses to produce. The numerical simulations imply that trade does not have a large impact on the number of surviving firms; but it does drive out the least-productive firms, raise the range of brands produced by each of the remaining firms, and raise welfare.

Yeaple uses a simple framework for studying ways in which geographic characteristics and firm heterogeneity impact the assembly and sourcing strategies of multinational corporations. In Chapter 7, he develops a theoretical model that contains three main ingredients. First, there are two regions: a home region in which companies are headquartered, and a foreign region composed of many areas arrayed in a "hub and spokes" configuration. Transport costs exist both interregionally and intraregionally, and these costs are lowest between the "hub" and its "spokes." Second, a final good is assembled from a continuum of intermediate inputs, the production of which entails fixed and variable costs. In addition, there exist plant-specific fixed costs. Third, firms face heterogeneous product demand. These companies choose the locations of assembly lines and of the source for intermediate inputs. This framework provides a rich set of predictions about the location of multinational affiliates based on the geographic characteristics of the various areas, the sourcing of intermediate inputs, and the export of both final goods and intermediate inputs by foreign affiliates. In particular, it emphasizes the role of regional centrality as an important factor in explaining the export patterns of multinationals and their affiliates, both to related and unrelated parties. It provides a flexible and tractable framework for studying sourcing strategies when geographic features are important.

Eaton, Eslava, Kugler, and Tybout develop new, stylized facts about export dynamics. In Chapter 8, they use rich transaction-level customs data from Colombia to study firm-specific export patterns, entry and exit into destination markets, and revenues from sales in these markets. They find that in a typical year, nearly half of Colombia's exporters did not export in the previous year. As a result, export sales are dominated by a small number of very large and stable exporters. Nevertheless, a fraction of the new exporters survive and rapidly expand their foreign sales. Over a period of less than a decade, the successful new exporters account for almost half of the total expansion of exports. Finally, exporters that add or drop markets follow certain geographic patterns. And the likelihood of survival in foreign markets depends on which markets are used as testing grounds for new exporters who wish to learn about their foreign-market potential.

In Chapter 9, Grossman and Helpman study a new reason for foreign sourcing: fair wage considerations. Their model features two types of workers, skilled and unskilled. While skilled workers can perform the tasks of the unskilled, there are tasks that only the skilled can perform. Every worker cares about relative pay in his own workplace. In particular, a worker is unhappy when paid a wage below his firm's average. As a result, firms compete for workers not only in terms of wages but also in terms of the employment mix, with the latter having productivity effects. This leads to equilibria in which otherwise identical firms may have different hiring practices, both in a closed and in an open economy. In this framework, offshoring may take place in situations in which it would not occur in the absence of relative wage concerns. Moreover, if the economic structure is such that offshoring takes place with and without relative wage concerns, the extent of offshoring is larger in the former case. In other words, relative wage concerns lead to more offshoring in order to ease the constraint they impose on the employment mix.

The final chapter, by Antràs, Garicano, and Rossi-Hansberg, discusses international offshoring in a model that focuses on host-country management skills and communication costs. These authors consider a general equilibrium North-South environment in which production requires time and knowledge, and agents with heterogeneous abilities form hierarchical teams. In this setup, low-skilled agents specialize in production while high-skilled agents specialize in management. Offshoring requires intermediate layers of local managers with "middle skills" in South in order to reduce the cost of transmitting knowledge within international teams. As a result, the distribution of skills in the host country plays an important role. Within-country communication costs are also an important determinant of international offshoring, because they affect the capacity of local managers to form local teams and therefore they also affect the opportunity cost of working for an international hierarchy. A major result of the analysis is that middle skills in the host country have a stronger impact on offshoring the worse is the host country's local communication technology. Using FDI inflows as a measure of offshoring and an index of the availability of communication technologies (constructed from data on telephone, computer, and Internet usage), the authors present suggestive cross-country evidence lending support to this prediction.

The themes of these chapters comprise the core of the new view of international trade and foreign direct investment, a view that has emerged over the last decade from studies of highly disaggregated datasets and new conceptualizations of the evolving patterns of international specialization. It is now understood that in the modern era, trade and investment are driven by business firms that differ from each other in technology and organizational form; that their sourcing strategies cross national borders and involve nontraditional forms of foreign direct investment; and that international trade has effected such fundamental changes in corporations as the move to flatter hierarchies, the decentralization of decision making, and the emergence of human capital as a stakeholder in firms. This new understanding has profound implications for the analysis of trade and investment policies and for the relationship between international trade and economic growth. Moreover, it provides a foundation for a better understanding of the relationship between trade, labor markets, and the distribution of income. Many of these issues will be explored in future research.

— 1 —

Contractual Frictions and Global Sourcing

POL ANTRÀS AND ELHANAN HELPMAN

1.1 Introduction

Insights from neoclassical trade theory and new trade theory have improved our understanding of the structure of foreign trade and investment. Recent developments in the world economy have sparked, however, an increased interest in new theoretical approaches designed to better understand the evidence about firms that organize production on a global scale. These developments include the growing role of multinational corporations in the global economy,[1] their engagement in more complex integration strategies,[2] and the growing share of intermediate inputs in trade flows.[3]

Although traditional theories allow for trade in intermediate inputs and for the emergence of international production networks,[4] they cannot explain some newly observed phenomena.[5] First, while the traditional approaches assume that firms are (for the most part) symmetrically structured within industries, the data exhibit substantial within-industry heterogeneity, both in the size distribution of firms and in their participation in foreign trade.[6] Second, in developing global-sourcing strategies, firms decide on where to locate the production of different parts of their value chains and also on the extent of their control over these activities. Which activities should they locate in the home country and which should they offshore? If they choose to offshore, should they engage in foreign direct investment (FDI) and import intermediate inputs within their boundaries or should they outsource the production of intermediates to independent foreign suppliers? As is well known from the work of Coase (1937), Williamson (1975, 1985), and Grossman and Hart (1986), these questions cannot be answered in a complete-contracting framework of the type used in traditional theories of international trade.

9

In Antràs and Helpman (2004) we developed a simple, two-country Ricardian model of international trade in order to address some of these issues. In our model, firms in the north develop differentiated products. Then they decide whether to integrate the production of intermediates or outsource them. In either case, firms have to decide in which country to source these inputs, in the high-cost country "North" or the low-cost country "South." Production entails relationship-specific investments by both the final-good producers (or product developers) and their suppliers, and we assumed that the nature of these investments does not enable the parties to specify them in an enforceable contract. As in the work of Grossman and Hart (1986), we envisioned a world in which incomplete contracting creates inefficiencies even when the production of intermediate inputs is carried out by integrated suppliers. The key difference between integration and outsourcing is that only the former gives the final-good producer property rights over the fruits of the relationship-specific investments.

Our model focused on the choices between integration and outsourcing and between domestic sourcing and foreign sourcing. In particular, we described an equilibrium in which firms with different productivity levels choose among the four feasible organizational modes: domestic outsourcing, domestic integration, foreign outsourcing (and thus imports of intermediate inputs at arm's length), and foreign integration (and thus FDI and intrafirm imports of inputs). We then studied the effects of variations in country and industry characteristics on the relative prevalence of these organizational forms.

In this chapter we generalize the Antràs and Helpman (2004) model to accommodate varying degrees of contractual frictions.[7] In particular, we adopt the formulation of partial contracting from Acemoglu, Antràs, and Helpman (2007). Final-good producers and their suppliers undertake a continuum of relationship-specific activities aimed at producing an intermediate input used in the production of the final good. A fraction of these activities is ex ante contractible while the rest cannot be verified by a court of law and therefore are noncontractible. Both parties are bound to perform their duties in the contractible activities, but they are free to choose how much they invest in the noncontractible activities. Moreover, a party can withhold its noncontractible services at the bargaining stage over the division of surplus if it is not satisfied with the outcome. Every party's expected payoff in the bargaining game determines its willingness to invest in the noncontractible activities. Suppliers of intermediate inputs do not expect to receive the full marginal return from their investment in non-contractible activities, and therefore tend to underinvest in these activities relative to a complete-contracting benchmark. The larger the fraction of noncontractible activities is, the larger the distortions in production are.

We allow the degree of contractibility to vary across inputs and countries.[8] As in Antràs and Helpman (2004), we describe equilibria in which firms with different productivity levels choose different ownership structures and supplier locations. We then study the effects of changes in the quality of contracting institutions on the relative prevalence of these organizational forms.

We begin the analysis with a closed economy in which an organizational choice boils down to outsourcing versus integration. We show that, as in our previous work, the relative importance of the inputs provided by different parties is a crucial determinant of the "make-or-buy" decision.[9] In particular, regardless of the degree of contractibility of the inputs, integration is profit maximizing if and only if the production process is sufficiently intensive in the input provided by the final-good producer. The new, interesting result is that the degree of contractibility of different inputs plays a central role in the integration decision. Improvements in the contractibility of an input provided by the final-good producer encourage outsourcing while improvements in the contractibility of an input provided by a supplier encourage integration. This contrasts with the transaction-costs literature (e.g., Williamson 1975, 1985), where any type of contractual improvement tends to favor outsourcing.

We next extend the analysis to a two-country world in which final-good producers can contract with suppliers in their home country, North, or a foreign country, South. Wages are higher in North, but North has better contracting institutions in the sense that larger fractions of activities are contractible in North. Although final-good producers always locate in North and make their investments there, we allow the contractibility of these investments to be a function of the location of suppliers. This reflects the notion that certain clauses of a contract may be harder to enforce when the contract governs an international transaction or when one of the parties resides in a country with weaker contracting institutions.

Having constructed equilibria in which firms with different productivity levels sort into different organizational forms, we proceed to study the effects of improvements in contractibility on the relative prevalence of these organizational forms. We first derive the result that improvements in contractibility in South raise the share of Northern firms that offshore the production of intermediate inputs. In contrast, improvements in contractibility in North reduce the share of offshoring firms. These results are in line with recent arguments that the quality of contracting institutions impacts comparative advantage (see Helpman [2006] for a summary); the work of Nunn (2007) provides empirical support.[10]

We also show, however, that the effect that changes in contractibility have on the relative prevalence of particular organizational forms depends importantly on the nature of the contractual improvements. In particular, better contracting in South, which raises offshoring, may reduce the relative prevalence of FDI if the institutional improvement disproportionately affects the contractibility of inputs provided by the final-good producer. And better contractibility in South may reduce the share of firms engaged in offshore outsourcing when the contractual improvements are biased toward inputs provided by suppliers rather than the final-good producer. One has to be mindful of the impact that improvements in legal systems have on the contractibility of specific inputs when predicting the prevalence of particular organizational forms.

The rest of the chapter is organized as follows. Section 1.2 develops our model of the firm in the presence of partial contracting. Section 1.3 studies the make-or-buy decision in a closed economy. Section 1.4 extends the analysis to a two-country world. Section 1.5 concludes.

1.2   Technology and Investment

In this section we generalize the model of the firm that we developed in Antràs and Helpman (2004) in order to accommodate varying degrees of contractual frictions. For this purpose, we first focus on a single firm that produces a brand of a differentiated product, for which it faces a demand function

$$q = Ap^{-1/(1-\alpha)}, \quad 0 < \alpha < 1,$$

where q is quantity, p is price, A measures the demand level, and α is a parameter that controls the demand elasticity; the larger α is, the larger the elasticity of demand $1/(1-\alpha)$ is. As is well known, this form of demand results from constant elasticity-of-substitution preferences for brands of a differentiated product. This demand function yields revenue

$$R = A^{1-\alpha}q^{\alpha}. \tag{1.1}$$

Output q is produced with two inputs, headquarter services X_h and an intermediate input X_m, using a Cobb-Douglas production function

$$q = \theta \left(\frac{X_h}{\eta_h} \right)^{\eta_h} \left(\frac{X_m}{\eta_m} \right)^{\eta_m}, \quad 0 < \eta_h < 1, \quad \eta_m = 1 - \eta_h,$$

where θ represents productivity, which may vary across firms, and η_h is a parameter that measures the technology's headquarter intensity. As in Antràs and Helpman (2004), both inputs are brand-specific. That is, X_h and X_m have to be designed to precisely fit the needs of this brand; otherwise the services derived from the inputs equal zero. Moreover, an input designed to fit this brand cannot be usefully employed in the production of other brands of the product.

We follow Acemoglu, Antràs, and Helpman (2007) in assuming that each one of the specialized inputs is produced with a set of activities indexed by points on the interval [0, 1], according to the Cobb-Douglas production function

$$X_j = \exp \left[\int_0^1 \log x_j(i) \, di \right], \quad j = h, m,$$

where $x_j(i)$ is the investment in activity i for input j. Investment in activities is input-specific: they can be used only to produce the input for which they were designed. We assume that activities connected with input j in the range $[0, \mu_j]$, $0 \le \mu_j \le 1$, $j = h, m$, are contractible, in the sense that the characteristics of these activities can be fully specified in advance in an *enforceable* ex ante contract. The remaining activities $(\mu_j, 1]$ are not contractible.

The final-good producer has to supply headquarter services and she has to hire a supplier for the intermediate input. The supplier of X_m can be the firm's employee or an outside agent. At this point we put aside the question of whether the firm integrates the production of the intermediate input or outsources it; we will deal with this question later. For now, note that in either case there is an agency problem, because *by assumption* the firm needs a supplier. The organizational form determines (1) fixed costs, to be specified later; (2) variable costs of investment c_j per unit $x_j(i)$ for $j = h, m$ and $i \in [0, 1]$, where c_h is borne by the final-good producer while c_m is borne by the supplier; (3) the fractions of contractible activities μ_j, $j = h, m$; and (4) the fraction $\beta_h \in (0, 1)$ of the revenue that the final-good producer obtains at the bargaining stage, and the fraction $\beta_m = 1 - \beta_h$ of the revenue that the supplier of X_m obtains. We will discuss the details of alternative organizational forms in due course.

The timing of events is as follows:

1. The final-good producer enters the industry and finds out her productivity level θ.

2. The final-good producer chooses to leave the industry or stay and produce.

3. If she chooses to stay, the final-good producer chooses an organizational form.

4. The final-good producer commits to invest $\{x_{hc}(i)\}_{i=0}^{\mu_h}$ in the contractible activities of headquarter services and she offers potential suppliers a contract, which stipulates the supplier's required investment in the contractible activities of the intermediate input $\{x_{mc}(i)\}_{i=0}^{\mu_m}$ and an upfront payment of τ_m to the supplier, which can be positive or negative.

5. A large pool of potential suppliers can earn income w_m, and they are willing to accept the firm's contract if the payoff from supplying X_m is at least as large as w_m. This payoff consists of the upfront payment τ_m plus the fraction β_m of the revenue that they expect to receive at the bargaining stage, minus the cost of the inputs $\{x_m(i)\}_{i=0}^{1}$. Potential suppliers apply for the firm's contract, and the firm chooses one supplier.

6. The supplier and the final-good producer simultaneously choose their investment levels $x_j(i) = x_{jc}(i)$ in the contractible activities $i \in [0, \mu_j]$, $j = h, m$, as specified in the contract, and both sides choose independently their remaining investment levels $x_j(i)$, $i \in (\mu_j, 1]$, $j = h, m$, in the noncontractible activities.

7. Output

$$q = \theta \left(\frac{\exp\left[\int_0^1 \log x_h(i)\, di\right]}{\eta_h} \right)^{\eta_h} \left(\frac{\exp\left[\int_0^1 \log x_m(i)\, di\right]}{\eta_m} \right)^{\eta_m} \quad (1.2)$$

is sold, and the resulting revenue is distributed between the final-good producer and the supplier in proportions β_h and β_m, respectively. (We will discuss the details of the bargaining later on.)

We seek to characterize a symmetric subgame perfect equilibrium (SSPE) of this 7-stage game.

To characterize an SSPE of this game, first consider stage 6, in which the final-good producer and the supplier each choose their investment levels in the noncontractible activities. Using the revenue function (1.1), the final-good producer's problem is

$$\max_{\{x_h(i)\}_{i=\mu_h}^1} \beta_h A^{1-\alpha} q^\alpha - c_h \int_{\mu_h}^1 x_h(i)\, di,$$

subject to equation (1.2), $x_j(i) = x_{jc}(i)$ for the contractible activities, and given investment levels $x_m(i)$ in the supplier's noncontractible activities. Similarly, the supplier's problem is

$$\max_{\{x_m(i)\}_{i=\mu_m}^1} \beta_m A^{1-\alpha} q^\alpha - c_m \int_{\mu_m}^1 x_m(i)\, di,$$

subject to equation (1.2), $x_j(i) = x_{jc}(i)$ for the contractible activities, and given investment levels $x_h(i)$ in the firm's noncontractible activities. The Nash equilibrium of this noncooperative game yields

$$x_j(i) = x_{jn} \equiv \left(\frac{\beta_j \eta_j}{c_j}\right) \alpha R, \quad \text{for } i \in (\mu_j, 1], \; j = h, m, \quad (1.3)$$

for the noncontractible activities. It follows that the investment in noncontractible activities is

$$x_j(i)^{1-\alpha\omega} = \alpha \theta^\alpha A^{1-\alpha} \eta_h^{-\alpha\eta_h} \eta_m^{-\alpha\eta_m} \left[\exp \sum_{\ell=h,m} \alpha\eta_\ell \int_0^{\mu_\ell} \log x_\ell(i)\, di\right]$$

$$\times \left(\frac{\beta_j \eta_j}{c_j}\right)^{1-\alpha\omega_k} \left(\frac{\beta_k \eta_k}{c_k}\right)^{\alpha\omega_k}, \quad \text{for } i \in (\mu_j, 1], \; j, k = h, m, \; k \neq j,$$

$$(1.4)$$

where $\omega_\ell = \eta_\ell(1-\mu_\ell)$ for $\ell = h, m$, and $\omega = \sum_{\ell=h,m} \omega_\ell$. Note that ω_h measures the importance of the noncontractible activities of headquarter services in the production of the final good; it represents the elasticity of output with respect to x_{hn}. Similarly, ω_m measures the importance of the noncontractible activities of the intermediate input in the production of the final good; it represents the elasticity of output with respect to x_{mn}. These measures of the impact of the noncontractible activities on the production of the final good play an important role in our applications of the model. From the definition of ω_ℓ, the noncontractible activities of input ℓ are more important the larger the weight η_ℓ of input ℓ is in the production function and the smaller the fraction of contractible activities μ_ℓ is. That is, ω_ℓ results from an interaction of technological features with contracting frictions.

For stage 5 of the game to generate a non-empty set of applicants for the supply of X_m, the final-good producer needs to offer a contract that satisfies the suppliers' participation constraint, which is

$$\beta_m R - c_m \int_0^1 x_m(i) \, di + \tau_m \geq w_m, \tag{1.5}$$

where the left-hand side represents a supplier's payoff from forming a relationship with the final-good producer and the right-hand side represents his outside option before he forms this relationship. In this participation constraint, the investment levels in the noncontractible activities satisfy equation (1.4); the investment levels in the contractible activities are $x_{jc}(i)$ for $i \in [0, \mu_j]$, $j = h, m$, as specified in the contract; and revenue R and output q are given by (1.1) and (1.2), respectively.

In stage 3, the final-good producer chooses the contract to maximize her payoff

$$\beta_h R - c_h \int_0^1 x_h(i) \, di - \tau_m,$$

subject to (1.1), (1.2), the participation constraint (1.5), and the incentive compatibility constraints (1.4). As long as there are no constraints on the upfront payment τ_m, the participation constraint is satisfied with equality at the solution to this problem. Therefore we can solve the upfront payment τ_m from the participation constraint treated as an equality and substitute the result into the final-good producer's objective function. Under these circumstances the final-good producer's choice of contractible investments is the solution to

$$\max_{\{x_h(i)\}_{i=0}^1, \{x_m(i)\}_{i=0}^1} \pi \equiv R - c_h \int_0^1 x_h(i) \, di - c_m \int_0^1 x_m(i) \, di - w_m,$$

subject to the incentive compatibility constraints (1.4) and the revenue and output equations (1.1) and (1.2). The solutions of $x_j(i)$ for $i \in [0, \mu_j]$, $j = h, m$, yield the contractible investment levels $x_{jc}(i)$ for $i \in [0, \mu_j]$,

$j = h, m$. Using the first-order conditions of the maximization problem together with (1.3) they can be expressed as

$$x_j(i) = x_{jc} \equiv \frac{1 - \alpha \sum_{\ell=h,m} \beta_\ell \omega_\ell}{1 - \alpha \omega} \left(\frac{\eta_j}{c_j}\right) \alpha R,$$

$$\text{for } i \in [0, \mu_j], \quad j = h, m. \tag{1.6}$$

Comparing this equation with (1.3) we obtain the following lemma.[11]

Lemma 1.1 *For every input $j = h, m$, investment in contractible activities is larger than investment in noncontractible activities, that is, $x_{jc} > x_{jn}$, for $j = h, m$.*

Evidently, when investment in contractible activities exceeds investment in noncontractible activities, the investment levels do not maximize overall profits, because the two types of investment are equally costly. Moreover, the relative investment levels in the contractible activities, $x_{hc}/x_{mc} = (\eta_h/c_h) / (\eta_m/c_m)$, are profit maximizing, while the relative investment levels in the noncontractible activities, $x_{hn}/x_{mn} = (\beta_h/\beta_m)(\eta_h/c_h) / (\eta_m/c_m)$, are not. The latter results from the fact that each party's return on its investment in noncontractible activities depends on its bargaining share β_j, and these shares are not necessarily equal. If they are equal, there is no distortion in the relative investment in noncontractible activities. Finally, note that the optimal investment levels for a profit-maximizing firm are $x_j(i) = (\eta_j/c_j) \alpha R$ for $j = h, m$. Therefore, in the equilibrium, the noncontractible activities are underinvested and the contractible activities are overinvested relative to the revenue level R.

This characterization of the contractible investment levels yields

$$x_{jc} = K_c \left(\frac{\eta_j}{c_j}\right)^{1 + \frac{\alpha \mu_j \eta_j}{1-\alpha}} \left(\frac{\eta_k}{c_k}\right)^{\frac{\alpha \mu_k \eta_k}{1-\alpha}}, \quad \text{for } j, k = h, m \text{ and } k \neq j, \tag{1.7}$$

where

$$K_c = \left(\frac{1 - \alpha \sum_{\ell=h,m} \beta_\ell \omega_\ell}{1 - \alpha \omega}\right)^{\frac{1-\alpha\omega}{1-\alpha}}$$

$$\left[\alpha \theta^\alpha A^{1-\alpha} \eta_h^{-\alpha\eta_h} \eta_m^{-\alpha\eta_m} \left(\frac{\beta_m \eta_m}{c_m}\right)^{\alpha\omega_m} \left(\frac{\beta_h \eta_h}{c_h}\right)^{\alpha\omega_h}\right]^{\frac{1}{1-\alpha}}.$$

This implies that the final-good producer's profits are

$$\pi = Z\Theta - w_m, \tag{1.8}$$

where $\Theta = \theta^{\alpha/(1-\alpha)}$ is an alternative measure of productivity, and

$$Z = (1-\alpha)\,A\left[\alpha^\alpha c_h^{-\alpha\eta_h} c_m^{-\alpha\eta_m} \frac{\beta_m^{\alpha\omega_m}\beta_h^{\alpha\omega_h}\left(1-\alpha\sum_{\ell=h,m}\beta_\ell\omega_\ell\right)^{1-\alpha\omega}}{(1-\alpha\omega)^{1-\alpha\omega}}\right]^{\frac{1}{1-\alpha}} \tag{1.9}$$

is a derived parameter, which is proportional to the demand level; it depends on the costs of inputs, on the bargaining shares, and on the importance of contractual frictions for headquarter services and intermediate inputs. As expected, the profits of the final-good producer are higher the higher the demand level A is, the lower the costs of inputs c_h and c_m are, and the less attractive the suppliers' outside option w_m is. In addition, her profits are lower the larger ω_h or ω_m is, which implies that her profits are higher the larger the fraction of contractible activities in headquarter services and/or in intermediate inputs is. These results are summarized in the following proposition.[12]

Proposition 1.1   *The profits of the final-good producer are decreasing in input costs c_j, $j = h, m$, declining in the outside option of suppliers, w_m, and increasing in the shares of contractible activities μ_j, $j = h, m$.*

Bearing in mind that $\beta_m = 1 - \beta_h$, note that profits are not monotonic in β_h; rather they are smallest when the revenue share of the final-good producer equals zero or one, and profits are higher for intermediate values. So consider the shares β_h and β_m that maximize profits. To find them, we maximize

$$\beta_m^{\alpha\omega_m}\beta_h^{\alpha\omega_h}\left(1-\alpha\sum_{\ell=h,m}\beta_\ell\omega_\ell\right)^{1-\alpha\omega},$$

subject to the constraint $\beta_h = 1 - \beta_m$, and $\beta_h \in (0, 1)$. The solution to this problem is unique; it is given by

$$\beta_j^* = \frac{\omega_j \left(1 - \alpha \omega_k\right) - \sqrt{\omega_h \omega_m \left(1 - \alpha \omega_h\right) \left(1 - \alpha \omega_m\right)}}{\omega_j - \omega_k}$$

$$\text{for } j, k = h, m, \quad k \neq j, \tag{1.10}$$

and it implies that $\left(\beta_h^* - \beta_m^*\right)\left(\omega_h - \omega_m\right) \geq 0$, with strict inequality holding when $\omega_h \neq \omega_m$. That is, the final-good producer wants to give the supplier less than half the revenue if and only if the noncontractible activities in m are less important than the noncontractible activities in h. Moreover, β_j^* is increasing in ω_j and declining in ω_k, $k \neq j$, and $\beta_h^* = \beta_m^* = 1/2$ for $\omega_h = \omega_m$. In other words, the final-good producer wants to give the supplier lower shares of the revenue the less important noncontractible activities in m are and the more important noncontractible activities in h are. Since $\omega_j = \left(1 - \mu_j\right)\eta_j$, it also implies that the final-good producer's optimal β_h^* is increasing in η_h, declining in μ_h, and increasing in μ_m. Finally, profits are rising with β_j for $0 < \beta_j < \beta_j^*$ and declining with β_j for $\beta_j^* < \beta_j < 1$. These results are summarized in the following proposition.

Proposition 1.2 *The optimal shares β_h^* and β_m^* have the following properties:*

1. *$\left(\beta_h^* - \beta_m^*\right)\left(\omega_h - \omega_m\right) \geq 0$, with strict inequality for $\omega_h \neq \omega_m$, and $\beta_h^* = \beta_m^* = 1/2$ for $\omega_h = \omega_m$.*
2. *β_h^* is increasing in η_h, declining in μ_h, and increasing in μ_m.*
3. *Profits are rising with β_j for $0 < \beta_j < \beta_j^*$ and declining with β_j for $\beta_j^* < \beta_j < 1$, $j = h, m$.*

We will use these results in the following analysis.

1.3   The Make-or-Buy Decision

We now consider the trade-off between integration and outsourcing, that is, whether to make the intermediate input in-house or to outsource it to an outside supplier. In this section, we focus on the case in which both choices are made in the same country, say, the home country of the final-good producer. In this event, input costs do not depend on the organizational form, nor do the degrees of contractual friction.[13] Moreover, the outside option of suppliers, w_m, does not depend on the make-or-buy decision.

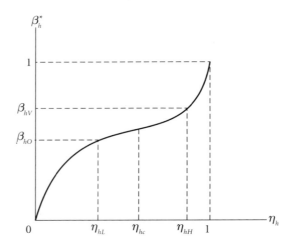

Figure 1.1 Bargaining shares and headquarter intensity.

Under the circumstances, we can focus on differences in the revenue shares β_j. In view of part (3) of proposition 1.2, the final-good producer prefers organizational forms with β_h closer to β_h^*.

Figure 1.1 depicts β_h^* as a function of η_h. In view of part (2) of proposition 1.2, this is an increasing function, and it is easy to verify that β_h^* approaches 0 when $\eta_h \to 0$, and β_h^* approaches 1 when $\eta_h \to 1$, as shown in the figure.

Now consider what determines the share β_h under outsourcing and integration. In stage 7 of the game, the investment levels $x_h(i)$ and $x_m(i)$ are predetermined and therefore so are the input levels X_h and X_m of headquarter services and components. At this stage, the supplier and the final-good producer bargain over the distribution of revenue R that they will receive when the final goods are sold in the market. Under outsourcing, X_m belongs to the supplier, while X_h belongs to the final-good producer. If the bargaining fails, output q equals zero and so does revenue. Moreover, given the high specificity of these inputs, which have no value outside the relationship, the outside option of every player equals zero. We assume that the parties engage in generalized Nash bargaining with a bargaining weight $\beta \in (0, 1)$ for the final-good producer and $1 - \beta \in (0, 1)$ for the supplier. Therefore the solution to the bargaining game, which gives every player his or her outside option plus the bargaining weight times the ex post gains from the relationship, delivers the final-good producer the payoff $0 + \beta (R - 0 - 0) = \beta R$. Namely, it gives her the fraction β of the revenue. By similar reasoning, the supplier gets $(1 - \beta) R$. It follows from this analysis that under outsourcing, the final-good producer gets the fraction

$$\beta_{hO} = \beta$$

of the revenue, while the supplier gets the fraction $\beta_{mO} = 1 - \beta$.

Next consider integration. Under this arrangement, the supplier is the final-good producer's employee, and therefore the supplier does not own the intermediate input. As a result, the outside option of the supplier equals zero. Following Grossman and Hart (1986), we assume that in the absence of the supplier's cooperation, the final-good producer, who owns both X_h and X_m, cannot produce as efficiently with these inputs on her own as she can with the cooperation of the supplier. In particular, we assume that the final-good producer can produce on her own only a fraction $\delta \in (0, 1)$ of the output that she can produce with the cooperation of the supplier, that is, δq instead of q, where q is given in (1.2). In these circumstances the revenue is $\delta^\alpha R$ instead of R, where $R = A^{1-\alpha} q^\alpha$ is the revenue generated by q (see (1.1)). It follows that now the outside option of the final-good producer is not zero but $\delta^\alpha R$, and this outside option is smaller the larger is the efficiency loss from the departure of the supplier. As a result, the final-good producer's payoff from bargaining is $\delta^\alpha R + \beta (R - \delta^\alpha R - 0) = \beta_{hV} R$, where

$$\beta_{hV} = \beta + (1 - \beta) \delta^\alpha$$

is the share of the revenue accruing to the final-good producer. The supplier obtains the revenue share $\beta_{mV} = 1 - \beta_{hV}$. Evidently, $\beta_{hV} > \beta = \beta_{hO}$, which means that the final-good producer gets a larger share of the revenue under integration than under outsourcing. In what follows, our analysis proceeds under the assumption that $\beta_{hV} > \beta_{hO}$.

Figure 1.1 depicts the revenue shares β_{hO} and β_{hV} and the headquarter intensities η_{hL} and η_{hH} for which each one of these shares maximizes profits. Part (3) of proposition 1.2 implies that all firms with intensity below η_{hL} prefer to outsource and all firms with intensity above η_{hH} prefer to integrate. By continuity, firms with intensity slightly above η_{hL} also prefer to outsource and firms with intensity slightly below η_{hH} also prefer to integrate. And we show in the Appendix that a unique critical intensity level exists between η_{hL} and η_{hH}, denoted in the figure by η_{hc}, at which a firm is just indifferent between outsourcing and integration. Firms with headquarter intensity below η_{hc} outsource, and those with intensity above η_{hc} integrate.[14] This result is similar to our result in Antràs and Helpman (2004).

In order to study the impact of the quality of legal systems on industrial structure, we need to understand how contractual frictions affect the make-or-buy decision. To this end first consider an improvement in contracting for intermediate inputs, reflected in an increase in μ_m, the fraction of contractible activities in the manufacturing of components. Part (2) of proposition 1.2 implies that this raises the optimal revenue share β_h. In Figure 1.1 this translates into an upward shift of the β_h^* curve. As a result, the critical intensity levels η_{hL} and η_{hH} decline. We show in the Appendix that the critical intensity level η_{hc} also declines.[15] The implication is that in response to improvements in contracting possibilities for components, more firms, that is, firms with a larger range of headquarter intensities, choose to integrate. The reason is that with better contracting in intermediate inputs, final-good producers are less dependent on the power of the incentives they can offer suppliers, and for this reason outsourcing—which gives the suppliers stronger incentives than integration—becomes less attractive.

Importantly, the opposite happens when contracting improves in headquarter services. In this case, part (2) of proposition 1.2 implies that the optimal revenue share β_h declines for every firm and the cutoff η_{hc} rises.[16] As a result, firms with a larger range of headquarter intensities choose outsourcing over integration. The reason is that with better contracting in headquarter services it becomes more important to give suppliers better incentives, because contractual frictions now play a relatively more important role in components. In response, more firms choose outsourcing, which gives the suppliers more powerful incentives.

These results are summarized in the following proposition.

Proposition 1.3 *Let fixed and variable costs be the same under integration and outsourcing. Then*

1. *There exists a unique headquarter-intensity cutoff $\eta_{hc} \in (0, 1)$ such that profits are higher under outsourcing for $\eta_h < \eta_{hc}$ and higher under integration for $\eta_h > \eta_{hc}$.*

2. *The cutoff η_{hc} is higher the larger μ_h is and the smaller μ_m is.*

This proposition implies that whenever sectors differ by headquarter intensity and organizational choices do not affect fixed and variable costs, the make-or-buy decision does not depend on a firm's productivity, only on its sectoral affiliation. All firms in low headquarter-intensity sectors choose outsourcing, and all firms in high headquarter-intensity sectors choose integration. Moreover, the fraction of sectors that choose integration is larger the larger the fraction of contractible activities in components is and the smaller the fraction of contractible activities in headquarter services is.

We next examine the impact of fixed costs on the make-or-buy decision of firms with different productivity levels. To this end, suppose that there are different fixed costs of running an integrated or an outsourcing enterprise, which we denote by F_V and F_O, respectively. Under these circumstances we can replace the profit function (1.8) with

$$\pi_i = Z_i \Theta - w_m - F_i, \quad \text{for } i = O, V, \tag{1.11}$$

where i represents the organizational form, and Z_i is the derived parameter Z when evaluated at $\beta_h = \beta_{hi}$ and the industry's η_h. At this point we take variable costs c_h and c_m to be the same for both organizational forms, and therefore for a given industry, Z_i varies only with β_{hi}. Proposition 1.3 implies that $Z_O > Z_V$ for $\eta_h < \eta_{hc}$ and $Z_O < Z_V$ for $\eta_h > \eta_{hc}$.

Following Antràs and Helpman (2004), we now assume that integration involves higher fixed costs than outsourcing. Two opposing forces determine these costs. On the one hand, managerial overload is larger in an integrated enterprise, because management has to pay attention to many more tasks. On the other hand, there are economies of scope in management. If the managerial overload imposes larger costs than the costs saved due to economies of scope, then $F_V > F_O$. In the opposite case, $F_V < F_O$.

For concreteness we assume $F_V > F_O$. Under the circumstances, profits from outsourcing are higher than profits from integration in all sectors with $\eta_h < \eta_{hc}$, independently of a firm's productivity level. The profit function π_O is depicted in Figure 1.2; it has an intercept at minus $w_m + F_O$ and a constant slope Z_O. The resulting profits are negative for $\Theta < \underline{\Theta}$. For this reason, only firms with higher productivity manufacture in this industry. We also depict in this figure the profit function from integration, π_V; it has a lower intercept because $F_V > F_O$ and a lower slope because $Z_V < Z_O$. This shows that in industries with low headquarter intensity, all profitable firms outsource.

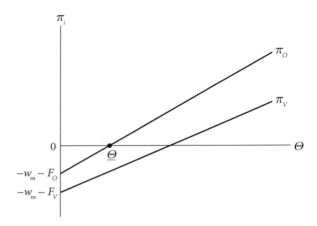

Figure 1.2 Profit function in a sector with $\eta_h < \eta_{hc}$.

Figure 1.3 depicts the two profit functions π_O and π_V in a sector with high headquarter intensity. Now the fixed costs still give outsourcing an advantage, as they did in the low headquarter-intensity sector. But this is partly offset by lower-power incentives to the supplier, which help the final-good producer (i.e., $Z_V > Z_O$). As a result, outsourcing dominates integration only for low-productivity firms, those with $\Theta < \Theta_O$.[17] It follows that firms with productivity below $\underline{\Theta}$ do not produce, those with productivity between $\underline{\Theta}$ and Θ_O outsource, and firms with productivity above Θ_O integrate.

Our results on the choice of organizational form by firms with different productivity levels are summarized in the following proposition.

Proposition 1.4 *Let variable costs be the same under integration and outsourcing and let fixed costs be higher under integration. Then*

1. *In every sector there exists a cutoff $\underline{\Theta}$ such that firms with productivity below $\underline{\Theta}$ do not produce.*

2. *In a sector with $\eta_h < \eta_{hc}$, all firms with productivity above $\underline{\Theta}$ outsource.*

3. *In a sector with $\eta_h > \eta_{hc}$, there exists a cutoff Θ_O such that all firms with productivity above this cutoff integrate. If this cutoff is above $\underline{\Theta}$, then all firms in the productivity range $\left(\underline{\Theta}, \Theta_O\right)$ outsource.*

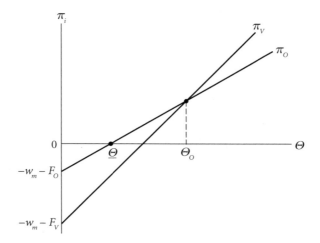

Figure 1.3 Profit function in a sector with $\eta_h > \eta_{hc}$.

This proposition shows how fixed-cost differences between organizational forms interact with productivity differences across firms in shaping sectoral make-or-buy decisions. In economies with higher fixed costs of integration, high-productivity firms integrate and low-productivity firms outsource in sectors with high headquarter intensity. In sectors with low headquarter intensity, all firms outsource.

Now consider the impact of contractual frictions on the relative prevalence of integration and outsourcing. Evidently, this analysis applies only to sectors with $\eta_h > \eta_{hc}$, in which the two organizational forms coexist. As in Antràs and Helpman (2004), we measure the prevalence of an organizational form by the fraction of firms that adopt it.

For this purpose, let the cumulative distribution function of productivity be $G(\Theta)$. Then in sectors with $\Theta_O > \underline{\Theta}$, the fraction of firms that integrate is

$$\sigma_V = \frac{1 - G\left(\Theta_O\right)}{1 - G\left(\underline{\Theta}\right)}.$$

Next suppose that Θ is distributed Pareto with shape parameter κ,[18] so that

$$G(\Theta) = 1 - \left(\frac{\Theta_{\min}}{\Theta}\right)^{\kappa} \quad \text{for } \Theta \geq \Theta_{\min} > 0 \text{ and } \kappa > 2. \quad (1.12)$$

Then

$$\sigma_V = \left(\frac{\underline{\Theta}}{\Theta_O} \right)^{\kappa}.$$

It follows that the share of integrating firms is larger the larger the ratio $\underline{\Theta}/\Theta_O$ is. From the definition of these cutoffs we find that

$$\underline{\Theta} = \frac{w_m + F_O}{Z_O},$$

$$\Theta_O = \frac{F_V - F_O}{Z_V - Z_O}.$$

Therefore, σ_V is larger the larger the ratio Z_V/Z_O is. We show in the Appendix that this ratio is decreasing in μ_h and increasing in μ_m. As a result, the share of outsourcing firms, which equals $1 - \sigma_V$, is increasing in μ_h and declining in μ_m. We therefore have the following proposition.

Proposition 1.5   *Let variable costs be the same under integration and outsourcing and let fixed costs be higher under integration. Then in sectors with $\eta_h > \eta_{hc}$ in which $\Theta_O > \underline{\Theta}$, the share of outsourcing firms is increasing in μ_h and declining in μ_m.*

It follows from this proposition that larger contractual frictions in headquarter services encourage integration and larger contractual frictions in components encourage outsourcing. For this reason, overall improvements in the quality of the legal system, which raise the fraction of contractible activities in both headquarter services and components, may raise the relative prevalence of integration or outsourcing.[19] A key insight from this proposition is that contractual improvements per se do not bias the industrial structure toward outsourcing, because the differential impact of the improvement on contractual frictions in the two inputs plays an important role.

Note that proposition 1.5 describes the impact of variations in contractual frictions on the prevalence of outsourcing even when there are general equilibrium effects, as long as the general equilibrium feedbacks do not impact the relative cost ratio $(w_m + F_O) / (F_V - F_O)$, because the unit costs c_h and c_m do not affect the Z_V/Z_O ratio, nor does the demand level A. It is therefore evident that this proposition holds in the general equilibrium of a one-factor economy, in which the fixed costs F_i, $i = O, V$, and w_m are proportional to the price of the factor. In fact, in this case we can think of w_m as the factor price.[20]

1.4 Foreign Sourcing

Next consider foreign sourcing. We assume that the final-good producer is located in North, which is a high-cost country. But North has good contracting institutions, so the fraction of activities that are contractible is larger in North. Now a firm is not required to source the intermediate input in its home country; it has a choice to source it in North or South. Unlike North, South is a low-cost country, but its contracting institutions are weaker and, therefore, smaller fractions of activities are contractible there. In what follows we denote with the superscript N variables that are affiliated with North and superscript S variables that are affiliated with South. Our assumption can therefore be represented by $\mu_j^N > \mu_j^S$ for $j = h, m$.

In addition, we assume that the final-good producer has to produce headquarter services in North, but she can produce intermediate inputs in North or South, with $c_m^S < c_m^N$. In either case, that is, independently of whether she produces components in North or South, she has the option to do so in-house or to outsource. When she chooses integration in South, she engages in foreign direct investment (FDI). When she chooses outsourcing in South, she engages in an arm's-length transaction. In the former case, there is intrafirm importing of components; in the latter case there is arm's-length importing of components.

To simplify the analysis, we assume that the revenue shares β_{hi}, $i = O, V$, are the same in North and South. As a result we can characterize the relative size of the cutoff η_{hc}, which now depends on whether components are produced in North or South. The cutoff η_{hc}^N is defined in the same way as before; it represents the headquarter intensity at which the final-good producer is indifferent between outsourcing and integration when the variable costs and fixed costs are the same in both cases, and the contractual frictions μ_j^N, $j = h, m$, are those prevailing in North. In other words, η_{hc}^N solves $Z_O^N = Z_V^N$, where in computing these Zs we use equation (1.9) evaluated at Northern variable costs. We have shown in the Appendix that the ratio Z_O^N / Z_V^N does not depend on the variable costs and that it declines in η_h. As a result the solution to η_{hc}^N is unique.

We now define analogously η_{hc}^S as the headquarter-intensity measure at which $Z_O^S = Z_V^S$, where Z_i^S represents the derived parameter Z in equation (1.9) evaluated at the unit cost of headquarter services in North, c_h^N, the unit cost of components in South, c_m^S, the Southern measure of contractual frictions for headquarter services, μ_h^S, and the Southern measure of contractual frictions for components, μ_m^S. Now too the cutoff η_{hc}^S does not depend on unit costs and the ratio Z_O^S/Z_V^S is declining in η_h. As a result, the cutoff η_{hc}^S is unique. The implication is that in industries with $\eta_h < \eta_{hc}^S$ we have $Z_O^S > Z_V^S$, and in industries with $\eta_h > \eta_{hc}^S$ we have $Z_O^S < Z_V^S$. It then follows that among the firms who choose to offshore the production of intermediate inputs, those with $\eta_h < \eta_{hc}^S$ prefer to outsource, and those with $\eta_h > \eta_{hc}^S$ prefer to integrate, unless the fixed costs of integration and outsourcing are not the same.

Note that the ratio Z_O^S/Z_V^S differs from Z_O^N/Z_V^N only as a result of the difference between μ_j^S and μ_j^N for $j = h, m$. In the previous section (see Appendix for a formal proof), we have established that Z_O/Z_V is decreasing in μ_m and increasing in μ_h. As a result, the lower contractibility of components in South, $\mu_m^S < \mu_m^N$, tends to make the ratio Z_O^S/Z_V^S higher than the ratio Z_O^N/Z_V^N. On the other hand, our formulation implies that foreign sourcing also reduces the contractibility of headquarter services even though these are produced in North, $\mu_h^S < \mu_h^N$. The idea is that, as in Antràs (2005), all parts of a contract governing an international transaction are relatively harder to enforce. The lower contractibility of headquarter services associated with offshoring tends to make the ratio Z_O^S/Z_V^S lower than the ratio Z_O^N/Z_V^N. Overall, whether Z_O^S/Z_V^S is higher or lower than Z_O^N/Z_V^N depends on the relative magnitude of $\mu_h^N - \mu_h^S$ and $\mu_m^N - \mu_m^S$. Because it seems natural that the contractibility of an intermediate input is disproportionately affected by the contracting institutions of the country in which this input is produced, in the remainder of the chapter we focus on situations in which the difference $\mu_h^N - \mu_h^S$ is low relative to the difference $\mu_m^N - \mu_m^S$. This allows us to establish the following result.

Proposition 1.6 *When $\mu_h^N - \mu_h^S$ is sufficiently smaller than $\mu_m^N - \mu_m^S$, the cutoff η_{hc} is higher when components are produced in South than when they are produced in North, that is, $\eta_{hc}^S > \eta_{hc}^N$.*

This proposition implies that when weak institutions in South have a stronger effect on the contractibility of components than headquarter services, then more sectors find outsourcing advantageous when they off-shore than when they do not.[21] A direct corollary of this proposition is as follows.

Corollary 1.1 *When $\mu_h^N - \mu_h^S$ is sufficiently smaller than $\mu_m^N - \mu_m^S$, the slopes of the profit functions satisfy:*

1. $Z_O^S > Z_V^S$ and $Z_O^N > Z_V^N$ for $\eta_h < \eta_{hc}^N$.
2. $Z_O^S > Z_V^S$ and $Z_O^N < Z_V^N$ for $\eta_{hc}^N < \eta_h < \eta_{hc}^S$.
3. $Z_O^S < Z_V^S$ and $Z_O^N < Z_V^N$ for $\eta_h > \eta_{hc}^S$.

We are now ready to characterize the joint offshoring and make-or-buy decisions. For this purpose we assume, as we did in the previous section, that the fixed costs of integration are higher than the fixed costs of outsourcing. Moreover, we assume that the fixed costs of offshoring are higher than the fixed costs of producing at home. In addition, we make the somewhat stronger assumption

$$F_V^S + w_m^S > F_O^S + w_m^S > F_V^N + w_m^N > F_O^N + w_m^N.$$

In this ordering, the fixed costs of doing business in South are substantially higher than the fixed costs of doing business in North, and this difference overwhelms the South's cost advantage in w_m. The resulting profit functions are

$$\pi_i^\ell = Z_i^\ell \Theta - w_m^\ell - F_i^\ell, \quad i = O, V, \text{ and } \ell = N, S. \tag{1.13}$$

As in Antràs and Helpman (2004), it is now useful to study the equilibrium in sectors that differ by headquarter intensity, η_h.

1.4.1 Low Headquarter-Intensity Sector

First consider an industry with headquarter intensity η_h smaller than η_{hc}^N. From corollary 1.1, this implies $Z_O^\ell > Z_V^\ell$ for $\ell = N, S$. Given that the overall fixed costs of integration $w_m^\ell + F_V^\ell$ are higher than the overall fixed costs of outsourcing $w_m^\ell + F_O^\ell$, it follows that in an industry with this headquarter intensity outsourcing dominates integration in North as well as in South, independently of a firm's productivity level, that is, $\pi_O^\ell > \pi_V^\ell$ for $\ell = N, S$ and all Θ. Under the circumstances, the effective choice is between outsourcing at home and outsourcing in South. Since the fixed

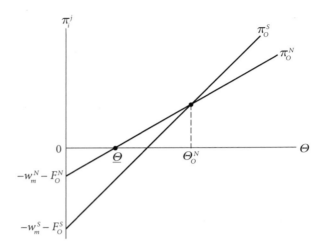

Figure 1.4 Profits from outsourcing when $\eta_h < \eta^N_{hc}$ and $Z^S_O > Z^N_O$.

costs of outsourcing in South are higher than the fixed costs of outsourcing in North, there is a trade-off between these two organizational forms only if $Z^S_O > Z^N_O$; otherwise outsourcing in South dominates outsourcing in North. But the slope differential between the two profit functions from outsourcing is driven by two considerations. On the one hand, the variable unit costs of producing components are lower in South, that is, $c^N_m > c^S_m$, which raises Z^S_O relative to Z^N_O. On the other hand, contractual frictions are higher in South, that is, $\mu^N_j > \mu^S_j$ for $j = h, m$, which reduces Z^S_O relative to Z^N_O. In other words, the marginal profitability from higher productivity can be higher or lower in South depending on differences in unit costs and in contractual frictions.[22] In industries with $Z^S_O < Z^N_O$, all firms outsource in North. In industries with $Z^S_O > Z^N_O$, high-productivity firms outsource in South.

Figure 1.4 depicts the trade-off for $Z^S_O > Z^N_O$. Firms with productivity below $\underline{\Theta}$ lose money either way, and they do not produce. Firms with productivity between $\underline{\Theta}$ and Θ^N_O outsource in North, and those with productivity above Θ^N_O outsource in South. This sorting pattern is similar to Antràs and Helpman (2004), except that now the case $Z^S_O < Z^N_O$ can also arise, in which all firms outsource in North. Note also that in the case depicted in the figure, it is possible that all firms will outsource in South if $\underline{\Theta} > \Theta^N_O$; otherwise the two organizational forms coexist in the industry.

We now calculate the fraction of firms that outsource in South—that is, the fraction of firms that offshore—assuming the Pareto distribution of productivity (1.12). This fraction is given by

$$\sigma_O^S = \left(\frac{\underline{\Theta}}{\Theta_O^N}\right)^\kappa,$$

where

$$\underline{\Theta} = \frac{w_m^N + F_O^N}{Z_O^N}, \tag{1.14}$$

and

$$\Theta_O^N = \frac{\left(F_O^S + w_m^S\right) - \left(F_O^N + w_m^N\right)}{Z_O^S - Z_O^N}. \tag{1.15}$$

It follows from these equations that σ_O^S is larger the larger the ratio Z_O^S/Z_O^N is. Naturally, this ratio is larger the larger the unit cost advantage of the South c_m^N/c_m^S is. Moreover, from proposition 1.1, the ratio Z_O^S/Z_O^N is larger the larger is the fraction of contractible activities in South, either μ_m^S or μ_h^S, and the smaller is the fraction of contractible activities in North, either μ_m^N or μ_h^N. In summary, we have the following proposition.

Proposition 1.7 *Consider an industry with $\eta_h < \eta_{hc}^N$. Then no firm integrates, and there exists a cutoff $\underline{\Theta}$ given by (1.14) such that firms with productivity $\Theta < \underline{\Theta}$ do not produce. In addition*

1. *If $Z_O^S < Z_O^N$, then all firms with $\Theta > \underline{\Theta}$ outsource in North.*
2. *If $Z_O^S > Z_O^N$, then there exists a cutoff Θ_O^N given by (1.15) such that all firms with $\Theta > \Theta_O^N$ outsource in South, and if $\Theta_O^N > \underline{\Theta}$, then all firms with $\Theta \in \left(\underline{\Theta}, \Theta_O^N\right)$ outsource in North.*
3. *If $\Theta_O^N > \underline{\Theta}$, then the fraction of offshoring firms is larger the larger are the fractions of contractible activities in South and the smaller are the fractions of contractible activities in North.*

A key implication of this proposition is that lower contractual frictions in South encourage offshoring, while lower contractual frictions in North discourage offshoring.

Although our emphasis in this chapter is on the roles played by contractual frictions, it is useful to note that two additional sectoral characteristics also affect the extent of foreign sourcing: productivity dispersion and headquarter intensity. As to productivity dispersion, Helpman, Melitz, and Yeaple (2004) show that it varies substantially across sectors. We have a natural measure of dispersion, embodied in the shape parameter κ of the Pareto distribution; productivity dispersion is larger the smaller this parameter is. It is evident from the formula for the share of offshoring firms, $\sigma_O^S = \left(\Theta / \Theta_O^N \right)^\kappa$, that this share is declining in κ. Therefore, offshoring is more prevalent in sectors with more productivity dispersion.

Next consider the impact of η_h on the extent of foreign sourcing. In Antràs and Helpman (2004) we found that offshoring is less prevalent in sectors with higher headquarter intensity. This is easily generalized in the current model, in which contractual frictions vary across inputs and countries. Suppose that contractual frictions vary across inputs but not across countries, i.e., $\mu_m^N = \mu_m^S = \mu_m$ and $\mu_h^N = \mu_h^S = \mu_h$, but μ_h differs from μ_m.[23] Then

$$\frac{Z_O^S}{Z_O^N} = \left(\frac{c_m^N}{c_m^S} \right)^{\alpha \left(1 - \eta_h \right)}.$$

Since unit variable costs of components are lower in South, it follows that this ratio is lower in sectors that are more headquarter intensive. Moreover, since σ_O^S is increasing with the ratio Z_O^S / Z_O^N, we conclude that outsourcing in South is less prevalent in sectors that are more headquarter intensive.

A novel feature of the more complex model is that this result may not hold when contractual frictions vary across countries. To illustrate, consider the case in which $\mu_m^N = \mu_h^N = \mu_h^S = 1$ and $\mu_m^S = 0$. That is, there are no contractual frictions in North, there are no contractual frictions in headquarter services in South, but no activities of components are contractible in South. Moreover, let $\alpha = 0.4$, $\beta_{hO} = 0.2$, and $c_m^N / c_m^S = 1.1$. Then the ratio Z_O^S / Z_O^N is declining in η_h. However, replacing the revenue share $\beta_{hO} = 0.2$ with $\beta_{hO} = 0.5$ implies that the ratio Z_O^S / Z_O^N is increasing in η_h.

1.4.2 Medium Headquarter-Intensity Sector

We next consider an industry with $\eta_h \in \left(\eta_{hc}^N, \eta_{hc}^S \right)$. Corollary 1.1 implies that in such an industry, outsourcing dominates integration in South,

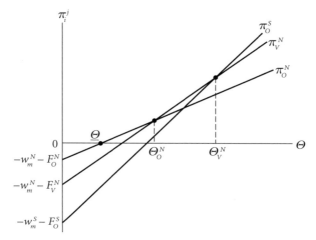

Figure 1.5 Profits from outsourcing and integration when $\eta_h \in \left(\eta_{hc}^N, \eta_{hc}^S \right)$ and $Z_O^S > Z_V^N$.

because $Z_O^S > Z_V^S$, but in North, integration dominates outsourcing for high-productivity firms, because $Z_V^N > Z_O^N$. Figure 1.5 presents the profit functions π_O^N and π_V^N, which describe the trade-offs in the make-or-buy decision of firms who choose to manufacture components in North; the fixed costs are higher for integration while the marginal profits from higher productivity are also higher from integration. The figure shows a cutoff $\underline{\Theta}$ below which firms lose money either way, and therefore they do not produce. Firms with productivity $\Theta \in \left(\underline{\Theta}, \Theta_O^N \right)$ make higher profits from outsourcing, and firms with productivity above Θ_O^N make higher profits from integration. Naturally, if the fixed costs of integration are very low, such that $\Theta_O^N < \underline{\Theta}$, then some low-productivity firms choose not to produce and all those who produce integrate.

Figure 1.5 also shows a profit function from outsourcing in South, π_O^S.[24] The fixed costs of outsourcing in South are higher than the fixed costs of integration in North. As a result, integration in North dominates outsourcing in South for all Θ whenever $Z_O^S \leq Z_V^N$. In other words, if the impact on profitability of the less favorable contractual environment in South is large enough, relative to the South's unit cost advantage c_m^N/c_m^S, so as to yield $Z_O^S \leq Z_V^N$, then no firm in this industry offshores. Instead the figure shows profits from outsourcing in South for $Z_O^S > Z_V^N$, which means that the South's unit cost advantage is large relative to its disadvantage in the contractual environment. But the figure exhibits a case in which the ratio $Z_O^S/Z_V^N > 1$ is not too large, so that the cutoff, Θ_V^N, at which profits from integration in North just equal profits from outsourcing in South, is larger than Θ_O^N. In this event, firms with productivity below $\underline{\Theta}$ do not produce, those with $\Theta \in \left(\underline{\Theta}, \Theta_O^N\right)$ outsource in North, those with productivity $\Theta \in \left(\Theta_O^N, \Theta_V^N\right)$ integrate in North, and those with higher productivity levels outsource in South. Also note that if Z_O^S/Z_V^N is higher, so as to imply $\Theta_V^N \in \left(\underline{\Theta}, \Theta_O^N\right)$, then no firm integrates in North. In this case a cutoff exists between $\underline{\Theta}$ and Θ_O^N such that firms between $\underline{\Theta}$ and this cutoff outsource in North and firms above this cutoff outsource in South.

We now focus on the case depicted in Figure 1.5, in which all three organizational forms that are feasible for a headquarter-intensity level of $\eta_h \in \left(\eta_{hc}^N, \eta_{hc}^S\right)$ coexist, that is, outsourcing in North, integration in North, and outsourcing in South. We wish to study the prevalence of these organizational forms. The share of firms that outsource in South is

$$\sigma_O^S = \left(\frac{\underline{\Theta}}{\Theta_V^N}\right)^\kappa, \tag{1.16}$$

where $\underline{\Theta}$ is again given by (1.14) and

$$\Theta_V^N = \frac{\left(F_O^S + w_m^S\right) - \left(F_V^N + w_m^N\right)}{Z_O^S - Z_V^N}. \tag{1.17}$$

It follows that this share is larger the larger the ratio $\left(Z_O^S - Z_V^N\right)/Z_O^N$ is. From proposition 1.1 we have that Z_O^S is increasing in μ_j^S for $j = h, m$, while Z_i^N is increasing in μ_j^N for $j = h, m, i = O, V$. In addition, the Z's corresponding to a particular sourcing location are not a function of the degree of contractibility in the other country. We can thus conclude that offshoring, which takes the form of outsourcing in our middle headquarter-intensity sector, is more prevalent the better the contractual environment in South is and the worse the contractual environment in North is.

The share of firms that outsource in North is

$$\sigma_O^N = 1 - \left(\frac{\underline{\Theta}}{\Theta_O^N}\right)^\kappa, \tag{1.18}$$

where

$$\Theta_O^N = \frac{F_V^N - F_O^N}{Z_V^N - Z_O^N}. \tag{1.19}$$

Evidently, this share does not depend on contractual frictions in South (μ_m^S or μ_h^S). As a result, the share of firms that integrate in North, given by

$$\sigma_V^N = \left(\frac{\Theta}{\Theta_O^N}\right)^\kappa - \left(\frac{\Theta}{\Theta_V^N}\right)^\kappa, \tag{1.20}$$

or simply $\sigma_V^N = 1 - \sigma_O^N - \sigma_O^S$, varies inversely with the share of firms that outsource in South and is thus decreasing in μ_m^S and μ_h^S.

The effect of Northern contracting institutions on the shares σ_O^N and σ_V^N is more complicated. First note that σ_O^N is decreasing in the ratio Z_V^N/Z_O^N, which in turn is increasing in μ_m^N and decreasing in μ_h^N. Hence, unlike in our low headquarter-intensity sector, an improvement in contracting institutions in North does not always lead to more firms outsourcing in North. The nature of this contracting improvement in North is important for the direction of the effect: better contractibility in headquarter services leads to relatively more outsourcing in North, but better contractibility in components leads to relatively less outsourcing. Finally, because both σ_O^N and σ_O^S are decreasing in μ_m^N, we conclude that the share of firms integrating in North is higher the higher the contractibility of components is in North. Interestingly, however, an improvement in the contractibility of headquarter services in North, which reduces foreign offshoring, does not always lead to an increase in the share of firms integrating in North.[25]

We can summarize our results for the intermediate headquarter-intensity sector as follows.

Proposition 1.8 *Consider an industry with $\eta_h \in \left(\eta_{hc}^N, \eta_{hc}^S\right)$. Then no firm integrates in South and there exists a cutoff $\underline{\Theta}$ given by (1.14) such that firms with productivity $\Theta < \underline{\Theta}$ do not produce. In addition, there exist two thresholds Θ_V^N and Θ_O^N, defined by (1.17) and (1.19), such that if $\Theta_V^N > \Theta_O^N > \underline{\Theta}$ then*

   1. Firms with productivity $\Theta \in \left(\underline{\Theta}, \Theta_O^N\right)$ outsource in North, those with productivity $\Theta \in \left(\Theta_O^N, \Theta_V^N\right)$ integrate in North, and firms with higher productivity outsource in South.

2. *The fraction of offshoring firms is larger (where offshoring takes the form of outsourcing), and the fraction of firms that integrate in North is smaller the larger the fractions of contractible activities are in South. The fraction of firms that outsource in North is not affected by contractual frictions in South.*

3. *The fraction of offshoring firms is smaller and the fraction of firms that source in North is larger the larger the fractions of contractible activities are in North. A disproportionate improvement in the contractibility of components in North may reduce, however, the share of firms that outsource in North, while a disproportionate improvement in the contractibility of headquarter services in North may reduce the share of firms that integrate in North.*

As in the low headquarter-intensity sector, we find in this case too that offshoring declines with contractual frictions in South and rises with contractual frictions in North. The main difference with the previous case is that the share of firms that outsource in North is now independent of contractibility in South and it no longer unambiguously increases when contracting institutions improve in North. Evidently, these differences stem from the fact that under the conditions of this proposition, offshoring competes with integration in North rather than with outsourcing in North.[26]

1.4.3 High Headquarter-Intensity Sector

Propositions 1.7 and 1.8 imply that in sectors with headquarter intensity $\eta_h < \eta_{hc}^S$, no foreign direct investment takes place; there can be integration in North but not in South. It follows that offshoring via integration can emerge only in sectors with relatively high headquarter intensity. So consider a sector with $\eta_h > \eta_{hc}^S$. Corollary 1.1 implies that in such a sector the marginal profitability of integration is higher than the marginal profitability of outsourcing in each one of the countries, that is, $Z_V^\ell > Z_O^\ell$ for $\ell = N, S$. In this case, all four organizational forms may coexist in equilibrium: outsourcing in North, integration in North, outsourcing in South, and integration in South (FDI). This is illustrated in Figure 1.6. Firms with Θ below $\underline{\Theta}$ do not produce, those with $\Theta \in \left(\underline{\Theta}, \Theta_O^N\right)$ outsource in North, those with $\Theta \in \left(\Theta_O^N, \Theta_V^N\right)$ integrate in North, those with $\Theta \in \left(\Theta_V^N, \Theta_O^S\right)$ outsource in South, and those with $\Theta > \Theta_O^S$ integrate in South, that is, they engage in foreign direct investment. Naturally, we can change the assump-

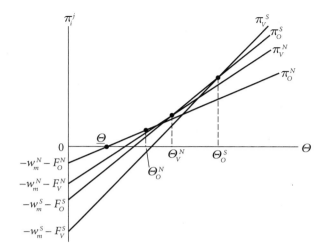

Figure 1.6 Profits from outsourcing and integration when $\eta_h > \eta_{hc}^S$: four organizational forms.

tions on fixed costs or the ranking of the marginal profits Z_i^j to eliminate one or more of the regimes in this case too. But their ranking by productivity will not be affected.

We next study the determinants of the relative prevalence of different organizational forms in an equilibrium in which all four forms coexist. Our first observation is that the shares of firms that outsource in North or integrate in North are given as before by (1.18) and (1.20), respectively. (Recall that these expressions were derived for intermediate headquarter-intensity sectors.) Because the thresholds Θ_V^N and Θ_O^N are also defined as before, by (1.17) and (1.19), respectively, we conclude that the effects of changes in contractibility on the shares σ_O^N and σ_V^N are identical to those in sectors with $\eta_h \in \left(\eta_{hc}^N, \eta_{hc}^S \right)$, as summarized in proposition 1.8.

It remains to discuss how the degree of contractibility of different inputs in different countries affects the relative prevalence of firms that outsource in South or engage in FDI there. A direct corollary of proposition 1.8 is that the overall share of firms that offshore, given by

$$\sigma_O^S + \sigma_V^S = \left(\frac{\Theta}{\Theta_V^N} \right)^\kappa , \tag{1.21}$$

is larger the larger contractibility is in South, and is lower the larger contractibility is in North.

How is the decrease in the share of firms that offshore distributed between firms that outsource and firms that engage in FDI when contractibility improves in North? To answer this question, note that

$$\sigma_V^S = \left(\frac{\underline{\Theta}}{\Theta_O^S} \right)^\kappa, \tag{1.22}$$

where $\underline{\Theta}$ is given by (1.14) and

$$\Theta_O^S = \frac{F_V^S - F_O^S}{Z_V^S - Z_O^S}. \tag{1.23}$$

It thus follows that the share σ_V^S is larger the larger the ratio $(Z_V^S - Z_O^S)/Z_O^N$ is. Evidently, the share of firms that do FDI falls as a result of increases in μ_j^N for $j = N, S$. Moreover, the fraction of offshoring firms that do FDI is given by

$$\frac{\sigma_V^S}{\sigma_O^S + \sigma_V^S} = \left(\frac{\Theta_V^N}{\Theta_O^S} \right)^\kappa, \tag{1.24}$$

which from (1.17) and (1.23) is an increasing function of $(Z_V^S - Z_O^S)/(Z_O^S - Z_V^N)$. We can thus conclude that an improvement of contractibility in North increases the prevalence of FDI relative to foreign outsourcing. Given that the share of firms engaged in FDI is negatively affected by such an improvement in contractibility in North, we also conclude that the share of firms that outsource falls. In sum, larger contractibility in North is associated with lower shares of both types of offshoring firms, with the decrease falling disproportionately on firms that outsource.

We noted above that an improvement in contracting institutions in South increases the share of firms that offshore. We next want to study the effects of this change on the relative prevalence of the two distinct types of offshoring: outsourcing and FDI. In doing so, it is important to distinguish between improvements in the contractibility of components and improvements in the contractibility of headquarter services.

Consider the former first. Remember that the share of firms that do FDI, σ_V^S, is increasing in the ratio $(Z_V^S - Z_O^S)/Z_O^N$, which we can write as $(Z_V^S/Z_O^S - 1)/(Z_O^N/Z_O^S)$. We have established above that both Z_O^S and the ratio Z_V^S/Z_O^S are increasing in μ_m^S. As a result, the share of firms that do FDI is increasing in the contractibility of components in South.

The effect of μ_m^S on σ_O^S is more complicated. From (1.21) and (1.22) we obtain

$$\sigma_O^S = \left(\frac{\Theta}{\Theta_V^N}\right)^\kappa - \left(\frac{\Theta}{\Theta_O^S}\right)^\kappa.$$

A larger contractibility of components in South makes foreign outsourcing relatively more profitable than integration in North ($\underline{\Theta}/\Theta_V^N$ falls), but it also decreases the profitability of outsourcing in South relative to FDI ($\underline{\Theta}/\Theta_O^S$ falls). The balance of these two effects is in general ambiguous, and we cannot rule out that increases in μ_m^S actually reduce the share of firms that outsource in South. Moreover, although the above discussion might have suggested that an improvement in the contractibility of components in South has a disproportionately large effect on FDI relative to outsourcing, it is possible to generate numerical examples in which the ratio σ_V^S/σ_O^S is actually decreasing in μ_m^S.[27]

We close by studying the effects of an improvement in the contractibility of headquarter services in South on the share of firms that outsource in South and the share of firms that engage in FDI. As noted above, the fraction of offshoring firms that do FDI, $\sigma_V^S/(\sigma_V^S + \sigma_O^S)$, is an increasing function of $(Z_V^S - Z_O^S)/(Z_O^S - Z_V^N)$. Rewriting this expression as $(Z_V^S/Z_O^S - 1)/(1 - Z_V^N/Z_O^S)$ shows that it is decreasing in μ_h^S. As a result, we conclude that an improvement in the contractibility of headquarter services in South increases the share of firms offshoring there, with a disproportionately positive effect on the share of firms that outsource in South. As a matter of fact, the disproportionate effect may be large enough to generate a negative relationship between μ_h^S and the share of firms that engage in FDI.

The results we obtained for the high headquarter-intensity sector can be summarized as follows.

Proposition 1.9 *Consider an industry with $\eta_h > \eta_{hc}^S$. Then there exists a cutoff $\underline{\Theta}$ given by (1.14) such that firms with productivity $\Theta < \underline{\Theta}$ do not produce. In addition, there exist three thresholds Θ_V^N, Θ_O^N, and Θ_O^S, defined by (1.17), (1.19), and (1.23), such that if $\Theta_V^N > \Theta_O^N > \underline{\Theta}$, then*

1. *Firms with productivity $\Theta \in (\underline{\Theta}, \Theta_O^N)$ outsource in North, those with productivity $\Theta \in (\Theta_O^N, \Theta_V^N)$ integrate in North, those with productivity $\Theta \in (\Theta_V^N, \Theta_O^S)$ outsource in South, and firms with higher productivity integrate in South.*

2. *The fraction of offshoring firms is larger and the fraction of firms that integrate in North is smaller, the larger are the fractions of contractible activities in South. The fraction of firms that outsource in North is not affected by contractual frictions in South. A disproportionate improvement in the contractibility of components in South may reduce the share of firms that outsource in South, while a disproportionate improvement in the contractibility of headquarter services in South may reduce the share of firms that integrate in South.*

3. *The fractions of offshoring firms, both offshore outsourcing firms and firms engaged in FDI, are smaller and the share of firms that source in North is larger, the larger are the fractions of contractible activities in North. A disproportionate improvement in the contractibility of components in North may, however, reduce the share of firms that outsource in North, while a disproportionate improvement in the contractibility of headquarter services in North may reduce the share of firms that integrate in North. Moreover, the fraction of outsourcers among the set of offshoring firms is larger the smaller the fractions of contractible activities μ_h^N and μ_m^N in North are.*

An important implication of this proposition is that a better contractual environment in South or a worse contractual environment in North do not equally encourage offshore outsourcing and FDI; they tend to encourage offshore outsourcing relatively more, except in cases in which the contractual improvement in South disproportionately affects the production of components.

1.5 Concluding Comments

In this chapter we have generalized the global sourcing model of Antràs and Helpman (2004) to accommodate varying degrees of contractual frictions. In the model, a continuum of firms with heterogeneous productivities decides whether to integrate or outsource intermediate inputs and in which countries to source the inputs. Final-good producers and their suppliers make relationship-specific investments, which are only partially contractible, both in an integrated firm and in an arm's-length relationship. The degree of contractibility can vary across countries and inputs.

Our model generates equilibria in which firms with different productivity levels chose different ownership structures and supplier locations. Assuming a Pareto distribution of productivity, we studied the effects of changes in the quality of contractual institutions on the relative prevalence of these organizational forms. We have shown that an improvement in contractual institutions in South raises the prevalence of offshoring, but it can reduce the relative prevalence of either FDI or offshore outsourcing if it disproportionately affects the contractibility of headquarter services or components, respectively. This result embodies one of the major messages of this chapter: the relative prevalence of alternative organizational forms depends not only on cross-country differences in contractibility, but also on the degree to which contractual institutions are biased toward inputs controlled by the final-good producer or other suppliers.

Although our model is partial equilibrium in scope, it can be embodied in a general equilibrium framework. Such an analysis might shed light on the sources of international income differences and their relationship to the structure of contractual frictions and the resulting trade and investment. Acemoglu, Antràs, and Helpman (2007) provide a first step in this direction by analyzing the impact of contractual frictions on technology choice and the resulting productivity levels, but their model does not feature trade in intermediate inputs nor foreign direct investment. For this reason it cannot address the issues discussed in this chapter. It is necessary to integrate the choice of technology with the choice of organizational form in order to obtain a unified theory that is suitable for the study of links between the quality of contractual institutions, productivity, and trade and investment.

Appendix

1A.1 Derivation of the Profit Function (1.8) and Proof of Lemma 1.1

In this Appendix we discuss properties of the solution to the final-good producer's optimization problem

$$\max_{\{x_h(i)\}_{i=0}^1, \{x_m(i)\}_{i=0}^1} \pi \equiv R - c_h \int_0^1 x_h(i)\, di - c_m \int_0^1 x_m(i)\, di - w_m,$$

subject to the incentive compatibility constraints (1.4) and the revenue and output equations (1.1) and (1.2). First note from (1.3) that

$$R - \sum_{\ell=h,m} c_\ell \left(1 - \mu_\ell\right) x_{\ell n} = \left(1 - \alpha \sum_{\ell=h,m} \beta_\ell \omega_\ell\right) R.$$

Therefore, the maximization problem can be expressed as

$$\max_{\{x_h(i)\}_{i=0}^{\mu_h}, \{x_m(i)\}_{i=0}^{\mu_m}} \pi \equiv \left(1 - \alpha \sum_{\ell=h,m} \beta_\ell \omega_\ell\right) R$$
$$- \sum_{\ell=h,m} c_\ell \int_0^{\mu_\ell} x_\ell(i)\, di - w_m, \qquad (1A.25)$$

subject to

$$R = \left(K_1 \left[\exp \sum_{\ell=h,m} \alpha \eta_\ell \int_0^{\mu_\ell} \log x_\ell(i)\, di\right]\right)^{\frac{1}{1-\alpha\omega}}, \qquad (1A.26)$$

where

$$K_1 = \alpha^{\alpha\omega} \theta^\alpha A^{1-\alpha} \eta_h^{-\alpha\eta_h} \eta_m^{-\alpha\eta_m} \left(\frac{\beta_m \eta_m}{c_m}\right)^{\alpha\omega_m} \left(\frac{\beta_h \eta_h}{c_h}\right)^{\alpha\omega_h}.$$

This representation of the revenue is obtained by substituting (1.4) into (1.2) and the result into (1.1). The first-order conditions (1.6) follow directly from this problem.

To prove lemma 1.1, note from (1.3) and (1.6) that $x_{jc} > x_{jn}$ if and only if

$$\frac{1 - \alpha \sum_{\ell=h,m} \beta_\ell \omega_\ell}{1 - \alpha\omega} > \beta_j.$$

But, since $\beta_\ell \in (0, 1)$ for $\ell = h, m$, the left-hand side is larger than 1 while the right-hand side is smaller than 1, implying $x_{jc} > x_{jn}$.

Using the expression for R from (1A.26), the first-order conditions (1.6) can be expressed as

$$x_{jc} = \frac{1 - \alpha \sum_{\ell=h,m} \beta_\ell \omega_\ell}{1 - \alpha\omega} \left(\frac{\eta_j}{c_j}\right) \alpha \left(K_1 x_{hc}^{\alpha\mu_h\eta_h} x_{mc}^{\alpha\mu_m\eta_m}\right)^{\frac{1}{1-\alpha\omega}}, \quad \text{for } j = h, m.$$

The solution to this system of equations yields (1.7).

Next, from (1A.25) we have

$$\pi = \left(1 - \alpha \sum_{\ell=h,m} \beta_\ell \omega_\ell\right) R - \sum_{\ell=h,m} c_\ell \int_0^{\mu_\ell} x_\ell(i)\,di - w_m.$$

Substituting (1.6) into this expression yields

$$\pi = (1-\alpha)\left(\frac{1 - \alpha \sum_{\ell=h,m}\beta_\ell \omega_\ell}{1 - \alpha\omega}\right) R - w_m.$$

Using (1A.26) together with (1.7) yields (1.8).   □

1A.2 Proof of Proposition 1.1

To prove proposition 1.1, first note from (1.8) that profits are trivially a decreasing function of input costs and the outside option of suppliers. To show that profits are decreasing in ω_j, $j = h, m$, requires more involved arguments. For this purpose, first note that π is decreasing in ω_j if and only if

$$\pi_\omega \equiv \frac{\beta_m^{\alpha\omega_m}\beta_h^{\alpha\omega_h}\left(1 - \alpha\sum_{\ell=h,m}\beta_\ell\omega_\ell\right)^{1-\alpha\omega}}{(1-\alpha\omega)^{1-\alpha\omega}}$$

is decreasing in ω_j. Taking logarithms of both sides and differentiating, we obtain

$$\frac{\partial \ln \pi_\omega}{\partial \omega_h} = \alpha \ln \beta_h - \alpha \ln\left(\frac{1 - \alpha\sum_{\ell=h,m}\beta_\ell\omega_\ell}{1-\alpha\omega}\right)$$

$$+ \frac{\alpha\left[1 - \alpha\beta_m\omega_m - \beta_h\left(1 - \alpha\omega_m\right)\right]}{1 - \alpha\sum_{\ell=h,m}\beta_\ell\omega_\ell}.$$

Moreover,

$$\frac{\partial^2 \ln \pi_\omega}{\partial \omega_h^2} = -\frac{\alpha^2\left[1 - \alpha\beta_m\omega_m - \beta_h\left(1 - \alpha\omega_m\right)\right]^2}{\left(1 - \alpha\sum_{\ell=h,m}\beta_\ell\omega_\ell\right)^2(1-\alpha\omega)} < 0,$$

because

$$1 - \beta_m\alpha\omega_m - \beta_h\left(1 - \alpha\omega_m\right) \geq 1 - \alpha\omega_m - \beta_h\left(1 - \alpha\omega_m\right)$$

$$= \left(1 - \beta_m\right)\left(1 - \alpha\omega_m\right) > 0.$$

Therefore

$$\frac{\partial \ln \pi_\omega}{\partial \omega_h} < \frac{\partial \ln \pi_\omega}{\partial \omega_h}\bigg|_{\omega_h=0} = g\left(\omega_m\right),$$

where

$$g\left(\omega_m\right) \equiv \alpha \ln \beta_h - \alpha \ln \left(\frac{1 - \alpha\beta_m\omega_m}{1 - \alpha\omega_m}\right) + \frac{\alpha\left[1 - \alpha\beta_m\omega_m - \beta_h\left(1 - \alpha\omega_m\right)\right]}{1 - \alpha\beta_m\omega_m}.$$

Next note that

$$g'\left(\omega_m\right) = -\frac{\alpha^2\left(1 - \beta_m\right)\left[1 - \beta_m\alpha\omega_m - \beta_h\left(1 - \alpha\omega_m\right)\right]}{\left(1 - \alpha\beta_m\omega_m\right)^2\left(1 - \alpha\omega_m\right)} < 0,$$

which implies

$$\frac{\partial \ln \pi_\omega}{\partial \omega_h} < g\left(0\right) = \alpha \ln \beta_h + \alpha\left(1 - \beta_h\right) < 0.$$

The last inequality results from the fact that $\ln \beta_h + 1 - \beta_h$ is maximized at $\beta_h = 1$, in which case $g\left(0\right)|_{\beta_h=1} = 0$. Yet $\beta_h \in (0, 1)$, and therefore we have the inequality.

We have thus proved that profits are declining in ω_h, and therefore they are rising in μ_h (because $\omega_h = (1 - \mu_h)\eta_h$). Symmetric arguments show that profits are also declining in ω_m and therefore increasing in μ_m.

Note finally that the only channel through which the parameters ω_h and ω_m affect profits is through the function Z in (1.9). Hence, it is also the case that Z is increasing in μ_h and μ_m. □

1A.3 Characterization of β_j^* and Proof of Proposition 1.2

In order to characterize β_j^*, note that substituting $\beta_k = 1 - \beta_j$ into

$$\beta_m^{\alpha\omega_m}\beta_h^{\alpha\omega_h}\left(1 - \alpha\sum_{\ell=h,m}\beta_\ell\omega_\ell\right)^{1-\alpha\omega}$$

and computing the partial derivative with respect to β_j yields an expression which is proportional to the polynomial

$$\left(\omega_j - \omega_k\right)\beta_j^2 - 2\omega_j\left(1 - \alpha\omega_k\right)\beta_j + \omega_j\left(1 - \alpha\omega_k\right).$$

Equating this polynomial to 0 yields the solution (1.10). First note that this solution can be expressed as

$$\beta_j^* = \sqrt{\omega_j \left(1 - \alpha\omega_k\right)} \frac{\left[\sqrt{\omega_j \left(1 - \alpha\omega_k\right)} - \sqrt{\omega_k \left(1 - \alpha\omega_j\right)}\right]}{\omega_j - \omega_k}$$

$$\text{for } j, k = h, m, \quad k \neq j,$$

and that for $k \neq j$, $\sqrt{\omega_j \left(1 - \alpha\omega_k\right)} > \sqrt{\omega_k \left(1 - \alpha\omega_j\right)}$ if and only if $\omega_j > \omega_k$. Under the circumstances, $\beta_j^* > 0$ for $j = h, m$, and since $\beta_h^* + \beta_m^* = 1$, it also implies $\beta_j^* < 1$. Second note that the second root of the quadratic equation from which β_j^* has been solved is

$$\beta_j^* = \frac{\omega_j \left(1 - \alpha\omega_k\right) + \sqrt{\omega_h\omega_m \left(1 - \alpha\omega_h\right)\left(1 - \alpha\omega_m\right)}}{\omega_j - \omega_k}$$

$$\text{for } j, k = h, m, \quad k \neq j,$$

and this root is larger than 1, because $\omega_j \left(1 - \alpha\omega_k\right) > \left(\omega_j - \omega_k\right)$. It follows that profits are rising with β_j for $0 < \beta_j < \beta_j^*$ and declining with β_j for $\beta_j^* < \beta_j < 1$.

To prove proposition 1.2 first note that L'Hôpital's rule implies $\beta_j^* \to 1/2$ when $\omega_j \to \omega_k$ for $k \neq j$. Second,

$$\left(\beta_h^* - \beta_m^*\right)\left(\omega_h - \omega_m\right)$$

$$= \omega_h \left(1 - \alpha\omega_m\right) + \omega_m \left(1 - \alpha\omega_h\right) - 2\sqrt{\omega_h\omega_m \left(1 - \alpha\omega_h\right)\left(1 - \alpha\omega_m\right)}$$

$$= \left[\sqrt{\omega_h \left(1 - \alpha\omega_m\right)} - \sqrt{\omega_m \left(1 - \alpha\omega_h\right)}\right]^2 \geq 0, \tag{1A.27}$$

with strict inequality holding when $\omega_h \neq \omega_m$, because in this case

$$\sqrt{\omega_h \left(1 - \alpha\omega_m\right)} \neq \sqrt{\omega_m \left(1 - \alpha\omega_h\right)}.$$

Moreover,

$$\left[\sqrt{\omega_h \left(1 - \alpha\omega_m\right)} - \sqrt{\omega_m \left(1 - \alpha\omega_h\right)}\right]\left(\omega_h - \omega_m\right) > 0 \quad \text{for } \omega_h \neq \omega_m.$$

Next, differentiate (1.A27) to obtain

$$\frac{\partial \left(\beta_h^* - \beta_m^*\right)}{\partial \omega_h} = \left(\frac{\beta_h^* - \beta_m^*}{\omega_h - \omega_m}\right) \sqrt{\frac{\omega_m \left(1 - \alpha \omega_m\right)}{\omega_h \left(1 - \alpha \omega_h\right)}}.$$

The previous arguments then establish that the right-hand side is strictly positive. It follows that β_h^* is strictly increasing in ω_h. A symmetric argument implies that β_m^* is strictly increasing in ω_m. Therefore β_h^* is strictly declining in ω_m. □

1A.4 Determinants of the Make-or-Buy Decision and Proof of Proposition 1.3

To formally prove proposition 1.3, we need to study the properties of the ratio Z_V/Z_O. From (1.9), we have

$$\frac{Z_V}{Z_O} = \left(\frac{1 - \beta_{hV}}{1 - \beta_{hO}}\right)^{\frac{\alpha \omega_m}{1-\alpha}} \left(\frac{\beta_{hV}}{\beta_{hO}}\right)^{\frac{\alpha \omega_h}{1-\alpha}} \left(\frac{1 - \alpha \sum_{\ell=h,m} \beta_{\ell V} \omega_\ell}{1 - \alpha \sum_{\ell=h,m} \beta_{\ell O} \omega_\ell}\right)^{\frac{1-\alpha\omega}{1-\alpha}}.$$

It is useful to work with the following monotonic transformation of Z_V/Z_O:

$$(1 - \alpha) \ln \left(\frac{Z_V}{Z_O}\right) = \alpha \omega_m \ln \left(\frac{1 - \beta_{hV}}{1 - \beta_{hO}}\right) + \alpha \omega_h \ln \left(\frac{\beta_{hV}}{\beta_{hO}}\right)$$

$$+ \left(1 - \alpha \left(\omega_h + \omega_m\right)\right) \ln \left(\frac{1 - \alpha \left(\beta_{hV} \omega_h + \left(1 - \beta_{hV}\right) \omega_m\right)}{1 - \alpha \left(\beta_{hO} \omega_h + \left(1 - \beta_{hO}\right) \omega_m\right)}\right). \quad (1A.28)$$

We will first prove that $\ln \left(Z_V/Z_O\right)$ is an increasing function of ω_h and a decreasing function of ω_m. This will immediately imply that Z_V/Z_O is increasing in η_h and μ_m and decreasing in η_m and μ_h.

Let us start with the effect of ω_m. Straightforward differentiation of (1A.28) delivers

$$(1 - \alpha) \frac{\partial \ln \left(Z_V / Z_O\right)}{\partial \omega_m}$$

$$= \alpha \ln \left(\frac{1 - \beta_{hV}}{1 - \beta_{hO}}\right) - \alpha \ln \left(\frac{1 - \alpha \left(\beta_{hV}\omega_h + \left(1 - \beta_{hV}\right) \omega_m\right)}{1 - \alpha \left(\beta_{hO}\omega_h + \left(1 - \beta_{hO}\right) \omega_m\right)}\right)$$

$$+ \frac{\left(1 - \alpha\omega_h\right) \alpha \left(1 - \alpha \left(\omega_h + \omega_m\right)\right) \left(\beta_{hV} - \beta_{hO}\right)}{\left(1 - \alpha \left(\beta_{hO}\omega_h + \left(1 - \beta_{hO}\right) \omega_m\right)\right) \left(1 - \alpha \left(\beta_{hV}\omega_h + \left(1 - \beta_{hV}\right) \omega_m\right)\right)}.$$

To show that $\partial \ln \left(Z_V / Z_O\right) / \partial \omega_m < 0$, we will proceed in two steps. We will first show that $\partial^2 \ln \left(Z_V / Z_O\right) / \partial \omega_m^2 < 0$ and then that, when evaluated at $\omega = 0$, $\partial \ln \left(Z_V / Z_O\right) / \partial \omega_m$ is negative.

Step 1: Simple though cumbersome differentiation delivers

$$(1 - \alpha) \frac{\partial^2 \ln \left(Z_V / Z_O\right)}{\partial \omega_m^2}$$

$$= - \frac{\left(1 - \alpha\omega_h\right) \left(\beta_{hV} - \beta_{hO}\right) \alpha^2}{\left(1 - \alpha \left(\beta_{hO}\omega_h + \left(1 - \beta_{hO}\right) \omega_m\right)\right)^2 \left(1 - \alpha \left(\beta_{hV}\omega_h + \left(1 - \beta_{hV}\right) \omega_m\right)\right)^2}$$

$$\times g \left(\alpha, \beta_{hV}, \beta_{hO}, \omega_h, \omega_m\right),$$

where

$$g \left(\alpha, \beta_{hV}, \beta_{hO}, \omega_h, \omega_m\right)$$
$$= \beta_{hV} + \beta_{hO} + 2\alpha\omega_h - \beta_{hV}\alpha\omega_m - 2\beta_{hV}\alpha\omega_h - \alpha\beta_{hO}\omega_m - 2\alpha\beta_{hO}\omega_h$$
$$+ 2\beta_{hV}\alpha\beta_{hO}\omega_m - 2\beta_{hV}\alpha\beta_{hO}\omega_h - 2\alpha^2\omega_m\omega_h + 3\beta_{hV}\alpha^2\omega_m\omega_h$$
$$+ 3\alpha^2\beta_{hO}\omega_m\omega_h - 4\beta_{hV}\alpha^2\beta_{hO}\omega_m\omega_h - \beta_{hV}\alpha^2 \left(\omega_h\right)^2 - \alpha^2\beta_{hO} \left(\omega_h\right)^2$$
$$+ 4\beta_{hV}\alpha^2\beta_{hO} \left(\omega_h\right)^2.$$

The function $g \left(\cdot\right)$ is somewhat complex, but we can show that it only takes positive values in the relevant domain. To see this, note that

$$\frac{\partial g \left(\cdot\right)}{\partial \omega_m} = - \alpha \left(\beta_{hV} \left(1 - \alpha\omega_h\right) \left(1 - \beta_{hO}\right) + \beta_{hO} \left(1 - \beta_{hV}\right) \left(1 - \alpha\omega_h\right)\right.$$

$$\left. + 2\alpha\omega_h \left(1 - \beta_{hO}\right) \left(1 - \beta_{hV}\right)\right) < 0,$$

and thus it suffices to check that $g\left(\alpha, \beta_{hV}, \beta_{hO}, \omega_h, 1\right)$ is positive. But this follows from

$$g\left(\alpha, \beta_{hV}, \beta_{hO}, \omega_h, 1\right)$$
$$= (1-\alpha)\left(\beta_{hV} - \beta_{hO} + 2\beta_{hO}\left(1 - \alpha\omega_h\right) + 2\alpha\omega_h\left(1 - \beta_{hV}\right)\right)$$
$$+ \left(2\beta_{hV}\beta_{hO}\left(1 - \alpha\omega_h\right) + \beta_{hV}\alpha\omega_h\left(1 - \beta_{hO}\right)\right.$$
$$\left. + \omega_h\beta_{hO}\alpha\left(1 - \beta_{hV}\right)\right)\alpha\left(1 - \omega_h\right),$$

which indeed is a sum of positive terms.

Step 2: Next we note that, when evaluated at $\omega_m = 0$, we have that $\partial\ln\left(Z_V/Z_O\right)/\partial\omega_m < 0$ if and only if

$$h\left(\beta_{hO}\right) = \alpha\ln\left(\frac{1 - \beta_{hV}}{1 - \beta_{hO}}\right) - \alpha\ln\left(\frac{1 - \alpha\beta_{hV}\omega_h}{1 - \alpha\beta_{hO}\omega_h}\right)$$
$$+ \frac{\alpha\left(1 - \alpha\omega_h\right)^2\left(\beta_{hV} - \beta_{hO}\right)}{\left(1 - \alpha\beta_{hO}\omega_h\right)\left(1 - \alpha\beta_{hV}\omega_h\right)} < 0.$$

But note that

$$h'\left(\beta_{hO}\right) = \frac{\alpha\left(1 - \alpha\omega_h\right)\left(\alpha\omega_h\left(1 - \beta_{hO}\right) + \beta_{hO}\left(1 - \alpha\omega_h\right)\right)}{\left(1 - \beta_{hO}\right)\left(1 - \alpha\beta_{hO}\omega_h\right)^2} > 0,$$

and thus $\beta_{hV} = \arg\sup h\left(\beta_{hO}\right)$ (remember that $\beta_{hO} \geq \beta_{hV}$ is not possible). Finally, note that $h\left(\beta_{hV}\right) = 0$, and thus it follows that $h\left(\beta_{hO}\right) < 0$ and $\partial\ln\left(Z_V/Z_O\right)/\partial\omega_m < 0$ for all $\omega_m \in (0, 1)$. This completes the proof that Z_V/Z_O is a decreasing function of ω_m.

The proof of $\partial\ln\left(Z_V/Z_O\right)/\partial\omega_h > 0$ is analogous, though we need not repeat all the steps. It suffices to note that letting $\hat{\beta}_{hV} = 1 - \beta_{hV}$ and $\hat{\beta}_{hO} = 1 - \beta_{hO}$, we can write (1A.28) as

$$(1-\alpha)\ln\left(\frac{Z_V}{Z_O}\right)$$
$$= -\alpha\omega_m\ln\left(\frac{\hat{\beta}_{hO}}{\hat{\beta}_{hV}}\right) - \alpha\omega_h\ln\left(\frac{1 - \hat{\beta}_{hO}}{1 - \hat{\beta}_{hV}}\right)$$
$$- \left(1 - \alpha\left(\omega_h + \omega_m\right)\right)\ln\left(\frac{1 - \alpha\left(\left(1 - \hat{\beta}_{hO}\right)\omega_h + \hat{\beta}_{hO}\omega_m\right)}{1 - \alpha\left(\left(1 - \hat{\beta}_{hV}\right)\omega_h + \hat{\beta}_{hV}\omega_m\right)}\right),$$

where $\hat{\beta}_{hO} > \hat{\beta}_{hV}$. Notice that this expression is analogous to the one we used to prove that $\partial \ln (Z_V/Z_O)/\partial \omega_m < 0$, but with negative signs throughout. We can thus conclude that Z_V/Z_O is increasing in ω_h.

Given these results, we can conclude that Z_V/Z_O is increasing in η_h and μ_m and decreasing in η_m. Next, we want to show that outsourcing is preferred to integration for a low-enough η_h, while the converse is true for a high-enough η_h. This follows from noting that when $\eta_h \to 0$, then $\omega_h \to 0$ and

$$(1 - \alpha) \ln \left(\frac{Z_V}{Z_O} \right) \to \alpha \omega_m \ln \left(\frac{1 - \beta_{hV}}{1 - \beta_{hO}} \right)$$

$$+ \left(1 - \alpha \omega_m \right) \ln \left(\frac{1 - \left(1 - \beta_{hV} \right) \alpha \omega_m}{1 - \left(1 - \beta_{hO} \right) \alpha \omega_m} \right).$$

Because $\beta_{hV} > \beta_{hO}$, using the fact that $(1 - ax)\, x^{a/(1-a)}$ is an increasing function of x for $a \in (0, 1)$ and $x \in (0, 1)$, we can conclude that

$$\left(\frac{1 - \beta_{hV}}{1 - \beta_{hO}} \right)^{\frac{\alpha \omega_m}{1 - \alpha \omega_m}} \left(\frac{1 - \left(1 - \beta_{hV} \right) \alpha \omega_m}{1 - \left(1 - \beta_{hO} \right) \alpha \omega_m} \right) < 1.$$

This implies that $Z_V/Z_O < 1$, and thus profits are higher under outsourcing in such a case (remember that fixed and variable costs are here assumed identical under integration and outsourcing). Similarly, when $\eta_h \to 1$, then $\omega_m \to 0$ and

$$(1 - \alpha) \ln \left(\frac{Z_V}{Z_O} \right) \to \alpha \omega_h \ln \left(\frac{\beta_{hV}}{\beta_{hO}} \right) + \left(1 - \alpha \omega_h \right) \ln \left(\frac{1 - \alpha \beta_{hV} \omega_h}{1 - \alpha \beta_{hO} \omega_h} \right).$$

Again, using the fact that $(1 - ax)\, x^{a/(1-a)}$ is an increasing function of x for $a \in (0, 1)$ and $x \in (0, 1)$, we can conclude that $\ln (Z_V/Z_O) > 0$ and profits are higher under integration in such a case.

Given the monotonicity of $\ln (Z_V/Z_O)$ and the two extreme cases $\eta_h \to 0$ and $\eta_h \to 1$, we can thus conclude that a unique headquarter-intensity cutoff $\eta_{hc} \in (0, 1)$ exists, such that profits are higher under outsourcing for $\eta_h < \eta_{hc}$ and higher under integration for $\eta_h > \eta_{hc}$.

To prove part (2) of proposition 1.3, it suffices to use the implicit-function theorem. The cutoff η_{hc} is implicitly defined by $Z_V/Z_O = 1$. Since

Z_V/Z_O is increasing in η_h, decreasing in μ_h, and increasing in μ_m, we can conclude that the cutoff η_{hc} is higher the larger μ_h is and the smaller μ_m is. □

1A.5 Numerical Example in Note 19

Remember that the ratio Z_V/Z_O is given by

$$\frac{Z_V}{Z_O} = \left(\frac{1 - \beta_{hV}}{1 - \beta_{hO}}\right)^{\frac{\alpha \omega_m}{1-\alpha}} \left(\frac{\beta_{hV}}{\beta_{hO}}\right)^{\frac{\alpha \omega_h}{1-\alpha}} \left(\frac{1 - \alpha \sum_{\ell=h,m} \beta_{\ell V} \omega_\ell}{1 - \alpha \sum_{\ell=h,m} \beta_{\ell O} \omega_\ell}\right)^{\frac{1-\alpha\omega}{1-\alpha}}.$$

Let $\alpha = 4/5$, $\beta_{hV} = 1/2$, $\beta_{hO} = 1/3$, and $\mu_h = \mu_m = \lambda = 1/4$. Then we have that when $\eta_h = 0.4$, we obtain $Z_V/Z_O = 1.027$, while when $\eta_h = 0.5$, we have $Z_V/Z_O = 1.193$. If we raise λ to $1/2$, we instead obtain $Z_V/Z_O = 1.03$ when $\eta_h = 0.4$, and $Z_V/Z_O = 1.125$ when $\eta_h = 0.5$. Hence, the effect of λ (and thus overall contractibility) on the ratio Z_V/Z_O is ambiguous.

ACKNOWLEDGMENTS

We thank Morten Olsen for excellent research assistance and Gianmarco Ottaviano for helpful comments. Helpman thanks the National Science Foundation for financial support.

NOTES

1. The gross product (value added) of multinational firms is roughly 25% of world GDP (UNCTAD 2000). Leaving out the value added generated by parent firms, about 10% of world GDP is accounted for by foreign affiliates, and this ratio has been increasing over time.

2. See UNCTAD (1998) and Feinberg and Keane (2003).

3. See for instance Hummels, Ishii, and Yi (2001) and Yeats (2001). Feenstra and Hanson (1996) estimate that the share of imported intermediates increased from 5.3% of total U.S. intermediate purchases in 1972 to 11.6% in 1990. Campa and Goldberg (1997) find similar evidence for Canada and the United Kingdom, but not for Japan.

4. See Helpman and Krugman (1985, ch. 11–13) and Jones (2000).

5. See Helpman (2006) for a review of the newly observed phenomena and theoretical attempts to explain them.

6. See Bernard and Jensen (1999) or Bernard et al. (2003) for evidence on heterogeneity in the exporting decision, and Bernard, Redding, and Schott (2005) for evidence on heterogeneity in the importing decision.

7. Using data on the activities of U.S. multinational firms, Yeaple (2006) presents evidence supporting some salient cross-industry implications of our model. In particular, he finds that the share of intrafirm imports in total U.S. imports (a measure of the relative prevalence of FDI over foreign outsourcing) is higher in industries with high research and development (R&D) intensity and high productivity dispersion. Although the generalized model developed in this chapter also implies a positive correlation between the share of intrafirm trade and productivity dispersion, it implies a more nuanced correlation with R&D intensity.

8. But we maintain the standard assumption that the set of available contracts does not vary with firm boundaries.

9. See also Grossman and Hart (1986) and Antràs (2003, 2005).

10. Nunn's (2007) estimates suggest that the impact of cross-country variation in contracting institutions on trade flows is of the same order of magnitude as the impact of cross-country variation in human capital.

11. For a derivation of the profit function and proof of lemma 1.1, see the Appendix.

12. For proofs of propositions 1.1, 1.2, and 1.3, see the Appendix.

13. One could, of course, allow μ_m to vary with the internalization decision, but we prefer to avoid this complication.

14. The last statement follows from the fact that the critical value η_{hc} is unique, as we show in the Appendix. Note that at this critical value, profits (1.8) are the same when the firm outsources or integrates, which means that the value of Z is the same under both organizational forms. Let $Z\left(\beta_h, \eta_h\right)$ be the value of Z when the final-good producer receives a fraction β_h of the revenue and headquarter intensity is η_h. Then the definition of β_h^* implies that $Z\left(\beta_{hO}, \eta_{hL}\right) > Z\left(\beta_{hV}, \eta_{hL}\right)$ and $Z\left(\beta_{hO}, \eta_{hH}\right) < Z\left(\beta_{hV}, \eta_{hH}\right)$. For this reason the continuity of the function $Z\left(\cdot\right)$ implies that there exists a critical value $\eta_{hc} \in \left(\eta_{hL}, \eta_{hH}\right)$ such that $Z\left(\beta_{hO}, \eta_{hc}\right) = Z\left(\beta_{hV}, \eta_{hc}\right)$. The uniqueness of η_{hc} results from the fact that the ratio $Z\left(\beta_{hO}, \eta_h\right) / Z\left(\beta_{hV}, \eta_h\right)$ is declining in η_h.

15. This stems from the fact that the ratio $Z\left(\beta_{hO}, \eta_h\right) / Z\left(\beta_{hV}, \eta_h\right)$ (defined in the previous note), which is declining in η_h at $\eta_h = \eta_{hc}$, also is declining in μ_m at $\eta_h = \eta_{hc}$.

16. The last result stems from the fact that the ratio $Z\left(\beta_{hO}, \eta_h\right) / Z\left(\beta_{hV}, \eta_h\right)$, which is declining in η_h at $\eta_h = \eta_{hc}$, is increasing in μ_h at $\eta_h = \eta_{hc}$.

17. Note that in sectors with η_h close to η_{hc}, the cutoff Θ_O is strictly above $\underline{\Theta}$, but in sectors with η_h close to 1, it can be below $\underline{\Theta}$. In the latter case, all profitable firms in the industry integrate.

18. There is a productivity distribution of θ, say $G_\theta(\cdot)$, and this distribution induces a distribution of $\Theta = \theta^{\alpha/(1-\alpha)}$, $G(\cdot)$. When θ is distributed Pareto with the shape parameter k, then Θ is also distributed Pareto with the shape parameter $\kappa = k\alpha/(1-\alpha)$.

19. To clarify this point, let λ be an index of the quality of a country's legal system and let $\mu_i(\lambda)$, $i = O, V$, be increasing functions of this index. Then the marginal effects $\mu_i'(\lambda)$, that is, the slopes of these functions, can differ substantially. We have no theory to tell how they differ, and it is clear from our analysis that there are differences that lead to a rise in the prevalence of outsourcing and other differences that lead to a rise in the prevalence of integration. Moreover, the shift in industrial structure may depend on sectoral characteristics, such as headquarter intensity. We show in the Appendix an example with $\mu_i(\lambda) = \lambda$ for $i = O, V$, in which the ratio Z_V/Z_O is rising in λ for $\eta_h = 0.4$ and declining in λ for $\eta_h = 0.5$, where both these η_h's are above η_{hc}.

20. In our analysis we have assumed that $F_V > F_O$. Suppose instead that the fixed costs of outsourcing are higher than the fixed costs of integration. In this case we obtain the following results. First, in every sector there exists a cutoff $\underline{\Theta}$ such that firms with productivity below $\underline{\Theta}$ do not produce. Second, in a sector with $\eta_h > \eta_{hc}$, all firms with productivity above $\underline{\Theta}$ integrate. Third, in a sector with $\eta_h < \eta_{hc}$ there exists a cutoff Θ_V such that all firms with productivity above this cutoff outsource, and if $\Theta_V > \underline{\Theta}$, then all firms in the productivity range $(\underline{\Theta}, \Theta_V)$ integrate. Finally, in an industry in which some firms integrate and some firms outsource, we find that the share of outsourcing firms is increasing in μ_h and declining in μ_m, just as in proposition 1.5. Hence, the effect of contractual frictions on the relative prevalence of integration or outsourcing is independent of the ranking of fixed costs.

21. Formally, the result follows from the fact that Z_O^ℓ/Z_V^ℓ is declining in η_h and μ_m^ℓ and increasing in μ_h^ℓ for $\ell = N, S$. Hence, by the implicit-function theorem, η_{hc}^ℓ is increasing in μ_h^ℓ and decreasing in μ_m^ℓ. For $\mu_h^N - \mu_h^S$ sufficiently smaller than $\mu_m^N - \mu_m^S$, we thus have that $\eta_{hc}^N < \eta_{hc}^S$.

22. In Antràs and Helpman (2004) we had no differences in contractual frictions, as a result of which we had $Z_O^S > Z_O^N$. There the assumption was $\mu_j^\ell = 0$ for $j = h, m$, and $\ell = N, S$.

23. Recall that in Antràs and Helpman (2004), $\mu_m^\ell = \mu_h^\ell = 0$ for $\ell = N, S$.

24. Since outsourcing in South dominates integration in South, we do not show the profit function from integration in South.

25. The reason is that this type of contracting improvement improves the profitability of integration in North relative to offshoring, but it reduces its profitability relative to outsourcing in North.

26. Note that as long as $Z_O^S > Z_V^N$, low enough fixed costs of outsourcing in South lead to an equilibrium in which low-productivity firms outsource in South and high-productivity firms outsource in North, with no firm integrating. In this type of equilibrium, offshoring competes with outsourcing in North, just as it does in sectors with $\eta_h < \eta_{hc}^N$.

27. For example, assume that $\alpha = 0.5$, $c_h^N = c_m^N = 1$, $c_h^S = c_m^S = 0.7$, $\eta = 0.5$, $\beta_O = 0.3$, $\beta_V = 0.5$, $\mu_h^N = \mu_h^S = 0.3$, and $\mu_m^N = 1$. In this case $Z_V^S > Z_O^S > Z_V^N > Z_O^N$ for $\mu_m^S = 0.5$ and $\mu_m^S = 0.7$, and the ratio $\left(Z_V^S - Z_O^S\right)/\left(Z_O^S - Z_V^N\right)$ is lower when $\mu_m^S = 0.7$ than when $\mu_m^S = 0.5$. Hence, an increase in μ_m^S can reduce the fraction of offshoring firms that engage in FDI.

REFERENCES

Acemoglu, Daron, Pol Antràs, and Elhanan Helpman. 2007. "Contracts and Technology Adoption." *American Economic Review* 97(3):916–43.

Antràs, Pol. 2003. "Firms, Contracts, and Trade Structure." *Quarterly Journal of Economics* 118(4):1375–1418.

———. 2005. "Incomplete Contracts and the Product Cycle," *American Economic Review* 95(4):1054–73.

Antràs, Pol, and Elhanan Helpman. 2004. "Global Sourcing." *Journal of Political Economy* 112(3):552–80.

Bernard, A. B., J. Eaton, J. B. Jensen, and S. Kortum. 2003. "Plants and Productivity in International Trade." *American Economic Review* 93(4, Sep.):1268–90.

Bernard, A. B., and J. B. Jensen. 1999. "Exceptional Exporter Performance: Cause, Effect, or Both?" *Journal of International Economics* 47(1):1–25.

Bernard, A. B., Stephen Redding, and Peter K. Schott. 2005. "Importers, Exporters, and Multinationals: A Portrait of Firms in the U.S. That Trade Goods." NBER working paper 11404.

Campa, Jose M., and Linda S. Goldberg. 1997. "The Evolving External Orientation of Manufacturing: A Profile of Four Countries." *Federal Reserve Bank of New York Economic Policy Review* 3(July 1997):53–81.

Coase, Ronald H. 1937. "The Nature of the Firm." *Economica* 4(16):386–405.

Feenstra, Robert C., and Gordon H. Hanson. 1996. "Globalization, Outsourcing, and Wage Inequality." *American Economic Review* 86(2):240–45.

Feinberg, Susan E., and Michael P. Keane. 2003. "Accounting for the Growth of MNC-Based Trade Using a Structural Model of U.S. MNCs." Mimeo, Yale University.

Grossman, Sanford J., and Oliver D. Hart. 1986. "The Costs and Benefits of Ownership: A Theory of Vertical and Lateral Integration." *Journal of Political Economy* 94(4):691–719.

Helpman, Elhanan. 2006. "Trade, FDI, and the Organization of Firms." *Journal of Economic Literature* XLIV(3):589–630.

Helpman, Elhanan, and Paul R. Krugman. 1985. *Market Structure and Foreign Trade*. Cambridge, MA: MIT Press.

Helpman, Elhanan, Marc J. Melitz, and Stephen R. Yeaple. 2004. "Export versus FDI with Heterogeneous Firms." *American Economic Review* 94(1):300–316.

Hummels, David, Jun Ishii, and Kei-Mu Yi. 2001. "The Nature and Growth of Vertical Specialization in World Trade." *Journal of International Economics* 54(June):75–96.

Jones, Ronald W. 2000. *Globalization and the Theory of Input Trade*. Cambridge, MA: MIT Press.

Nunn, Nathan. 2007. "Relationship Specificity, Incomplete Contracts and the Pattern of Trade." *Quarterly Journal of Economics* 122(2):569–600.

UNCTAD. 1998. *World Investment Report: Trends and Determinants*. New York and Geneva: United Nations Conference on Trade and Development.

———. 2000. *World Investment Report: Cross-Border Mergers and Acquisitions and Development*. New York: United Nations.

Williamson, Oliver E. 1975. *Markets, Hierarchies: Analysis, Antitrust Implications*. New York: Free Press.

———. 1985. *The Economic Institutions of Capitalism*. New York: Free Press.

Yeaple, Stephen R. 2006. "Offshoring, Foreign Direct Investment, and the Structure of U.S. International Trade," *Journal of the European Economic Association* 4(2–3):602–11.

Yeats, Alexander J. 2001. "Just How Big Is Global Production Sharing?" In *Fragmentation: New Production Patterns in the World Economy*, eds. Sven W. Arndt and Henryk Kierzkowski. New York: Oxford University Press.

— 2 —

The Boundaries of the Multinational Firm:
An Empirical Analysis

NATHAN NUNN AND DANIEL TREFLER

2.1 Introduction

This volume is the culmination of a rich and recent research agenda into the determinants of intrafirm trade. Unlike the older literature on international trade in the presence of imperfect competition, for example, Helpman and Krugman (1985), the current literature provides a much more intellectually satisfying notion of what constitutes a firm. It thus provides us with deeper insights into which elements of international trade are done internally to the firm (multinational or intrafirm trade) and which are done outside the boundaries of the firm. Seminal contributions include McLaren (2000), Antràs (2003, 2005), Grossman and Helpman (2002, 2003, 2004, 2005), and Antràs and Helpman (2004).

In this chapter we are particularly interested in a strand of the literature that examines the relationship between a multinational firm and its supplier. Each contributes a customized input that is noncontractible. As a result, there is a classic holdup problem and the multinational must decide whether to vertically integrate its supplier or outsource to its supplier. One narrow strand of the literature—the one we will be dealing with—treats the difference between these two organizational forms as the difference between the outside options of the multinational in the event that the holdup problem cannot be resolved through bargaining. This treatment of the difference between vertical integration and outsourcing originates with Antràs (2003) and appears again in Antràs and Helpman (2004, 2008).

This literature yields three important insights into the determinants of the share of total U.S. imports that are intrafirm, that is, the share that is imported by U.S. multinationals from their foreign affiliates. First, Antràs (2003) argues that when the U.S. headquarters firm provides the bulk of the noncontractible inputs, underinvestment in inputs is reduced by highly incentivizing the headquarters firm. Vertical integration provides such incentives because it allows the headquarters firm to control at least some of the supplier's inputs even if bilateral bargaining breaks down. In contrast, when the foreign supplier provides the bulk of the noncontractible inputs, the foreign supplier must be highly incentivized. This is done by outsourcing: outsourcing strips the headquarters firm of any control over the supplier's inputs and thus strengthens the bilateral bargaining position of the supplier. In short, the share of U.S. imports that are intrafirm is increasing in the share of (noncontractible) inputs provided by the U.S. headquarters firm. This logic is a specific instance of the larger property rights approach to the firm, for example, Grossman and Hart (1986).

The second prediction about the share of total U.S. imports that is intrafirm is developed in Antràs and Helpman (2004). They start with the well-known fact that firms display heterogeneous productivities as described, for example, in Bernard and Jensen (1997). Antràs and Helpman (2004) also argue that the fixed costs of producing abroad are lower when outsourcing to a foreign supplier than when using foreign direct investment (vertical integration). Since only the most productive firms capture the market share needed to offset the high costs of vertical integration, not all firms identified by Antràs (2003) as candidates for vertical integration will in fact integrate. Only the most productive will. Thus, the share of U.S. imports that are intrafirm will be large when two conditions are simultaneously satisfied: (1) the share of inputs provided by the headquarters firm is large (as in Antràs 2003) and (2) firm productivity is high.

The third prediction about intrafirm trade appears in Chapter 1 of this volume (Antràs and Helpman 2008). While Antràs (2003) and Antràs and Helpman (2004) assume that inputs are completely noncontractible, Antràs and Helpman (2008) allow inputs to be partially contractible. This leads to a surprising result. The typical view is that where property rights are strong, outsourcing is more prevalent. Antràs and Helpman (2008) arrive at the opposite conclusion, at least for some parameter values. The logic is simple. As foreign property rights improve so that the supplier's share of noncontractible inputs falls, the party that requires *relatively* more incentives becomes the headquarters firm. These incentives are provided through vertical integration. Improved property rights lead to internalization!

Using data on U.S. intrafirm and arm's-length imports for 5,423 products imported from 210 countries, we examine these determinants of the share of U.S. imports that are intrafirm. Our conclusions mirror the three predictions listed above.

1. In terms of the Antràs (2003) mechanism, we find support for the role of the share of headquarter inputs. This support is stronger than that found in the only two extant empirical studies of the issue, namely, Antràs (2003) and Yeaple (2006).[1]

2. We find strong support for the Antràs and Helpman (2004) prediction that intrafirm trade is largest where headquarter inputs are important *and* productivity is high.

3. We also find support for the Antràs and Helpman (2008) prediction about increased internalization due to an improved contracting environment for the supplier's inputs.

The chapter is organized as follows. Sections 2.2, 2.3, and 2.4 examine the predictions of Antràs (2003), Antràs and Helpman (2004), and Antràs and Helpman (2008) respectively. Section 2.5 concludes.

2.2 The Boundary of the Firm and the Role of η (Antràs 2003)

We begin by reviewing the salient features of the Antràs (2003) model from the perspective of the empirical work to follow. A U.S. firm produces a brand of a differentiated product. Demand is generated by CES preferences. To produce the good, the firm *must* use two inputs, those produced by the U.S. firm (h for *h*eadquarters) and those produced by a foreign supplier (m for inter*m*ediates). Output of the final good is given by a Cobb-Douglas production function with two key parameters: a Hicks-neutral productivity parameter θ and the cost share of the input provided by the firm η. Specifically,

$$q = \theta \left(\frac{h}{\eta}\right)^{\eta} \left(\frac{m}{1-\eta}\right)^{1-\eta}. \tag{2.1}$$

The two inputs are entirely customized. Customization raises quality to a threshold that allows the final good to be sold to consumers. Unfortunately for the U.S. firm and its foreign supplier, quality is not observable or contractible. This is modelled by assuming that the investments in customization are noncontractible. Equally unfortunate for the firm and its supplier, customization has no value outside of the relationship. Thus, there is a standard holdup problem. After the investments in customization have been made there is renegotiation over how the ex post quasi-rents from the relationship will be shared.

Let β be the generalized Nash share of the ex post quasi-rents from the relationship that go to the U.S. firm. The U.S. firm receives this share plus its outside option. The role of the organizational form (vertical integration versus outsourcing) is that it alters the outside option received by the U.S. firm in the event of a bargaining breakdown in the renegotiation stage. What are the various outside options? If there is no agreement, the supplier earns nothing, regardless of the organizational form. The outside option is also 0 for the U.S. firm in an outsourcing relationship. However, for a firm that has vertically integrated with its supplier, no agreement means that the firm can still produce some output by "forcing" its now-disgruntled supplier to do at least some work. Vertical integration is therefore a way for the firm to improve its outside option in the case of a bargaining breakdown.

This difference in the firm's outside options under the two organizational forms leads to a trade-off. Vertical integration allows the firm to grab a larger share of the pie, but it leads to a smaller pie because of underinvestment by the supplier. This is modelled mathematically as follows. Let the subscripts $k = V, O$ denote the organizational form with V for vertical integration and O for outsourcing. Recall that β is the share of the ex post quasi-rents that goes to the firm. Let R_k be the revenue generated when there is an agreement. If there is no agreement, the firm can only sell a portion δ of the final output. With CES preferences and constant markup $1/\alpha$, this generates a revenue of $\delta^\alpha R_V$. Therefore, the firm receives its outside option $\delta^\alpha R_V$ plus a share β of the quasi-rents $(R_V - \delta^\alpha R_V)$. That is, the firm receives $[\delta^\alpha + \beta(1 - \delta^\alpha)]R_V$. Let $\beta_V = \delta^\alpha + \beta(1 - \delta^\alpha)$ be the firm's share of revenues under vertical integration. Under outsourcing, the outside option is 0 and the quasi-rents are R_O so that the firm receives $0 + \beta(R_O - 0) = \beta R_O$. Let $\beta_O = \beta$ be the firm's share of total revenues under outsourcing. The upshot of all this is the central result that the organizational form alters the U.S. firm's share of revenue. In particular, $\beta_V > \beta_O$.

The timing of the game played by the U.S. firm and its foreign supplier is simple. The two match, and the U.S. firm chooses the organizational form. Then investments in customized inputs are made. Finally, the initial contract is renegotiated, and, if there is agreement, the product is sold.

Both the U.S. firm and the foreign supplier invest and hence each must worry about the other's underinvestment. Where η is large, the surplus generated by the relationship is particularly sensitive to the amount of investment undertaken by the U.S. firm. To reduce the degree of underinvestment by the U.S. firm, the firm must be given a large share of the revenue. This share is largest under vertical integration because $\beta_V > \beta_O$. This is a specific instance of the Grossman and Hart (1986) property-rights theory of the firm, where residual control rights are allocated to the U.S. firm. In contrast, when η is small, the surplus generated by the relationship is particularly sensitive to the amount of investment undertaken by the supplier. To reduce supplier underinvestment, the supplier must be given a large share of the revenue. Outsourcing accomplishes this because $1 - \beta_O > 1 - \beta_V$.

Proposition 1 in Antràs (2003) shows that there is a unique value of η—call it η_c—such that the U.S. firm prefers vertical integration for $\eta > \eta_c$ and prefers outsourcing otherwise.

Hypothesis 2.1   *There exists a unique cutoff η_c with the following property: If $\eta > \eta_c$, then the firm will vertically integrate with the supplier. If $\eta < \eta_c$, then the firm will outsource from the supplier.*

We will refer to this dependence of organizational form on η as the "Antràs effect."

2.2.1 Data Sources

To investigate hypothesis 2.1 we use data on intrafirm and total trade from the U.S. Census Bureau. Importers bringing goods into the United States are required by law to report whether or not the transaction is with a related party. This information allows us to identify whether imports are intrafirm (related party) or at arm's length (nonrelated party). See the Appendix for details. The trade data are at the 6-digit Harmonized System (HS6) level for the years 2000 and 2005. We are grateful to Andy Bernard for drawing our attention to these data. See Bernard, Jensen, and Schott (2005) for an example of how the data have been used.

Our key dependent variable is intrafirm imports as a share of total U.S. imports. Let g index industries, and let M_{Vg} be the value of intrafirm U.S. imports in industry g. The V subscript is for vertical integration. Let M_{Og} be the value of arm's-length U.S. imports in industry g. The O subscript is for outsourcing. $M_{Vg} + M_{Og}$ is total U.S. imports and

$$\frac{M_{Vg}}{M_{Vg} + M_{Og}} \qquad (2.2)$$

is intrafirm imports as a share of total U.S. imports of good g.

A drawback of our Census data relative to the Bureau of Economic Analysis (BEA) data on multinationals is that we do not know whether the U.S. importer is the U.S.-owned parent or the foreign-owned affiliate. To address this, we also report results based on a restricted sample of countries. A country is included in the restricted sample if at least two-thirds of intrafirm U.S. imports from the country are imported by U.S. parents. For example, only 3% of U.S. intrafirm imports from Japan are imports by U.S. parents from their foreign affiliates so that Japan is excluded from the restricted sample. Data on intrafirm U.S. imports by country and parent (U.S. versus foreign) are from Zeile (2003) and pertain to 1997. The countries in the full sample are reported in Appendix tables 2A.1 and 2A.2. Countries not in the restricted sample are marked with an asterisk.[2]

Data on the inputs provided by the U.S. firm are from the Bartelsman and Gray (1996) database. For each U.S. 4-digit SIC industry in 1996, the database provides information on capital K_g, employment L_g, capital intensity $\ln K_g/L_g$, nonproduction workers S_g, and skill intensity $\ln S_g/L_g$ (as in Berman, Bound, and Griliches 1994). Note that we use 1996 industry-level data, but the trade data are for 2000 and 2005. In translating the HS6 data into 4-digit SIC data, we keep only HS6 codes that go into a unique SIC code. As a result, we are left with 370 of the 400+ possible SIC codes.

2.2.2 Examining Hypothesis 2.1 (Antràs 2003): Cross-Industry Analysis

Antràs (2003) examined hypothesis 2.1 using BEA data on intrafirm U.S. imports as a share of total U.S. imports. He related this share to capital intensity, a proxy for η. Following Antràs and Helpman (2004), we might also want to proxy η by skill intensity. Antràs (2003) worked at the 2-digit SIC level with 28 industries. We start by examining his relationship using the Census data with its 370 industries. In particular, we consider the following cross-industry regression:

Table 2.1 The determinants of the share of intrafirm imports in total imports—by industry

	Full sample		Restricted sample	
	2000	2005	2000	2005
Capital intensity, $\ln K_g/L_g$	.264**	.295**	.169**	.188**
	(.050)	(.049)	(.053)	(.053)
Skill intensity, $\ln S_g/L_g$	.199**	.219**	.105*	.105*
	(.050)	(.049)	(.053)	(.053)
R^2	.14	.17	.05	.06
Number of observations	370	370	367	367

Note: This table reports estimates of (2.3). The dependent variable is $M_{Vg}/(M_{Vg} + M_{Og})$, U.S. intrafirm imports as a share of total U.S. imports. 4-digit SIC industries are the unit of observation. Standardized "beta" coefficients are reported. Robust standard errors appear in parentheses. The symbols ** and * indicate significance at the 1% and 5% levels, respectively. See Section 2.2.1 "Data Sources" for a description of the restricted sample.

$$\frac{M_{Vg}}{M_{Vg} + M_{Og}} = \gamma_0 + \gamma_{K/L} \ln K_g/L_g + \gamma_{S/L} \ln S_g/L_g + \varepsilon_g, \quad (2.3)$$

where $\ln K_g/L_g$ is capital intensity and $\ln S_g/L_g$ is skill intensity. We estimate equation (2.3) separately for 2000 and 2005, the two years for which the data are available to us.

Estimates of equation (2.3) appear in Table 2.1. Column 1 reports estimates using trade data from 2000, and column 2 uses data from 2005. Using data from either year, both variables are positive and statistically significant.[3] The capital intensity result confirms the findings of Antràs (2003) and Yeaple (2006) for our sample.[4] Antràs (2003) and Yeaple (2006) do not consider skill intensity: we find that skill-intensive industries tend to import more within firm boundaries. In contrast, the Antràs and Yeaple studies find that the share of intrafirm imports tends to be higher in R&D-intensive industries. At our level of industrial disaggregation, there are no measures of R&D intensity. It is possible that our skill-intensity variable is picking up the importance of R&D for the integration versus outsourcing decision.

Columns 3 and 4 report the estimates using our restricted sample of exporting countries to construct industry aggregates. The sample consists of countries for which intrafirm U.S. imports are dominated by U.S. parents.

As shown, the results are similar to the results for the larger sample, except that the estimated magnitudes of the coefficients are smaller.

Because we report standardized "beta" coefficients, one can easily assess and compare the magnitudes of the coefficients for the capital and skill measures. The coefficients for capital suggest that a one standard-deviation increase in capital results in a 0.169 to 0.295 standard-deviation increase in the share of intrafirm imports. This is an economically large effect. The estimated coefficient for skill is somewhat smaller, ranging from 0.105 to 0.219.

A problem with the above approach is that it assumes that we can aggregate across exporting countries. Yet as Schott (2004) notes, this may be seriously misleading because an HS6 good produced in a poor country may be very different from an HS6 good produced in a rich country. To address this, we now turn to a different approach than that of Antràs (2003) and Yeaple (2006). Let M_{Vgc} be the value of U.S. intrafirm imports of good g that are imported from country c. Let M_{Ogc} be the corresponding value of arm's-length U.S. imports. Then $M_{Vgc} + M_{Ogc}$ is the total U.S. imports of good g from country c and $M_{Vgc}/(M_{Vgc} + M_{Ogc})$ is the intrafirm import-share of good g imported from country c. We estimate a regression that pools across industries and countries:

$$\frac{M_{Vgc}}{M_{Vgc} + M_{Ogc}} = \gamma_c + \gamma_{K/L} \ln K_g/L_g + \gamma_{S/L} \ln S_g/L_g + \varepsilon_{gc}. \quad (2.4)$$

In this regression we control for exporter heterogeneity by allowing for country fixed effects γ_c. Further, g now subscripts HS6 products rather than 4-digit SIC industries.

The results appear in Table 2.2. Because our variables of interest, $\ln K_g/L_g$ and $\ln S_g/L_g$, vary only at the 4-digit SIC industry level while the unit of observation is a country and HS6 good, we report standard errors clustered at the 4-digit SIC level. The estimates, consistent with the cross-industry estimates of Table 2.1, show that the capital and skill intensity of an industry are positively correlated with the share of intrafirm trade. This is true in both 2000 and 2005. It is also true for the full sample and the restricted sample of exporting countries. Overall, these results combined with the cross-industry results of Table 2.1 provide considerable support for hypothesis 2.1.

Table 2.2 The determinants of the share of intrafirm imports in total imports—by country and industry

	Full sample		Restricted sample	
	2000	2005	2000	2005
Capital intensity, ln K_g/L_g	.073**	.061**	.055**	.058**
	(.019)	(.016)	(.017)	(.017)
Skill intensity, ln S_g/L_g	.085**	.079**	.077**	.075**
	(.017)	(.015)	(.019)	(.016)
Country fixed effects	Yes	Yes	Yes	Yes
R^2	.12	.12	.10	.10
Number of observations	110,355	115,781	38,229	41,790

Note: This table reports estimates of equation (2.4). The dependent variable is $M_{Vgc}/(M_{Vgc} + M_{Ogc})$, U.S. intrafirm imports as a share of total U.S. imports. An observation is an HS6-country pair. Standardized "beta" coefficients are reported. Standard errors clustered at the 4-digit SIC industry level appear in parentheses. The symbols ** and * indicate significance at the 1% and 5% levels, respectively. All regressions include country fixed effects. See Section 2.2.1 "Data Sources" for a description of the restricted sample.

2.3   Productivity Heterogeneity (Antràs and Helpman 2004)

Examining the data on intrafirm imports one finds that $M_{Vgc}/(M_{Vgc} + M_{Ogc})$ is rarely either 0 or 1 as predicted by the Antràs theory. An obvious explanation is aggregation bias. However, simple versions of aggregation bias are not consistent with the data. For one, Bernard, Jensen, and Schott (2005) show that even though only one third of U.S. trade is done within the firm, U.S. multinationals account for 90% of all U.S. trade. Thus, it would seem that individual multinationals trade both within the firm and between firms. Further, Bernard, Jensen, and Schott (2006) show that at the 10-digit HS level (HS10), multinationals typically conduct both intrafirm and arm's-length trade, sometimes even to the same destination country. Feinberg and Keane (2006) offer additional evidence on this subject. In their study of trade between U.S. firms and their Canadian affiliates, they find the following. Only 12% of these relationships are pure horizontal relationships, and only 19% are pure vertical relationships. Fully 69% of these relationships involve two-way trade flows, what Helpman (2006) calls "complex integration strategies." Thus, simple aggregation bias cannot be the entire story. An explanation in terms of heterogeneity seems more likely.

In particular, Antràs and Helpman (2004) introduce productivity heterogeneity in order to generate entirely novel predictions about the determinants of the share of imports that are intrafirm. To this end they append the Antràs framework to the Melitz (2003) model. Productivity heterogeneity means that θ in equation (2.1) varies across firm-supplier relationships. Let $\overline{\pi}_k$ be variable profits for a firm with $\theta = 1$ that uses organizational form $k = V, O$. Then as is well known, profits for a firm with productivity θ that adopts organizational form k are linear in $\theta^{\alpha/(1-\alpha)}$:

$$\pi_k(\theta) = \theta^{\alpha/(1-\alpha)}\overline{\pi}_k - F_k, \qquad (2.5)$$

where F_k is the fixed costs of offshoring using organizational form k. Antràs (2003) assumes that all firms have the same productivity ($\theta = 1$) and the same fixed costs ($F_V = F_O$). Under these assumptions, the Antràs effect states that $\overline{\pi}_V > \overline{\pi}_O$ if and only if $\eta > \eta_c$, that is, the U.S. firm prefers vertical integration to outsourcing when the firm's share of inputs is large. Heterogeneity of productivity by itself does not alter this conclusion—it simply magnifies the advantages (or disadvantages) of vertical integration.[5]

However, when the fixed costs of outsourcing vary across organizational forms, then productivity heterogeneity matters. How heterogeneity matters depends on whether $F_V - F_O$ is positive or negative. Since the results depend transparently on the sign of $F_V - F_O$, we only present the results under Antràs and Helpman's preferred assumption, namely, $F_V > F_O$. They reason that vertical integration creates a need to supervise the production of intermediate inputs, thus creating managerial overload.

Figure 2.1 illustrates what happens when heterogeneity is introduced. The figure plots profits under outsourcing $\pi_O(\theta)$ and vertical integration $\pi_V(\theta)$. From Antràs (2003, lemma 3), we know that $\overline{\pi}_V/\overline{\pi}_O$ is increasing in η and equals 1 for $\eta = \eta_c$. This together with equation (2.5) implies that $\pi_V(\theta)$ is steeper than $\pi_O(\theta)$ for $\eta > \eta_c$ and flatter for $\eta < \eta_c$. From the left-hand panel of Figure 2.1 where $\eta < \eta_c$, it must be that outsourcing is always preferred to vertical integration—the Antràs effect and the lower fixed costs of outsourcing both work in favor of outsourcing.

When $\eta > \eta_c$, as in the right-hand panel of Figure 2.1, $\pi_V(\theta)$ is steeper than $\pi_O(\theta)$. It follows that the two curves must cross. Firms with productivity to the right of the crossing point will vertically integrate. Firms to the left will outsource. The tension here is that fixed costs push for outsourcing while the Antràs effect pushes for vertical integration. Since the Antràs

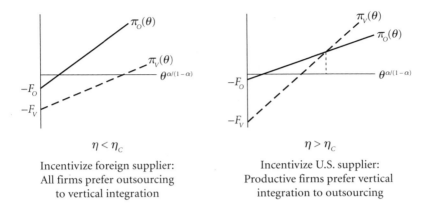

Figure 2.1 The outsourcing decision with productivity heterogeneity.

effect is greatest for the most productive firms, the Antràs effect dominates for productive firms.

All of this leads to an interesting empirical prediction about the share of U.S. imports that are intrafirm, that is, about $M_{Vgc}/(M_{Vgc} + M_{Ogc})$. The share should depend on an interaction of η with θ. When $\eta < \eta_c$, we have $M_{Vgc} = 0$ so that an increase in θ has no effect on $M_{Vgc}/(M_{Vgc} + M_{Ogc}) = 0$. Where $\eta > \eta_c$, an increase in θ increases $M_{Vgc}/(M_{Vgc} + M_{Ogc})$. This suggests that in industries with firms that tend to have large values of θ, we should see a larger share of firms that vertically integrate.

Antràs and Helpman (2004) formalize this by assuming that the distribution of productivities θ within an industry is described by the Pareto distribution, that is, by the cumulative distribution function

$$G(\theta) = 1 - \left(\frac{\theta}{b}\right)^{\lambda}, \quad \theta \geq b > 2. \tag{2.6}$$

Note that for the Pareto distribution, the mean and variance of θ are increasing in λ. Consider the case where $\eta > \eta_c$ as in the right-hand panel of Figure 2.1. Antràs and Helpman (2004, 573) show that an increase in λ (a rise in the mean and variance of θ) leads to a rise in the share of firms that vertically integrate. Empirically, this means a rise in $M_{Vgc}/(M_{Vgc} + M_{Ogc})$. On the other hand, when $\eta < \eta_c$, as in the left-hand panel of Figure 2.1, an increase in λ has no effect on $M_{Vgc}/(M_{Vgc} + M_{Ogc})$, which is 0 independent of λ.

Moving to an empirical counterpart of λ, let x_g^θ be some measure of productivity dispersion in industry g. We will describe x_g^θ in detail shortly. Helpman, Melitz, and Yeaple (2004) and Yeaple (2006) use productivity dispersion x_g^θ as a measure of λ, and we follow suit. We can now offer an empirically oriented hypothesis that comes out of the Antràs-Helpman model.

Hypothesis 2.2   *Assume $F_V > F_O$. Let x_g^θ be the dispersion of θ across firms within industry g.*

1. *If $\eta < \eta_c$, then dispersion does not affect the intrafirm share of imports:*

$$\frac{\partial M_{Vgc}/(M_{Vgc} + M_{Ogc})}{\partial x_g^\theta} = 0.$$

2. *If $\eta > \eta_c$, then dispersion increases the intrafirm share of imports:*

$$\frac{\partial M_{Vgc}/(M_{Vgc} + M_{Ogc})}{\partial x_g^\theta} > 0.$$

2.3.1 Examining Hypothesis 2.2 (Antràs and Helpman 2004)

To construct our measure of productivity dispersion x_g^θ, we follow Helpman, Melitz, and Yeaple (2004) and Yeaple (2006) as closely as possible given the more limited data available to us. With CES utility and the production function that we have been using, more-productive firms have larger sales and exports. Using firm sales as a measure of firm productivity, Helpman, Melitz, and Yeaple (2004) and Yeaple (2006) construct estimates of the dispersion of firm productivity using the standard deviation of firm sales across all firms within an industry. (Their level of industry aggregation allows for only 51 or 52 industries.) We do not have firm-level data. Instead, we construct sales of "notional" firms from U.S. export data as follows. Let g index HS6 goods. Let $v(g)$ be an HS10 good that feeds into HS6 good g. The v stands for the variety of the HS6 good. Let c index the destination country for U.S. exports. Let l index the location within the United States from which the exports were shipped. We define an industry as an HS6 product g and we define the sales of a notional firm as the exports of an HS10 good $v(g)$ exported from U.S. location l to destination country

c. Let $X_{v(g),l,c}$ be these exports. Our measure of productivity dispersion within industry g is just the standard deviation of $\ln X_{v(g),l,c}$:

$$x_g^\theta \equiv \sqrt{\mathbf{V}(\ln X_{v(g),l,c})}, \qquad (2.7)$$

where $\mathbf{V}$ is the variance operator. The variance is calculated across all triplets $(v(g), l, c)$ that feed into HS6 industry g.[6]

As a robustness check we also use a second method of constructing the sales of a notional firm. Since a single firm may export to more than one country, we aggregate across export destinations and define sales of a notional firm as exports $X_{v(g),l} \equiv \Sigma_c X_{(v(g),l,c)}$. We then construct dispersion as[7]

$$x_g^\theta \equiv \sqrt{\mathbf{V}(\ln X_{v(g),l})}. \qquad (2.8)$$

To test hypothesis 2.2, we estimate how the relationship between productivity dispersion x_g^θ and intrafirm imports varies with headquarter intensity. We do not expect the second derivative to be linear. It will be 0 when η is small and positive when η is large. In addition, we do not know where the cutoff level η_c will be. Because of this, we pursue the following estimation strategy: Rank our 370 4-digit SIC industries by headquarter intensity. (Headquarter intensity will be measured by either skill intensity or capital intensity.) Based on this ranking, divide the 370 industries into five quintiles of 74 industries each. Let $p = 1, \ldots, 5$ index quintiles, with $p = 1$ being the least headquarters-intensive quintile. Finally, let $I_{gp}^\eta = 1$ if industry g is in quintile p and $I_{gp}^\eta = 0$ otherwise.

We consider a regression that allows the relationship between dispersion and intrafirm imports to differ by quintile:

$$\frac{M_{Vgc}}{M_{Vgc} + M_{Ogc}} = \gamma_c + \gamma_{K/L} \ln K_g/L_g + \gamma_{S/L} \ln S_g/L_g + \sum_{p=1}^{5} \gamma_{\eta p} I_{gp}^\eta$$

$$+ \sum_{p=1}^{5} \gamma_{\theta \eta p} (x_g^\theta \cdot I_{gp}^\eta) + \varepsilon_{gc}. \qquad (2.9)$$

The primary coefficients of interest are the $\gamma_{\theta \eta p}$. Hypothesis 2.2 states that for low η and hence low p, the impact of dispersion should be zero. That is, $\gamma_{\theta \eta p} = 0$ for low p. Hypothesis 2.2 also states that for high η and hence high p, the impact of dispersion should be positive. That is, $\gamma_{\theta \eta p} > 0$ for high p. Since we do not know which quintile p contains the cutoff η_c, we cannot be more precise about what "low" and "high" p means. We will let the data answer this.

The equation (2.9) regression also includes capital intensity, skill intensity, headquarter-intensity dummies (I^{η}_{gp}), and country fixed effects.

Table 2.3 reports results for 2005 intrafirm trade data. The results for 2000 are similar. In columns 1–3 we measure productivity dispersion using equation (2.7). In columns 4–7 we measure productivity dispersion using equation (2.8). In the first column we examine the effect of productivity dispersion averaged across all industries, regardless of their headquarter intensities. That is, we impose that all five $\gamma_{\theta\eta p}$ are equal. The average effect is positive and highly significant. The estimated coefficient of .09 suggests that a one-standard-deviation increase in the dispersion measure increases the proportion of within-firm imports by 2.9 percentage points. Because our variable of interest x^{θ}_g is an industry-specific measure, we include country fixed effects and adjust the estimated standard errors for clustering across countries within each HS6 industry.

In the second and third columns, we allow the effect of dispersion to differ depending on the headquarter intensity of the industries. In column 2 we measure headquarter intensity by skill intensity S_g/L_g. In column 3 we measure headquarter intensity by capital intensity K_g/L_g. Consistent with hypothesis 2.2, we observe a significant jump in the magnitude of the estimated coefficient when moving from the first quintile to the second quintile. After this, the estimated coefficient remains essentially constant. That is, we find that $0 \leq \hat{\gamma}_{\theta\eta 1} < \hat{\gamma}_{\theta\eta 2} \approx \hat{\gamma}_{\theta\eta 3} \approx \hat{\gamma}_{\theta\eta 4} \approx \hat{\gamma}_{\theta\eta 5}$. F-tests cannot reject the null hypothesis of the equality of any pair of coefficients among $\hat{\gamma}_{\theta\eta 2}$, $\hat{\gamma}_{\theta\eta 3}$, $\hat{\gamma}_{\theta\eta 4}$, or $\hat{\gamma}_{\theta\eta 5}$. However, F-tests do reject the null hypothesis of equality between $\hat{\gamma}_{\theta\eta 1}$ and either $\hat{\gamma}_{\theta\eta 2}$, $\hat{\gamma}_{\theta\eta 3}$, $\hat{\gamma}_{\theta\eta 4}$, or $\hat{\gamma}_{\theta\eta 5}$. These results provide dramatic confirmation of hypothesis 2.2. They also suggest that the η_c cutoff is relatively low, somewhere near the first and second quintiles of the distribution of headquarter intensity.

We further examine the robustness of our results in columns 4 to 6 where we report the same results using the alternative measure of productivity dispersion from equation (2.8). The results using the two different measures of productivity dispersion are very similar.

In the final column of the table, we show that the results are similar when we use our restricted sample of countries. The sample ensures that most of

Table 2.3 Productivity dispersion as a determinant of the share of intrafirm imports in total imports

		Productivity dispersion calculated using $X_{v(g),l,c}$			Productivity dispersion calculated using $X_{v(g),l}$			
Headquarter intensity measure:			S_g/L_g	K_g/L_g		S_g/L_g	K_g/L_g	K_g/L_g
Productivity dispersion, x_g^θ		.09**			.08**			
		(.006)			(.005)			
Productivity dispersion interactions:								
Low η,	$(x_g^\theta \cdot I_{g1}^\eta)$		.03**	.03**		.04**	.01	.04**
			(.010)	(.009)		(.011)	(.011)	(.011)
Low-mid η,	$(x_g^\theta \cdot I_{g2}^\eta)$		.11**	.13**		.10**	.10**	.11**
			(.014)	(.083)		(.009)	(.013)	(.022)
Mid η,	$(x_g^\theta \cdot I_{g3}^\eta)$		.11**	.12**		.10**	.11**	.12**
			(.016)	(.014)		(.012)	(.010)	(.017)
Mid-high η,	$(x_g^\theta \cdot I_{g4}^\eta)$		.11**	.09**		.09**	.08**	.07**
			(.015)	(.015)		(.011)	(.010)	(.016)
High η,	$(x_g^\theta \cdot I_{g5}^\eta)$		.11**	.11**		.09**	.10**	.13**
			(.014)	(.013)		(.011)	(.011)	(.017)
Skill, capital intensity controls		Yes	Yes	Yes	Yes	Yes	Yes	Yes
Headquarter indicators I_{gp}^η		Yes	Yes	Yes	Yes	Yes	Yes	Yes
Country fixed effects		Yes	Yes	Yes	Yes	Yes	Yes	Yes
R^2		.12	.13	.13	.12	.13	.13	.11
Number of observations		115,436	115,436	115,436	115,433	115,433	115,433	41,682

Note: This table reports estimates of equation (2.9). The dependent variable is $M_{Vgc}/(M_{Vgc} + M_{Ogc})$, the share of U.S. intrafirm imports in total U.S. imports. The unit of observation is an HS6-country pair in 2005. x_g^θ is a measure of productivity dispersion across "notional" firms in industry g. For the definition of x_g^θ, see equation (2.7) for columns 1–3 and equation (2.8) for columns 4–7. I_{gp}^η for $p = 1, \ldots, 5$ is a dummy for whether the industry's headquarter intensity is in the pth quintile of the headquarter-intensity distribution. Headquarter intensity is measured by either skill or capital intensity—see the column headings. All regressions include controls for capital intensity $\ln K_g/L_g$, skill intensity $\ln S_g/L_g$, five headquarter-intensity indicator variables I_{gp}^η, and country fixed effects. The symbols ** and * indicate significance at the 1% and 5% significance levels, respectively. The final column uses the restricted sample that is described in Section 2.2.1 under "Data Sources."

the intrafirm imports are done by firms with U.S. parents. The final column reports estimates using the same specification as in the adjacent column 6. For the other specifications, the restricted sample estimates are also similar to the full sample estimates.

Overall, the evidence from Table 2.3 provides support for hypothesis 2.2. We find that there is indeed a cutoff level of headquarter intensity. For industries with headquarter intensity greater than this cutoff, productivity dispersion increases the share of intrafirm imports. For industries with headquarter intensity below the cutoff, the estimated relationship is much weaker and close to zero. Because the cutoff is quite low, this suggests that the empirically relevant case from Antràs and Helpman (2004) is the high-η specification.

2.4   Partially Incomplete Contracting (Antràs and Helpman 2008)

Antràs and Helpman (2008) introduce the possibility that the inputs supplied by the U.S. firm and its foreign supplier are partially contractible. The input of the foreign supplier (m in equation (2.1)) is assumed to be produced from a continuum of activities. Only a fraction μ_m^S of these activities are contractible. The remaining activities are not contractible. Likewise, the input of the U.S. firm (h in equation (2.1)) is assumed to be produced from a continuum of activities and only a fraction μ_h^S of these activities are contractible. With this setup, all of the previous results carry through, though the cutoff η_c shifts somewhat. Let η_c' be the new cutoff.

The introduction of partial contractibility offers many new insights, one of which deals with the intrafirm share of U.S. imports $M_{Vgc}/(M_{Vgc} + M_{Ogc})$. Antràs and Helpman (2008) show that as the contractibility of the foreign supplier's inputs improves (μ_m^S rises), there are two offsetting effects on the intrafirm share of U.S. imports. To understand the first effect, we must introduce the possibility that the U.S. firm can produce in the United States and not just abroad. This is shown in the top panel of Figure 2.2 where we are assuming $\eta > \eta_c'$. (If $\eta < \eta_c'$, then $M_{Vgc} = 0$ as in hypotheses 2.1 and 2.2.) There are now two productivity cutoffs. One determines whether the U.S. firm will produce abroad or in the United States. This cutoff occurs where the profits from foreign outsourcing are zero: $\pi_O(\theta) = 0$. The second cutoff is the one we saw in the last section and demarcates the decision whether to outsource abroad or vertically integrate abroad. It oc-

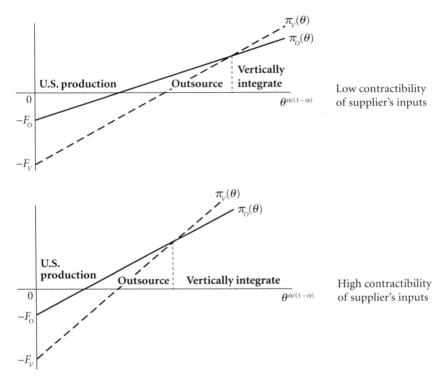

Figure 2.2 Improved contractibility of the foreign supplier's inputs.

curs where the profits from vertical integration and outsourcing are equal: $\pi_V(\theta) = \pi_O(\theta) = 0$.

Now consider the effects of an improvement in the contractibility of foreign intermediate inputs. This raises the profitability of foreign operations and, in particular, increases the term $\bar{\pi}_k$ in equation (2.5). Since $\bar{\pi}_k$ is the slope of the Figure 2.2 profit functions $\pi_k(\theta)$, an improvement in foreign contractibility makes the lines in Figure 2.2 rotate counter-clockwise around their fixed vertical intercepts. This is shown in the bottom panel of Figure 2.2. As a result of the improvement in foreign contractibility, the two cutoffs shift left. This impacts the intrafirm share of U.S. imports in two ways.

Hypothesis 2.3   *Assume $F_V > F_O$ and consider an increase in the contractibility of the foreign supplier's inputs (a rise in μ_m^S).*

1. *If $\eta > \eta'_c$, then there are two offsetting effects of improved contractibility on the intrafirm share of U.S. imports.*

    (a) *The "Standard Effect": U.S. production migrates abroad where it is outsourced. This increases arm's-length U.S. imports and thus lowers the intrafirm share of U.S. imports.*

    (b) *The "Surprise Effect": The most productive outsourcing relationships become vertically integrated into the U.S. firm's organization. For these relationships, intrafirm imports increase at the expense of arm's-length imports, thus raising the intrafirm share of U.S. imports.*

2. *If $\eta < \eta'_c$, then the intrafirm share of U.S. imports $M_{Vgc}/(M_{Vgc} + M_{Ogc}) = 0$ and is independent of the contractibility of the supplier's inputs.*

The surprising effect is, well, surprising. However, once stated, the insight is simple. With a better contracting environment for inputs produced by the foreign supplier, it is no longer as important to incentivize the foreign supplier. This makes it *relatively* more important to incentivize the U.S. firm. Thus, improved contracting abroad leads the U.S. firm to internalize previously outsourced activities.

Antràs and Helpman (2008) show that the sum of the standard and surprise effects can push the intrafirm share of U.S. imports either up or down. This means that in a regression of the intrafirm share of U.S. imports on foreign contracting institutions, a positive coefficient indicates that the surprise effect is more important than the standard effect while a negative coefficient indicates the opposite.[8]

2.4.1 Examining Hypothesis 2.3 (Antràs and Helpman 2008)

In the Antràs and Helpman (2008) model, μ^S_m measures the proportion of contractible "activities" involved in producing the input. We interpret "activities" as the components or intermediate inputs used in the production of the input. Following this logic, we use Nunn's (2007) measure of the proportion of each industry's intermediate inputs that are relationship-specific and therefore susceptible to potential contracting problems. Denote Nunn's measure by z_g. Because we want a measure that is increasing in the completeness of contracts, we use 1 minus the fraction of inputs that are relationship-specific, which we denote by $(1 - z_g)$.

The relationship-specificity measure from Nunn (2007) provides variation across industries in contractibility, but in Antràs and Helpman's model, contractibility varies across industries and countries. We capture variation in contracting across countries using the "rule of law" variable from the *Governance Matters V* database (Kaufmann, Kraay, and Mastruzzi 2006). The variable measures the enforcement of contracts and the overall quality of a country's legal system. The original measure ranges from -2.5 to $+2.5$ and is increasing in the quality of the contracting environment. We normalize the measure to be between 0 and 1 (like the industry measure z_g) by adding 2.5 and dividing by 5. We denote the normalized variable by r_c.

To capture the interaction between the relationship-specificity of industries and the overall contracting environment in the country, we use the interaction of the industry and country measures:

$$x_{gc}^{\mu} \equiv r_c \times (1 - z_g). \tag{2.10}$$

This provides a country- and industry-specific measure of contractual completeness that captures in a simple way the notion that both the inherent contractibility of an industry's production process and the overall quality of a country's contracting environment matter. It also captures the intuition that a country's judicial quality matters more in industries with relationship-specific, customized, intermediate inputs.

Hypothesis 2.3 states that in a regression of the intrafirm share of U.S. imports on x_{gc}^{μ}, the coefficient should vary across industries. In industries with $\eta < \eta_c'$, the coefficient should be zero. In industries with $\eta > \eta_c'$, the coefficient should be positive or negative depending on the size of the standard and surprise effects. To model this nonlinearity, we proceed as in the previous section. We group industries into five quintiles based on the value η, that is, on the size of industries' skill intensities $\ln S_g/L_g$ or capital intensities $\ln K_g/L_g$. Let the $p = 1, \ldots, 5$ subscripts denote the quintiles and let I_{gp}^{η} be a binary indicator of whether industry g is in quintile p.

We estimate the following equation:

$$\frac{M_{Vgc}}{M_{Vgc} + M_{Ogc}} = \gamma_g + \gamma_c + \sum_{p=1}^{5} \gamma_{\mu\eta p} \, (x_{gc}^{\mu} \cdot I_{gp}^{\eta}) + \varepsilon_{gc} \tag{2.11}$$

where the $(x_{gc}^{\mu} \cdot I_{gp}^{\eta})$ are the five primary regressors and the $\gamma_{\mu\eta1}, \ldots, \gamma_{\mu\eta5}$ are the corresponding coefficients.

The fact that x_{gc}^{μ} varies across goods and countries allows us to include good fixed effects γ_g and country fixed effects γ_c. Of course, with these fixed effects included we can no longer test hypotheses 2.1 and 2.2, which are about the industry-specific characteristics $\ln S_g/L_g$, $\ln K_g/L_g$, and x_g^{θ}. Also, because of the good fixed effects, the headquarter-indicator variables I_{gp}^{η} are subsumed in the industry fixed effects.

Estimates of (2.11) appear in Table 2.4.[9] Column 1 reports the average relationship between contractual completeness and intrafirm imports across

Table 2.4 Contractual completeness as a determinant of the share of intrafirm imports in total imports

Headquarter intensity measured by:	Full sample			Restricted sample		
	S_g/L_g	K_g/L_g		S_g/L_g	K_g/L_g	
Contractual completeness, x_{gc}^{μ}	.10*			.12		
	(.043)			(.071)		
Contractual completeness interacted with:						
Low η, $(x_{gc}^{\mu} \cdot I_{g1}^{\eta})$		−.03	−.12		.05	−.13
		(.047)	(.070)		(.077)	(.116)
Low-mid η, $(x_{gc}^{\mu} \cdot I_{g2}^{\eta})$		.01	−.05		.04	−.00
		(.048)	(.050)		(.079)	(.085)
Mid η, $(x_{gc}^{\mu} \cdot I_{g3}^{\eta})$		.11*	−.04*		.13	−.02
		(.046)	(.051)		(.079)	(.083)
Mid-high η, $(x_{gc}^{\mu} \cdot I_{g4}^{\eta})$		.09	.10*		.14	.18*
		(.047)	(.048)		(.084)	(.086)
High η, $(x_{gc}^{\mu} \cdot I_{g5}^{\eta})$		.29**	.11*		.24*	.10
		(.065)	(.045)		(.111)	(.073)
Good fixed effects	Yes	Yes	Yes	Yes	Yes	Yes
Country fixed effects	Yes	Yes	Yes	Yes	Yes	Yes
R^2	.22	.22	.22	.26	.26	.26
Number of observations	111,768	111,768	111,768	40,428	40,428	40,428

Note: This table reports estimates of equation (2.11). The dependent variable is $M_{Vgc}/(M_{Vgc} + M_{Ogc})$, the share of U.S. intrafirm imports in total U.S. imports. The unit of observation is a country and HS6 good in 2005. x_{gc}^{μ} of equation (2.10) is a measure of contractual incompleteness for industry g in country c. I_{gp}^{η} for $p = 1, \ldots, 5$ is a dummy for whether the industry's headquarter intensity is in the pth quintile of the headquarter-intensity distribution. All regressions include HS6 good fixed effects and country fixed effects. Because the contracting regressor is at the NAICS level, standard errors are clustered. The symbols ** and * indicate significance at the 1% and 5% significance levels, respectively. The restricted sample is described in Section 2.2.1, "Data Sources."

all industries. We find a positive, marginally significant, relationship, which implies that the "surprise effect" slightly dominates the "standard effect."

Columns 2 and 3 allow the estimated effects to differ by headquarter intensity. Although the coefficients are not precisely estimated, the general pattern that emerges is that for low headquarter-intensive industries, there is no relationship between contractibility and intrafirm imports. For higher headquarter-intensive industries, the relationship between contract completeness and intrafirm imports is positive. The relevant cutoff appears to be between the 2nd and 3rd quintiles when headquarter intensity is measured with skill intensity, and between the 3rd and 4th quintiles when capital intensity is used.

Columns 4 to 6 report estimates using the restricted sample of exporting countries, that is, the sample dominated by U.S.-owned parents. The results are similar. There appears to be no relationship between contractibility and intrafirm imports in low headquarter-intensive industries, and a positive relationship in high headquarter-intensive industries. Overall, these results are perfectly consistent with Antràs and Helpman's (2008) model.

2.5   Conclusion

Antràs (2003) proposed that we think of the boundaries of the firm—of the choice between outsourcing on the one hand and vertical integration, foreign direct investment, and multinationals on the other—in the property-rights terms of Grossman and Hart (1986). The central assumption of the Antràs approach is that vertical integration allows the U.S. firm to partially control the customized, intermediate inputs produced by its foreign supplier. The central implication is that we should see vertical integration in industries that intensively use the headquarter inputs produced by the U.S. firm. We analyzed this implication using Census data on U.S. intrafirm and arm's-length imports of 5,423 products from 210 countries in 2000 and 2005. As predicted by Antràs, we found that skill- and capital-intensive industries have a higher ratio of intrafirm imports to total imports. This is true even after controlling for exporter fixed effects. Our results extend those of Antràs (2003) and Yeaple (2006) who both used a much smaller number of industries and countries.

Antràs and Helpman (2004) extended the original Antràs model to allow for (1) firm-level heterogeneity in productivities and (2) fixed costs that are higher for vertical integration than for outsourcing. The extension implies that the intrafirm share of U.S. imports will be highest for firms with two characteristics: (a) high headquarter intensity η and (b) high productivity θ. We found very strong evidence to support this implication.

Antràs and Helpman (2008) extended their earlier model to allow for partial contractibility of the foreign supplier's inputs. An improvement in contractibility has two effects. The standard effect is that it encourages arm's-length transactions. The surprise effect is that it makes the *relative* noncontractibility of the U.S. firm's inputs all the more pressing, thus encouraging vertical integration and more intrafirm imports. This surprise effect should only appear for the most productive firms. This is exactly what we found.

In short, this chapter provides rich support for the central predictions in Antràs (2003) and Antràs and Helpman (2004, 2008) about U.S. intrafirm imports as a share of total U.S. imports.

Appendix

2A.1 Data Description

Data on intrafirm and total trade are from the U.S. Census Bureau. The trade data are at the 6-digit Harmonized System (HS6) level for the years 2000 and 2005. Each shipment imported into the United States is accompanied by a form that asks about the value of the shipment, the HS10 code, and whether or not the transaction is with a related party, that is, whether or not the transaction is intrafirm or at arm's length.

Two parties are related if one owns at least 6% of the other. There is an oft-used alternative data set on intrafirm trade, namely, the BEA's multinationals database. In the BEA data, a 10% ownership stake is used to define intrafirm transactions. However, the BEA data provide two pieces of evidence to suggest that a 6% threshold is large enough to ensure a controlling stake. First, only 5% of intrafirm BEA imports involve ownership positions of less than 10%. See Table 11 in Mataloni and Yorgason (2006). Thus, if an ownership position is at least 6%, then it is likely that it is at least 10%. Second, for a very large proportion of ownership positions in the BEA data, once the position is more than 10%, it is also more than 50%. (Authors' calculations from the BEA data available on the Web.) Thus, although the threshold ownership stake is only 6% in our data, it is safe to say that in most cases it is a controlling stake.

The capital intensity $\ln K_g / L_g$ and skill intensity $\ln S_g / L_g$ measures are constructed using data from Bartelsman and Gray (1996). The data are from the United States in 1996, with industries classified at the 4-digit SIC87 level.

We use U.S. export data to construct productivity dispersion measures x_g^θ. The data are from the U.S. Department of Commerce CD *U.S. Exports History: Historical Summary 2000–2004*. x_g^θ is based on 2004 export data for the 2005 regressions and 2000 export data for the 2000 regressions. The data report the value of U.S. bilateral imports and exports. The data are also disaggregated by the geographic location within the United States from which the products are exported. When goods are exported overland, the location is the U.S. customs port where the surface carrier crosses the border. When goods are exported by sea or by air, then the location is the U.S. customs port where the merchandise is loaded onto the carrier that is taking the merchandise out of the United States. Finally, when goods are exported by post, the location is the U.S. post office where the merchandise is mailed. There are 46 locations coded in the data.

The industry measures of relationship-specificity are from Nunn (2007). We use Nunn's first measure of relationship-specificity, z_i^{rs1}, and we use the most recent year for which the measure is available, 1997. The measure is classified according to the 1997 I-O classification, which is based on the 6-digit NAICS classification. The country measures of rule of law are from the *Governance Matters V* database (Kaufmann, Kraay, and Mastruzzi 2006). This measure is from 2005.

The regressions have a maximum of 210 countries, depending on the specific equation being estimated. A list of the countries organized by per capita GDP in 2005 (from the *World Development Indicators*) is given in Table 2A.1. Table 2A.2 reports a list of the remaining countries in the sample for which no income data are available. These countries are listed alphabetically in the table.

ACKNOWLEDGMENTS

Both authors thank the Canadian Institute for Advanced Research (CIFAR) for its support. We also thank Pol Antràs, Rob Feenstra, Elhanan Helpman, Gene Grossman, Wilhelm Kohler, and Marc Melitz for insightful comments. We are especially grateful to Joel Blit for facilitating construction of the database.

Table 2A.1 Countries in the sample, ordered by 2005 real per capita GDP

Income	Country	Income	Country
516	Sierra Leone	2,004	Angola
594	Malawi	2,004	Guinea
620	Tanzania	2,045	Pakistan
622	Burundi	2,058	Ghana
648	Congo, Dem. Rep. (Zaire)	2,227	Cambodia*
663	Guinea-Bissau	2,338	Papua New Guinea*
695	Ethiopia	2,407	Lesotho
716	Niger	2,499	Bolivia
788	Madagascar	2,523	Vietnam*
807	Yemen	2,614	Georgia
867	Zambia	2,644	Honduras
898	Eritrea	2,804	Vanuatu*
899	Congo	2,885	India
917	Mali	3,316	Indonesia*
1,003	Benin	3,318	Syria
1,006	Central African Republic	3,340	Nicaragua
1,047	Kenya	3,642	Ecuador
1,061	Nigeria	3,769	Armenia
1,074	Burkina Faso	3,817	Azerbaijan
1,104	Tajikistan	3,826	Jamaica
1,137	Mozambique	3,870	Egypt
1,160	Rwanda	3,961	Morocco
1,359	Uganda	3,964	Guatemala
1,369	Nepal*	4,034	Sri Lanka*
1,412	Togo	4,080	Guyana
1,425	Ivory Coast	4,241	Philippines
1,574	Senegal	4,308	Jordan
1,589	Moldova*	4,423	Paraguay
1,667	Solomon Islands*	4,575	Albania*
1,718	Uzbekistan	4,633	El Salvador
1,719	Bangladesh	5,158	Samoa*
1,779	Kyrgyz Republic	5,182	Swaziland
1,783	Mauritania	5,186	Dominica
1,786	Comoros	5,219	Peru
1,791	Sudan	5,264	Cape Verde
1,796	Laos*	5,364	Lebanon
1,830	Gambia	5,419	China*
1,832	Djibouti	5,554	Venezuela*
1,889	Mongolia*	5,575	Fiji*
1,898	Zimbabwe	5,812	St. Lucia
1,921	Chad	5,877	Ukraine
1,998	Cameroon	5,880	St. Vincent and the Gren.

Table 2A.1 *(continued)*

Income	Country	Income	Country
6,069	Algeria	13,439	Slovak Republic*
6,075	Macedonia*	14,024	Oman
6,087	Gabon	15,304	Seychelles
6,201	Belize	15,453	Hungary*
6,406	Belarus*	17,351	Malta*
6,463	Bosnia-Herzegovina	17,815	Kuwait
6,669	Colombia	17,837	Czech Republic*
6,689	Panama	18,040	Portugal*
6,818	Namibia	18,840	Korea, South*
6,838	Kazakhstan	19,078	Bahrain
6,846	Dominican Republic	19,244	Slovenia*
6,916	Iran	20,407	Greece*
7,125	Turkey	20,959	Cyprus
7,139	Tunisia	21,518	New Zealand*
7,233	Tonga*	22,109	United Arab Emirates
7,372	Grenada	22,408	Israel*
7,424	Bulgaria*	23,019	Spain*
7,435	Thailand*	25,804	Singapore
7,531	Brazil	25,899	Italy*
7,793	Romania*	26,013	Germany*
8,658	Uruguay	26,884	Japan*
8,714	Costa Rica	26,929	France*
9,010	Mexico	27,150	Sweden*
9,101	Russia*	27,527	Finland*
9,140	Botswana	27,876	Australia*
9,444	Malaysia	28,326	United Kingdom*
9,993	Chile	28,327	Hong Kong*
10,286	South Africa	28,579	Belgium*
10,710	Latvia*	28,732	Canada
11,054	Mauritius	29,216	Netherlands*
11,196	Trinidad and Tobago	29,331	Denmark*
11,204	Croatia*	29,664	Austria*
11,567	Antigua and Barbuda	30,365	Switzerland*
11,924	Poland*	30,376	Iceland*
12,046	Lithuania*	35,341	Norway*
12,222	Argentina	35,684	Ireland
12,706	Saudi Arabia*	64,299	Luxembourg*
13,377	Estonia*		

Note: Countries are ordered by 2005 real per capita GDP from the *World Development Indicators*. An asterisk indicates that the country is not in the restricted sample of countries.

Table 2A.2 Countries in the sample without income data, ordered alphabetically

Afghanistan	Guadeloupe	New Caledonia*
Andorra*	Haiti	Niue*
Anguilla	Iraq	Palau*
Aruba*	Kiribati*	Qatar
Bahamas	Korea, North*	Reunion
Barbados	Liberia	San Marino*
Bermuda	Libya	Sao Tome and Principe
Bhutan*	Liechtenstein*	Serbia and Montenegro*
British Virgin Islands	Macao*	Somalia
Brunei*	Maldives*	St. Kitts and Nevis
Cayman Islands	Marshall Islands*	Suriname*
Cook Islands*	Martinique*	Taiwan*
Cuba	Micronesia*	Timor, East*
Equatorial Guinea	Monaco*	Turkmenistan
French Guiana	Myanmar*	Turks and Caicos Islands
French Polynesia*	Nauru*	Tuvalu*
Greenland	Netherlands Antilles	West Bank

Note: Countries are ordered alphabetically. An asterisk indicates that the country is not in the restricted sample of countries.

NOTES

1. Feenstra and Hanson (2005) also provide support for the property-rights approach in an international trade context.

2. It is evident from the table that the countries for which a large share of intrafirm imports are imports from foreign-owned parents are higher-income countries. An alternative strategy therefore is to restrict high-income countries from the sample. We have also done this using data from the *World Development Indicators*. Although we do not report the results here, they are qualitatively identical to the results we obtain from either our full sample or our restricted sample.

3. The results are similar if either capital intensity or skill intensity enter separately in the estimating equation.

4. To remind the reader, the differences between our estimates and those of the Antràs and Yeaple studies are that (1) our data have 370 industries, much more than the 23 used by Antràs and the 51 used by Yeaple and (2) we have import data for 210 exporting countries, much more than the 28 exporters considered by Antràs and the 58 exporters considered by Yeaple. In addition,

Yeaple uses only U.S. parents whereas we are forced to include foreign parents. Our restricted sample eliminates most of the foreign parents.

5. That is, if $F_V = F_O$ then $\pi_V(\theta) > \pi_O(\theta) \Leftrightarrow \overline{\pi}_V > \overline{\pi}_O$ and it remains true that the firm prefers vertical integration if and only if $\eta > \eta_c$.

6. See Helpman, Melitz, and Yeaple (2004, 307) for an explanation of how the standard deviation of the log of firm sales recovers the parameter λ.

7. Alternatively, one could approximate a notional firm's exports by exports of an HS10 variety to a particular country from any location in the United States. This would be a more appropriate measure if firms exported goods from multiple locations in the United States. Using this alternative measure produces results that are qualitatively identical to what we report below.

8. An alternative interpretation that one can take from the Antràs and Helpman (2008) model is that improved contracting institutions increase μ_m^S, but increase μ_h^S even more. In this case, the standard effect leads to a rise in the intrafirm import share, and the surprise effect leads to a fall in the intrafirm import share. In our view, improved contracting for developing countries is best thought of in terms of a disproportional increase in μ_m^S. We thus ignore this alternative interpretation.

9. Note that the measure of contract intensity is only available at the 6-digit NAICS level, not the HS6 level. We therefore adjust the standard errors for clustering across HS6 goods within 6-digit NAICS industries in our estimating equations.

REFERENCES

Antràs, Pol. 2003. "Firms, Contracts, and Trade Structure." *Quarterly Journal of Economics* 118:1375–1418.

———. 2005. "Incomplete Contracts and the Product Cycle." *American Economic Review* 95:1054–73.

Antràs, Pol, and Elhanan Helpman. 2004. "Global Sourcing." *Journal of Political Economy* 112:552–80.

———. 2008. "Contractual Frictions and Global Sourcing." Chapter 1, this volume.

Bartelsman, Eric J., and Wayne Gray. 1996. "The NBER Manufacturing Productivity Database." Technical working paper no. 205, National Bureau of Economic Research.

Berman, Eli, John Bound, and Zvi Griliches. 1994. "Changes in the Demand for Skilled Labor within U.S. Manufacturing: Evidence from the Annual Survey of Manufactures." *Quarterly Journal of Economics* 109:367–97.

Bernard, Andrew B., and J. Bradford Jensen. 1997. "Exporters, Skill Upgrading, and the Wage Gap." *Journal of International Economics* 42:3–31.

Bernard, Andrew B., J. Bradford Jensen, and Peter Schott. 2005. "Importers, Exporters, and Multinationals: A Portrait of Firms in the U.S. That Trade Goods." Working paper no. 11404, National Bureau of Economic Research.

————. 2006. "Transfer Pricing by U.S.-Based Multinational Firms." Working paper no. 12493, National Bureau of Economic Research.

Feenstra, Robert C., and Gordon H. Hanson. 2005. "Ownership and Control in Outsourcing to China: Estimating the Property-Rights Theory of the Firm." *Quarterly Journal of Economics* 120:729–61.

Feinberg, Susan E., and Michael P. Keane. 2006. "Accounting for the Growth of MNC-Based Trade Using a Structural Model of U.S. MNCs." *American Economic Review* 96:1515–58.

Grossman, Gene M., and Elhanan Helpman. 2002. "Integration versus Outsourcing in Industry Equilibrium." *Quarterly Journal of Economics* 117:85–120.

————. 2003. "Outsourcing versus FDI in Industry Equilibrium." *Journal of the European Economic Association* 1:317–27.

————. 2004. "Managerial Incentives and the International Organization of Production." *Journal of International Economics* 63:237–62.

————. 2005. "Outsourcing in a Global Economy." *Review of Economic Studies* 72:135–59.

Grossman, Sanford J., and Oliver D. Hart. 1986. "Costs and Benefits of Ownership: A Theory of Vertical and Lateral Integration." *Journal of Political Economy* 94:691–719.

Helpman, Elhanan. 2006. "Trade, FDI and the Organization of Firms." *Journal of Economic Literature* 44:589–630.

Helpman, Elhanan, and Paul R. Krugman. 1985. *Market Structure and Foreign Trade: Increasing Returns, Imperfect Competition, and the International Economy.* Cambridge, MA: MIT Press.

Helpman, Elhanan, Marc J. Melitz, and Stephen R. Yeaple. 2004. "Export versus FDI with Heterogeneous Firms." *American Economic Review* 94:300–16.

Kaufmann, Daniel, Aart Kraay, and Massimo Mastruzzi. 2006. "Governance Matters V: Governance Indicators for 1996–2005." Working paper, World Bank.

Mataloni Jr., Raymond J., and Daniel R. Yorgason. 2006. "Operations of U.S. Multinational Companies: Preliminary Results from the 2004 Benchmark Survey." *Survey of Current Business* 86:37–68.

McLaren, John. 2000. "Globalization and Vertical Structure." *American Economic Review* 90:1239–54.

Melitz, Marc J. 2003. "The Impact of Trade on Intra-Industry Reallocations and Aggregate Industry Productivity." *Econometrica* 71:1695–1725.

Nunn, Nathan. 2007. "Relationship-Specificity, Incomplete Contracts, and the Pattern of Trade." *Quarterly Journal of Economics* 122:569–600.

Schott, Peter. 2004. "Across-Product versus Within-Product Specialization in International Trade." *Quarterly Journal of Economics* 119:647–78.

Yeaple, Stephen R. 2006. "Offshoring, Foreign Direct Investment, and the Structure of U.S. Trade." *Journal of the European Economic Association* 4:602–11.

Zeile, William J. 2003. "Trade in Goods within Multinational Companies: Survey-Based Data and Findings for the United States of America." Mimeo, U.S. Bureau of Economic Analysis.

— 3 —

Contract Enforcement, Comparative Advantage, and Long-Run Growth

GIANMARCO I. P. OTTAVIANO

3.1 Introduction

From a historical perspective there is increasing agreement that institutions (such as contract enforcement, investor protection, and constitutions) have played a key role in shaping the international pattern of economic development, and, still today, developed countries typically feature better institutions than developing ones (see, e.g., La Porta et al. 1998; Acemoglu, Johnson, and Robinson 2002). A growing stock of empirical evidence also suggests that institutions (especially, contract enforcement) affect the international pattern of comparative advantage and, thus, sectoral specialization as well as trade flows. For instance, Antràs (2003) shows that, when investments related to the labor input are harder to share than investments in physical capital, incomplete contract enforcement can explain why capital-intensive goods are transacted within the boundaries of multinational firms, while labor-intensive goods are traded at arm's length. Levchenko (2004) shows that, when some industries rely on institutions more than others, international differences in institutions act as a source of comparative advantage. Nunn (2007) combines a sectoral measure of intensity in relationship-specific investment with data on trade flows and judicial quality. He finds that countries with good contract enforcement specialize in the production of goods for which relationship-specific investments are more important. Costinot (2006) argues that better institutions and more-educated workers are complementary sources of comparative advantage in more complex industries.

So far the effects of institutional quality on economic development and comparative advantage have been investigated separately. The aim of the present chapter is to propose a theoretical framework in which trade patterns and growth rates are jointly determined by international differences in contract enforcement that affect firms' organizational choices. In a two-country dynamic Ricardian model with endogenous innovation à la Taylor (1993), and in hold-up problems à la Grossman and Helpman (2002), the value chain consists of two activities, innovation and production. Entry in the market happens through R&D, and firms face two decisions. The *location decision* concerns where to locate R&D labs and production plants. The *ownership decision* concerns whether innovation and production should be performed within the same vertically integrated structure or not. While the former decision is driven by comparative advantage and wage differences, the latter is driven by a trade-off between the diseconomies of scope associated with vertical integration and the hold-up frictions associated with outsourcing. These are allowed to vary between countries due to quality differences in contract enforcement, and across industries depending on their potential for technological improvement. In this framework, the quality of contract enforcement drives the ownership decision between insourcing and outsourcing. The ownership structure then affects the returns to innovation, research intensity, and growth. The resulting adjustments in the balance of payments cause movements in relative wages that impact on the location decision and, therefore, on the pattern of sectoral specialization and international trade.

General equilibrium effects due to balance-of-payments adjustments are the key channel through which the ownership decision influences the location decision. These effects materialize when innovation and production take place in different countries so that royalty payments from labs to plants cross international borders. In this case, through its impact on royalties, the ownership decision affects wages and location. As a result, when correlated with the sectoral potential for technological improvement, the pattern of comparative advantage determines the relative prevalence of alternative organizational forms in the two countries. The pattern of specialization also depends on the differences across countries in the quality of the contractual environment.

The proposed theoretical framework can be used to investigate several alternative scenarios. For concreteness, this chapter focuses on a specific situation in which a developing country ("South") trades with a developed one ("North") that has an advantage in innovation relative to production, a comparative advantage in industries with higher growth potential, and better contract enforcement. In equilibrium, industries endogenously sort into five organizational forms depending on comparative advantage: outsourcing from Southern innovators to Southern producers; outsourcing from Northern innovators to Southern producers; production in South by vertically integrated Northern innovators; outsourcing in North by Northern innovators; production in North by vertically integrated Northern innovators.

Two shocks are analyzed: an improvement of contract enforcement in South (*institutional convergence*) and a generalized increase in the growth potential of all industries (*systemic innovation*). On impact, the former leads to an increase in the share of industries that innovate in North but produce in South. As the profits of offshored plants increase, royalty payments from South to North surge. The balance of payments is maintained by a rise in Southern net exports and an associated increase in the shares of industries innovating or producing in South as Southern wages fall. If the relative advantage of North in innovation is pronounced, the range of industries producing in South increases more than the range of industries innovating there, thus fostering offshoring from North to South. Moreover, if diseconomies of scope are strong, the fraction of offshoring firms that outsource also increases. Turning to systemic innovation, when the potential for technological improvement goes up in all industries, the share of industries that outsource goes down both in North and South. This effect is due to larger hold-up losses for innovators, and it is stronger in South due to weaker contract enforcement. If the diseconomies of scope are small and international legal asymmetries large, many industries shift from outsourcing to vertical integration, royalty payments rise, and, as before, the balance of payments is maintained through larger net exports from South associated with lower Southern wages and a larger share of industries choosing South for innovation or production. Again, more industries offshore if the Northern relative advantage in innovation is pronounced. On the contrary, if diseconomies of scope are large and legal asymmetries small, few industries shift to vertical integration, royalty payments fall, and the balance of payments is maintained through smaller Southern net exports, higher Southern wages and smaller shares of industries selecting South for innovation or production. Fewer industries offshore if the Northern relative advantage in innovation is pronounced.

To summarize, better Southern institutions unambiguously foster outsourcing and a relocation of industries from North to South. Systemic innovation unambiguously fosters vertical integration. However, it may have different effects on relocation depending on the strength of the dis-economies of scope and the extent of institutional asymmetries as these determine the share of industries that undergo organizational restructuring. As to growth, if relative wages do not change much, the aggregate return to innovation increases whenever royalties increase. This maps into higher research intensity and a faster growth rate.

The model combines two well-established approaches. The first is the incomplete contracting approach to the theory of the firm due to Grossman and Hart (1986) as well as Hart and Moore (1990). This approach has been applied to trade theory in the wake of Grossman and Helpman (2002) and has given rise to a thriving literature, surveyed by Helpman (2006). The second is Grossman and Helpman's (1991) and Aghion and Howitt's (1998) approach to endogenous growth through rising product quality. This approach has been applied to Ricardian trade by Taylor (1993). In this respect, there are few contributions strictly related to the present paper. Acemoglu and Zilibotti (1999) and Martimort and Verdier (2000, 2004) as well as Francois and Roberts (2003) study the qualitative impact on economic growth of changes in the internal organization of firms. Acemoglu and Zilibotti (1999) link the level of economic development to the level of information available in an economy, as this determines the importance of agency costs. Martimort and Verdier (2000, 2004) present a Schumpeterian growth model in which firms face agency costs due to the existence of asymmetries of information and discuss the two-way relationships between the structure of internal transaction costs, organizational technologies, and macroeconomic growth, focusing on the formation of vertical collusions inside those firms (*bureaucratization*). Francois and Roberts (2003) analyze how growth interacts with the production relationships between firms and workers in an incomplete-contracting environment. They show that changes in the technological parameters may have unexpected impacts on growth through their effects on contractual arrangements. In Acemoglu, Aghion, and Zilibotti (2006), firms closer to the technology frontier have a stronger incentive to outsource production in order to concentrate on more valuable R&D. Finally, Naghavi and Ottaviano (2006) study the effects of outsourced production on growth in a closed-economy model of incomplete contracts and increasing product diversity when R&D and production are performed by independent firms. The closest contribution to the present chapter is Acemoglu, Antràs, and Helpman (2006) who investigate the channels through which institutional parameters determine countries' comparative advantages by affecting firms' decisions on technology adoption and organizational forms. They find that weaker contract enforcement leads to the adoption of less advanced technologies. Their model of technology adoption is, however, essentially static. Moreover, the ownership and location decisions are treated separately. In short, none of the foregoing models deals with Ricardian trade and simultaneously with both the ownership and the location decisions in a general-equilibrium, endogenous-growth framework.

The rest of the chapter is organized in four sections. Section 3.2 presents the model. Section 3.3 characterizes its general equilibrium. Section 3.4 deals with comparative statics. Section 3.5 concludes.

3.2   The Model

Consider a given set of industries indexed $z \in [0, 1]$ that employ labor as their only primary factor. The industries operate in two countries, South and North. Variables pertaining to the former bear no label, while those pertaining to the latter are labeled by an asterisk. In the two countries there are given measures (numbers) of workers, L and L^*, each supplying one unit of labor inelastically. All income belongs to workers, so L and L^* also represent the numbers of consumers in the two countries. The presentation will focus on South with analogous expressions holding for North.

3.2.1 Consumption

All consumers share the same preferences and, within countries, also the same income. The preferences of the representative Southern consumer are captured by the following utility function:

$$U = \int_0^\infty e^{-\rho t} \ln D(t) dt, \tag{3.1}$$

where $\rho > 0$ is the rate of time preference. Instantaneous consumption $\ln D(t)$ consists of a CES basket comprising the outputs (products) of all industries $z \in [0, 1]$:

$$\ln D(t) = \int_0^1 \ln [x(z, t)] dz, \tag{3.2}$$

where $x(z, t)$ is the consumption of the product of industry z and all industries absorb the same expenditure share.

Borrowing and lending is free in a perfectly integrated international capital market where a riskless bond exists, bearing interest rate $r(t)$. Intertemporal utility maximization then yields the standard consumption-smoothing result:

$$\frac{\dot{E}(t)}{E(t)} = r(t) - \rho, \tag{3.3}$$

where $E(t)$ is expenditures and $\dot{E}(t) \equiv dE(t)/dt$. Moreover, instantaneous utility maximization also implies that consumption is allocated across industries depending on their prices:

$$x(z, t) = \frac{E(t)}{p(z, t)}. \tag{3.4}$$

3.2.2 Production

In any industry z the value chain consists of two activities, innovation and production, with the former inventing new technology vintages for the latter. As a result of repeated innovations, in a generic instant t there are several vintages available for production whose efficiency is a decreasing function of their age with the same efficiency gap between any pair of contiguous vintages. This allows one to rank all vintages in increasing order of efficiency along a *technology ladder* from the oldest to the youngest. Specifically, let $a(z, j) = a(z)\phi(j, z)$ be the unit input requirement of the vintage that occupies the generic position j along the technology ladder of industry z. Then, the productivity ratio of vintage $j + 1$ to vintage j, namely $\phi(j, z)/\phi(j + 1, z) > 1$, identifies the constant *step* of the industry technology ladder (*potential for technological improvement*). At $t = 0$ the same vintage $j = 0$ is available in both countries with unit input requirements $a(z, 0) = a(z)\phi(0, z)$ in South and $a^*(z, 0) = a(z)^*\phi(0, z)$ in North.

After invention, the properties of the latest and thus most efficient vintage remain known only to its inventor (*leader*) until the next vintage is discovered. When this happens, the properties of the formerly leading vintage become common knowledge. These knowledge spillovers will sustain technological progress in the long run. Market structure is modelled as an oligopolistic Bertrand competition so that the incumbent leader maximizes its profit by quoting a price that is just low enough to prevent anybody else from selling at all (*limit pricing*). As a result, the leader is the only supplier in the industry. It faces two choices. First, it may supply the product on its own (vertical integration) or it may contract the use of its vintage to an independent producer (outsourcing). This is the ownership decision. Second, no matter whether the leader selects integration or outsourcing, it may choose whether production should take place in the same country as innovation or in the other country (offshoring). This is the location decision. As in Antràs and Helpman (2004), the combination of the ownership and the location decisions determines the overall organizational form of the industry.

Both ownership structures have pros and cons. Vertical integration incurs diseconomies of scope as the combination of innovation and production within the boundaries of the same firm sacrifices the efficiency gains of specialized production. Outsourcing faces hold-up problems instead, due to incomplete contracts. In particular, in each period the inventor has to find a producer to contract. It is assumed that producers can enter and exit the market freely and there are many of them potentially active. While the inventor is thus surely matched, all matches are destroyed every period. Production takes place only after the matched parties have signed a contract and the leader has revealed the properties of its vintage to the producer. The contract is incomplete because those properties are unobservable to third parties, which makes it possible for the producer to renege on the contract and exploit the leader's vintage without being prosecuted. Crucially, if that happens, it is too late for the leader to find a substitute for the producer or to produce on its own. On the other hand, reneging bears some costs for the producer too as the vintage technology cannot be exploited to its full potential without the support of its inventor. These circumstances affect the outside options of the two parties at the ex post bargaining stage, which takes place after the innovator reveals the properties of the vintage to the producer but before the latter actually produces.

Formally, diseconomies of scope are captured by assuming that, under vertical integration, the technological step equals $\lambda(z)$, whereas under outsourcing it equals $\alpha\lambda(z)$ with $\alpha \in (1, \infty)$. The hold-up problem is modeled through ex post instantaneous Nash bargaining assuming that, when used outside the contractual relation, the technological step is reduced to $\beta\lambda(z)$ with $\beta \in (1/\lambda(z), 1)$. Accordingly, β can be interpreted as an inverse measure of the quality of the contractual environment. For simplicity, the ex post bargaining weight of the producer is set to zero. Under limit pricing, different technological steps imply different markups over marginal cost and therefore different profits. In the case of vertical integration, the markup equals $\lambda(z)$, which yields profits

$$\Pi_V(z) = \left[1 - \frac{1}{\lambda(z)}\right][E(t) + E^*(t)]. \tag{3.5}$$

When production is outsourced, there are two possible outcomes. In the first, the producer reneges and uses the leading vintage to supply the market on its own. This reduces the efficiency of the vintage and therefore the price the producer can command. In this case, the markup becomes $\beta\lambda(z)$ with profits

$$\Pi_R(z) = \left[1 - \frac{1}{\beta\lambda(z)}\right][E(t) + E^*(t)]. \tag{3.6}$$

In the second outcome, the producer keeps its contractual commitment with the innovator and, thanks to its support, productivity is higher than under vertical integration by a factor $\alpha \in (1, \infty)$. This implies that the markup equals $\alpha\lambda(z)$ with profits

$$\Pi_M(z) = \left[1 - \frac{1}{\alpha\lambda(z)}\right][E(t) + E^*(t)]. \tag{3.7}$$

This expression identifies the joint surplus from the outsourcing contract that has to be shared between the innovator and the producer through ex post Nash bargaining. Since its bargaining weight is zero, the producer is left as well off as if it had reneged while the residual surplus is appropriated by the innovator. Hence, the former gets $\Pi_R(z)$ whereas the latter gets $\Pi_O(z) \equiv \Pi_M(z) - \Pi_R(z)$. Results (3.6) and (3.7) then imply

$$\Pi_O(z) = \left(\frac{1}{\beta} - \frac{1}{\alpha}\right)\frac{E(t) + E^*(t)}{\lambda(z)}. \tag{3.8}$$

Anticipating this, the leader chooses to outsource whenever $\Pi_O(z) - \Pi_V(z) > 0$ or equivalently, by (3.5) and (3.8), whenever

$$\lambda(z) < 1 + \frac{1}{\beta} - \frac{1}{\alpha}. \tag{3.9}$$

In words, outsourcing is preferred when the technological step is small (small $\lambda(z)$), the diseconomies of scope are strong (large α), and the quality of the contractual environment is good (small β). The reason is that, while under vertical integration profits (3.5) are an increasing function of the technological step, under outsourcing they are a decreasing function of

$\lambda(z)$. This is due to the fact that a larger step raises the outside option of the producer (3.6) more than the joint surplus from the outsourcing contract (3.7). The more so, the worse the quality of the contractual environment and the weaker the gains from specialized production.

3.2.3 Innovation

The innovation technology is Poisson with an arrival rate that varies proportionately with R&D efforts. Specifically, in industry z the Southern innovation technology is such that an R&D effort of intensity $i(z)$ exerted for a time interval dt faces a probability $i(z)dt$ of moving the state-of-the-art technology one step forward. This research effort is financed by issuing equity claims that give right to the flow profit associated with market leadership in case of success, and nothing otherwise. Well-diversified equity holders finance the R&D effort as long as the expected benefits equal the associated costs. The former are given by the expected stock value of industry leadership $v(z)i(z)dt$, the latter by the wage w multiplied by the unit labor requirement $a_I(z)$ and the R&D intensity $i(z)dt$. Positive and finite R&D intensity $i(z) \in (0, \infty)$ therefore requires that

$$v(z) = wa_I(z),\tag{3.10}$$

where time dependence is left implicit. To simplify the notation, this will be the convention henceforth.

Due to financial arbitrage, equities have to grant the same rate of return as the riskless bond. For industries with R&D in South, that happens whenever

$$r = \frac{R(z)}{v(z)} + \frac{\dot{v}(z)}{v(z)} - i(z),\tag{3.11}$$

where $R(z)$ is the leadership dividend for (i.e., the profit accruing to) the innovator, $\dot{v}(z)$ is the associated capital gain, and $i(z)$ is the probability that leadership is lost to the next innovator. The dividend $R(z)$ depends on both the ownership and the location decisions.

Mutatis mutandis, analogous results apply to North. The analysis below will focus on three types of international asymmetries in terms of the following: the production technological parameters, $a^*(z)$ versus $a(z)$; the R&D technological parameters, $a_I^*(z)$ versus $a_I(z)$; and the contractual parameters, β^* versus β.

3.2.4 Comparative Advantage

To simplify notation, define

$$n_V(z) \equiv 1 - \frac{1}{\lambda(z)}, n_M(z) \equiv 1 - \frac{1}{\alpha\lambda(z)}, \tag{3.12}$$

where $n_V(z)$ and $n_M(z)$ are the operating margins under integration and outsourcing respectively. Then define

$$\theta(z) \equiv 1 - \left[1 - \frac{1}{\beta\lambda(z)}\right] \bigg/ \left[1 - \frac{1}{\alpha\lambda(z)}\right], \text{ and} \tag{3.13}$$

$$\theta^*(z) \equiv 1 - \left[1 - \frac{1}{\beta^*\lambda(z)}\right] \bigg/ \left[1 - \frac{1}{\alpha\lambda(z)}\right].$$

These capture the weakness of the outside options of the producers in the two countries and are therefore measures of the quality of national contractual environments. They range from 0 to 1, with both decreasing in $\lambda(z)$ since the producer's outside option is stronger when the technology step is larger. Note that $dn_V(z)/d\lambda(z) > 0$, $dn_M(z)/d\lambda(z) > 0$, $d\theta(z)/d\lambda(z) < 0$, and $d\left[n_M(z)\theta(z)\right]/d\lambda(z) < 0$. Accordingly, the ownership decision rule (3.9) leading to outsourcing becomes

$$n_V(z) < n_M(z)\theta(z) \text{ and } n_V(z) < n_M(z)\theta^*(z), \tag{3.14}$$

for production in South and North respectively. Finally, define the relative input requirements in production and innovation as

$$A(z) \equiv \frac{a^*(z)\phi(0, z)}{a(z)\phi(0, z)}, RD(z) \equiv \frac{a_I^*(z)}{a_I(z)}. \tag{3.15}$$

In principle, the functions $A(z)$ and $RD(z)$ may take any shape. The same is true for $\lambda(z)$ and thus for $\theta(z)$ and $\theta^*(z)$. Moreover, β may be larger or smaller than β^*. To avoid a proliferation of subcases that would make the analysis taxonomic without adding much insight, the following assumptions are made:

1. $RD(z) < A(z)$ so that North has an advantage in innovation relative to production;

2. $RD'(z) < 0$ and $A'(z) < 0$ so that in terms of both innovation and production, North has a comparative advantage in high-z industries;

3. $RD'(z) < A'(z)$ so that Northern comparative advantage in high-z industries is stronger for innovation than for production;

4. $\lambda'(z) > 0$ so that Northern comparative advantage is positively correlated with industries' technological steps;

5. $\beta > \beta^*$ and hence $\theta(z) < \theta^*(z)$ so that North offers a better contractual environment.

Taken together, all these assumptions depict a situation in which North is more developed than South, as it exhibits better legal institutions, a relative advantage in innovation, and a comparative advantage in industries with more room for technological improvement.

3.3   General Equilibrium

The general equilibrium of the model is represented in Figure 3.1 under the above assumptions 1–5.[1] The top panel, where the $BP(z)$ curve represents the balance of payments (see Section 3.3.3 for its derivation), is the same as Figure 1 in Taylor (1993, 234) with the industry index z and relative Southern wage w/w^* on the horizontal and the vertical axes respectively. This panel shows that the *location decision* generates a Ricardian pattern of specialization according to which South performs innovation in industries $z \in [0, Z_I]$ and production in industries $z \in [0, Z_P]$, whereas North performs innovation in industries $z \in [Z_I, 1]$ and production in industries $z \in [Z_P, 1]$, with $Z_I < Z_P$. Industries $z \in [Z_I, Z_P]$ are characterized by offshoring since innovation takes place in North and production in South. The solid $A(z)$ curve corresponds to the situation at time 0 and shows that initially South features front-line technologies in innovation and production up to industries Z_I and Z_P respectively. For industries above these thresholds, front-line technologies belong to North. Free entry in R&D implies that only innovators in the country where the innovation technology is front line are able to raise funds in the capital market. Accordingly, innovation is only implemented on Southern products for $z \in [0, Z_P]$ and Northern products for $z \in [Z_P, 1]$. Thus, as time passes, Z_P does not change and $A(z)$ rotates clockwise around it, as exemplified by the dash-dotted curve.

The bottom panel of Figure 3.1 shows the outcome of the *ownership decision* as determined by the quality of the contractual environment in the two countries. It shows that, when production is located in South, out-

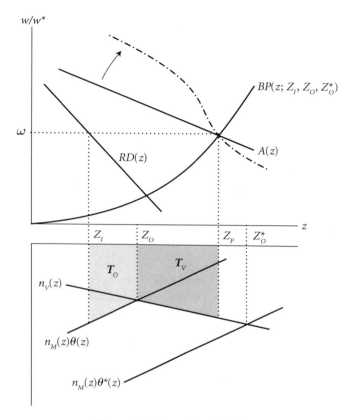

Figure 3.1 General equilibrium.

sourcing is selected for industries $z \in [0, Z_O]$ and vertical integration for industries $z \in [Z_O, 1]$. Analogously, when production takes place in North, outsourcing is selected for industries $z \in [0, Z_O^*]$ and vertical integration for industries $z \in [Z_O^*, 1]$. The ranking $Z_O < Z_O^*$ reflects the fact that the hold-up problem associated with outsourcing is more severe in South as this has the poorer contract enforcement.

Crossing the location and the ownership decisions gives the equilibrium organizational forms and the associated relative wage ω. While the location and the ownership thresholds are ranked $Z_I < Z_P$ and $Z_O < Z_O^*$ respectively, there is no unambiguous ordering of the former with respect to the latter. Figure 3.1 is drawn under the additional assumption that $Z_I < Z_O <$

$Z_P < Z_O^*$, and this ranking will be used from now on. The specific results derived will naturally follow from this specific ranking. However, nothing in the analysis in general relies on them, as other cases are relatively straightforward to examine once the selected case is understood. For parsimony, this is left to the interested reader.

Considering the two panels together allows one to partition the industries into five groups depending on their organizational form: outsourcing from Southern innovators to Southern producers for $z \in [0, Z_I]$; outsourcing from Northern innovators to Southern producers for $z \in [Z_I, Z_O]$; production in South by vertically integrated Northern innovators for $z \in [Z_O, Z_P]$; outsourcing in North by Northern innovators for $z \in [Z_P, Z_O^*]$; production in North by vertically integrated Northern innovators for $z \in [Z_O^*, 1]$. Since $\lambda'(z) > 0$ by assumption, the industries are allocated from the first to the fifth groups in increasing order of magnitude of their technological steps. Finally, the areas T_O and T_V in Figure 3.1 represent royalty payments from Southern producers to Northern innovators when these decide to offshore production. The former area concerns transactions between independent firms; the latter concerns transactions between divisions of the same vertically integrated firm.

3.3.1 Piecewise Notation

With industries sorted into five organizational forms, a compact description of the equilibrium can be achieved by turning to piecewise notation. In particular, define the following two piecewise functions that are relevant for production

$$\eta(z) = \begin{cases} \theta(z) \\ 1 \\ \theta^*(z) \\ 1 \end{cases}, \quad n(z) = \begin{cases} n_M(z) \\ n_V(z) \\ n_M(z) \\ n_V(z) \end{cases} \quad \text{for } z \in \begin{cases} [0, Z_O] \\ [Z_O, Z_P] \\ [Z_P, Z_O^*] \\ [Z_O^*, 1] \end{cases}. \quad (3.16)$$

Hence, profits accruing to innovators can be written as $R(z) = \eta(z)n(z)(E + E^*)$. Define also a third piecewise function that is relevant for innovation

$$\delta(z) = \begin{cases} wa_I(z) \\ w^*a_I^*(z) \end{cases} \quad \text{for } z \in \begin{cases} [0, Z_I] \\ [Z_I, 1] \end{cases}. \quad (3.17)$$

3.3.2 Research Intensity and Expenditures

Let us pick labor in South as the numeraire ($w = 1$), so that the Southern wage is constant ($\dot{w} = 0$). In the steady state expenditures and the Northern wage also have to be constant: $\dot{E} = \dot{E}^* = \dot{w}^* = 0$. The consumption-smoothing result (3.3) then implies $r = \rho$, and the arbitrage condition (3.11) can be rewritten as

$$i(z) = \frac{\eta(z)n(z)(E + E^*)}{\delta(z)} - \rho, \tag{3.18}$$

which reveals that research intensity varies across industries depending on their organizational form as captured by $\eta(z)n(z)$ and $\delta(z)$. Research intensity (3.18) is increasing in world expenditures, which can be evaluated by equating world labor income $wL + w^*L^*$ to the sum of the wage bills paid for production and innovation:

$$wL + w^*L^* = (E + E^*) \int_0^1 [1 - n(z)]\,dz + (E + E^*) \int_0^1 \eta(z)n(z)dz$$

$$- \rho \int_0^1 \delta(z)dz.$$

This yields steady state expenditures as labor income plus dividend payments from leading vintages:

$$E + E^* = \Lambda^{-1}\left[wL + w^*L^* + \rho \int_0^1 \delta(z)dz \right], \tag{3.19}$$

where $\Lambda \equiv \int_0^1 \{1 - [1 - \eta(z)]n(z)\}\,dz < 1$ measures world innovators' profit loss due to limited contract enforcement. This loss has a positive impact on expenditures (3.19) as it diverts resources away from R&D investment. When the quality of the contractual environment is at its best (i.e., $\eta(z) = 1$), $\Lambda = 1$ and expenditures are independent from ownership decisions.

3.3.3 Balance of Payments

In the top panel of Figure 3.1 a key role is played by the upward-sloping curve representing the balance of payments. This is found by imposing the current account balance,

$$\left[Z_P E^* - \left(1 - Z_P\right) E \right] = -\Lambda^{-1} \rho \left[s \int_{Z_I}^1 \delta(z)dz - (1-s) \int_0^{Z_I} \delta(z)dz \right]$$

$$+ \left(E + E^* \right) \int_{Z_I}^{Z_P} \eta(z)n(z)dz, \qquad (3.20)$$

where s is the Southern share of world assets.

To understand the derivation of (3.20), one has to keep in mind that Z_P and $\left(1 - Z_P\right)$ are the shares of products supplied by South and North respectively. Then, on the left-hand side of (3.20), given Northern expenditures E^* and Southern expenditures E, $Z_P E^*$ is Northern demand for Southern products, whereas $\left(1 - Z_P\right) E$ is Southern demand for Northern products. Hence, the left-hand side is South's trade balance. When negative, this must be exactly matched by net service payments from South to North. These appear on the right-hand side. Since industries $z \in [0, Z_I]$ innovate in South and $(1 - s)$ is the Northern share of world assets, the term $\Lambda^{-1}\rho(1 - s) \int_0^{Z_I} \delta(z)dz$ represents dividend payments from Southern labs to Northern investors. Vice versa, $\Lambda^{-1}\rho s \int_{Z_I}^1 \delta(z)dz$ represents dividend payments from Northern labs to Southern investors. Lastly, as industries $z \in [Z_I, Z_P]$ innovate in North but produce in South, the second term on the right represents royalty payments from Southern plants to Northern labs that arise due to offshoring.

Using

$$E = \Lambda^{-1} \left[wL + \rho s \int_0^1 \delta(z)dz \right] \quad \text{and}$$

$$E^* = \Lambda^{-1} \left[w^*L^* + \rho(1 - s) \int_0^1 \delta(z)dz \right],$$

the balance-of-payments (3.20) condition can be rewritten as

$$\frac{w}{w^*} = \frac{Z_P - \int_{Z_I}^{Z_P} \eta(z)n(z)dz}{1 - Z_P + \int_{Z_I}^{Z_P} \eta(z)n(z)dz} \frac{L^* + \rho A_I^*(Z_I)}{L + \rho A_I(Z_I)}, \qquad (3.21)$$

with $wA_I(Z_I) \equiv \int_0^{Z_I} \delta(z)dz$ and $w^*A_I^*(Z_I) \equiv \int_{Z_I}^1 \delta(z)dz$. Expression (3.21) defines the balance-of-payments schedule $BP(z)$ depicted in Figure 3.1.

3.3.4 Location and Ownership

The equilibrium conditions of the model represented in Figure 3.1 can be summarized as follows. First, given the relative wage w/w^*, the industry which is indifferent as to where to innovate determines the innovation location threshold Z_I such that

$$\frac{w}{w^*} = RD(Z_I).$$ (3.22)

Second, given the relative wage, the industry which is indifferent as to where to produce determines the production location threshold Z_P such that

$$\frac{w}{w^*} = A(Z_P).$$ (3.23)

Third, the industry which is indifferent whether to outsource production or not in South determines the Southern ownership threshold Z_O such that

$$n_V(Z_O) = n_M(Z_O)\theta(Z_O).$$ (3.24)

Fourth, the industry which is indifferent whether to outsource production or not in North determines the Northern ownership threshold Z_O^* such that

$$n_V(Z_O^*) = n_M(Z_O^*)\theta^*(Z_O^*).$$ (3.25)

Finally, given the four thresholds, the balance of payments (3.21) determines the relative wage. Accordingly, expressions (3.21) to (3.25) generate a system of five equations in the five unknowns Z_I, Z_P, Z_O, Z_O^*, and w/w^*. Recalling that $w = 1$ by choice of numeraire, the solutions for those variables can be used in (3.19) and (3.18) to obtain the equilibrium values of expenditures and research intensities.

3.3.5 Growth Rate

The equilibrium research intensities determine the overall growth rate of the world economy. To see this, recall that the innovation pattern is such that each industry experiences occasional innovations whose arrivals are governed by independent Poisson processes. The technological evolution of each industry is therefore both choppy and random with an expected number of discoveries in a time interval of length t equal to $i(z)t$. At the aggregate level, however, the law of large numbers kicks in and technological progress is both smooth and nonrandom with a constant fraction of industries upgrading their vintages each period by their respective steps $1/[1 - n(z)]$. As a result, the average price of products falls steadily and, since equilibrium expenditures are constant, such price reduction maps into increasing consumption. In particular, the consumption index (3.2) grows at the constant growth rate

$$g = - \int_0^1 \ln[1 - n(z)]i(z)dz, \qquad (3.26)$$

where $1/[1 - n(z)]$ is the technological step in industry z, $- \ln[1 - n(z)]$ is the utility value of the associated reduction in price, and $i(z)$ is the industry's research intensity.

Hence, the technological step $1/[1 - n(z)]$ has both an indirect and a direct effect on growth. On the one hand, a larger step raises R&D intensity and thus the probability of technological breakthroughs in each period. On the other hand, a larger step increases the contribution of each breakthrough to aggregate productivity.

3.4   Technology and Institutions

General equilibrium effects due to balance-of-payments adjustments are the key channel through which the ownership decision affects the location decision. They materialize only when innovation and production take place in different countries so that royalty payments from plants to labs cross international borders. In this case, through its impact on royalties, the ownership decision affects wages and location. As a result, the pattern of comparative advantage determines the relative prevalence of alternative organizational forms in the two countries and their patterns of specialization depend on the differences across countries in terms of contractual enforcement. To see this, consider again Figure 3.1 and assume that $RD(z) = A(z)$ so that $Z_I = Z_P$ and $\int_{Z_I}^{Z_P} \eta(z)n(z)dz = 0$. In this case, no industry innovates in North and produces in South, so royalty payments do not cross international borders. As (3.21) is independent from Z_O, the location and the ownership decisions are unrelated.

Several comparative statics experiments can be investigated starting from an initial situation like the one depicted in Figure 3.1. Sections 3.4.1 and 3.4.2 focus on two scenarios: an increase in the technological-step parameter $\lambda(z)$ across all industries (*systemic innovation*) and an improvement in the quality of the contractual environment in South (*institutional convergence*). The first scenario shows what changes when industries can react to a technological shock not only in terms of location as in Taylor (1993) but also in terms of ownership structure. The second scenario shows how the model can be used to study the general equilibrium effects of institutional changes when these affect industrial organization.

3.4.1 Systemic Innovation

When $\lambda(z)$ increases uniformly across all industries, both curves $n_M(z)\theta(z)$ and $n_M(z)\theta^*(z)$ shift toward the horizontal axis as producers' outside options strengthen. These shifts are larger the larger the differences $(1/\beta - 1/\alpha)$ and $(1/\beta^* - 1/\alpha)$ respectively, so $n_M(z)\theta(z)$ shifts more than $n_M(z)\theta^*(z)$. On the other hand, as $\lambda(z)$ increases, $n_V(z)$ moves away from the horizontal axis as innovators see their competitive lead increase. These movements are depicted in the bottom panel of Figure 3.2, which shows Z_O and Z_O^* falling as some industries turn from outsourcing to vertical integration. The figure also shows that, if α is small and β is much smaller than β^*, smaller Z_O raises the royalty payments T_O and T_V on impact as many offshored industries restructure from outsourcing to vertical integration. Given (3.21), larger royalties shift the balance-of-payments schedule $BP(z)$ downward in the top panel, thus causing a fall in the Southern relative wage as well as a rise in both Z_I and Z_P. This is due to the fact that higher royalties yield an incipient external deficit for South, which is compensated by import substitution in both innovation and production. Hence, a generalized increase in the potential for technological improvement affects both the ownership and the location decisions by expanding the ranges of industries that innovate and produce in South.

If $RD(z)$ is much steeper than $A(z)$, an increase in $\lambda(z)$ also implies that the range of Southern producing industries rises more than the range of Southern innovating industries, thus fostering offshoring. Moreover, the fraction of offshored industries that outsource shrinks. This is the case when the relative advantage of North in innovation is very pronounced.

On the other hand, if α is large and β is close to β^*, few industries shift from outsourcing to vertical integration, royalty payments go down, and the $BP(z)$ curve shifts upward. As before, fewer industries outsource but an incipient Southern external surplus leads to export substitution in both

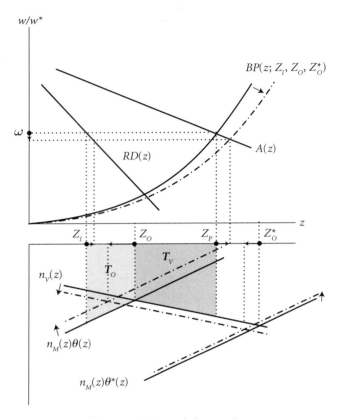

Figure 3.2 Systemic innovation.

innovation and production with rising Southern relative wages. In this case, if $RD(z)$ is much steeper than $A(z)$, the number of offshoring industries falls.

3.4.2 Institutional Convergence

Turning to institutional change, Figure 3.3 depicts the effects of improved contractual enforcement in South as captured by weaker outside options for local producers (smaller β). In the bottom panel, this shifts $n_M(z)\theta(z)$ away from the horizontal axis, which on impact increases royalty payments T_O and T_V from South to North. The reason is the reduction in the ex post bargaining power of Southern producers, which generates a transfer from

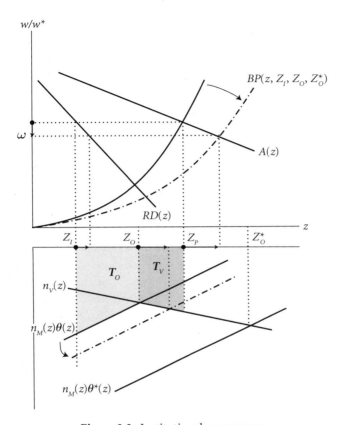

Figure 3.3 Institutional convergence.

them to Northern innovators. Accordingly, the Southern ownership threshold Z_O increases and some offshoring industries restructure from vertical integration to outsourcing. The Northern ownership threshold Z_O^* is, instead, unaffected. General equilibrium effects materialize through the movement of the balance-of-payments schedule $BP(z)$. As in the case of systemic innovation, richer royalties shift $BP(z)$ downward, which reduces the Southern relative wage and raises both the innovation location threshold Z_I and the production location threshold Z_P.

Hence, better Southern contract enforcement expands the shares of industries that innovate and produce in South. If $RD(z)$ is much steeper than $A(z)$, the range of Southern producing industries increases more than the range of Southern innovating ones, thus fostering offshoring. Moreover, if the gains from specialized production are large (large α), the fraction of offshoring firms that outsource increases.

As to growth, if relative wages do not change much, the aggregate return to innovation increases whenever royalties increase. This maps into higher research intensity and a faster growth rate.

3.5   Conclusion

This chapter has modeled the organizational choices of firms in dynamic industries characterized by *creative destruction* due to ongoing technology improvement. In the proposed model, the value chain of each industry consists of two tasks, innovation and production. In a two-country world, the organizational form is the result of two types of decisions. The location decision determines where innovation and production take place. This decision is driven by relative and comparative advantages. Offshoring arises when the two tasks are separated in different countries within the same industry. The ownership decision determines whether the two tasks are performed within the boundaries of the same firm (vertical integration) or by independent firms (outsourcing). This decision is driven by a trade-off between efficiency gains from specialization and hold-up problems from limited contract enforcement. The two decisions interact in the aggregate through the balance of payments jointly affecting the wages in the two countries, their expenditure levels, and overall research intensity.

The model is able to generate several comparative statics results. The analysis has focused on two scenarios based on the assumption that one of the two countries is more developed than the other in that it has a relative advantage in innovation with respect to production, a comparative advantage in production in industries characterized by a larger potential for technological improvement, and better contract enforcement. The first scenario has studied a generalized increase in the technological improvement potential across all industries (systemic innovation). The second experiment has considered an increase in the quality of the contractual environment in the less-developed country (institutional convergence).

Additional assumptions are needed to pin down how aggregate research intensity and, thus, the aggregate growth rate respond to such changes in technology and institutions. Further work along these lines is a first direction for future research. Also, for simplicity, the industries' potentials for technological improvement have been kept exogenously given. Another direction of future research is to endogenize it, possibly exploiting the formal connections between the adopted growth model and the static model with heterogeneous firms by Bernard et al. (2003).

ACKNOWLEDGMENTS

I am indebted to seminar participants at the University of Oslo and at the Université Libre de Bruxelles for comments. I am grateful to Pol Antràs, Micael Castanheira, Paola Conconi, Jonathan Eaton, Elhanan Helpman, Dalia Marin, Kjetil Storesletten, and Thierry Verdier for helpful discussions.

NOTES

1. The equilibrium analysis focuses on the steady state of the model. Grossman and Helpman (1991) prove that a model like the present one reaches its steady state instantaneously.

REFERENCES

Acemoglu, Daron, Philippe Aghion, and Fabrizio Zilibotti. 2006. "Distance to Frontier, Selection, and Economic Growth." *Journal of the European Economic Association* 4:37–74.

Acemoglu, Daron, Pol Antràs, and Elhanan Helpman. 2007. "Contracts and Technology Adoption." *American Economic Review* 97:916–43.

Acemoglu, Daron, Simon Johnson, and James Robinson. 2002. "Reversal of Fortune: Geography and Institutions in the Making of the Modern World Income Distribution." *Quarterly Journal of Economics* 117:1231–94.

Acemoglu, Daron, and Fabrizio Zilibotti. 1999. "Information Accumulation in Development." *Journal of Economic Growth* 4:5–38.

Aghion, Philippe, and Peter Howitt. 1998. *Endogenous Economic Growth*. Cambridge, MA: MIT Press.

Antràs, Pol. 2003. "Firms, Contracts, and Market Structure." *Quarterly Journal of Economics* 118:1375–1418.

Antràs, Pol, and Elhanan Helpman. 2004. "Global Sourcing." *Journal of Political Economy* 112(3):552–80.

Bernard, Andrew, Jonathan Eaton, Bradford Jensen, and Samuel Kortum. 2003. "Plants and Productivity in International Trade." *American Economic Review* 93:1268–90.

Costinot, Arnaud. 2006. "On the Origins of Comparative Advantage." Mimeo, UC San Diego.

Francois, Patrick, and Joanne Roberts. 2003. "Contracting Productivity Growth." *Review of Economic Studies* 70:59–85.

Grossman, Sanford, and Oliver Hart. 1986. "The Costs and Benefits of Ownership: A Theory of Vertical and Lateral Integration." *Journal of Political Economy* 94:691–719.

Grossman, Gene, and Elhanan Helpman. 1991. *Innovation and Growth in the Global Economy*. Cambridge, MA: MIT Press.

———. 2002. "Integration vs. Outsourcing in Industry Equilibrium." *Quarterly Journal of Economics* 117:85–120.

Hart, Oliver, and John Moore. 1990. "Property Rights and the Nature of the Firm." *Journal of Political Economy* 98:1119–58.

Helpman, Elhanan. 2006. "Trade, FDI, and the Organization of Firms." *Journal of Economic Literature* 44:589–630.

La Porta, Rafael, Florencio Lopez-de-Silanes, Andrei Shleifer, and Robert Vishny. 1998. "Law and Finance." *Journal of Political Economy* 106:1113–55.

Levchenko, Andrei. 2007. "Institutional Quality and International Trade." *Review of Economic Studies* 74(3):791–819.

Martimort, David, and Thierry Verdier. 2000. "The Internal Organization of the Firm, Transaction Costs and Macroeconomic Growth." *Journal of Economic Growth* 5:315–40.

———. 2004. "The Agency Cost of Internal Collusion and Schumpeterian Growth." *Review of Economic Studies* 71:1119–41.

Naghavi, Alireza, and Gianmarco I.P. Ottaviano. 2006. "Outsourcing, Complementary Innovations and Growth." CEPR discussion paper no. 5925.

Nunn, Nathan. 2007. "Relationship-Specificity, Incomplete Contracts and the Pattern of Trade." *Quarterly Journal of Economics* 122:569–600.

Taylor, M. Scott. 1993. "'Quality Ladders' and Ricardian Trade." *Journal of International Economics* 34:225–43.

— 4 —

The Dynamics of Firm-Level Adjustment to Trade Liberalization

JAMES A. COSTANTINI AND MARC J. MELITZ

4.1 Introduction

Recent evidence on firm-level adjustments to trade liberalization have documented that firms jointly make innovation and export-market–participation decisions (see Trefler 2004; Bustos 2005; Verhoogen 2008; Aw, Roberts, and Winston 2007). Another now large and established research agenda using microlevel production data has confirmed time and again the strong self-selection of more-productive firms into export markets. More recently, another branch of this literature has found some evidence for a "learning by exporting" phenomenon, whereby firms improve their productivity subsequent to export market participation (see, for instance, Delgado, Farinas, and Ruano 2002; Girma, Greenaway, and Kneller 2004; Topalova 2004; de Loecker 2006; and the survey in López 2005).

In this chapter, we build a dynamic model of firm-level adjustment to trade liberalization that jointly addresses all of these features. Our model captures the self-selection of more-productive firms into export markets, the joint export-market–participation and innovation decisions, and the continuing innovation of other firms following their entry into export markets.[1] We thus explain how some potentially conflicting results concerning the direction of causation between export participation and productivity (based on whether productivity improvements are observed prior to or subsequent to export-market participation) can be reconciled within a single model that recognizes that these decisions are jointly considered by firms, and jointly affected by trade liberalization.

Our model shows how some important nontechnological factors, such as the pace and anticipation of trade liberalization, can fundamentally affect this perceived causation link between export status and productivity. For example, we show that the anticipation of trade liberalization tends to

107

bring forward the decision to innovate relative to the export-market participation, and how a more abrupt pace of liberalization amplifies these effects. Our model also highlights the potential empirical pitfalls of analyzing current-period industrial performance as a response to the concurrent trade costs during periods of trade liberalization. Our model shows how the current industrial response not only depends on those concurrent trade costs, but also, inextricably, on the firms' prior expectations about those trade costs, and their expectations for their changes in the future. Although we emphasize that "true" learning by exporting (in the literal sense that firms learn from their foreign-market experience) cannot be inferred based on the timing of export-market entry, we do not mean to dismiss the potential relevance of such a learning channel.[2]

In order to capture these complex, dynamic effects involving changes in expectations about future outcomes, we build a model with heterogeneous firms that incorporates both idiosyncratic firm uncertainty (future productivity is stochastic) and forward-looking decisions subject to sunk costs. All of the forward-looking firm decisions concerning entry, exit, export, and innovation incorporate a sunk-cost component. We focus on the interaction between the firm decisions to undertake a large, one-off innovation and the decision to enter the export market. The benefit of this innovation is a one-time stochastic jump in productivity (relative to the default productivity transition). Given firm heterogeneity, this leads to a sorting of firms into innovators and noninnovators in a very similar way to the sorting that occurs with export-market participation.[3] Naturally, this induces a large amount of overlap between exporting and innovation across the productivity distribution (high-productivity firms undertake both). We will therefore focus on the transition paths into these activities, and the relative timing of the export and innovation decisions.

We characterize both the stationary equilibrium, given an invariant level of trade costs, and the equilibrium transition path, given any arbitrary path of trade liberalization from a high trade-cost stationary state to a new one with lower cost. The initial and final stationary states do not necessarily have the same sorting of firms into innovation and export. For example, some firms with intermediate productivity levels innovate ahead of the export decision when facing sufficiently high trade costs but reverse this ordering in an environment with low-enough trade costs.

We analyze the transition dynamics between two such stationary states from high to low trade costs. The transition dynamics are largely shaped by the way the firms' value of undertaking innovation and/or exports is affected by the future evolution of trade costs, and the associated anticipated industry response. As these firm decisions are subject to sunk costs (irreversibility) along with idiosyncratic firm uncertainty, they will critically depend on the firms' anticipation concerning future liberalization (when it is announced, and the pace of liberalization once undertaken). We will contrast trade liberalization scenarios that differ along these timing dimensions.

We rely on numerical methods to solve for these equilibria. Since we do not know of any previously developed computational methods to solve this type of dynamic problem with a large number of firms, we develop a general computational algorithm that can be used to solve a wide set of related dynamic industry evolution models.[4] We describe this algorithm in detail in the Appendix.

4.2   Model Setup

As highlighted above, we develop our model to analyze the evolution of an industry comprised of heterogeneous firms in response to trade liberalization. The firms in the industry are distinguished by their productivity. We focus on two interdependent firm policies: innovation involving a stochastic jump in firm productivity, and export-market participation. Clearly, these policies are both affected by trade liberalization, which increases the returns to both activities. We investigate how these policy choices respond to the timing of trade liberalization: whether the liberalization is anticipated by the firms, and whether the liberalization, once started, occurs abruptly or gradually. We analyze this model in a partial equilibrium setting with respect to the industry: we assume a demand system for the industry as a whole, and a perfectly elastic labor supply to the industry at the economy-wide wage.

The core elements of the model are based on Melitz (2003), reintroducing the stochastic evolution of firm productivity from Hopenhayn (1992). In addition, we add the innovation option subject to sunk costs. We then computationally solve this extended model for its stationary equilibrium along with any transition paths between two stationary states. We next describe each part of the model, the equilibrium, and how we calibrate the model based on the empirical literature.

4.2.1 Demand

Consumer preferences for the differentiated varieties in the industry exhibit Constant Elasticity of Substitution (CES) with elasticity $\sigma > 1$. There is a continuum of varieties $\omega \in \Omega$. Let

$$P_t = \left[\int_{\omega \in \Omega} p_t(\omega)^{1-\sigma} \right]^{1/(1-\sigma)}$$

be the CES price index for the aggregated differentiated good

$$Q_t \equiv \left[\int_{\omega \in \Omega} q_t(\omega)^{(\sigma-1)/\sigma} \right]^{\sigma/(\sigma-1)}$$

at time t, where $p_t(\omega)$ and $q_t(\omega)$ are the price and quantity consumed of the individual varieties ω. We further assume that overall demand for the differentiated good Q_t is generated by $Q_t = AP_t^{-\eta}$, where A is an exogenous demand parameter for the industry (constant over time), and $\eta < \sigma$ is the industry price elasticity of demand. Demand for an individual variety ω is then $q_t(\omega) = Q_t P_t^{\sigma} p_t(\omega)^{-\sigma} = AP_t^{\sigma-\eta} p_t(\omega)^{-\sigma}$.

4.2.2 Production

Each variety is produced by a firm with productivity $v \in \Upsilon$ (which we now also use as the index for varieties). Labor is the only factor of production, and we normalize the wage level to unity. Firms produce with a technology exhibiting constant marginal cost $1/v$, along with an overhead per-period fixed cost F (measured in labor units). Given the demand system and a continuum of competing firms, all firms set a constant markup $\sigma/(\sigma - 1)$ over marginal cost. The per-period profit for production sold in the domestic market is

$$\pi_t^D(v) = \frac{(\sigma - 1)^{\sigma-1}}{\sigma^{\sigma}} AP_t^{\sigma-\eta} v^{\sigma-1} - F. \tag{4.1}$$

4.2.3 Productivity Evolution and Innovation

The firms' productivity evolves stochastically in each time period with a known martingale process. In addition, firms have a one-time opportunity to innovate. We denote the firms that have not innovated as A firms, and firms that have exercised their innovation option as B firms.[5] The benefit of innovation is a one-time evolution of productivity based on a more favor-

able (and known) probability distribution than the alternative of no innovation. Note that a firm only benefits from this better productivity draw
once. However, given the subsequent martingale evolution process, this
productivity gain is long lasting. We choose the same martingale process
for both A and B firms. New innovators expect a subsequent productivity draw at a given percentage above their current productivity. The sunk
innovation cost is stochastic, but independent and identically distributed
(i.i.d.) in every period (with different realizations across firms). The real-
ization of this sunk cost is either S^B with probability γ^B or infinite: in the
latter case, the firm cannot innovate. Hence, only a proportion γ^B of firms
can consider innovating in any given period.[6]

4.2.4 Trade

Firms have the opportunity to export. We consider a symmetric, two-
country world where exporters incur three additional costs: a per-unit
(iceberg) trade cost, τ_t; a per-period fixed cost to export, F^X; and a sunk
cost to enter the export market, S^X. There are no sunk costs to exit the
export market (though subsequent reentry into the export market would
require, again, payment of the sunk cost to enter the export market). In
this chapter, we only consider trade liberalization involving the per-unit
trade cost; hence, this is the only trade cost indexed by time. Based on the
symmetric, foreign-demand setup discussed above, in each time period
that a firm chooses to export, the firm generates profits from export $\pi_t^X(v)$
given by

$$\pi_t^X(v) = \frac{(\sigma - 1)^{\sigma-1}}{\sigma^\sigma} A P_t^{\sigma-\eta} \left(\frac{v}{\tau_t} \right)^{\sigma-1} - F^X. \tag{4.2}$$

4.2.5 Value Functions and Firm Policy Decisions

We now discuss the firm policy decisions. Within each time period, the
timing of events is as follows (and is illustrated in Figure 4.1). First, firms
decide whether to continue in the industry or exit. This is based on the
maximization of firm value $V_t(v, z)$, with state $z \in \{AD, BD, AX, BX\}$
referring to firm technology and export status. The firm compares the
value of continuing, $V_t^C(v, z)$, to the value of exit, which we set to zero for
simplicity:

$$V_t(v, z) = \max \left[0, V_t^C(v, z) \right]. \tag{4.3}$$

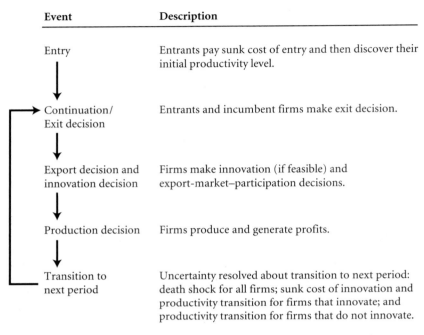

Event	Description
Entry	Entrants pay sunk cost of entry and then discover their initial productivity level.
Continuation/ Exit decision	Entrants and incumbent firms make exit decision.
Export decision and innovation decision	Firms make innovation (if feasible) and export-market–participation decisions.
Production decision	Firms produce and generate profits.
Transition to next period	Uncertainty resolved about transition to next period: death shock for all firms; sunk cost of innovation and productivity transition for firms that innovate; and productivity transition for firms that do not innovate.

Figure 4.1 Timing and description of events within time periods.

Continuing firms maximize their value by optimally choosing innovation and export policies. Firms operating with technology A have the option of innovating and switching to technology B. Firms also choose whether to start exporting, continue exporting, or stop exporting. Lastly, firms discount next-period profits at the exogenous rate β, and internalize the exogenous probability δ of a death-inducing shock (which is independent of productivity v and state z).[7] The firm policy choices must satisfy the Bellman equation:

$$V_t^C(v, z) = \max_{z'} \left\{ \pi_t(v, z') - S^B I^B(z, z') - S^X I^X(z, z') \right.$$

$$\left. + \beta (1 - \delta) \int_{v \in \Upsilon} V_{t+1}(v', z') dG \left[v' \mid v, I^B(z, z') \right] \right\}, \quad (4.4)$$

where

$$\pi_t(v, z') = \begin{cases} \pi_t^D(v) & \text{if } z' \in \{AD, BD\} \\ \pi_t^D(v) + \pi_t^X(v) & \text{if } z' \in \{AX, BX\} \end{cases}$$

represents total firm per-period profit, and

$$I^B(z, z') = \begin{cases} 1 & \text{if } z \in \{AD, AX\}, z' \in \{BD, BX\} \\ 0 & \text{otherwise} \end{cases}$$

and

$$I^X(z, z') = \begin{cases} 1 & \text{if } z \in \{AD, BD\}, z' \in \{AX, BX\} \\ 0 & \text{otherwise} \end{cases}$$

are indicators for new innovators and exporters. $G\left[v' \mid v, I^B(z, z')\right]$ is the firm-productivity stochastic-evolution process, where $E[v' \mid v, 0] = v$.

The optimal firm policies from (4.4) can be summarized by a set of transition productivity cutoffs from state z to z' or exit. For a given z, the range of possible productivity levels v will be partitioned into segments representing next-period choice of z' or exit. Clearly, the exit segment will always encompass the lowest productivity levels up to a cutoff. Some other rankings are clear: the choice to transition to, respectively, AX or BX (whenever feasible) will always occur at higher v than the transition to, respectively, AD or BD (again, whenever feasible). In other words, among both innovators and noninnovators, relatively more-productive firms choose to export. Absent an upper bound on productivity v, the same logic applies to the B states relative to their respective A states (relatively more-productive firms choose to innovate). However, since we use a finite productivity grid in our numerical methods (with an upper bound on productivity), the dominance of the B state is reversed for productivity levels right below the upper bound: there is no incentive to innovate for a firm for which productivity cannot increase any further. In all our numerical simulations, we choose a high enough upper bound on the productivity grid such that there are essentially no firms in this situation. The dominance of the B states over their respective A states is thus quantitatively verified.

Yet there are also some rankings of transition states that will critically vary with the level of trade costs (most prominently, the transitions from the AD state to either the BD or AX states). In an environment with high enough trade costs, firms who are just productive enough to transition out of their current AD state will choose to innovate ($ADBD$ transition). As trade costs fall, the export option becomes relatively more attractive, and those firms who are just productive enough to transition out of AD may choose to transition to AX instead (export, but not innovate).[8] Our numerical calibration will feature this reversal in the transition rankings from *AD*. We describe and motivate these transitions in greater detail later, along with the other simulation results.

4.2.6 Entrants

At the start of each period, new entrants can potentially enter the industry. An entrant pays a sunk cost of entry, S, and then realizes its initial productivity draw from a known invariant distribution $G_E(v)$. Entry is not otherwise restricted. Entrants arrive into the industry in the *AD* state. Thereon, entrants are indistinguishable from incumbent firms with the same productivity and policy state. A prospective entrant therefore faces a net value of entry

$$V_t^E = \int_{v \in \Upsilon} V_t(v, AD) dG_E(v) - S.$$

When this value is negative, entry is unprofitable.

4.3   Equilibrium

Let $\mu_{z,t}$ represent the measure function for producing firms with state z in period t, over sets of productivity levels v. This function summarizes all information on the distribution of producing firms across productivity levels, as well as the total mass of producing firms in state z, $M_{z,t} = \mu_{z,t}(\Upsilon)$. A dynamic equilibrium is characterized by a time path for the price index $\{P_t\}$, the measure of firms in each state, $\{\mu_{z,t}\}$, and the mass of entrants $\{M_{E,t}\}$. Note that a choice of $\{P_t\}$ uniquely determines the time path for $\{V_t^C(v, z)\}$ and thus determines all the optimal choices for any firm, given its productivity v and state z. An equilibrium $\{P_t\}$, $\{\mu_{z,t}\}$, and $\{M_{E,t}\}$ must then satisfy the following three conditions:

1. Firm value maximization: All firms' choices for exit or continuation, and given the latter, for z' (export or innovation) conditional on v and z must satisfy (4.3) and (4.4). In the aggregate, this means that $\mu_{z,t}$ is entirely determined by $\mu_{z,t-1}$ and the choices for $\{P_t\}$ and $\{M_{E,t}\}$: starting with a mass and distribution of firms at time $t - 1$, a share δ of firms receive the exogenous death shock, while the remaining $(1 - \delta)$ share of firms receive their new productivity draw. To these firms are

added the $M_{E,t}$ new entrants to the AD state, with a distribution determined by $G_E(v)$. All firms make their endogenous exit decisions, and the continuing firms make their innovation or export decision (the optimal choice for z' given v and z). This entails a distribution and mass of firms for every state. In equilibrium this must match the chosen $\mu_{z,t}$.

2. Free entry: In equilibrium, the net value of entry V_t^E must be non-positive, since there is an unbounded pool of prospective entrants and entry is not restricted beyond the sunk entry cost. Furthermore, entry must be zero whenever V_t^E is negative.

3. Aggregate industry accounting: The mass and distribution of firms over productivity levels (aggregating over states) implies a mass and distribution of prices (applying the profit-maximizing markup rule to firm marginal cost $1/v$). Aggregating these prices into the CES price index must yield the chosen P_t in every period.

4.3.1 Stationary Equilibrium

A time-invariant level of trade costs τ leads to a stationary equilibrium with a time-invariant price index P, measure of firms μ_z, and mass of entrants M_E. In such a stationary equilibrium, entry must be positive since there is always an exogenous component to exit. Thus V_t^E must be zero in this equilibrium. Although an equal mass of firms enter and exit, their distributions over productivity and states will not generally match. This is due to the productivity-transition dynamics among incumbent firms (which also induce transitions across states). Jointly, these productivity and state transitions, along with the distribution of entrants and exiting firms, lead to a stationary distribution of firms for every state.

4.3.2 Equilibrium along Trade Liberalization Transition

We consider the equilibrium along a transition driven by a liberalization of trade that reduces the trade cost τ_t. Firms are initially in a stationary equilibrium, as described in Section 4.3.1. At the end of one of these stationary time periods, trade liberalization is announced. We analyze the anticipation effects of such an announcement by varying the time between it and the time the first drop in trade cost occurs. The trade cost can then drop abruptly or gradually. Thereafter, the trade cost remains constant at its new lower level. The equilibrium then converges to this new stationary equilibrium with lower τ.

We compare three trade-liberalization scenarios that vary along these timing dimensions, while keeping the same preliberalization and postliberalization stationary states (thus, the same cumulative drop in τ):

1. An unanticipated, abrupt drop in trade cost (UA): there is no anticipation period, and the full difference in τ between the two stationary states occurs from one period to the next.

2. An anticipated, abrupt drop in trade costs (AA): very similar to the unanticipated case, but with a lag period between the time the liberalization is announced and the time it takes effect.

3. An anticipated gradual drop in trade costs (AG): the same anticipation period as in the previous AA scenario, but then followed by a gradual drop in the trade costs until the same final postliberalization τ is reached.

We consider how firm policies and hence the industry equilibrium evolve over a long enough set of time periods such that, by the final period, the industry is arbitrarily close to its stationary equilibrium, consistent with the new, lower trade costs. Thus, a summary description of the total long-run change in the industry is provided by a comparison of the stationary states generated by the initial and final set of parameters. The equilibrium path for the price index $\{P_t\}$, measure of firms $\{\mu_{z,t}\}$, and entrants $\{M_{E,t}\}$ will thus begin at their old stationary levels, remain constant until trade liberalization is announced, then follow a transition path until they reach the new stationary state levels, and remain constant thereafter. During the transition, as opposed to the stationary states, the net value of entry may be negative, resulting in periods of zero entry. Since we will consider scenarios with fewer firms (across states) in the postliberalization stationary state—relative to the preliberalization stationary state—such periods of zero entry will occur whenever the change in trade cost is large and abrupt.

4.3.3 Calibration

We search for the equilibrium paths of $\{P_t\}$, $\{\mu_{z,t}\}$, and $\{M_{E,t}\}$ using numerical methods. The Appendix provides a description of the algorithm used. In essence, we first compute the values of P, μ_z, and M_E in the old and new stationary equilibria. The algorithm then iterates over candidate equilibrium paths for $\{P_t\}$ and $\{M_{E,t}\}$. The choice for $\{P_t\}$ determines all of the policy choices for any incumbent firm (this is the crucial benefit of abstracting from strategic interactions in our monopolistic competition equilibrium). Since μ_z in the old stationary state is known, we can thus compute $\{\mu_{z,t}\}$ based on those policy choices, and the choice for the number of entrants. In turn, we can then compute a new price index $\{P_t\}$ based on the distribution and mass of firms (which implies a distribution of prices). We iterate until this new price path $\{P_t\}$ matches the prior choice of the candidate $\{P_t\}$.

We next describe how we set the parameters of the model to run the model simulations. The model is calibrated to reflect the findings from the recent empirical literature on the effect of trade on firms and industries, and typical patterns of firm dynamics within industries, in particular the following: Bernard and Jensen (1999, 2006), Bartelsman, Scarpetta, and Schivardi (2003), Trefler (2004), Bustos (2005), and de Loecker (2006). The matching between the calibration choices and the empirical literature is described in more detail in Tables 4.1–4.3.

We first describe the grid over time periods and productivity levels on which to run the model (see Table 4.1). We set each time period to correspond to one month. This is relatively short, as compared to the typical time unit used empirically of one year, thus smoothing out the dynamic processes. We set the total number of time periods to 200 (i.e., around 17 years) as this is long enough to ensure that by the final period, the industry will have converged close to the stationary equilibrium corresponding to the final set of parameters. Note that we do not impose this final stationary state as the end point: rather, we allow the industry to evolve toward it.

We consider two aspects of the timing of the change in trade policy: the extent of preannouncement of the policy and the time required to implement the change in policy. Reflecting the timing of policy changes discussed in the empirical literature, we compare the three scenarios previously described (UA, AA, AG). In all three scenarios, the trade costs initially change after a period of three years. For the UA scenario, this change is unanticipated. For the AA and AG scenarios, this change is anticipated at the beginning of year one (with year zero the old stationary state). Once the trade costs change, in the UA and AA cases, the drop in τ occurs immediately, over a period of one month. For the AG case, the gradual change in τ is linear over a period of three years, and then τ is constant at the new stationary state thereafter.

Table 4.1 Calibration: Model timing and productivity grid

Variable	Empirical evidence	Explanation of model calibration
Time path of trade policy		
Duration of time periods (t)	Most empirical data is annual data.	Set each time period to correspond to one month, so time period is short relative to typical empirical unit of analysis. Set total number of time periods such that by the final period, the industry will have converged close to the final stationary state.
Timing of policy change	Typical timeframes are zero to three years anticipation of policy change[c] and around two to four years to implement.	Set announced policy change to start after 36 periods (i.e., three years) after announcement. Set abrupt change as one-period (i.e., one month) transition, and gradual as 36-period transition (i.e., three years).
Discount rate (β)		Set at 5% per year, thus 0.4% per month (i.e., per time period).
Productivity grid		
Productivity (v)	Relative size of largest to smallest firms often over 100x.[b,f]	Set v range to [0.7, 3] to allow a sufficiently broad range of firm sizes, as relative firm size determined by productivity $v^{\sigma-1}$.
Normalization		
Wage per period (w)		Normalize monthly wage to one.

Note: The references to the empirical literature are as follows:
[a] Bernard and Jensen (1999)
[b] Bartelsman, Scarpetta, and Schivardi (2003)
[c] Trefler (2004)
[d] Bustos (2005)
[e] Bernard and Jensen (2006)
[f] de Loecker (2006)

We set the productivity range to $v = [0.7, 3]$. This grid size is exogenous to any firm decisions. Hence, we set a sufficiently wide range such that this encompasses the range of productivity levels relevant to firms in the endogenous, equilibrium-size distribution. In particular, this grid is set such that the exit cutoffs are sufficiently above the lower bound, and that virtually no firms have productivity levels close to the upper bound. The resulting size distribution of firms (for the range of trade costs considered) exhibits a 75th to 25th percentile size ratio around 2, a 90th to 10th percentile size ratio around 4, and standard deviation of log size around 0.6. This represents a smaller amount of size heterogeneity than found in most empirical studies of firm size across industries.[9] We stick with this lower level of size heterogeneity for two reasons: first, our model is meant to capture the equilibrium dynamics for a narrowly defined industry, probably narrower than the classifications used in economy-wide studies of firm-size distributions. Second, we acknowledge that there are many other sources of heterogeneity across firms that induce differences in firm size not directly related to the productivity or product quality channel from our model. Our model is therefore intended to capture a subset of firm-level differences that induce the empirical heterogeneity in firm size. We set the number of productivity grid points to 600, high enough that there are sufficient grid points to minimize any effects from the discreteness of the grid. For instance, a finer grid allows for the productivity cutoffs to more smoothly adjust over time.

Next we discuss the demand and production parameters (see Table 4.2). The main demand parameters are the price elasticity of demand for the aggregate industry output, which we set to $\eta = 1.5$, and elasticity of substitution between varieties, which we set to $\sigma = 4$. The overhead cost $F = 9$ is set such that, on average, firms devote 20% of their labor cost to overhead.

We set the range of variable trade costs to $\tau = 1.35$ and $\tau = 1.05$ in the initial and final stationary states. This reduction of 30% corresponds to the typical reduction in trade costs for industries most affected by trade reforms, though we intentionally choose to model a substantial liberalization reform. In addition, we set the relative levels of variable, fixed, and sunk costs of trade to lead to a range of 15% to 45% of exporting firms, across the two stationary states. These percentages are within empirical ranges for the proportion of exporters across sectors. Specifically, we set the fixed costs of trade to $F^X = 10$ and the sunk costs of trade to $S^X = 2.4$. Hence, the fixed

Table 4.2 Calibration: Demand, production, and trade costs

Variable	Empirical evidence	Explanation of model calibration
Demand		
Elasticity of demand (η)		Set to 1.5.
Elasticity of substitution (σ)		Set to 4.
Production		
Fixed costs (F)	Skilled workers are ~16% of workforce, with an additional 6% in continuing exporters.[d]	Set $F = 9$ so that for firms on average fixed labor cost is around 20% of total labor cost.
Trade costs		
Variable, fixed, and sunk costs of trade (τ, F^X, and S^X)	Range of evidence on extent of drop in trade costs: maximum drop in duty is from over 10% to 1% over 8 years;[c] maximum 30% to 20% drop in freight and duty costs over 10 years, with average 10% to 8% drop;[e] and drop from 12% to 11% average external tariff over 3 years, but within Mercosur, drop is from range of 0% to 22% down to around 0%.[d]	Set τ to drop from 1.35 to 1.05. Set F^X to 10 and S^X to 2.4.
Proportion of exporters	Exporters rise for (f) from 33% to 48% of firms, and for (d) from 38% to 54%. Proportion of firms per year becoming exporters: 11% for (f), 10% for (e) and 4% for (d) (in sample of mostly large firms). Proportion of exporters per year that stop exporting: 15% for (e) and 0.5% for (d) (in sample of mostly large firms).	Set trade cost to result in rise in proportion of exporters from around 15% to 45% of firms.

Note: The references to the empirical literature are as follows:
[a] Bernard and Jensen (1999)
[b] Bartelsman, Scarpetta, and Schivardi (2003)
[c] Trefler (2004)
[d] Bustos (2005)
[e] Bernard and Jensen (2006)
[f] de Loecker (2006)

costs of trade are comparable in magnitude to the per-period fixed costs. The relatively low sunk costs of trade ease firms' shift in and out of export status, as there is empirical evidence of substantial transitions by firms in and out of the export market.

Next we discuss our choices for the productivity transitions (see Table 4.3). First the death shock: we set this at 15% per year, which is higher than the firm-level exit rates observed empirically (of around 3%–7% per year). However, the model can also be interpreted as focused on product lines, and we would expect higher exit rates for these more disaggregated units of analysis. For firms that do not innovate, we set the stochastic productivity transition based on a lognormal distribution. For each firm, the draw is from a distribution with mean corresponding to the current firm's productivity. The standard deviation is the same across all firms (with truncation of extreme changes in productivity, in part to avoid accumulation of firms at the edge of the productivity grid). Thus each firm has the same probability of experiencing a similar percent increase or decline in productivity.[10] For firms that do innovate, we set the average increase in productivity to 10% above their current productivity. The new productivity is again drawn from a lognormal distribution (with truncation of extreme outcomes). The expected increase in productivity is comparable to the empirical evidence on the increase in productivity for firms entering the export market. We set the sunk costs of innovation to $S^B = 300$ whenever innovation is feasible, which occurs with a $\gamma_B = 0.5$ probability (i.i.d. over time for every potential innovator). This sunk cost is equivalent to a per-period interest charge of around 14% of the level of fixed costs (at our 5% annual discount rate β). If innovation is not feasible, then firms choose their next-best alternative. Note that this effect of γ_B, which is modeled to induce some smoothing in the distribution of firms close to the innovation cutoff, will be short lived: over the course of one year, virtually all firms $(1 - 0.5^{12} > 0.999)$ who wish to innovate (in each month of the year) will be able to do so.

Finally, we specify the distribution of potential entrants over productivity levels as lognormal with $\log(0.8)$ mean and 0.2 standard deviation, restricted to the [0.7, 3] productivity grid (see Figure 4.2 and Table 4.3). The endogenous exit-productivity cutoffs will always be above the 0.7 productivity lower bound so that some entrants with low productivity draws around this cutoff choose to immediately exit and not produce. Overall, in our simulations, entrants enter with an average productivity lower than that of incumbent firms (for which average productivity is always above

Table 4.3 Calibration: Evolution of productivity and entry

Variable	Empirical evidence	Explanation of model calibration
Productivity transitions		
Death shock (δ)	Exit rate is ~3% per year,[f] and ~3% to 7% per year.[b]	Set to 15% per year (with additional exit from firm productivity dropping below exit-productivity cutoff), thus 1.4% per month (i.e., per time period).
Transition for firms (except for *A* firms investing to become *B*)		Productivity evolves according to truncated lognormal evolution with mean $\log(v)$ and 0.02 standard deviation (hence, mean zero change in productivity). Also, truncate increase/decrease to future productivity to within $\pm 20\%$ of current v.
Investment		
Transition for *A* firms that invest to become *B*	Trade opening impact on plants of ~14% improvement in productivity.[c] Also, ~9% immediate impact on productivity.[f] Note these include the impact of any change in technology that occurred so as to export. Indeed, many new exporters seem to increase technology spending.[d]	Productivity evolves according to truncated lognormal evolution with mean $\log(1.1v)$ and 0.02 standard deviation (hence, mean $+10\%$ change in productivity). Also, truncate increase/decrease to future productivity to within $\pm 50\%$ of current v.
Sunk cost of investment (S^B and γ^B)		Set $S^B = 300$ with probability $\gamma^B = 0.5$, which correponds to a monthly interest charge of 1.3 (i.e., around 14% of per-period fixed costs); otherwise S^B is infinite.

Table 4.3 (*continued*)

Variable	Empirical evidence	Explanation of model calibration
Entrants		
Entrant size	Entrants are smaller than incumbents on average. Also, around 50% of entrants survive to 7 years, with 20% hazard in year 1 and around 10% hazard thereafter. [b]	Set entrants as distributed lognormal, with mean log(0.8) and 0.2 standard deviation, over the productivity grid (hence generating truncated distribution). This results in entrants with lower average productivity and higher exit rates, relative to incumbents.
Entry sunk cost (S)		Set $S = 60$, which correponds to a monthly interest charge of 0.2 (i.e., around 3% of per-period fixed costs).

Note: The references to the empirical literature are as follows:
[a] Bernard and Jensen (1999)
[b] Bartelsman, Scarpetta, and Schivardi (2003)
[c] Trefler (2004)
[d] Bustos (2005)
[e] Bernard and Jensen (2006)
[f] de Loecker (2006)

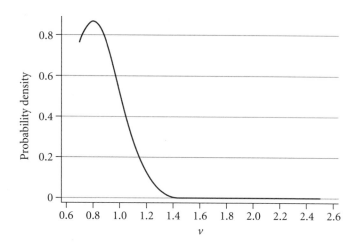

Figure 4.2 Productivity distribution of entrants.

$v = 1.15$). Thus, our simulations replicate the robust empirical findings that recent entrants are on average smaller, and exhibit higher exit rates than incumbent firms. The entry sunk cost is set to $S = 60$, which is equivalent to a per-period interest charge of 3% of fixed costs (at our 5% annual discount rate β).

4.4   Simulated Results

We now describe the numerical properties of the two stationary states with the preliberalization high trade cost $\tau = 1.35$ and the postliberalization low trade cost $\tau = 1.05$. One defining characteristic of these equilibria concerns the cutoff productivity levels that determine the key firm policy decisions for exit, export, and innovation. These cutoffs are shown in Table 4.4. The first two columns of each panel show the productivity range along with the transition decision (the range for which no transition occurs is indicated by a dash, "—"). The third column indicates the yearly transition flows to each of the other possible states. These flows are expressed as a percentage of the number of firms in the originating state.[11] As we previously discussed, the rankings of the firm decision rules across productivity are such that exit (the endogenously driven component) is always at the bottom, and the BX option is always at the top.[12] However, the level of trade cost significantly affects the relative benefits of innovation and export-market participation. This is most clearly seen in the optimal decision of AD firms that have not yet undertaken either activity and jointly consider both of these options following favorable productivity shocks (top part of Table 4.4). The productivity cutoffs in the left panel show that the preliberalization trade cost $\tau = 1.35$ is high enough that exporting is relatively unattractive prior to innovation: AD firms receiving positive productivity shocks will predominantly choose to innovate, but not export. A tiny fraction of firms receiving large positive shocks choose to undertake both. Still, no firms choose to export but not innovate—and thus all exporters in the preliberalization stationary state have innovated.[13] With lower trade costs, exporting becomes more attractive to midlevel productivity firms. Given our calibration for the postliberalization stationary state, there are then some AD firms who choose to export but not innovate, following a productivity increase. Given large enough productivity increases, these AD firms then choose to jointly innovate and export. There are thus no longer any transitions from AD to BD: a decision to innovate but not export by some AD firms.[14] The transitions from AX in Table 4.4 show that this state is mostly transitional, with

Table 4.4 Firm cutoff rules and transition flows in the stationary states

Transitions from AD

Pre			Post		
v range	To	Flow	v range	To	Flow
0.70–0.88	Exit	14.3%	0.70–0.91	Exit	22.2%
0.88–1.30	—	—	0.91–1.17	—	—
1.30–1.40	BD	4.6%	1.17–1.19	AX	16.8%
1.40+	BX	0.2%	1.19+	BX	4.1%

Transitions from AX

Pre			Post		
v range	To	Flow	v range	To	Flow
			0.70–0.91	Exit	0.0%
	(No AX firms)		0.91–1.13	AD	80.8%
			1.13–1.19	—	—
			1.19+	BX	201.7%

Transitions from BD

Pre			Post		
v range	To	Flow	v range	To	Flow
0.70–0.89	Exit	0.7%	0.70–0.92	Exit	6.9%
0.89–1.42	—	—	0.92–1.17	—	—
1.42+	BX	65.7%	1.17+	BX	35.3%

Transitions from BX

Pre			Post		
v range	To	Flow	v range	To	Flow
0.70–0.89	Exit	0.0%	0.70–0.92	Exit	0.0%
0.89–1.37	BD	20.0%	0.92–1.13	BD	6.1%
1.37+	—	—	1.13+	—	—

firms either moving on to *BX* (if things go well) or back down to *AD* (if they do not): the annual flows from *AX* to either of these states are large (recall that the annual flows are cumulations of twelve monthly simulation periods) as the productivity band to remain in *AX* is relatively narrow.

Since firms do not have an option to "un-innovate" (transition from a *B* state back to an *A*), the rankings of the transition decisions for innovators

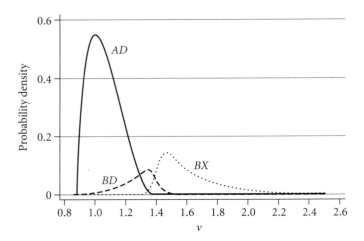

Figure 4.3 Preliberalization steady-state distribution of firm productivity.

in the bottom half of Table 4.4 are straightforward: the lowest productivity firms exit, the highest productivity firms export, and the remaining firms choose to only serve their domestic market (including the decision to exit the export market and forego the sunk export cost for *BX* firms receiving bad productivity shocks). The cutoff ranges for the transitions between *BD* and *BX* also highlight the important effects arising from the combination of sunk export market costs and firm-level uncertainty concerning future productivity: these jointly generate an export-market hysteresis band. Both the pre- and postliberalization stationary states feature such a band, within which non-exporters (*BD*) and exporters (*BX*) both choose to maintain their current state. There is also a very similar export-market hysteresis band between *AD* and *AX* firms in the postliberalization stationary state. *AD* firms also face option values to waiting when considering the decision to innovate in the preliberalization stationary state. Absent any uncertainty concerning future productivity, some *AD* firms would choose to innovate: innovation generates a positive net-present-value activity for those firms (but one that is less than the option value of waiting).[15]

Figures 4.3 and 4.4 show the distribution of firms over productivity for each state in the pre- and postliberalization stationary states, respectively. Figure 4.5 combines the firm productivity distributions across states. The top panel of Table 4.5 quantitatively summarizes how the firms are dis-

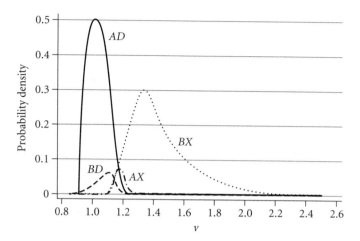

Figure 4.4 Postliberalization distribution of firm productivity.

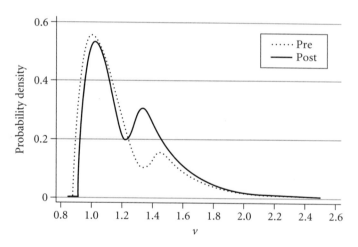

Figure 4.5 Combined distribution of firm productivity across steady states.

tributed across the two stationary states, and also shows that there are fewer total firms (across states) in the postliberalization stationary state (although there are more competing imported varieties in the latter). The overall and striking difference between the two firm distributions across states is the substantial shift from *AD* firms to *BX* firms (in terms of both the range

Table 4.5 Distribution of firms and transitions across states

Stationary states	# firms	Firm distribution				Transitions				
		AD	BD	AX	BX	ADBD	ADAX	ADBX	BDBX	AXBX
Pre	570	77%	8%	0%	15%	4%	0%	0%	5%	0%
Post	446	51%	4%	3%	42%	0%	9%	2%	2%	6%

UA		Firm distribution				Transitions				
Year	# firms	AD	BD	AX	BX	ADBD	ADAX	ADBX	BDBX	AXBX
0	570	77%	8%	0%	15%	4%	0%	0%	5%	0%
1	570	77%	8%	0%	15%	4%	0%	0%	5%	0%
2	570	77%	8%	0%	15%	4%	0%	0%	5%	0%
3	570	77%	8%	0%	15%	4%	0%	0%	5%	0%
4	473	59%	2%	4%	35%	0%	16%	6%	8%	10%
5	441	55%	2%	3%	40%	0%	10%	2%	1%	7%
6	438	53%	2%	3%	42%	0%	9%	2%	1%	6%
7	439	52%	3%	3%	42%	0%	9%	2%	1%	6%
8	440	52%	3%	3%	42%	0%	9%	2%	1%	6%

AA		Firm distribution				Transitions				
Year	# firms	AD	BD	AX	BX	ADBD	ADAX	ADBX	BDBX	AXBX
0	570	77%	8%	0%	15%	4%	0%	0%	5%	0%
1	619	79%	8%	0%	13%	3%	0%	0%	4%	0%
2	628	78%	9%	0%	13%	4%	0%	0%	5%	0%
3	597	75%	10%	0%	15%	9%	0%	0%	8%	0%
4	461	57%	2%	3%	39%	0%	11%	4%	14%	6%
5	412	50%	2%	3%	45%	0%	10%	2%	1%	6%
6	421	51%	2%	3%	44%	0%	9%	2%	1%	6%
7	428	51%	3%	3%	43%	0%	9%	2%	1%	6%
8	433	51%	3%	3%	43%	0%	9%	2%	1%	6%

AG		Firm distribution				Transitions				
Year	# firms	AD	BD	AX	BX	ADBD	ADAX	ADBX	BDBX	AXBX
0	570	77%	8%	0%	15%	4%	0%	0%	5%	0%
1	599	78%	8%	0%	14%	3%	0%	0%	5%	0%
2	605	78%	8%	0%	14%	3%	0%	0%	5%	0%
3	615	78%	8%	0%	14%	4%	0%	0%	5%	0%
4	592	76%	7%	0%	17%	6%	0%	0%	9%	0%
5	529	69%	5%	0%	26%	8%	1%	1%	10%	1%
6	452	58%	3%	1%	38%	2%	6%	5%	4%	3%
7	417	51%	2%	3%	44%	0%	10%	2%	1%	6%
8	424	51%	2%	3%	44%	0%	9%	2%	1%	6%

and mass of the distributions), when moving from the pre- to postliberalization stationary state. When we analyze the dynamics along the trade-liberalization equilibrium between these two stationary states, we will pay particular attention to the transition paths for this substantial group of firms moving between the two states. The right-hand side of Table 4.5 highlights the subset of transitions most relevant for the trade-liberalization equilibrium: transitions out of AD and into BX. In order to make these firm-transition flows comparable, they are expressed as percentages of the total number of firms across states (and not relative to the number of firms in the originating state, as was the case for Table 4.4). As in Table 4.4, the flows are annual, accumulating twelve monthly simulation periods.

4.4.1 Trade Liberalization

The contrast between the two stationary states already highlights how trade costs affect the relative benefits of innovation and export-market participation (and hence also highlights how the decision to innovate is inextricably linked to the export decision). We now analyze the transition dynamics between these two stationary states, paying particular attention to how these dynamics are affected by the anticipation and pace of liberalization. We investigate the effects of the three different trade-liberalization scenarios that involve the same long-run transition between the two stationary states, as previously described. The first scenario is an unanticipated, abrupt lowering of the trade costs, UA; the second scenario involves the same abrupt change in trade costs, but anticipated three years ahead, AA; and the third scenario is an anticipated but gradual change in trade costs, AG. In all cases, variable trade cost τ first decreases at the beginning of the fourth year. In the case of the anticipated liberalizations, this is announced at the beginning of the first year. The gradual liberalization occurs over a period of three years, whereas the abrupt liberalization occurs from one month to the next.

As described above, our model numerically solves for the full range of firm responses to the liberalization at monthly frequencies. Figure 4.6 shows the response of the price index P_t at this monthly frequency. Table 4.5 reports annual averages for the evolution in the number of firms and their distributions across each state (AD, BD, AX, BX), as well as the key transition flows out of AD and into BX at annual frequencies for all three scenarios. In all cases, year zero represents the old stationary state. Although we simulate the response over a period of seventeen years (to make sure that the end of the simulation corresponds nearly exactly to the new stationary

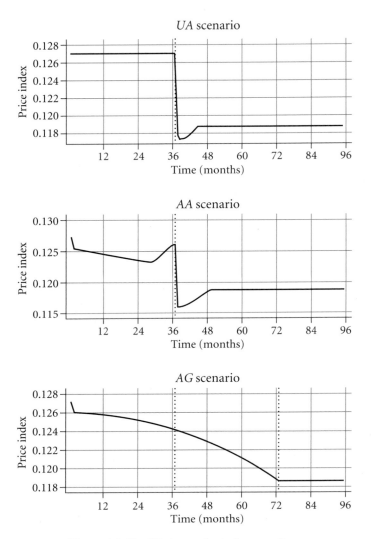

Figure 4.6 Equilibrium price index over time

state), we only report the first eight years as, in all three scenarios, that is enough to get back to an industry equilibrium that is very close to the new stationary state (with very few year-to-year variations in later years).

In the case of the unanticipated liberalization (*UA*), all years preceding the drop in trade costs follow the old stationary-state equilibrium. Entry

drops to zero for ten months following the drop in trade costs to accommodate the lower number of producers in the new long-run stationary state.
Immediately following the drop in trade costs, over a third of the *AD* firms
immediately enter the export market. Of these new exporters, a third innovate jointly with the export decisions (*ADBX* transition) while two thirds
do not innovate immediately upon entering the export market (*ADAX*
transition). The transitions into *BX* show that a large portion of *BD* firms
also immediately begin exporting (this flow represents almost all of the existing *BD* firms). Lastly, a large portion of the new *AX* exporters choose to
innovate shortly after their export-market–entry decision: the large *ADAX*
transitions are accompanied by large *AXBX* transitions, with very few firms
remaining as *AX* for very long. Thus, we can summarize the transition
paths of the new exporters by noting that most of them innovate either concurrent with, or subsequent to, their export-market–entry decision.

We now describe the transition path for a similar case of abrupt liberalization, but where this liberalization is now anticipated three years ahead
of time. It is clear from the response of the price index that this anticipation not only affects the firms' expectations for the future, but also
their current behavior. This is most drastically exhibited by the behavior
of the low-productivity *AD* firms that start exiting as soon as the news of
trade liberalization is announced. Figure 4.7 shows the response of the exit-
productivity cutoff for *AD* firms. The main force behind the exit of these
low-productivity firms is not the endogenous response of the price, but
the direct effect of the change in those firms' option value to remain active
in the industry—given future liberalization. In fact, even if the price index
did not change at all during the first three years prior to liberalization (but
stayed fixed at the old stationary equilibrium), the response of the exit cutoff would be essentially as it is depicted. The news of future liberalization
has a dramatic effect on the low-productivity firms' option value to remain
active. The probability that these firms will survive past the first three years
is now drastically reduced, and hence the option value of waiting for better
productivity draws is driven to zero (the closer to the expected liberalization, the closer the option value is driven to zero).

For similar reasons, the option values to invest for *AD* firms and to
export for *BD* firms are substantially affected by the prospect of future
liberalization.[16] The high-productivity *AD* firms know that they will almost surely be innovating postliberalization (and exporting), and the high-
productivity *BD* firms know that they will almost surely be exporting

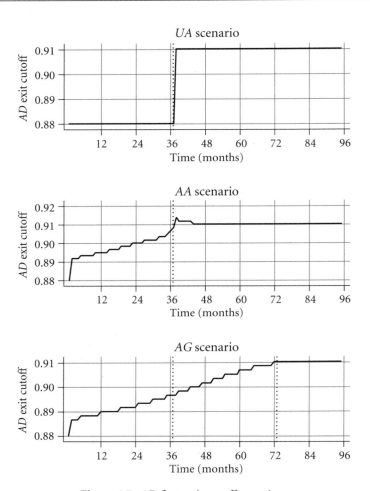

Figure 4.7 *AD* firm exit cutoff over time

postliberalization. Thus, their option value of waiting to do so also goes to zero as the liberalization date approaches, inducing those *AD* firms to innovate (transition to *BD*) and those *BD* firms to export (transition to *BX*). This is clearly reflected in the transitions in Table 4.5, although our parameterization suggests that this effect is only quantitatively important for the year preceding liberalization (the percentage of firms that transition from *AD* to *BD* increases from 4% to 9%, and that of firms that transition from *BD* to *BX* increases from 5% to 8%). After liberalization in year four, almost all the *BD* firms enter the export market, and the transition flows and distribution of firms across states very quickly approximates that of the unanticipated liberalization scenario. The crucial difference is that the anticipation of future liberalization induces many new exporters to innovate ahead of liberalization, and thus also ahead of their anticipated, but yet unrealized, entry into the export market.

In this case of anticipated, abrupt trade liberalization, entry drops to zero for several periods: for the six months preceding the drop in τ, and for just over a year following the drop. Preceding the drop in τ, the exit threshold rises. Just after the drop in τ, the exit threshold continues to rise and overshoots the long run level, only returning down to the long-run level nine months after the drop in τ. As entrants are typically smaller than incumbents (and initially start out as *AD* firms), the value of entry is sensitive to this pattern in the exit cutoff. The lack of entry contributes to the reduction in the number of firms in the industry (and, in particular, at lower productivity levels): hence the steep rise in the price index prior to liberalization. Postliberalization, the price drops below the long-run level. One reason is that there is an immediate large switch of *BD* firms into the export market, which drives down industry price. In effect, "too many" incumbent firms remain in the industry, in the hope that their productivity evolves favorably: for instance, there is no sudden shift of *AD* firms into exit. With the prospect of the shakeout of *AD* firms, the value of entry is negative. Over time, this firm "overhang" is whittled away and entry eventually resumes.

Lastly, we turn to the scenario of the anticipated gradual liberalization. If this liberalization is gradual enough, as is the case with our current calibration, then the anticipation of liberalization does not have any noticeable effects on the firms' transitions between states prior to the start of liberalization—although it is still important enough to be significantly reflected in the endogenous price-index response and in the exit behavior of the least productive firms. Also, the transition process is sufficiently gradual that entry remains positive in all periods, unlike the other two scenarios with abrupt changes in trade costs.

However, the anticipated future course of liberalization does significantly affect the firm's transitions between states once liberalization begins. A series of unanticipated drops in trade costs would induce firms to start exporting whenever profitable to do so (and innovate concurrently or later as that becomes profitable too), but would not induce firms to innovate ahead of their expected entry into export markets. Yet, this is exactly what is reflected in the transitions reported in Table 4.5 for this scenario. As liberalization begins, we witness the same substantial response in the transitions from AD to BD. These firms then subsequently enter the export market and transition from BD to BX. As in the case of the anticipated abrupt liberalization, some BD firms are induced to enter the export market as their option value of waiting to export falls, though this effect is harder to separate from the direct effect of the drop in trade costs in the current scenario.

4.5   Conclusion

In this chapter, we build a dynamic model of firm-level adjustment to trade liberalization that jointly addresses firms' decisions to innovate and/or to enter the export market. We analyze the equilibrium transition from an initial stationary state with high trade costs, comparing scenarios that differ in the extent to which the trade liberalization is anticipated by firms and how fast the trade costs drop once the liberalization starts. The comparison across the trade liberalization scenarios shows how some important non-technological factors, such as the pace and anticipation of trade liberalization, can fundamentally affect the perceived causation link between export status and productivity. For example, we show that the anticipation of trade liberalization tends to bring forward the decision to innovate relative to export-market participation, and how a more abrupt pace of liberalization amplifies these effects. Thus, our model shows how the current industrial response not only depends on concurrent trade costs, but also, inextricably, on the firms' prior expectations about those current trade costs, and their expectations for future trade costs. More generally, our model highlights the potential empirical pitfalls of analyzing current-period industrial performance as a response to the concurrent trade costs during periods of trade liberalization.

Appendix

4A.1   Model Algorithm

We describe below the algorithm for numerically solving the model, focusing on the equilibrium conditions required and the sequence of calculations performed. The demand structure leads to monopolistic competition. In particular, this means that each firm in each time period t needs only know industry aggregate outcomes for industry price P from time t onward, $\{P_t, \ldots, P_T\}$, to determine its specific policies conditional on its current productivity v and policy state $z = \{AD, BD, AX, BX\}$, where A and B refer to firm choice of technology, and D and X to firm choice of whether to export or not. Firm policy choices are whether to $\{Continue, Exit\}$, and, if continuing, whether to switch policy state.

The algorithm comprises three steps. Step 1 is to set parameters. Step 2 is to compute the firm policies and firm-size distribution $\mu_{z,1}$ corresponding to the initial parameter values, the initial stationary state equilibrium at $t = 1$. Within Step 2, there is an iteration over the aggregate price for the stationary state P_1. Step 3 computes the firm policies and firm-size distribution for the evolution from the initial stationary state through to period T. Within Step 3, there is an iteration over the price path $\{P_2, \ldots, P_T\}$.

1. Set initial parameters, including for industry characteristics and grid structure.

2. P_1 iteration

   • Choose candidate value for P_1.
   • Firm value and policy iteration
     ▪ Compute profit $\pi(v)$ at each productivity v, based on the specific demand system and production function chosen.
     ▪ Pick a candidate value function $V_1(v, z)$.
     ▪ Determine $\{Continuation/Exit\}$ and choice of policy state z at each $\{v, z\}$.
     ▪ The set of firm policies over continuation and choice of policy state imply a next-iteration value for the value function, $V_1'(v, z)$, based on computing the value of continuing and comparing to the value of exit.
     ▪ Check whether new $V_1'(v, z)$ is sufficiently close to $V_1(v, z)$.
       * If not, continue iteration with $V_1'(v, z)$.
       * If close enough, return to P_1 iteration.
   • Check the value of entry. As seek equilibria with positive entry, the condition should be close to zero. Compute firm-size distribution $\mu_{z,1}$.
     ▪ If close enough to zero, P_1 iteration is complete.
     ▪ If not, then adjust candidate P_1 accordingly: if condition is positive, lower P_1; if negative, raise P_1.

3. $\{P_2, \ldots, P_T\}$ iteration

- Choose candidate value for $\{P_2, \ldots, P_T\}$.
  - Compute price corresponding to stationary state at final parameter values.
  - Set initial guess for $\{P_2, \ldots, P_T\}$ based on prices corresponding to initial and final parameter values.
- Firm value and policy iteration
  - Firm value and policy iteration for $t = T$:
    * Compute profit $\pi_T(v)$ at each productivity v, based on the specific demand system and production function chosen.
    * Pick a candidate value function $V_T(v, z)$.
    * Determine $\{Continuation/Exit\}$ and choice of policy state z at each $\{v, z\}$.
    * The set of firm policies over continuation and choice of policy state imply a next-iteration value for the value function, $V_T'(v, z)$, based on computing the value of continuing and comparing to the value of exit.
    * Check whether new $V_T'(v, z)$ is sufficiently close to $V_T(v, z)$.
      – If close enough, return to $\{P_2, \ldots, P_T\}$ iteration.
      – If not, continue iteration with $V_T'(v, z)$.
  - Firm value and policy iteration for $t = \{2, \ldots, T - 1\}$:
    * Compute profit $\pi_t(v)$ at each productivity v, based on the specific demand system and production function chosen.
    * Iterate back to compute $V_{T-1}(v, z)$ based on $\pi_{T-1}(v)$ and $V_T'(v, z)$, and period T policies, based on computing the value of continuing and comparing to the value of exit. Hence, determine period $T - 1$ policies $\{Continuation/Exit\}$ and choice of policy state z.
    * Iterate back to period $t = 2$.
- Compute value of entry.
- Compute the size distribution of firms $\mu_z = \{\mu_{z,2}, \ldots, \mu_{z,T}\}$ consistent with the computed firm policies.
  - Compute $\mu_{z,2}$ based on $\mu_{z,1}$ and firm policies computed for $t = 2$.
  - Determine number of entrants:
    * If value of entry negative for $t = 2$, set entry to zero.
    * If value of entry is nonnegative, set entry such that
      – Case 1: If the distribution of incumbents implies a price below P_2, then entry is zero, as adding entrants would further distance the firm distribution from the current value of price path.

– Case 2: If the distribution of incumbents implies a price above P_2, then add entrants until the firm distribution (including entrants) implies a price equal to P_2.

▪ Iterate forward to compute $\mu_z = \{\mu_{z,3}, \ldots, \mu_{z,T}\}$.

• Check whether price path $\{P_2, \ldots, P_T\}$ is close enough to an equilibrium:

▪ Objective function to assess equilibrium comprised of two parts

 * The first part measures the distance between the price path and the price implied by the distribution of firms: $(P^{max} - P)$.

 * The second part measures an equivalent gap based on the value of entry: $(P^{fe} - P)$.

 – This is zero if value of entry is negative (to capture instances when this value is close to zero but negative, we consider this to be zero if the ratio of value of entry to the sunk cost of entry is larger than -10^{-4}).

 – This is negative if the value of entry is positive. We calculate P^{fe} as what the price would need to change to, in the time period in question, in order to close part of the gap in value of free entry. Hence, if value of entry is positive, the price change is negative so as to lower profitability and thus lower the value of entry. The adjustment is moderated by the extent to which price adjustments for future periods (which have been determined, as the algorithm work backs through time periods) are for increases or decreases in prices.

 * The objective function is then the Euclidian distance of these two measures: $((P^{max} - P)^2 + (P^{fe} - P)^2)^{\frac{1}{2}}$.

▪ If objective function is not sufficiently small, construct new candidate price path.

 * The suggested price adjustment is the average of $(P^{max} - P)$ and $(P^{fe} - P)$.

 * The actual price adjustment is only part of the suggested price adjustment, to reduce the risk of cycling over successive iterations of the price path.

ACKNOWLEDGMENTS

We are grateful to Robert Feenstra, Elhanan Helpman, and Esteban Rossi-Hansberg for helpful discussions and suggestions. We also greatly benefited from all the discussions at the book conference where the chapter was originally presented.

NOTES

1. Alvarez and López (2005) find empirical support for all three types of firm behavior. Yeaple (2005) and Ederington and McCalman (2008) have theoretically analyzed the joint technology adoption and export decisions of firms, when there are no ex ante differences between them. Chaney (2005) investigates the dynamics of firm entry and productivity with heterogeneous firms, immediately following an unanticipated opening to trade (from autarky). He shows how this leads to an overshooting of productivity due to the sluggish response of exit. Our model confirms these findings following certain types of trade liberalization, starting from an open economy environment. Our chapter is most closely related to Atkeson and Burstein (2006), who also analyze the joint innovation and export decisions of firms in a dynamic model of trade with heterogeneous firms. Atkeson and Burstein (2006) consider a continuous type of innovation activity (performed by all firms at varying intensities) whereas we consider a one-off innovation opportunity, such as the adoption of a new technology or a major product-quality upgrade or redesign.

2. We intentionally constructed our model without any such learning channel to highlight that this is not needed in order to explain the microlevel evidence on the relative timing of export-market entry and productivity gains. The existence of such a channel remains an open empirical question. To our knowledge, only Crespi, Criscuolo, and Haskel (2008) find some evidence for learning by exporting that is not based on the timing of export-market entry.

3. Bustos (2005) and Verhoogen (2008) both report how measures of firm innovation, for example the reported adoption of new technologies or ISO certification, are strongly correlated with firm productivity and export status.

4. A seminal contribution to the computation of such equilibria with a small number of firms under oligopoly is Pakes and McGuire (1994), following the development of the theoretical version of the model in Ericson and Pakes (1995). Both papers study an industry closed to foreign trade. Erdem and Tybout (2003) extend the work of Pakes and McGuire (1994) to the case of an import-competing industry. The computational methods we develop in the current chapter are radically different as they apply to a monopolistically competitive sector with a large number of competing firms (where the mass of firms evolves endogenously). These methods have also been concurrently used in Costantini (2006) to study the effects of credit constraints on industrial evolution. Similar methods applied to a continuous innovation decision in a general equilibrium setting have also recently been developed by Atkeson and Burstein (2006).

5. For simplicity, we allow A firms only a one-time choice to become a B firm. A more general setup could allow repeated innovation by firms, or possibly allow B firms to invest to scrap their innovation and transition back to an A firm.

6. We introduce γ^B only to generate a smoother firm distribution across productivity.

7. Thus, there is both endogenous exit (due to a bad productivity shock) and exogenous exit due to the death shock.

8. Clearly, those AD firms receiving high enough productivity-transition draws will choose to both innovate and export the $ADBX$ transition.

9. For instance, the standard deviation of log size ranges from 0.79 to 1.27 for selected five-digit Portuguese manufacturing industries (Cabral and Mata 2003), and varies between 0.9 to 0.95 for Dutch manufacturers over the period 1978 to 1998 (Marsili 2006).

10. Note that, although the productivity transition has no effect on the firm's expected productivity, this is not true for the effect on the firm's expected profit. The profit function rises steeply with productivity—hence in expectation, profits rise with a productivity shock. The death shock in part compensates for this effect (otherwise no firm would ever want to exit). Another modeling alternative would be to specify a mean-reverting productivity transition.

11. Note that these flows represent the accumulation of transitions over twelve monthly simulation periods, so these flows can be greater than 100% for originating states that are transitory for most firms. The exogenous exit flows due to the death shock δ (independent across productivity) are not represented.

12. As we previously noted, the use of a productivity upper bound implies that the benefits of innovation are worthless to a firm with productivity at the upper-bound threshold. This implies that BX is not the best option for noninnovators with productivity levels right below this threshold. Our calibration is such that the productivity upper bound $v \leq 3$ is high enough that there are virtually no firms close to this productivity range (see distribution plots, discussed later in this section). Thus, the effect of the upper bound on the incentives to innovate is immaterial in our calibrations—and is consequently ignored in the transition decisions in Table 4.4.

13. To be precise, the number of AX firms is not exactly zero: due to the i.i.d. probability of infeasible innovation (γ_B draw), a tiny fraction of AD firms, who wish to both export and innovate, are constrained to only export until their γ_B draw is reversed. However, the fraction of firms concerned is so minute, and the transition via AX so transitory, that the number of AX firms is essentially zero up to a rounding error.

14. The bottom half of Table 4.4 shows that there are still some BD firms in the postliberalization stationary state. These firms all transition to BD from the BX

state: some *BX* firms subsequently receive bad productivity shocks and exit the export market, transitioning to *BD*.

15. There is no hysteresis band associated with this option value as *BD* firms can not un-innovate.

16. There are virtually no *AX* firms, so no purpose in considering the innovation option for those firms. Also, the *AX* state is not attractive to *AD* firms, who would rather innovate first at the higher trade costs—hence no reason to consider the option value of exporting for *AD* firms.

REFERENCES

Alvarez, R., and R. A. López. 2005. "Exporting and Performance: Evidence from Chilean Plants." *Canadian Journal of Economics* 38(4):1384–1400.

Atkeson, A., and A. Burstein. 2007. "Innovation, Firm Dynamics, and International Trade." NBER working paper 13326.

Aw, B. Y., M. J. Roberts, and T. Winston. 2007. "Export Market Participation, Investments in R&D and Worker Training, and the Evolution of Firm Productivity." *The World Economy* 30(1):83–104.

Bartelsman, E., S. Scarpetta, and F. Schivardi. 2003. "Comparative Analysis of Firm Demographics and Survival: Micro-level Evidence for the OECD Countries." OECD Economics Department working paper no. 348.

Bernard, A., and B. Jensen. 1999. "Exceptional Exporter Performance: Cause, Effect or Both?" *Journal of International Economics* 47:1–25.

———. 2006. "Trade Costs, Firms and Productivity." *Journal of Monetary Economics* 53(2006):917–37.

Bustos, P. 2005. "The Impact of Trade on Technology and Skill Upgrading: Evidence from Argentina." Working paper, CREI and Universitat Pompeu Fabra.

Cabral, L. M. B., and J. Mata. 2003. "On the Evolution of the Firm Size Distribution: Facts and Theory." *The American Economic Review* 93(4):1075–90.

Chaney, T. 2005. "Productivity Overshooting: The Dynamic Impact of Trade Opening with Heterogeneous Firms." Mimeo, University of Chicago.

Costantini, J. 2006. "Impact of Financial Development on Firm Growth and Firm Size Distribution." Working paper, INSEAD.

Crespi, G., C. Criscuolo, and J. Haskel. 2008. "Productivity, Exporting and the Learning-by-Exporting Hypothesis: Direct Evidence from UK Firms." *Canadian Journal of Economics* 41:619–38.

Delgado, M., J. C. Farinas, and S. Ruano. 2002. "Firm Productivity and Export Markets: A Non-Parametric Approach." *Journal of International Economics* 57(2):397–422.

De Loecker, J. 2006. "Do Exports Generate Higher Productivity? Evidence from Slovenia." *Journal of International Economics* 73: 69–98.

Dixit, R., and J. Stiglitz. 1977. "Monopolistic Competition and Optimum Product Diversity." *The American Economic Review* 67(3, Jun):297–308.

Ederington, J., and P. McCalman. 2008. "Endogenous Firm Heterogeneity and the Dynamics of Trade Liberalization." *Journal of International Economics* 74:422–40.

Erdem, E., and J. Tybout. 2003. "Trade Policy and Industrial Sector Responses: Using Evolutionary Models to Interpret the Evidence." Brookings Trade Forum 2003, NBER working paper 9947.

Ericson, R., and A. Pakes. 1995. "Markov-Perfect Industry Dynamics: A Framework for Empirical Work." *Review of Economic Studies, 1995* 62(1):53–82.

Girma, S., D. Greenaway, and R. Kneller. 2004. "Does Exporting Increase Productivity? A Microeconometric Analysis of Matched Firms." *Review of International Economics* 12(5):855–66.

Hopenhayn, H. 1992. "Entry, Exit and Firm Dynamics in the Long Run." *Econometrica* 60(5, Sep):1127–50.

López, R. A. 2005. "Trade and Growth: Reconciling the Macroeconomic and Microeconomic Evidence." *Journal of Economic Surveys* 19(4):623–48.

Marsili, O. 2006. "Stability and Turbulence in the Size Distribution of Firms: Evidence from Dutch Manufacturing." *International Review of Applied Economics* 20(2):255–72.

Melitz, M. 2003. "The Impact of Trade on Aggregate Industry Productivity and Intra-Industry Reallocations." *Econometrica* 71(6):1695–1725.

Pakes, A., and P. McGuire. 1994. "Computing Markov-Perfect Nash Equilibria: Numerical Implications of a Dynamic Differentiated Product Model." *RAND Journal of Economics* 25(4, Winter):555–89.

Topalova, P. 2004. "Trade Liberalization and Firm Productivity: The Case of India." IMF working paper.

Trefler, D. 2004. "The Long and Short of the Canada-U.S. Free Trade Agreement." *The American Economic Review* 94(4, Sep):870–95.

Verhoogen, E. 2008. "Trade, Quality Upgrading and Wage Inequality in the Mexican Manufacturing Sector." *Quarterly Journal of Economics* 123:489–530.

Yeaple, S. R. 2005. "Firm Heterogeneity, International Trade, and Wages." *Journal of International Economics* 65(1):1–20.

— 5 —

Competing in Organizations

Firm Heterogeneity and International Trade

DALIA MARIN AND THIERRY VERDIER

5.1 Introduction

Until recently, international trade theory treated firms as a black box. The firm is characterized by a production function according to which the factors of production (capital, labor) are transformed into consumption goods. Moreover, these firms are assumed to be of equal size and productivity. In reality, however, firms consist of organizations with an inner life and differ in size, productivity, and type of firm organization.

Firm heterogeneity in size and productivity in the same industry are now widely recognized in various empirical firm-level studies (Bernard and Jensen 1999; Clerides, Lach, and Tybout 1998). A number of recent papers have introduced firm heterogeneity into models of international trade (Melitz 2003; Bernard et al. 2003; Melitz and Ottaviano 2008). In all these specifications, the basic ingredients are the same. Firms face an exogenous ex ante distribution of potential productivity levels. After uncertainty is realized, entry and competition provide an endogenous mechanism for selection of the equilibrium distribution of productivity within an industry. Trade integration, affecting somewhat the degree of market competition, leads to a reallocation to high-productivity firms within a sector, with an increase in aggregate productivity providing additional sources of gains from trade for economies.[1]

But what determines differences in productivity and size across firms in the same industry in the first place? Several empirical studies have attempted to clear away productivity differences among firms through better measures of inputs (capital, material, skills) and explicit measures of technology such as research and development or information and communication technologies. But an unexplained residual remains. A recent study

142

by Bloom and Van Reenen (2006) attempts to explain these residual differences in firm performance by differences in management practices across firms and countries. Using an elaborate measure of management quality, they find that better management practices are significantly associated with higher productivity, profitability, sales growth, and firm-survival rates in four countries: the United States, United Kingdom, France, and Germany.

In this chapter we focus on understanding the sources of firms' ex ante heterogeneity and their implications for competition and international trade. We consider the firms' mode of organization as one natural candidate for the source of firms' productivity heterogeneity. The type of organization may well explain differences in management practices described in Bloom and Van Reenen (2006). We take a first look at the relationship between corporate organization and productivity in Figure 5.1. The figure plots the pattern between firms' productivity (captured by firms' sales per worker) and firms' mode of organization. We capture corporate organization by the level of centralization of decision making inside the corporation. Firms are ranked by their level of centralization over several corporate decisions. The numbers in Figure 5.1 are averages over several corporate decisions ranging between 1 and 5, with 1 as a central decision taken at the CEO level at the top of the organization and 5 as a decentral decision taken at the divisional level.[2]

The pattern appears to be inverted U-shaped with the most productive firms having a management style in which both headquarters as well as middle managers are involved in the decision making inside the corporation.[3] This pattern raises the question—what forces explain the relationship between the observed diversity in corporate organization on the one hand and the pattern of heterogeneity among firms in productivity on the other? More specifically, do firms differ in terms of size and productivity because they adopt different types of organizations? Or is the reverse the case—that firms have different organizations because they differ in size and productivity?

In earlier work (Marin and Verdier 2003b, 2008a) we investigate the second link by focusing on how factor endowments on the one hand and international competition on the other are affecting firm size and the mode of organization firms choose. We find that firms that are neither too skill intensive nor too labor intensive will choose firm organizations in which power is delegated to the divisional level to keep middle managers' initiative alive. We also find that larger, more profitable firms will delegate decision

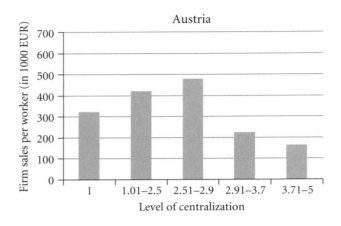

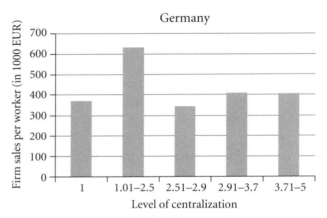

Figure 5.1 Firm productivity and level of centralization.

control to empower their middle managers. In this chapter we are reversing the question by asking how firms' organizational choices determine heterogeneity across firms in size and productivity in the same industry. We develop a model in which firms' choice of corporate organization is affecting firm performance and the nature of competition in international markets. We introduce organizational choices in a Krugman cum Melitz and Ottaviano model of international trade (Krugman 1980). Our model simultaneously determines firms' organizational choices and heterogeneity across firms in size and productivity. More precisely, we combine within-industry heterogeneity of Melitz (2003) and Melitz and Ottaviano (2008) with power in the firm of Marin and Verdier (2008a, 2008b). This allows us to study the impact of corporate organization on firm productivity and on the nature of competition in international markets. Moreover, it allows us to analyze the impact of international trade on aggregate productivity in an industry.

This chapter contributes in several respects to this literature. Antràs and Helpman (2004) ask how an exogenous distribution of productivity among firms determines organizational choices on sourcing. Melitz (2003) introduces firm productivity heterogeneity into a Krugman (1980) model of trade under monopolistic competition by an exogenous equilibrium distribution of productivity. We endogenize firm heterogeneity in a Melitz and Ottaviano (2008) model by firms' choice of organization. Our model generates an endogenous mix of firms with different productivity and size levels, which is driven by their organizational choices.

Our model predicts intrafirm reallocations from high-cost to low-cost firms resulting in an increase in average productivity of an industry following episodes of trade liberalizations similar to Melitz (2003). However, the mechanism by which this occurs is entirely different. Rather than through the exit of the least productive firms, trade liberalization increases average productivity by inducing CEOs or owners in firms to monitor more, leading to a larger fraction of firms in which CEOs have "real power" in firms and in which they choose the cost-minimizing project. Hence, the productivity effect arises inside firms rather than through reallocation between firms.

However, in contrast to Melitz (2003), a trade shock may or may not increase average productivity depending on the corporate equilibrium that emerges in the economy. Interestingly, we find that the toughness of competition in the market becomes endogenous and depends on who—headquarters or middle managers—has power inside firms. A large enough trade shock may lower productivity in the liberalizing country by inducing a change in corporate equilibrium from a P-organization to an A-organization in which power is delegated to middle managers to promote their incentives to find new projects for the firm. In this case, the shift in the organizational equilibrium toward management empowerment reduces the toughness of competition with larger markups and equilibrium profits. Aggregate productivity declines for two reasons. First, it declines because principals monitor less, leading to a smaller fraction of firms in which principals or owners have real power in firms. Second, it declines because competition becomes less intense, helping a larger share of high-cost firms survive in the market. Hence, in an empowerment equilibrium that promotes the creation of ideas for new projects, competition takes place in quality (more varieties) rather than in price. This way this chapter adds two new internal margins of trade adjustment—the monitoring margin and the organizational margin—to the external margin proposed by Melitz.[4]

The chapter is organized in the following sections. Section 5.2 presents the basic model of monopolistic competition in a closed economy. Section 5.3 determines the optimal mode of firm organization. Section 5.4 incorporates the model of firm organization into the framework of monopolistic competition described in Section 5.2. Section 5.5 determines the industry equilibrium with free entry. Section 5.6 shows how the choice of organization determines heterogeneity of firms in terms of size and productivity in the same industry. The section also shows how the nature of competition in international markets depends on the corporate equilibrium that emerges in the economy. The section then determines the productivity dispersion in the different organizational equilibria. Section 5.7 examines how a trade shock affects aggregate productivity. Section 5.8 concludes.

5.2   The Closed Economy

5.2.1 Demand Side

Consider an economy with L consumers. Consumer preferences are defined over a continuum of differentiated varieties indexed by $i \in \Omega$ and a homogeneous good chosen as the numeraire as in Melitz and Ottaviano (2008). They are given by

$$U = q_0 + \beta \int_{i \in \Omega} q_i \, di - \frac{1}{2}\gamma \int_{i \in \Omega} q_i^2 \, di - \frac{1}{2}\eta \left[\int_{i \in \Omega} q_i \, di \right]^2$$

where q_0 and q_i are, respectively, consumption of the numeraire good and consumption of variety i of the differentiated sector. The demand parameters β, γ, and η are positive with β and η giving the substitution between the differentiated varieties and the numeraire, and the parameter γ as the degree of product differentiation between the varieties. Let p_i be the price of variety i. We assume that consumers have positive demands for the numeraire good. Then standard utility maximization gives the individual inverse demand function

$$p_i = \beta - \gamma q_i - \eta Q^c,$$

where Q^c is total consumption level over all varieties

$$Q^c = \int_{i \in \Omega} q_i di.$$

Noting N, the measure of the set of varieties Ω with positive demands, and $\overline{p}$, the average price index

$$\overline{p} = \frac{1}{N} \int_{i \in \Omega} p_i di,$$

it follows that

$$\overline{p} = \beta - \frac{\gamma}{N} Q^c - \eta Q^c = \beta - \frac{\gamma + N\eta}{N} Q^c.$$

Hence, the market demand q_i for variety i is given by:[5]

$$q_i = L q_i = \frac{\beta L}{\gamma + N\eta} - \frac{L}{\gamma} p_i + \frac{N\eta}{\gamma + N\eta} \frac{L}{\gamma} \overline{p}. \tag{5.1}$$

Note that in this linear demand system for varieties, the price elasticity of demand is now also driven by the toughness of competition in the market, induced either by a lower average price for varieties $\overline{p}$ or more product varieties N. The price elasticity of demand increases with lower $\overline{p}$ and larger N.[6]

5.2.1.1 Production

The numeraire good 0 is produced with constant returns to scale (one unit of good 0 requires one unit of labor) and under perfect competitive conditions. Each variety of the differentiated good is produced under monopolistically competitive conditions. Suppose that a given variety i is produced with marginal cost c_i; then profits for that variety can be written as

$$\pi_i = q_i (p_i - c_i).$$

The profit-maximizing output level $q_i = q(c_i)$ and price level $p_i = p(c_i)$ are related to each other by

$$q_i = q(c_i) = \frac{L}{\gamma} \left[p(c_i) - c_i \right]. \tag{5.2}$$

The profit-maximizing price can be written as

$$p(c_i) = \frac{1}{2}\left[c_i + \frac{\beta\gamma}{\gamma + N\eta} + \frac{N\eta}{\gamma + N\eta}\,\overline{p}\right], \tag{5.3}$$

with the (absolute) markup over price as

$$m(c_i) = p(c_i) - c_i = \frac{1}{2}\left[\frac{\beta\gamma}{\gamma + N\eta} + \frac{N\eta}{\gamma + N\eta}\,\overline{p} - c_i\right]. \tag{5.4}$$

The average price $\overline{p}$ and average cost of firms $\overline{c}$ can be expressed as

$$\overline{p} = \frac{\overline{c} + \frac{\beta\gamma}{\gamma+N\eta}}{\frac{2\gamma+N\eta}{\gamma+N\eta}} \tag{5.5}$$

$$\overline{c} = \frac{1}{N}\int_{i\in\Omega} c_i\,di, \tag{5.6}$$

and equilibrium profits of a firm with cost c_i are given by

$$\pi(c_i) = \frac{L}{4\gamma}\left[c_D - c_i\right]^2, \tag{5.7}$$

where c_D is the cutoff cost level

$$c_D = \frac{2\beta\gamma}{2\gamma + N\eta} + \frac{N\eta}{2\gamma + N\eta}\,\overline{c}, \tag{5.8}$$

reflecting the cost level of a firm that is just indifferent about leaving or remaining in the industry and earns zero profits. Firms with cost $c_i < c_D$ earn positive profits. The cutoff cost level c_D captures the toughness of competition in an industry. It declines when competition is tougher with more firms around (larger N), with more low-cost firms in the market (lower average costs $\overline{c}$), and when varieties are closer substitutes (smaller γ).[7]

5.3   Power in the Firm

In this section we examine how firms decide over the mode of organization. We consider a firm with a simple hierarchy consisting of a CEO (the principal P) hiring a division manager (the agent A) to implement a production project. There are m potential and a priori identical projects (or ways to produce a good). Payoffs are ex ante unknown to both parties. Among the m projects, there is one that yields the highest possible benefit B for the principal and one that yields the highest possible benefit b for the agent. Let

αB be the principal's expected benefit when the agent's preferred project is implemented with ($0 \leq \alpha \leq 1$). Assume, for simplicity, that the agent's expected benefit when the principal's preferred project is implemented is 0. The lower α, the larger the conflict of interest between the principal and her agent. Hence, α is a parameter that captures the power struggle in the firm.

B and b are supposed to be known ex ante, though the parties do not know ex ante which project yields such payoff. We assume also that, among the m projects, there are some with very high, negative payoffs to both parties, implying that choosing a project randomly without being informed is not profitable to both agents who instead prefer to do nothing (project 0). This aspect, together with the fact that each uninformed party prefers to rubber-stamp the other informed party's suggestion to do nothing, implies that private information about payoffs gives decision control to the informed party. In this case, the informed party has *real power* rather than *formal power* in the firm. Thus, there are two sources of power in the firm, because it is allocated to the manager—*formal authority,* which is ex ante contractible, or, because the manager is better informed, *real authority.*[8]

Parties may acquire information on the payoff structure in the following way. By spending some resource cost

$$g_P(E) = g \frac{E^2}{2}$$

the principal P learns the payoff structure of all projects with probability E and remains uninformed with probability $1 - E$. Similarly, by exerting some effort

$$g_A(e) = ke \text{ with } e \in [0, \bar{e}], \ k < b,$$

the agent learns the payoff structure of all projects with probability e and remains uninformed with probability $1 - e$.

We assume that the principal is risk neutral and that the agent is infinitely risk averse with respect to income. Therefore, the agent is not responsive to monetary incentives and he agrees to receive a fixed wage w equal to his opportunity cost. His incentives to gather information on projects will be directly related to the private nonpecuniary benefit b he gets from his "best" project.

Firms can choose between three organizational types: a P-organization in which the CEO or owner has formal power, an A-organization in which the CEO or owner delegates formal power to the agent, and an O-organization in which the principal has formal power and in which the agent exerts minimum effort. The O-organization can be thought of as a single managed firm (run by the principal) without an internal hierarchy.

Decisions are taken in the following sequence. The principal allocates formal power to herself (P-organization) or to the agent (A-organization). Then the two parties simultaneously collect information about projects' payoff. The party who does not have decision power suggests a project (or nothing) to the other party. Finally, the party with power rubber-stamps the other party's suggestion or selects an alternative project or decides to do nothing. Hence, the party with formal authority, whenever informed, picks her preferred project. When she remains uninformed ex post, that party rubber-stamps the suggestion of the other party who, whenever informed, has real authority over the project choice and gets his preferred project implemented. When neither party has information on the payoff structure, no project is undertaken by the firm.

Let us look then at the equilibrium informational efforts of the two parties under each organization. We first compute the Nash equilibria in information collection and the resulting payoffs under each organization. Then we examine which of these organizations yields higher utility to the principal and is preferred by her.

5.3.1 P-organization

We start with the case where the principal has formal power in the firm and the agent participates actively in the management of the firm (i.e., $e > 0$). When the principal has formal power, the expected payoffs $U_P(E, e)$ for the principal and $v_P(E, e)$ for the agent are given by

$$U_P(E, e) = EB + (1 - E)e\alpha B - g_P(E) - w$$
$$v_P(E, e) = (1 - E)eb - g_A(e).$$

With probability E, the principal becomes fully informed about her payoffs and picks her preferred project with monetary payoff B, while the agent receives 0. With probability $1 - E$, the principal remains uninformed about payoffs. The agent may then learn, with probability e, the payoff structure and suggest his best project to the principal (who accepts it). The principal receives a monetary payoff αB while the agent gets his best private benefit b. Or the agent may remain also uninformed, in which case, no project is undertaken.

The first-order conditions of the two parties with respect to efforts E and e are

$$\text{Principal: } B(1 - e\alpha) = gE \text{ and Agent: } e = \begin{cases} \bar{e} & \text{if } k \leq b(1 - E) \\ 0 & \text{if } k > b(1 - E) \end{cases}. \quad (5.9)$$

The conditions highlight the trade-off between the principal's control and the agent's initiative. The principal supervises more, the higher her stake in the project (the larger B), the larger the conflict of interest between the principal and the agent (the lower α), and the lower the agent's effort e. The agent, in turn, has more initiative the higher her stake (the larger b) and the lower the principal's interference (the lower E). Thus, control comes with the cost of losing the agent's initiative.

The Nash equilibrium level of efforts of this game are given by

$$e_P^* = \bar{e}, \text{ and } E_P^* = \frac{B(1 - \bar{e}\alpha)}{g} \quad \text{when } B \leq \tilde{B}_P(\alpha) \quad (5.10)$$

$$e_P^* = 0, \text{ and } E_P^* = \frac{B}{g} \quad \text{when } B > \tilde{B}_P(\alpha)$$

with

$$\tilde{B}_P(\alpha) = \frac{g(1 - k/b)}{1 - \bar{e}\alpha}.$$

$\tilde{B}_P(\alpha)$ captures the threshold level of profits at which the agent's initiative is fully crowded out when the principal has formal power. For payoffs over $\tilde{B}_P(\alpha)$, the principal exerts an effort E_P^* that kills the initiative of the agent to acquire information. A P-organization with active participation of the agent prevails, therefore, only when $B < \tilde{B}_P(\alpha)$. The equilibrium expected utility of the principal under this organization is then

$$u_P(B) = U_P \left(\frac{B(1 - \bar{e}\alpha)}{g}, \bar{e} \right)$$

or, after substituting (5.10)

$$u_P(B) = \frac{B^2(1 - \alpha\bar{e})^2}{2g} + \bar{e}\alpha B - w. \quad (5.11)$$

5.3.2 O-organization

Alternatively, whenever profits are sufficiently large (i.e., $B > \widetilde{B}_P(\alpha)$), (5.10) implies that the agent does not actively engage in the firm (i.e., $e = 0$) in an organization with formal power in the hands of the principal. We denote such an organization as an *O-organization*. In this case, after substituting (5.10), the equilibrium expected utility of the principal is

$$u_O(B) = U_P\left(\frac{B}{g}, 0\right) = \frac{B^2}{2g} - w. \tag{5.12}$$

5.3.3 A-organization

Consider now the case in which the principal delegates decision control to the agent and the agent has formal power in the firm. Now the principal is prevented from overruling the agent's decision when both have acquired information. The two parties' expected payoffs are then

$$U_A(E, e) = e\alpha B + (1 - e)EB - g_P(E) - w$$
$$v_A(E, e) = eb - g_A(e).$$

Now the agent chooses his preferred project when informed. When the principal is informed and the agent is uninformed, the principal suggests her preferred project, which is then implemented by the agent. For $b > k$, the Nash equilibrium effort levels are[9]

$$e_A^* = \bar{e} \text{ and } E_A^* = \frac{B(1 - \bar{e})}{g}. \tag{5.13}$$

A comparison of the effort levels reveals that the agent's initiative is better promoted under the A-organization than under the P-organization. Actually under our specification, the agent will always provide maximum effort under the A-organization while his initiative will be killed under the P-organization for sufficiently large profits for the principal.

After substituting (5.13), the equilibrium expected utility of the principal under the A-organization is

$$u_A(B) = U_A\left(\frac{B(1 - \bar{e})}{g}, \bar{e}\right) = \frac{B^2(1 - \bar{e})^2}{2g} + \bar{e}\alpha B - w. \tag{5.14}$$

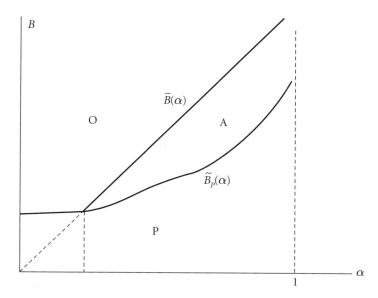

Figure 5.2 The optimal organization of the firm.

5.3.4 The Optimal Firm Organization

We turn now to determine the optimal firm organization. We ask how the parties' informational efforts respond to exogenous changes in the payoff B and in the conflict parameter α under each organization. We will make B and α endogenous in the next section. We illustrate the trade-offs the firm faces in its organizational choice with the help of Figure 5.2.

The $\tilde{B}_P(\alpha)$ curve relates the profit level to the incentives inside the firm and thus to the costs of having control in the firm. Recall that the $\tilde{B}_P(\alpha)$ curve represents the threshold level of profits at which the effort incentive of the agent is killed under the P-organization. $\tilde{B}_P(\alpha)$ is upward sloping in α because with an increase in α, the conflict of interest between the principal and the agent declines (the preferences between the principal and the agent become more similar). At a given profit level B, the principal intervenes less when the agent's preferred project is less in conflict with her objectives. Therefore, the profit level at which the agent's initiative is crowded out goes up. In the area below the $\tilde{B}_P(\alpha)$ line, the P-organization keeps the agent's initiative alive, while in the area above $\tilde{B}_P(\alpha)$, the agent does not exert any effort under the O-organization.

The $\bar{B}(\alpha)$ line relates the profit level to the market environment of the firm and thus captures the gain of having control in terms of the firms' profits. It is defined by $\bar{B}(\alpha) = \frac{2g\alpha}{2-\bar{e}}$ as the threshold level of profits at which the principal is indifferent between the O-organization with $e = 0$ and the A-organization with the agent's maximum initiative $\bar{e}$.[10] $\bar{B}(\alpha)$ is upward sloping in α because with an increase in α, the conflict declines, making delegating power to the agent less costly to the principal. Therefore, the level of profits at which the principal is indifferent between the P-organization and the A-organization goes up.

For profit levels below the $\tilde{B}_P(\alpha)$ curve, the benefit of control outweighs the costs, and the firm chooses the P-organization. In fact, at low levels of profits there is no trade-off between control and initiative, since the agent's initiative can be kept alive under the P-organization. At low profit levels, the principal monitors and intervenes little because her stakes are small and she cares little. Hence, the P-organization gives sufficient initiative to the agent. For profit levels in between the $\tilde{B}_P(\alpha)$ and the $\bar{B}(\alpha)$ curve, the cost of control outweighs the benefit, and the firm opts for the A-organization. There is a trade-off between control and initiative and the principal delegates formal power to the agent to keep his initiative, and the A-organization emerges as the optimal mode of organization. For profit levels above the $\bar{B}(\alpha)$ curve, the benefit of control again outweighs the costs, and the firm chooses the O-organization and loses the initiative of the agent. At high profit levels, there is again no trade-off between control and initiative. The principal's stakes are so large that she intervenes even under the A-organization, leading to minimum effort by the agent even when he is given formal power in the organization. Therefore, the principal might as well keep control by choosing the O-organization.[11]

5.4   Competition and the Power Struggle

We incorporate now the choice of firm organization into the production side described in Section 5.2.1.1. We endogenize profits B and the power struggle in firms α in this section. Recall the distinction between formal and real power in the firm. There are two types of firms depending on who— the principal or the agent—has *real* (as opposed to formal) power in the organization. More precisely, assume that the firms in which the principals' preferred project is implemented produce the good with production cost $c_i = c_B$. Call these firms "real P-organizations." Similarly the firms in which the agent's preferred project is implemented produce the good with larger production cost $c_i = c_b = \varphi c_B$ and $\varphi > 1$. Call these firms "real A-organizations." The idea here is that the agent does not always choose the cost-minimizing project but rather the one that is best for him and maximizes his perks. Thus, even in a formal P-organization in which the principal keeps formal control, the agent's preferred high-cost project may get implemented. This will happen when the principal decides not to get informed and to rubber-stamp the agent's suggestion. We then have, ex post, a real A-organization in a formal P-organization.

From (5.7) we can then rewrite the principal's profits when her best project is implemented as

$$B = \pi(c_B) = \frac{L}{4\gamma} \left[c_D - c_B \right]^2 = \frac{Lc_B^2}{4\gamma} \left[\tilde{c}_D - 1 \right]^2 \text{ with } \tilde{c}_D = \frac{c_D}{c_B}. \quad (5.15)$$

$\tilde{c}_D$ is the cost gap between firms with zero profits c_D and the low-cost P-organizations c_B. The smaller this gap, the harder it is to earn positive profits in the market. Thus, $\tilde{c}_D$ reflects the toughness of competition that a firm faces. Similarly, the conflict parameter α can also be expressed as a function of the cost gap $\tilde{c}_D$

$$\alpha = \frac{\pi(c_b)}{\pi(c_B)} = \left[\frac{\tilde{c}_D - \varphi}{\tilde{c}_D - 1} \right]^2. \quad (5.16)$$

The smaller $\tilde{c}_D$, the tougher is the competition in the market and the larger is the conflict of interest between the principal and her agent (the smaller α). The power struggle in firms becomes more intense with a decline in relative profits between an A-organization $\pi(c_b)$ (in which the agent runs the firm) and a P-organization $\pi(c_B)$ (in which the principal has power in the firm). Relative profits between these two types of firms decline with tougher competition, because high-cost A-organizations' revenues go down by more than revenues of low-cost P-organizations. A-organizations try to fight the loss in revenue s by lowering markups by more than P-organizations. Hence, with more intense competition, it matters more who runs the firm, and delegation of power to the agent becomes more costly to firms.

Low-cost, real P-organizations set lower prices p, produce larger outputs q, and earn higher revenues r and profits π than high-cost, real A-organizations, as can be seen from the following expressions:

$$q_B = q(c_B) = L\,c_B\,\frac{\widetilde{c}_D - 1}{2\gamma} \quad \text{while } q_b = q(c_b) = L\,c_B\,\frac{\widetilde{c}_D - \varphi}{2\gamma}$$

$$p_B = p(c_B) = c_B\,\frac{\widetilde{c}_D + 1}{2} \quad \text{while } p_b = p(c_b) = c_B\,\frac{\widetilde{c}_D + \varphi}{2}$$

$$r_B = r(c_B) = \frac{Lc_B^2}{4\gamma}\left(\widetilde{c}_D^2 - 1\right) \quad \text{while } r_b = r(c_b) = \frac{Lc_B^2}{4\gamma}\left(\widetilde{c}_D^2 - \varphi^2\right)$$

$$\pi_B = \pi(c_B) = \frac{Lc_B^2}{4\gamma}\left[\widetilde{c}_D - 1\right]^2 \quad \text{while } \pi_b = \pi(c_b) = \frac{Lc_B^2}{4\gamma}\left[\widetilde{c}_D - \varphi\right]^2.$$

However, low-cost, real P-organizations do not pass on all of the cost differential to consumers in the form of lower prices. They also set higher markups than high-cost, real A-organizations. This can be seen by expressing the markup of real P-organizations and real A-organizations, respectively, as a function of $\widetilde{c}_D$:

$$m_B = m(c_B) = c_B\,\frac{\widetilde{c}_D - 1}{2}, \quad \text{and} \quad m_b = m(c_b) = c_B\,\frac{\widetilde{c}_D - \varphi}{2}.$$

The two relationships (5.15) and (5.16) describe how the toughness of competition, given by the threshold parameter $\widetilde{c}_D$, jointly affects profits and the power struggle inside the firm. Eliminating $\widetilde{c}_D$, they define a relationship between B and α that has to be satisfied by any firm. From (5.15) we get

$$\widetilde{c}_D = 1 + \frac{2}{c_B}\sqrt{\frac{\gamma}{L}}\,\sqrt{B},$$

and from (5.16) we have

$$\widetilde{c}_D = \frac{\varphi - \sqrt{\alpha}}{1 - \sqrt{\alpha}}.$$

Therefore, the relationship between B and α is given by

$$B = \widehat{B}(\alpha) = \left[\frac{\varphi - 1}{1 - \sqrt{\alpha}}\right]^2 \frac{L}{\gamma}\frac{c_B^2}{4}. \tag{5.17}$$

5.5   Industry Equilibrium

In this section we derive the industry equilibrium with free entry for a given choice of firm organization.[12] The timing of events is as follows. In a first stage, firms decide whether or not to enter the market and to hire an agent to monitor projects. At this stage, there is free entry. In a second stage, firms decide who has *formal* power in the organization by choosing between the formal P-organization and the formal A-organization. In a third stage, information collection efforts are realized by the two parties, and a project is selected. This, in turn, determines who has *real* power in the organization. Finally there is production and consumption.

The free-entry conditions for a given choice of firm organization can be written as $\max\{u_P(B), u_A(B), u_O(B)\} = 0$ where $u_P(B)$, $u_A(B)$, and $u_O(B)$ are the profit levels of the firm under each organization P, A, or O as given, by (5.11), (5.14), and (5.12) respectively. The "max" argument in the free-entry conditions reflects the fact that each firm decides about its optimal type after market entry. We normalize $w = 1$. Three types of free-entry equilibria are possible:

1. *Equilibrium with P-organization and $e_P^* = \overline{e}$.*
   The free-entry condition in such a regime is

$$u_P(B) = g\frac{(E_P^*)^2}{2} + \overline{e}\alpha B - 1 = 0. \tag{5.18}$$

This gives a unique positive solution $B_P = B_P^*(\alpha)$, which is the profit level required to make a firm indifferent between entering and not entering the market as a formal P-organization. Obviously, an equilibrium in this regime exists if and only if $B_P^*(\alpha) \leq \widetilde{B}_P(\alpha)$.

2. *Equilibrium with A-organization and $e_A^* = \overline{e}$.*
   The free-entry condition in such a regime is

$$u_A(B) = g\frac{(E_A^*)^2}{2} + \overline{e}\alpha B - 1 = 0. \tag{5.19}$$

The free-entry condition gives a similarly unique positive solution $B_A = B_A^*(\alpha)$. An equilibrium in this regime exists if and only if $\widetilde{B}_P(\alpha) \leq B_A^*(\alpha) < \overline{B}(\alpha)$.

3. *Equilibrium with O-organization and $e_P^* = 0$.*
   Finally the free-entry condition in such a regime is

$$U_0(B) = g\frac{(E_0^*)^2}{2} - 1 = 0, \tag{5.20}$$

which gives the solution $B_P = \sqrt{2g}$. Such an equilibrium exists when $\sqrt{2g} > \overline{B}(\alpha)$.

Note that for all values of α, $B_A^*(\alpha) > B_P^*(\alpha)$. The formal A-organization, by giving less formal power to the principal, is less efficient than the formal P-organization. Hence, firms require a larger recurrent profit B to enter the market with a formal A-organization compared to a formal P-organization to cover the fixed cost of market entry (i.e., the wage rate for the middle manager $w = 1$).[13]

5.6   Firm Heterogeneity

The model generates, ex post, an endogenous pattern of heterogeneity across firms in size and productivity in the same industry. This arises in the following way. Firms choose the type of organization. This choice allocates formal power to principals (P- or O-organization) or agents (A-organization). The type of organization, in turn, determines the amount of information collection undertaken by principals and agents, which in turn determines the probability of success of finding a project for the firm. It also determines who—headquarters or middle managers—have real power in firms. Firm heterogeneity in productivity or costs in an industry arise because even under a formal P-organizational equilibrium (in which all firms in an industry adopt an organization in which principals have formal power in the corporation), there will be a share of firms in which agents have real power (real A-organizations) when principals in these firms decide not to become informed and to follow the suggestion for projects of their informed middle managers. Principals then implement the high-cost projects preferred by middle managers. Similarly, in a formal A-organizational equilibrium (in which all firms in an industry delegate formal power to their middle managers), there will be a share of firms in which principals have real power (real P-organizations) when middle managers implement low-cost projects suggested by informed principals. This way the number of low-cost P-organizations and high-cost A-organizations in an industry is endogenous and depends crucially on the organizational equilibrium that emerges in the economy and on the amount of information collection by principals and agents.

5.6.1 Competition in a P-equilibrium

We now show that the nature of competition in a market becomes endogenous and depends on the corporate equilibrium organization that emerges. Note that by the law of large numbers, given a number of entrants M in the industry, only $N = M[E + (1 - E)e]$ of them have information on how to produce. We can express average costs and cost dispersion in an industry under the P- and A-organizational equilibria.[14] Average marginal costs in an industry $\bar{c}$ become a function of the organizational mix of firms (which is the share of low-cost P-organizations and high-cost A-organizations in an industry, respectively).

5.6.1.1 Average Costs and the Toughness of Competition

Consider first the formal P-organizational equilibrium in which firms choose the P-organization as the optimal mode of organization. Average marginal costs in an industry can then be expressed as

$$\bar{c}^P(E) = \frac{ME}{M[E + (1 - E)\bar{e}]} c_B + \frac{M(1 - E)\bar{e}}{M[E + (1 - E)\bar{e}]} c_b$$

$$= \frac{[E + (1 - E)\bar{e}\varphi]}{[E + (1 - E)\bar{e}]} c_B. \tag{5.21}$$

With probability E, the principal gets informed and chooses the project with high costs c_B. With probability $(1 - E)e$, the principal does not get informed and the agent gets informed, in which case he chooses the project with high costs c_b. Under the law of large numbers, $\frac{E_p}{[E_p + (1 - E_p)e]}$ and $\frac{(1 - E_p)\bar{e}}{[E_p + (1 - E_p)e]}$ equal the fraction of low-cost, real P-organizations and high-cost, real A-organizations in the economy. Call these fractions the organizational mix of firms in an industry.

We can then express the toughness of competition in the market when principals have formal power in firms as the zero-profit cutoff cost level

$$\tilde{c}_D^P = \tilde{c}_D^P(E, N) = \frac{2\beta\gamma/c_B}{2\gamma + N\eta} + \frac{N\eta}{2\gamma + N\eta} \frac{[E + (1 - E)\bar{e}\varphi]}{[E + (1 - E)\bar{e}]},$$

with $N = M[E + (1 - E)\bar{e}]$ as the "effective" number of varieties produced.[15] The toughness of competition increases ($\tilde{c}_D^P$ declines) with the number of varieties N and with the amount of information collection by principals E (with the share of low-cost, real P-organizations). In fact, an increase in E biases the organizational mix between low-cost, real P-organizations and high-cost, real A-organizations in favor of the low-cost P-organizations. As a result, average costs in an industry $\bar{c}^P(E)$ decline and the toughness of competition in the economy increases.

5.6.1.2 Cost Dispersion

The variance of costs in an industry under the P-organization can be expressed as a function of E

$$V_P(E) = \frac{E}{[E + (1 - E)\bar{e}]} \left[c_B - \bar{c}^P(E) \right]^2$$
$$+ \frac{(1 - E)\bar{e}}{[E + (1 - E)\bar{e}]} \left[c_b - \bar{c}^P(E) \right]^2,$$

which can be rewritten to

$$V_P(E) = \frac{E(1 - E)\bar{e} \ [\varphi - 1]^2}{[E + (1 - E)\bar{e}]^3} c_B^2.$$

Differentiating $V_P(E)$ reveals that the function is bell shaped. More precisely,

$$\frac{dV_P(E)}{dE} \leq 0 \text{ if and only if } E^2(1 - \bar{e}) - 2E + \bar{e} \leq 0.$$

Hence there exists a value $\overline{E}_P(\bar{e}) \in \,]0, 1[$ such that $V_P(E)$ is increasing in E if and only if $E \leq \overline{E}_P(\bar{e})$.[16]

5.6.2 Competition in an A-equilibrium

5.6.2.1 Average Costs and the Toughness of Competition

Similarly, in a formal A-organizational equilibrium in which the A-organization maximizes profits of firms, average marginal costs in an industry are

$$\bar{c}^A(E) = \frac{M\bar{e}}{M[\bar{e} + (1 - \bar{e})E]} c_b + \frac{M(1 - \bar{e})E \ c_B}{M[\bar{e} + (1 - \bar{e})E]} c_B$$
$$= \frac{[E + (\varphi - E)\bar{e}]}{[E + (1 - E)\bar{e}]} c_B, \tag{5.22}$$

with $\frac{\bar{e}}{[E_A + (1 - E_A)\bar{e}]}$ and $\frac{E(1 - \bar{e})}{[E + (1 - E_A)\bar{e}]}$ as the fraction of high-cost, real A-organizations and low-cost, real P-organizations in the economy.

The toughness of competition in the market when principals delegate formal power to middle managers can be expressed as

$$\tilde{c}_D^A = \tilde{c}_D^A(E, N) = \frac{2\beta\gamma/c_B}{2\gamma + N\eta} + \frac{N\eta}{2\gamma + N\eta} \frac{[E + (\varphi - E)\bar{e}]}{[E + (1 - E)\bar{e}]}.$$

Comparing the cutoff cost levels in the two organizational equilibria reveals that $\tilde{c}_D^P < \tilde{c}_D^A$. Competition is tougher in a P-equilibrium compared to an A-equilibrium as principals monitor more in the former (an increase in E), which biases the organizational mix in favor of the low-cost P-organizations with $\bar{c}^P(E) < \bar{c}^A(E)$.

5.6.2.2 Cost Dispersion

Similarly, in a formal A-organizational equilibrium, the cost dispersion is given by

$$V_A(E) = \frac{(1 - \bar{e})E}{[\bar{e} + (1 - \bar{e})E]} \left[c_B - \bar{c}^A(E)\right]^2 + \frac{\bar{e}}{[\bar{e} + (1 - \bar{e})E]} \left[c_b - \bar{c}^A(E)\right]^2,$$

which can be rewritten to

$$V_A(E) = \frac{E\bar{e}(1 - \bar{e})\,[\varphi - 1]^2}{[E + (1 - E)\bar{e}]^3} c_B^2.$$

Differentiating $V_A(E)$ shows that the function is bell shaped. More precisely

$$\frac{dV_A(E)}{dE} \leq 0 \text{ if and only if } \bar{e} - 2(1 - \bar{e})E \leq 0.$$

$V_A(E)$ is increasing in E if and only if $E \leq \overline{E}_A(\bar{e}).$[17]

Comparing the variances $V_P(E)$ and $V_A(E)$ in the two organizational equilibria for a given value of E it is clear that for $E \neq 0$,

$$V_P(E) \leq V_A(E) \text{ if and only if } \bar{e} \leq E.$$

Hence, for the same effort level E, the P-organizational equilibrium exhibits less cost dispersion than an A-organizational equilibrium if the firm or principal is more efficient than the agent in collecting information.

The two variance functions are plotted in Figure 5.3. As can be seen, the cost dispersion under a P-organization is first increasing faster and then decreasing faster with E than that of the A-organization. The intuition for this pattern is as follows. In any organizational regime (P or A), a higher effort

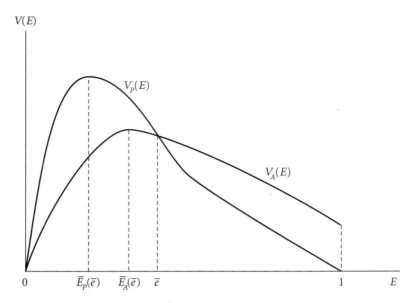

Figure 5.3 Cost dispersion in organizational equilibria.

of information collection E of the firm implies more firms with high costs c_B. As average costs move away from c_b toward c_B, we have a decrease in the wedge $\left[c_B - \overline{c}(E)\right]^2$ and conversely an increase in the wedge $\left[c_b - \overline{c}(E)\right]^2$. Now, in a P-organizational equilibrium, because the firm has formal power, the fraction of low-cost firms (i.e., with c_B) is more sensitive to a change in E than in an A-organizational equilibrium. Hence, $\left[c_B - \overline{c}(E)\right]^2$ and $\left[c_b - \overline{c}(E)\right]^2$ are more sensitive to a change in the principal's effort E in the P-organization compared to the A-organization.[18]

At low levels of E, wedges of type $\left[c_B - \overline{c}(E)\right]^2$ do not have much weight in the variance terms $V_P(E)$ and $V_A(E)$. Hence, much of the comparison between $V_P(E)$ and $V_A(E)$ is driven by the behavior of wedges $\left|c_b - \overline{c}^P(E)\right|$ and $\left|c_b - \overline{c}^A(E)\right|$. It follows that the variance of costs under a P-organizational equilibrium is increasing faster than the same variance under an A-organizational equilibrium. Conversely, when E is close to 1, variations in $\left[c_B - \overline{c}(E)\right]^2$ explain much of the shape of the variances $V_P(E)$ and $V_A(E)$. Thus, at large values of E, the cost dispersion under the P-organization declines faster with E than under the A-organization.

We are now in a position to examine how trade integration affects the pattern of firm heterogeneity in an industry. We focus on the effect on the first moment of the distribution (i.e., average productivity) and discuss two new internal margins of adjustments of trade: the monitoring margin and the organizational margin.

5.7 Trade Integration and Aggregate Productivity

Consider two countries H and F, which are identical in all dimensions but market size with $L_H > L_F$. Assume that there is free trade between H and F. Perfect trade integration is equivalent to an increase in market size from L_H or L_F to $L_H + L_F$. A change in market size L affects the productivity of the economy via two channels. First, a change in L affects the distribution between high- and low-cost firms. Second, a change in L affects the optimal pattern of organization. Hence, trade integration triggers a productivity effect *within* a given organizational equilibrium (P or A) and *across* organizational equilibria when the trade shock induces firms to change their equilibrium organization. We now discuss each effect in turn.[19]

5.7.1 The Monitoring Margin of Trade Adjustment

Consider first a small trade shock. A small increase in market size L increases firms' outputs and profits, inducing firm entry, tougher competition, and smaller markups. With increased competition, delegation of power inside the firm becomes more costly and tends to increase the power struggle between principals and managers (lower α). A larger conflict of interest in firms, and bigger profits, in turn, stimulate monitoring by principals (increased effort E), making it more likely that the initiative of the agent is crowded out under the central P-organization. When the trade shock is not too large, profits and the power struggle in firms increase only a little and principals monitor only a little under the P-organization. Hence, principals' monitoring does not kill the initiative of agents and firms keep the P-organization. As long as the trade shock is not too large, no change in corporate organization occurs.[20]

The effect of a small trade shock on average productivity or, equivalently, on average costs in an industry is illustrated in Figure 5.4. The figure plots how average costs in an industry in the two organizational equilibria P and A, $\bar{c}^P(E)$ and $\bar{c}^A(E)$, are affected by a change in E (which affects the

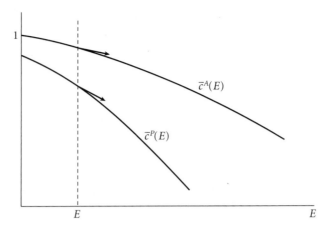

Figure 5.4 Average costs in an industry and organizational equilibria.

fraction of low-cost, real P-organizations in the economy). Three things are noteworthy. First, for a given value of E, average costs in a P-organizational equilibrium $\bar{c}^P(E)$ are always below average costs in an A-organizational equilibrium $\bar{c}^A(E)$. The reason is simply that the fraction of low-cost firms is larger in a P-equilibrium than in an A-equilibrium. Second, both $\bar{c}^P(E)$ and $\bar{c}^A(E)$ are declining with E, as an increase in E is directly related to an increase in the fraction of low-cost firms in both regimes. Third, $\bar{c}^P(E)$ declines more sharply with an increase in E than $\bar{c}^A(E)$ (i.e., $\bar{c}^P(E)$ is steeper than $\bar{c}^A(E)$), because the fraction of low-cost firms is larger in a P-organizational equilibrium than in an A-organizational equilibrium. Formally, this can be seen from differentiating (5.21) and (5.22) with respect to E

$$\frac{d\bar{c}^P(E)}{dE} = -\frac{(\varphi - 1)e}{[E + (1 - E)e]^2}c_B \text{ and } \frac{d\bar{c}^A(E)}{dE} = -\frac{(\varphi - 1)e(1 - e)}{[E + (1 - E)e]^2}c_B.$$

(5.23)

A small trade shock increases equilibrium profits B within an organizational equilibrium. This induces more monitoring of E_P or E_A by principals. As a result, the population of active firms is biased toward real P-organizations at the expense of real A-organizations. This reallocation from high-cost firms to low-cost firms reduces average production costs in an industry within each organizational regime. Furthermore, a small trade shock increases the conflict of interest between firms and managers in the corporation. As can be seen from (5.9), within the P-organizational equilibrium, the increase in the power struggle in firms also increases monitoring of E_P by principals, reducing even further the average production costs $\bar{c}^P(E)$ within this equilibrium. From this discussion we may conclude the following.

Statement 5.1   *A small trade shock increases average productivity by inducing the monitoring margin of trade adjustment. As a result, the fraction of low-cost P-organizations increases at the expense of high-cost A-organizations. Average productivity increases more in a formal P-organizational equilibrium than in a formal A-organizational equilibrium.*

5.7.2 The Organizational Margin of Trade Adjustment

Consider now a large trade shock. When the trade shock is large, profits and the power struggle in firms become sufficiently large that the stakes rise and principals in firms start to monitor intensively and kill the initiative of agents under the P-organization. To prevent this from happening, principals delegate formal power to agents to keep their initiative alive, and the A-organization emerges as the new corporate equilibrium.[21]

To assess the impact of a change in organization from P to A on aggregate productivity, three distinct effects have to be evaluated. They are illustrated in Figure 5.5. Quadrant I reproduces Figure 5.4, while quadrant II plots the principal's monitoring under the two organizational equilibria $E_P(B)$ and $E_A(B)$ as a function of profits B.

The first effect is the *composition effect* between low-cost P-organizations and high-cost A-organizations across organizational equilibria P and A. In fact, for a given value of monitoring E by firms, an A-organizational equilibrium is more likely to provide agents with real power in the firm compared to a P-organizational equilibrium. Hence, at a given value of E, an A-equilibrium has a larger fraction of high-cost real A-organizations than low-cost real P-organizations. This is reflected in quadrant I by the fact that $\bar{c}^A(E)$ is always above $\bar{c}^P(E)$ for all levels of E.

The second effect is the *monitoring effect* across organizational equilibria P and A. At a given profit level B, a formal P-organization monitors more than a formal A-organization (i.e., $E_P(B) > E_A(B)$ as can be seen from (5.9) and (5.13)). This is illustrated in quadrant II of Figure 5.5 by the fact that $E_P(B)$ is always above $E_A(B)$.

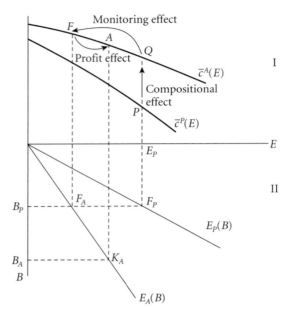

Figure 5.5 Average costs in an industry across organizational equilibria.

Finally, the last effect is the *profit effect*. Indeed, given that a formal A-organization is less efficient that a formal P-organization at any value of recurrent profit, it follows that the required profits under free entry in A-equilibrium $B_A = B_A^*(\alpha_A)$ are larger than the required profit $B_P = B_P^*(\alpha_P)$, in a P-equilibrium. From this it follows that the value of monitoring in formal A-organizations $E_A = (1 - e)B_A/g$ is larger than in formal P-organizations $E_P = (1 - e\alpha_P)B_P/g$. This is illustrated in quadrant II of Figure 5.5 by the fact that B_A is below B_P on the vertical axis.

Now we are ready to see how the three effects together influence average costs across organizational equilibria from P to A. We simply need to compare the values of $\bar{c}^A(E_A)$ corresponding to point A with $\bar{c}^P(E_P)$ corresponding to point P. The *composition effect* is shown in quadrant I by a vertical move from point P on $\bar{c}^P(E)$ to point Q on $\bar{c}^A(E)$ for the same value of monitoring E_P. This effect clearly contributes to an increase in average costs when the corporate equilibrium shifts from a P-organization to an A-organization.

The *monitoring effect* is illustrated in quadrant II by a horizontal move from point F_P with coordinates (E_P, B_P) on the line $E_P(B)$ to point F_A

on the line $E_A(B)$ with coordinates $(E_A(B_P), B_P)$. This effect is shown in quadrant I by a move from Q to F along $\bar{c}^A(E)$. This effect also increases average costs across organizational equilibria from P to A.

Finally, the *profit effect* is illustrated in quadrant II by a move from F_A to point K_A along the line $E_A(B)$, increasing profits from B_A to B_P. This effect is shown in quadrant I by a move from point F to A along the $\bar{c}^A(E)$ curve. The profit effect reduces average costs when the industry shifts from a P-organization to an A-organization and thus works in the opposite direction to the two other effects. Overall, a trade-induced change in organization from P to A has an ambiguous effect on productivity and depends on the relative size of each of the three effects. Note that the profit effect has to be strong enough to compensate for the first two effects. When the profit effect is not too large,[22] it is likely that a shift in corporate organization from a P-equilibrium to an A-equilibrium in response to a large trade shock will lower average productivity in the economy. This discussion can be summarized in the following statement.

Statement 5.2 *A large trade shock induces the organizational margin of trade adjustment. Its impact on average productivity can be decomposed into three effects: the composition effect, the monitoring effect, and the profit effect. The composition and monitoring effects both tend to decrease average productivity with an increase in market size L, and the profit effect tends to increase average productivity. When the profit effect is not too large, a move from a P-organizational equilibrium to an A-organizational equilibrium is likely to reduce average productivity.*

Statements 5.1 and 5.2 can be finally summarized in Figure 5.6, which describes the evolution of average costs in the economy as a function of market size L. The curve has three parts: $\bar{c}^P(L)$, $\bar{c}^A(L)$, and $\bar{c}^O(L)$, depending on the organizational equilibrium P, A, or O. From statement 5.1, we know that average costs are declining within an organizational equilibrium and the curves $\bar{c}^P(L)$ and $\bar{c}^A(L)$ are declining with market size. In the O-equilibrium, the average-cost curve becomes $\bar{c}^O(L) = c_B$, as all active firms are low-cost real P-organizations. At some threshold value of $L = \widehat{L}$, the A-organization emerges as a new equilibrium and the economy shifts from a P-organization to an A-organization. This shift introduces a discontinuity in average costs. When the profit effect is not too large compared to the other two effects, average costs go up (and productivity declines) with an increase in market size, as is illustrated in Figure 5.6. Hence, average

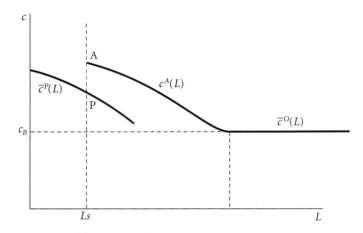

Figure 5.6 Average costs in an industry and market size.

costs (or productivity) are not necessarily a decreasing monotonic function of market size, since firms may find it optimal to shift from a low-cost organizational equilibrium to a high-cost organizational equilibrium with an accompanied increase in average costs in an industry.

As a result, a sufficiently large trade shock may induce an equilibrium in the liberalizing country in which managers are empowered to create ideas for new projects. Average productivity declines at the industry level, since managers will implement projects that maximize their interest. These projects are not necessarily cost minimizing. Furthermore, in the empowerment equilibrium, competition becomes less intense and less sensitive to price. Recently, Melitz (2003) has shown that trade integration brings average productivity gains through reallocation from high-cost to low-cost firms. Our findings suggest, however, that this will not necessarily be the case when firms are allowed to choose their organization endogenously. Under some circumstances, firms may opt for organizations that are conducive to new ideas and that adapt less well to price and cost competition.

5.8   Conclusion

This chapter develops a theory that investigates how firms' organizational choices are affecting firm performance and the nature of competition in international markets. Firm heterogeneity arises by the type of organization firms choose, which, in turn, allocates power to headquarters or middle managers. The power allocation in firms, in turn, determines the amount of information collection that firms undertake. The number of low-productivity and high-productivity firms in an industry evolves endogenously, depending on the corporate equilibrium that emerges in the economy. We find that competition is less intense in markets in which principals delegate power to their middle managers. We also identify two new internal margins of trade adjustment, which determine whether or not trade liberalizations lead to productivity gains.

ACKNOWLEDGMENTS

We thank Elhanan Helpman, Stephen Yeaple, and the CEPR Globalization and the Organization of Firms and Markets (February 2007) conference participants for helpful comments. Part of the chapter was written when Dalia Marin visited the Stern School of Business of New York University. She is grateful for the hospitality there and for the stimulating discussions. Financial support by the Volkswagen Foundation through the network grant "Globalization and the Organization of Firms and Markets" and by the German Science Foundation through Sonderforschungsbereich GESY SFB/TR 15 and through the research grant DFG-MA-1823/3-1 is gratefully acknowledged.

NOTES

1. For a recent survey, see Bernard et al. (2007).
2. The corporate decisions include the decisions over acquisitions, finances, new strategy, transfer pricing, a new product, R&D expenditures, the budget, hiring more than 10% of current personnel, hiring two workers, change of supplier, price increase of product, product price, moderate wage increase, firing of personnel, and hiring a secretary. For a ranking of these decisions and the description of the data, see Marin and Verdier (2008a) and Marin (2006).
3. We will later define an organization in which headquarters as well as the division level make decisions (level of centralization of around 3) as a P-organization. In terms of the model, this is an organization in which the principal runs the firm with the cooperation of the agent. We define an organization to be centrally organized as an O-organization (level of centralization of around 1) which is a single, managed firm run by the principal alone. Finally, we define an organization to be decentrally organized as an A-organization run by the divisional manager (level of centralization of around 5).
4. Bustos (2005) finds evidence for another internal margin—the innovation margin of trade adjustment—to be present in Argentina. Chen, Imbs, and Scott (2006) find positive productivity effects in the short run but not in the long run from trade liberalizations in industrialized countries.

5. Expression in (5.1) is valid whenever $q_i > 0$, which will be the case when

$$p_i \leq \frac{1}{\gamma + \eta N} \left(\gamma \beta + \eta N \overline{p} \right).$$

6. For details, see Melitz and Ottaviano (2008).

7. See Melitz and Ottaviano (2008) for more details.

8. As emphasized by Aghion and Tirole (1997), the amount of information acquisition is at the heart of the distinction between "formal" and "real" decision power in firms.

9. When the agent receives a strictly positive benefit $\beta b > 0$ with the principal's preferred project, there exists as well a threshold $\widetilde{B}_A$ given by

$$\widetilde{B}_A = \frac{g(1 - k/b)}{\beta(1 - \overline{e})}$$

and such that the agent's initiative is killed under the A-organization when $B > \widetilde{B}_A$. Intuitively, above the threshold level $\widetilde{B}_A$, the principal's stakes are so high that she acquires information E_A^* leading to a high probability of intervention, which, in equilibrium, leads again to the minimum agent's effort $e_A^* = 0$.

10. This is the relevant comparison because the principal always prefers the P-organization with $\overline{e}$ compared to the A-organization with $\overline{e}$.

11. For a formal proof see proposition 1 in Marin and Verdier (2008a).

12. In Marin and Verdier (2008a) we determine the free-entry corporate equilibria in which firms choose the profit-maximizing mode of organization and in which they have an incentive to enter the market with this organization.

13. For more details, see Marin and Verdier (2008a). When the cost differential $\varphi - 1$ between high-cost and low-cost firms is not too large (such that high-cost firms make positive recurrent profits in a monopolistic equilibrium with low-cost firms), we show in Marin and Verdier (2008a) that there exists at least one free-entry organizational equilibrium (B^e, α^e) (defined by the free-entry conditions (5.18), (5.19), and (5.20) and the condition (5.17) on $\widehat{B}(\alpha)$) such that (a) firms choose optimally their organizations, (b) firms maximize profits by choosing the level of production and price, and (c) there is free entry.

14. Note that in an O-organizational equilibrium, there is no firm heterogeneity. In this equilibrium only projects discovered by the firm or principal are implemented and thus all active firms have the same cost-minimizing technology with production cost c_B. Therefore, only the organizational equilibria P and A have to be examined.

15. When M firms enter, not all of them find a profitable project to produce, and hence the effective number of successful firms is N.

16. Formally, $\overline{E}_P(\overline{e})$ is the root between 0 and 1 of the equation $E^2(1 - \overline{e}) - 2E + \overline{e} = 0$.

17. $\overline{E}_A(\overline{e}) = [\overline{e}/2(1 - \overline{e})]$, and one can show that $\overline{E}_A(\overline{e}) > \overline{E}_P(\overline{e})$ as drawn in Figure 5.3.

18. Formally this can be seen from the following expressions:

$$\left|c_B - \overline{c}^P(E)\right| = \frac{(1 - E)\overline{e}}{[E + (1 - E)\overline{e}]}(\varphi - 1)c_B \quad \text{and}$$

$$\left|c_b - \overline{c}^P(E)\right| = \frac{E}{[E + (1 - E)\overline{e}]}(\varphi - 1)c_B$$

for the P-equilibrium and

$$\left|c_B - \overline{c}^A(E)\right| = \frac{\overline{e}}{[E + (1 - E)\overline{e}]}(\varphi - 1)c_B \quad \text{and}$$

$$\left|c_b - \overline{c}^A(E)\right| = \frac{E(1 - \overline{e})}{[E + (1 - E)\overline{e}]}(\varphi - 1)c_B$$

for the A-equilibrium. Indeed, $\left|c_B - \overline{c}^P(E)\right|$ declines faster with E than $\left|c_B - \overline{c}^A(E)\right|$, while $\left|c_b - \overline{c}^P(E)\right|$ increases faster with E than $\left|c_b - \overline{c}^A(E)\right|$.

19. In Marin and Verdier (2008a) we derive the conditions under which a change in L triggers a change in corporate organization.

20. For details on the comparative statics of a change in market size, see Section 4 in Marin and Verdier (2008a).

21. See Marin and Verdier (2008a), Section 4 for the conditions under which an increase in market size triggers a shift from the P-organization to the A-organization.

22. Whether the shift in equilibrium profits across organizational equilibria is large or small depends on how efficient the agent is in collecting information. The less efficient the agent is in information collection (i.e., $e \ll 1$), the smaller is the gap between the free-entry profit curves B_P^* and B_A^* under the two equilibria P and A. Intuitively, when the agent is not too efficient at getting information on projects, he is unlikely to have real power in the firm. Hence, it is not too costly to give him formal power in the firm either. In such a case, the shift in equilibrium profits across regimes is small and, therefore, average costs are likely to increase with a move from a P- to an A-organizational equilibrium.

REFERENCES

Aghion, P., and J. Tirole. 1997. "Formal and Real Authority in Organizations." *Journal of Political Economy* 105(1):1–29.

Antràs, P., and E. Helpman. 2004. "Global Sourcing." *Journal of Political Economy* 112:552–80.

Bernard, A., J. Eaton, B. Jensen, and S. Kortum. 2003. "Plants and Productivity in International Trade." *American Economic Review* 93(4):1268–90.

Bernard, A., and B. Jensen. 1999. "Exceptional Exporter Performance: Cause, Effect, or Both?" *Journal of International Economics* 47(1):1–25.

Bernard, A., J. B. Jensen, S. Redding, and P. Scott. 2007. "Firms in International Trade." *Journal of Economic Perspectives* 21(3):105–30.

Bloom, N., and J. Van Reenen. 2006. "Measuring and Explaining Management Practices across Firms and Countries." Discussion paper no. 5581, Centre for Economic Policy Research, London.

Bustos, P. 2005. "The Impact of Trade on Technology and Skill Upgrading." Mimeo. Evidence from Argentina, CREI, Peompeu Fabra.

Chen, N., J. Imbs, and A. Scott. 2006. "The Dynamics of Trade and Competition." Mimeo, University of Warwick, HEC Lausanne and London Business School.

Clerides, S., S. Lach, and J. Tybout. 1998. "Is Learning by Exporting Important? Micro-dynamic Evidence from Colombia, Mexico and Morocco." *Quarterly Journal of Economics* 113(3):903–47.

Dixit, A., and J. Stiglitz. 1977. "Monopolistic Competition and Optimum Product Diversity." *American Economic Review* 67(3):297–308.

Krugman, P. 1979. "Increasing Returns, Monopolistic Competition, and International Trade." *Journal of International Economics* 9:469–79.

———. 1980. "Scale Economies, Product Differentiation, and the Pattern of Trade." *American Economic Review* 70:950–59.

Marin, D. 2006. "A New International Division of Labour in Europe: Outsourcing and Offshoring to Eastern Europe." *Journal of the European Economic Association*, papers and proceedings, May.

Marin, D., and T. Verdier. 2003a. "Globalization and the 'New Enterprise.'" *Journal of the European Economic Association* 1(2/3):337–44.

———. 2003b. "Globalization and the Empowerment of Talent." CEPR Discussion paper no. 4129, Centre for Economic Policy Research, London.

———. 2008a. "Corporate Hierarchies and the Size of Nations: Theory and Evidence." CEPR Discussion paper no. 6734, Centre for Economic Policy Research, London.

———. 2008b. "Power Inside the Firm and the Market: A General Equilibrium Approach." *Journal of the European Economic Association* 6(4):752–88.

Melitz, M. 2003. "The Impact of Trade on Aggregate Industry Productivity and Intra-Industry Reallocations." *Econometrica* 71(6):1695–1726.

Melitz, M., and G. Ottaviano. 2008. "Market Size, Trade and Productivity." *Review of Economic Studies* 75:295–316.

— 6 —

Optimal Choice of Product Scope
for Multiproduct Firms
under Monopolistic Competition

ROBERT C. FEENSTRA AND HONG MA

6.1   Introduction

Recent literature in trade has begun to explore multiproduct firms. As documented by Bernard, Redding, and Schott (2006a), 41% of U.S. manufacturing firms produce in multiple, five-digit SIC industries, accounting for 91% of total sales. Using a large and unique dataset that contains product UPC barcodes, Broda and Weinstein (2007) also show that the majority of product creation and destruction happens within the boundaries of the firm. The concentration of sales in very large, multiproduct firms is even more apparent when we look at their exports sales. Bernard, Jensen, Redding, and Schott (2007) show that the top 1% of U.S. trading firms account for over 80% of total trade in 2000. Over 10% of exporters and 20% of importers are trading 10 or more harmonized system (HS) products, and these firms account for about 90% of export and import value. Furthermore, these authors show that two variables—the variation in the number of exporters and exported products per firm—explain most of the "gravity" results in trade: these two variables decline sharply with distance, and increase with importer income, whereas the average export value (per product and per firm) is actually increasing in distance and decreasing in importer income. Thus, the extensive margin of exporting firms is explaining much of the variation in the value of exports.

On the theoretical side, multiproduct firms have received attention for some years in the industrial organization literature (e.g., Brander and Eaton 1984). The earliest paper we are aware of in the trade literature is Helpman (1985), who analyzes how a multinational will expand over multiple product lines. Like later authors, Helpman does not take into account the implied effect on the markups of the firms, but uses the constant elasticity of substitution (CES) assumption with constant markups. Specifically, he assumed that the demand facing a firm producing product j is

$$y_j = k p_j^{-\eta},$$

where η is the elasticity of demand. The constant k would normally depend on the CES price index for the market, which leads to higher markups for multiproduct firms and also a "cannibalization" effect of increasing product varieties. By holding k constant, multiproduct firms charge the same markup as single product firms and do not consider the cannibalization effect. Instead, Helpman relies on diseconomies of scope to limit firms' expansion into new product lines.

The simplification by Helpman (1985) also occurs in more recent literature dealing with CES preferences. Brambilla (2006) presents an application of the Melitz (2003) model to investigate the introduction of new varieties by multiproduct firms, with empirical application to multinationals in China. She ignores the interaction in demand of the products produced by a firm, using constant markups like Helpman. Similarly, Bernard, Redding, and Schott (2006b) theoretically investigate multiple products using a Melitz approach but assume that a firm's products are in different categories of goods, so there is no cannibalization effect in demand, and markups are constant. Allanson and Montagna (2005) propose a multiproduct version of the standard Dixit-Stiglitz (1977) model using nested two-tier CES preferences but again ignore the interaction of multiple products in demand.

Departing from CES preferences, Nocke and Yeaple (2006) use a partial equilibrium inverse-demand curve $P(q)$ for every product produced by a firm. They likewise do not take into account the effect of increases in a firm's varieties on the demand for its existing products. They also assume decreasing returns to the range of products: the marginal cost of each variety is increasing in the number of varieties managed by one firm. That approach allows for a solution for the range of production for each firm, even without any interaction in demand.

From this brief summary, it is fair to say that there has been a reluctance in the trade literature to allow for cannibalization effects with multiple products per firm, at least in a CES setting. Endogenous markups have been introduced using alternative preferences: in particular, the linear-quadratic utility function from Melitz and Ottaviano (2005). Eckel and Neary (2006) use that approach and no longer treat the aggregate output (or price) index as exogenous. Instead, markups are endogenous and a cannibalization effect operates since a larger output of one variety tends to lower the demand for all other varieties. This gives a multiproduct firm an incentive to restrict its range of varieties. Eckel and Neary (2006) also introduce an incentive on the cost side, whereby each firm has a *core competence* in one particular variety, and the marginal cost of a new variety is greater, the more distant its deviation from the "core competence."

In comparison, our model returns to the conventional CES preferences but relaxes the constant aggregate price index assumption. We will show that it is both tractable and interesting to remove this assumption. Initially, we solve for the equilibrium in a model where firms have identical costs, in the spirit of the early work of Krugman (1979, 1980), but allowing for multiple products per firms. That identical-cost model is closest to the business-group model of Feenstra, Huang, and Hamilton (2003) and Feenstra and Hamilton (2006). In that work, a group of firms (or equivalently, a firm with multiple products) jointly maximized profits in upstream and downstream markets, choosing optimal prices and product scope in each, and free entry of groups was assumed. It turns out the multiple equilibria are present in the model, with different organizations of the business groups.[1] That result followed from the simultaneous upstream and downstream competition between groups. The model presented in this chapter departs from Feenstra and Hamilton by assuming that firms produce and sell in only the downstream sector, and by focusing on the comparison of autarky to international trade.

After analyzing the model with identical costs, we turn to a version of the model where firms have heterogeneous costs, as in Melitz (2003). Firms still choose their range of products optimally, and for that reason, cannot be treated as "small" relative to the market. The solution to the model cannot use the law of large numbers as applied by Melitz (2003); instead, we analyze the equilibrium with a combination of analytical and numerical results. We show analytically that the optimal number of varieties takes an inverted U-shape with respect to their market shares: the greatest range of product varieties is produced by firms with a midlevel of market share. When trade is opened, the larger market size reduces the cannibalization effect and expands the optimal scope of products. We show numerically that the number of firms in equilibrium is rather insensitive to the market size, but less-efficient firms are forced to exit due to trade, so the larger market is accommodated by more-efficient firms that produce more varieties per firm on average.

6.2   Preferences and Demand

There are L consumers (workers) in the economy, each endowed with one unit of labor. The utility function is

$$U = y_0 + \rho \ln(Y), \quad \rho < 1, \tag{6.1}$$

where y_0 is the consumption of an outside good, which is treated as numeraire. Y represents the consumption index for the horizontally differentiated products. As often used in the monopolistic competition model, the consumption index Y takes a CES form over a continuum of varieties:

$$Y = \left[\int_o^N y(i)^{\frac{\eta-1}{\eta}} di \right]^{\frac{\eta}{\eta-1}}, \tag{6.2}$$

where $y(i)$ is the quantity consumed of variety i, $\eta > 1$ is the elasticity of substitution between output varieties, and N is the total number of varieties.

We will assume that each firm $j = 1, \ldots, M$ produces a positive mass of products $N_j > 0$. Without loss of generality, we arrange the order of products so that firm 1 produces the first N_1 varieties, firm 2 produces the next N_2 varieties, and so on. Letting $N \equiv \sum_{j=1}^{M} N_j$ denote the total mass of product varieties, the consumption index Y becomes

$$Y = \left[\int_0^{N_1} y(i)^{\frac{\eta-1}{\eta}} di + \int_{N_1}^{N_1+N_2} y(i)^{\frac{\eta-1}{\eta}} di + \cdots \int_{N-N_M}^{N} y(i)^{\frac{\eta-1}{\eta}} di \right]^{\frac{\eta}{\eta-1}}.$$

$$\tag{6.2'}$$

The market for the numeraire good y_0 is competitive, and production requires one unit of labor for each unit of output, implying that the wage rate $w = 1$. Utility maximization under the typical budget constraint gives the familiar form of aggregate demand for each variety within the differentiated good sector,[2]

$$y(i) = \frac{R}{P^{1-\eta}} p(i)^{-\eta}, \tag{6.3}$$

where $R = \rho L$ denotes the aggregate expenditure on this sector, and the price index P is

$$P = \left[\int_0^{N_1} p(i)^{1-\eta}\, di + \int_{N_1}^{N_1+N_2} p(i)^{1-\eta}\, di + \cdots \int_{N-N_M}^N p(i)^{1-\eta}\, di \right]^{\frac{1}{1-\eta}}.$$

$$(6.4)$$

Each firm j chooses the continuum of prices $p(i)$ for its product varieties of mass N_j. We simplify this optimal control problem by assuming that each firm has the same marginal cost for all its varieties, so it charges the same price for them. Letting $p_j = p(i)$ for firm j's mass of N_j varieties, then the aggregate price index in (6.4) can be written as,

$$P = \left[\int_0^{N_1} p_1^{1-\eta} di + \int_{N_1}^{N_1+N_2} p_2^{1-\eta} di + \cdots \int_{N-N_M}^N p_M^{1-\eta}\, di \right]^{\frac{1}{1-\eta}}$$

$$= \left(\sum_{j=1}^M N_j p_j^{1-\eta} \right)^{\frac{1}{1-\eta}}.$$

$$(6.4')$$

Notice that a change in p_j for firm j will affect the aggregate price index P, provided that the mass of products N_j produced by firm j is strictly positive. Differentiating (6.3), the elasticity of demand for each variety $y_j = y(i)$ produced by firm j, with respect to the price p_j, is

$$\frac{\partial y_j}{\partial p_j} \frac{p_j}{y_j} = -[\eta(1 - s_j) + s_j],$$

$$(6.5)$$

where s_j denotes the market share of its products:

$$s_j = \frac{N_j y_j p_j}{\sum_{i=1}^M N_i y_i p_i} = \frac{N_j p_j^{1-\eta}}{\sum_{i=1}^M N_i p_i^{1-\eta}}.$$

$$(6.6)$$

We see from (6.5) and (6.6) that the elasticity of demand differs from η whenever $N_j > 0$. Moreover, larger firms face lower demand elasticity.

6.3 Production with Identical Costs

Firms maximize profits by choosing optimal prices p_j and product range N_j:

$$\max_{(p_j, N_j) \geq 0} \prod_j = N_j y_j (p_j - \phi) - (k_0 + k_1 N_j),$$

$$(6.7)$$

where k_0 is a fixed "headquarters cost," k_1 is the fixed cost of adding a marginal product into the product line, and y_j is the demand for the variety, with marginal cost ϕ and price p_j. In this section, the costs are identical across firms, while in sections 6.4 and 6.5 we will introduce heterogeneity in marginal costs, like Melitz (2003).

To choose its optimal price, the firm takes the aggregate price index into consideration when making pricing decisions, so its perceived price elasticity of demand is no longer a constant but equals that shown in (6.5) and (6.6). Then the optimal choice of p_j is

$$p_j = \left[\frac{1}{(\eta - 1)(1 - s_j)} + 1 \right] \phi. \tag{6.8}$$

Thus, the demand elasticity and the markup are both *endogenously* determined. As implied by (6.5) and (6.8), a firm with higher market share would face less elastic demand and therefore be able to set higher markups.

Optimization over the product range N_j gives

$$y_j(p_j - \phi) - s_j y_j(p_j - \phi) = k_1. \tag{6.9}$$

The first term on the left of (6.9) gives the marginal benefit of adding a marginal variety. But adding this variety will reduce the demand for other varieties produced by the same firm, which is shown by the second term on the left. The larger the market share of the firm, the more severe is this cannibalization effect.

We can use (6.8) in (6.9) to obtain

$$y_j \phi = (\eta - 1)k_1. \tag{6.10}$$

Condition (6.10) can be recognized as the zero-profit condition in a CES model with single-product firms, when the markup is $\eta/(\eta - 1)$ and the fixed costs are k_1. In our model, it follows from the first-order conditions for price and the scope of varieties.

The optimum number of varieties is obtained by writing firm j's market share as

$$s_j = \frac{N_j y_j p_j}{R} = \left[1 + \frac{1}{(\eta - 1)(1 - s_j)} \right] \frac{N_j y_j \phi}{R}$$

$$= \left[1 + \frac{1}{(\eta - 1)(1 - s_j)} \right] \frac{(\eta - 1)N_j k_1}{R}, \tag{6.11}$$

where the second equality follows from (6.8) and the third equality from (6.10). Firm j's optimal scope is then given by

$$N_j = \left[\frac{s_j(1 - s_j)}{\eta - (\eta - 1)s_j} \right] \frac{R}{k_1}, \tag{6.12}$$

where R is the total market expenditure with $R = \rho L$.

We will use the subscript "0" to denote the free-entry equilibrium, which satisfies

$$\Pi_0 = N_0 y_0 (p_0 - \phi) - (k_0 + k_1 N_0) = 0. \tag{6.13}$$

Multiplying the equality in (6.9) by N_0, we get

$$N_0 y_0 (p_0 - \phi)(1 - s_0) - k_1 N_0 = 0. \tag{6.14}$$

Then comparing (6.13) and (6.14), we obtain

$$1 - s_0 = \frac{k_1 N_0}{k_0 + k_1 N_0} > 0, \tag{6.15}$$

from which we obtain another (implicit) solution for the equilibrium number of varieties for each firm:

$$N_0 = \frac{k_0}{k_1} \left(\frac{1}{s_0} - 1 \right) > 0. \tag{6.16}$$

We still need to solve for the market share in the zero-profit equilibrium. Notice that with identical firms, all active firms will end up with the same market share. Using (6.8) and (6.12), firm j's optimized profits can be rewritten as

$$\Pi_j = \left[\frac{s_j^2}{\eta - (\eta - 1)s_j} \right] R - k_0. \tag{6.17}$$

In the zero-profit equilibrium, (6.17) becomes

$$\Pi_0 = \left[\frac{s_0^2}{\eta - (\eta - 1)s_0} \right] R - k_0 = 0, \tag{6.18}$$

which gives an expression for s_0:

$$s_0 = \frac{\sqrt{(\eta - 1)^2 k_0^2 + 4\eta k_0 R} - (\eta - 1)k_0}{2R}. \tag{6.19}$$

The firms' market share, s_0, is a function of the market size $R = \rho L$ and the headquarters cost k_0. An increase in the country size L leads to a *lower* level of zero-profit market share s_0. On the other hand, a larger headquarter cost requires a larger cutoff market share and thus an upward impact on active firms' market shares (recall, all firms have the same market share). That is[3]

$$\frac{\partial s_0}{\partial L} < 0 \quad \text{and} \quad \frac{\partial s_0}{\partial k_0} > 0. \tag{6.20}$$

Taking into account the endogeneity of the market shares s_0, using (6.16) we can also obtain the impact of the market size L and the headquarters investment k_0 on the range of products for each firm:

$$\frac{\partial N_0}{\partial L} > 0 \quad \text{and} \quad \frac{\partial N_0}{\partial k_0} \overset{>}{\underset{<}{}} 0. \tag{6.21}$$

The headquarters fixed costs lead to a higher market share for the zero-profit firm in (6.20): it must be selling a positive mass of product $N_0 > 0$ with market share $s_0 > 0$ in order to cover the fixed costs $k_0 > 0$. As market size grows, however, the fixed costs are then relatively less important, and the borderline market share s_0 falls. But the range of products N_0 produced by the borderline firm continues to grow. The indeterminacy of the impact of the headquarters investment k_0 on the range of products N_0 comes from the indeterminacy of the relationship between N_0 and s_0: when k_0 is low, relatively more firms could stay in the market (each takes a small share, see (6.22) below), so an increase in k_0 would require a rise in the market share of each firm, resulting in variety expansion of each active firm; but when only a few firms are in the market (each takes a substantial share), an increase in k_0 would again raise the market share, but this time leading to a reduction in variety range. This corresponds to the cannibalization effect of the with-firm brand competition: when the currently existing brands already take a large share in the market, it may not be wise to add another brand since it subtracts demand from other brands of the same firm more than from other competitors.

The number of firms active in equilibrium is readily solved from

$$M s_0 = 1 \tag{6.22}$$

so that $M = 1/s_0$. It follows from (6.20) that

$$\frac{\partial M}{\partial L} > 0 \quad \text{and} \quad \frac{\partial M}{\partial k_0} < 0. \tag{6.23}$$

An increase in country size (due to the opening of trade) leads to lower market share s_0, and as a result, the total number of firms M in the equilibrium is increasing in market size. The intuition for this result is similar to that discussed just above: as market size grows, the fixed costs become relatively less important, so the market share s_0 of the zero-profit firms falls. As a result, there is room for more firms in the market.

We can follow Krugman (1979) to obtain a solution for the number of firms *in each country* from the full-employment condition. The total labor input required for each firm j is

$$L_j = k_0 + N_j(k_1 + \phi y_j). \tag{6.24}$$

Notice that the total labor utilized in this industry is ρL, so the total number of firms in each country is

$$M = \frac{\rho L}{L_j} = \frac{\rho L}{k_0 + N_j(k_1 + \phi y_j)} = \frac{\rho L}{k_0 + N_0 \eta k_1}, \tag{6.25}$$

where the first equality follows the full employment condition, the second equality applies the definition of labor usage, while the last equality is from (6.10) with all firms having the same product range $N_j = N_0$ in equilibrium.

Consider, now, the thought experiment in Krugman (1979) where trade is opened between two identical countries. That leads to a doubling of the market size (i.e., from L to $2L$), so from (6.23), the total number of firms selling to consumers increases compared to the number of firms in each country in autarky. Since an increase in market size stimulates firms to expand their varieties (from (6.21)), then from (6.25), we see the number of firms producing in each country necessarily falls with the opening of trade. This effect is also observed in Krugman (1979), but in his work, the existence of this effect is due to the more general specification of the utility (the demand curve should be less convex than a constant-elasticity curve). Using CES utility with single-product firms would make that effect disappear. In contrast, the CES utility function is still utilized in our model, while the endogeneity of the demand elasticity comes from our multiple-products-per-firm assumption.

These results are summarized by the following proposition.

Proposition 6.1 *With identical marginal costs and positive headquarters fixed costs, increasing the market size through international trade leads to*

1. *The world number of surviving firms exceeds the number of firms in either country in autarky, while the number of producing firms in each country falls after trade relative to the number in autarky*

2. *An expansion in the range of varieties produced by each firm*

3. *No change in the quantity supplied of each variety (from (6.10))*

4. *An improvement in consumer welfare due to both (1) and (2)*

It is also worth noting that the welfare gains of consumers in (4) come from the increases in total available varieties due to (1) and (2), which result in a fall in the price index defined in (6.4'). Besides this "love of variety" gain, each firm also charges lower markups due to the diminishing market share after trade (as L rises, s_0 falls in (6.20), which reduces prices), which is another source of gains from trade that is absent from conventional CES trade models.

Interestingly, after trade opening, while the number of local producers is reduced, they supply a larger number of varieties in total. We therefore obtain the following result.

Corollary 6.1   *In the setting specified in proposition 6.1, an increase in market size due to trade leads to an expansion in the varieties produced by surviving firms that dominates the decrease in the number of local firms, so that the number of varieties produced in each country expands.*

Proof.   From (6.25), the total number of varieties supplied by local producers is

$$M N_0 = \frac{\rho L}{k_0 + N_0 \eta k_1} N_0 = \frac{\rho L}{(k_0/N_0) + \eta k_1},$$

where M is the number of local producers, and N_0 is the number of varieties produced by each firm. Opening trade leads to a larger N_0, and hence a larger $M N_0$.   □

6.4   Production with Heterogeneous Costs

We now assume that firms are heterogeneous in their marginal cost of production ϕ, as in Melitz (2003). For simplicity, we also assume no headquarters costs. We suppose that firms' productivity $1/\phi$ is drawn from a Pareto distribution with support $[1/\phi^{\max}, \infty)$ and with shape parameter γ. Thus the marginal cost ϕ follows the distribution specified as $F(\phi) = (\phi/\phi^{\max})^\gamma$, where $\phi^{\max}$ is the highest possible marginal cost. Not all entrants will stay in the market and produce: firms with a high draw of marginal costs might not be profitable. In order to describe the equilibrium of the model, we need to be careful about the information that firms have and the timing of moves.

Specifically, in a *short-run* equilibrium, we take as given the number of entering firms M_e, which is a nonstochastic variable. Given M_e, there will be a simultaneous and independent draw of marginal costs $\phi(M_e) = (\phi_1, \phi_2, \ldots, \phi_{M_e})$ for the M_e firms. These marginal costs are common knowledge to the firms who have entered the market, and they will each choose their optimal prices according to the same first-order condition that we had earlier:

$$p_j = \left[\frac{1}{(\eta - 1)(1 - s_j)} + 1 \right] \phi_j. \tag{6.26}$$

Optimization over the product range N_j also gives a similar equation as in (6.9):

$$y_j(p_j - \phi_j) - s_j y_j (p_j - \phi_j) \begin{cases} = k_1 & \text{if } N_j > 0 \\ \leq k_1 & \text{if } N_j = 0 \end{cases}. \tag{6.27}$$

The first term on the left of (6.27) gives the marginal benefit of adding a marginal variety. But adding this variety will reduce the demand for other varieties produced by the same firm, which is shown by the second term on the left. The larger the market share of the firm, the more severe is this cannibalization effect. The net benefit should be balanced by the fixed costs of adding a marginal variety. But for very inefficient firms, their net benefit from adding an additional variety can never cover the corresponding fixed costs, hence we have the inequality specified in the second line on the right of (6.27).

Subject to these choices of price and product range, we will check whether the profits of all firms are nonnegative. If not, then we assume that the highest-cost firm exits the market, and we check whether the profits for the remaining firms are all nonnegative. If not, we assume that the next-highest-cost firm exits the market, and so on. This procedure is repeated until enough high-cost firms have exited so that the remaining firms have nonnegative profits. We summarize this equilibrium procedure with the definition of the short-run equilibrium.

Definition 6.1   *Given the number of entrants M_e, a short-run equilibrium has prices and product ranges chosen according to (6.26) and (6.27), and exit of enough of the highest-cost firms so that the profits of the remaining firms are nonnegative.*

To see how the short-run equilibrium is computed in practice, suppose that firms $j = 1, 2, \ldots, M$ have positive profits with a positive choice of product range, so the equality in (6.27) holds. Then we can use that equality with (6.26) to obtain

$$y_j \phi_j = (\eta - 1)k_1. \tag{6.28}$$

From (6.28), and applying (6.3) and (6.26), we can readily solve for

$$\phi_j = P \left(1 + \frac{1}{(\eta - 1)(1 - s_j)} \right)^{-\eta/(\eta-1)} \left[\frac{R}{(\eta - 1)k_1} \right]^{1/(\eta-1)}. \tag{6.29}$$

Suppose that firm $j = 0$ earns zero profits and has $N_0 = 0$ and $s_0 = 0$, so (6.29) becomes

$$\phi_0 = P \left(1 + \frac{1}{(\eta - 1)} \right)^{-\eta/(\eta-1)} \left[\frac{R}{(\eta - 1)k_1} \right]^{1/(\eta-1)}. \tag{6.29'}$$

Condition (6.29′) gives the marginal cost of the borderline firm that is just able to produce a single product (or negligible share of products), and still breaks even. We can compare (6.29) to (6.29′) to get the relative costs of firms as related to their market shares:

$$\frac{\phi_j}{\phi_0} = \left(\frac{1 + \frac{1}{(\eta-1)(1-s_j)}}{1 + \frac{1}{(\eta-1)}} \right)^{-\eta/(\eta-1)}. \tag{6.30}$$

Let $\tau_j = \phi_j/\phi_0$ denote the relative cost ratio, so lower τ represents higher productivity, and then from (6.30) we can express firm j's market size s_j as a function:

$$s(\tau_j) = \left[1 - \frac{1}{1 + \eta(\tau_j^{-(\eta-1)/\eta} - 1)} \right] \text{ with } \tau_j \leq 1. \tag{6.31}$$

Obviously $s'(\tau_j) < 0$, so the more productive firm has larger market share.

Given the number of entrants M_e, and the productivity draw $\phi(M_e) = (\phi_1, \phi_2, \ldots, \phi_{M_e})$, we can easily check whether these firms all earn nonnegative profits by checking whether the market shares implied by (6.31) add up to less than unity. That is, take the highest-cost firm among the $j = 1, 2, \ldots, M_e$ draws of productivity, labeled as $j = 0$, and hypothesize that it earns zero profits with $N_0 = 0$ and $s_0 = 0$. Expressing all other relative marginal costs as $\tau_j = \phi_j/\phi_0$, then the market share for the remaining firms are computed from (6.31). If market shares sum to exactly unity, then we have found a short-run equilibrium. If the market shares sum to less than unity, then evidently all firms can stay in the market, but our initial hypothesis that profits are zero and $s_0 = 0$ for the highest-cost firm is not true. Instead, that firm can have a positive market share $s_0 > 0$, in which case the market shares of the other firms are computed as

$$s(\tau_j) = 1 - \frac{1}{\left(\eta - 1 + \frac{1}{(1-s_0)}\right) \tau_j^{-(\eta-1)/\eta} - \eta + 1}, \tag{6.32}$$

which is derived in the same manner as (6.31) but allowing for a positive market share $s_0 > 0$ for the highest-cost firm. Then the equilibrium is determined by solving for s_0 from the equation

$$\sum_{j=1}^{M_e} s(\tau_j) = \sum_{j=1}^{M_e} \left(1 - \frac{1}{\left(\eta - 1 + \frac{1}{(1-s_0)}\right) \tau_j^{-(\eta-1)/\eta} - (\eta - 1)} \right) = 1, \tag{6.33}$$

where $\tau_j = 1$ for the highest-cost firm.

On the other hand, if the initial hypothesis that profits are zero with $s_0 = 0$ for the highest-cost firms results in a sum of market shares from (6.31) that *exceeds* unity, then the highest-cost firm cannot earn nonnegative profits. So the least efficient firm is dropped, and we take the firm with second-highest marginal costs and hypothesize that it has zero profits with $s_0 = 0$. We then check whether the sum of market shares in (6.31) of the remaining firms is less than or equal to unity. If the sum of market shares equals unity, then we have found a short-run equilibrium; if it is less than unity, then we use (6.33), but without the highest-cost firm, to determine the equilibrium; and if the sum is more than unity, then we also need to drop the firm with second-highest marginal costs. This procedure is repeated until we arrive at the number of firms $M \le M_e$ that survive in the short-run equilibrium for that particular draw of marginal costs $\phi(M_e) = (\phi_1, \phi_2, \ldots, \phi_{M_e})$.[4] In practice we will always have $M < M_e$ in equilibrium, so the market shares are determined by

$$\sum_{j=1}^{M} s(\tau_j) = \sum_{j=1}^{M} \left(1 - \frac{1}{\left(\eta - 1 + \frac{1}{(1-s_0)} \right) \tau_j^{-(\eta-1)/\eta} - (\eta - 1)} \right) = 1, \quad (6.33')$$

where $\tau_j = 1$ for the highest-cost firm that survives in equilibrium, with market share s_0.

We are now in a position to identify the conditions that must be satisfied in the *long-run* equilibrium, where the expected profits of firms are nonpositive. Using (6.12) (which still holds with heterogeneous costs) and (6.26), firm j's optimized operating profit can be rewritten as

$$\prod(\tau_j) = \left[\frac{s(\tau_j)^2}{1 + (\eta - 1)(1 - s(\tau_j))} \right] R, \quad (6.34)$$

for any relative costs τ_j. We have already seen how the market shares are determined in a short-run equilibrium, and these can be used in (6.34) to determine profits for the surviving firms. Then the expected profits are computed by taking the average of (6.34) over firms and then taking the expected value over all draws of $\phi(M_e) = (\phi_1, \phi_2, \ldots, \phi_{M_e})$:

$$\text{Expected profits} = E \left\{ \frac{1}{M_e} \sum_{j=1}^{M_e} \prod(\tau_j) \right\}, \quad (6.35)$$

where we adopt the notation that $\prod(\tau_j) = 0$ for all firms $j = M + 1, \ldots M_e$ that do not survive in each short-run equilibrium. Notice that expected profits in (6.35) depend on the number of entrants M_e in several ways: that number is the dimension of the productivity vector $\phi(M_e) = (\phi_1, \phi_2, \ldots, \phi_{M_e})$, which is drawn for each short-run equilibrium; and it is also used to form the average of profits in (6.35). For the second reason, we expect that (6.35) is declining in the number of entering firms, at least as M_e gets sufficiently large: too many entrants will lower the probability that any firm survives, and lower expected profits. Then the long-run equilibrium is determined by the following definition.

Definition 6.2   *A long-run equilibrium is the smallest number of entering firms M_e such that the expected profits in (6.35) are greater than or equal to* *the fixed cost of entry k_e, and where the addition of one more entrant lowers the expected profits to strictly less than k_e.*

In practice, the long-run equilibrium is determined by taking repeated draws of the productivity vector $\phi(M_e) = (\phi_1, \phi_2, \ldots, \phi_{M_e})$, for given M_e. For each draw, we compute a short-run equilibrium, and its associated profits from (6.34). Averaging these over many draws, we obtain expected profits in (6.35). In order to determine the long-run equilibrium number of entrants, we would need to repeat this procedure for various choices of M_e, until definition 6.2 is satisfied. In practice, the numerical problem is simplified because for any choice of M_e, the short-run equilibrium does not depend on market size, which does not enter equations (6.31)–(6.33′). The market size enters profits in (6.34) in a linear fashion. This means that after taking many draws of the productivity vector and computing expected profits in (6.34) for one market size, the solution for another market size is obtained in direct proportion. So for any choice of M_e, it is fairly easy to find a market size R and fixed entry cost k_e that result in M_e being a long-run equilibrium.

Before turning to the computation of the equilibria, we can identify several analytical properties. The first property follows from our description above.

Lemma 6.1 *The number of surviving firms M in the short-run equilibrium depends on the number of entering firms M_e and their particular draws of marginal cost, but does not depend on the market size L.*

Notice that the market size does not enter into formulas (6.31)–(6.33′), which proves this lemma. As we discuss in the next section, the number of entering firms in the long-run equilibrium certainly does depend on market size. With the doubling of market size, for example, we will find numerically that the equilibrium number of entrants M_e also doubles. But we will further find that many of these firms do not survive for any draw of productivities, so that larger markets do not actually support more firms; instead, they will support more varieties per firm.

The result that larger markets support more varieties per firm can be seen from the optimal product range in (6.12) (which still holds with heterogeneous costs). Given a draw of productivities $\phi(M_e) = (\phi_1, \phi_2, \ldots, \phi_{M_e})$

and a corresponding short-run equilibrium, lemma 6.1 tells us that changing the market size $R = \rho L$ will have no impact on the equilibrium market shares. Therefore, from (6.12) it is immediate that the product range for each market share will expand in direct proportion to the market size.

Lemma 6.2   *Given the number of entering firms M_e and their particular draws of marginal cost in a short-run equilibrium, the range of varieties produced by each firm is in proportion to the market size L.*

What about the relationship between the product range and firms' productivities? Differentiating (6.12), given a fixed market size R, shows that there is an inverted U-shaped relationship between market share and the number of products, where N_j reaches its maximum when the market share is

$$s = \frac{\sqrt{\eta}}{\sqrt{\eta} + 1}. \tag{6.36}$$

Lemma 6.3   *There is an inverted U-shaped relationship between firms' productivities and the range of varieties they choose to produce.*

To explain this result: more-productive firms always have higher market share, as shown by (6.31); however, there is no monotonic relationship between firms' productivity level and their choices on product range. From (6.27), we know that having a higher market share means that firms are hurt more from the cannibalization effect. For this reason, the incentive to expand product lines weakens as productivity rises. Thus, the relationship between productivity and the range of products is nonmonotonic: firms at an intermediate level of productivity develop the largest range of products, while the most productive and least productive firms have smaller ranges.

We now turn to the numerical calculation of the long-run equilibrium to describe further properties of the model with heterogeneous costs.

6.5   Numerical Solution with Heterogeneous Costs

One key deviation of our model from the Melitz (2003) model with heterogeneous productivities is that in our case, firms are no longer small relative to the market. Dropping the assumption that firms are small enough relative to the market means that we can no longer use the law of large numbers

Table 6.1 A sample short-run equilibrium: Profits, variety numbers, and market size

	Firm number	Marginal cost	Market share	$R = 1{,}000$		$R = 2{,}000$		$R = 4{,}000$	
				Profit	Varieties	Profit	Varieties	Profit	Varieties
	1	3.580	0.489	67.085	14.048	134.169	28.095	268.338	56.191
	2	3.746	0.411	42.871	12.278	85.741	24.555	171.483	49.110
Short-	3	4.214	0.067	0.797	2.213	1.594	4.426	3.188	8.853
run,	4	4.256	0.021	0.074	0.695	0.149	1.390	0.297	2.781
$M_e = 7$	5	4.264	0.012	0.025	0.405	0.050	0.809	0.100	1.618
	6	4.465	0.000	0.000	0.000	0.000	0.000	0.000	0.000
	7	4.953	0.000	0.000	0.000	0.000	0.000	0.000	0.000

Note: Parameters take the values $k_1 = 5$, $k_e = 10$, $\gamma = 5$, and $\eta = 6$.

to get closed-form solutions in the long-run equilibrium for the market aggregates, such as the average productivity and the like. Nonetheless, the properties of the long-run equilibrium can still be derived using a simple numerical experiment.

We follow steps described in Section 6.4 in this numerical application. Specifically, we first choose the short-run number of entrants M_e, which is nonstochastic. Each of those M_e entrants will draw a marginal cost parameter ϕ from a cost distribution with Pareto density $F(\phi) = (\phi/\phi^{\max})^\gamma$, where we will arbitrarily let the upper bound of marginal cost $\phi^{\max} = 5$. We also choose the shape parameter $\gamma = 5$ for now. Recalling that a larger shape parameter implies less-dispersed cost distribution, we will also experiment with different values of γ later in this section. The other key parameter is the elasticity of substitution between varieties η—we first set $\eta = 6$ and will experiment with other values. For other parameters, we set the fixed costs of introducing each variety at $k_1 = 5$ and the sunk costs of entry at $k_e = 10$.

Table 6.1 gives an example of the short-run equilibrium where the nonstochastic number of entrants is fixed at $M_e = 7$, given parameters as specified above. With seven firms entering the market, they are randomly assigned marginal cost parameters like those in the second column of Table 6.1. Then the remaining columns show the outcome of market competition. In this example, it turns out that only five firms survive, with the two highest-cost firms dropping out. It is clear from this example that market shares do not depend on market size, since from (6.31) to (6.33), firms' market shares only depend on their relative marginal costs to the

Table 6.2 Market size and long-run equilibrium number of entrants

Market size	Long-run number of entrants	Number of surviving firms				Expected profits
R	Long-run M_e	M_{min}	M_{max}	M_{mean}	M_{median}	Sunk cost $k_e = 10$
4,000	64	2	6	3.00	3	10.63
2,000	32	2	6	2.90	3	10.26
1,000	16	2	7	2.97	3	10.32
500	8	2	8	3.08	3	10.09

Note: Parameters take the values $k_1 = 5$, $k_e = 10$, $\gamma = 5$, and $\eta = 6$, with 500 draws of marginal costs.

cutoff firm and the cutoff firm's market share. It is also clear that the profits and varieties are in direct proportion to the market size, which is exactly what is implied from (6.12) and (6.34).

The short-run equilibrium in Table 6.1 is not necessarily a long-run equilibrium, because potential entrants may still see net benefits from entry. As long as the expected profits in the market are greater than the entry costs, firms will keep on entering the market. This process continues until M_e reaches the point where adding one more entrant leads to expected profits less than entry costs. We illustrate the long-run equilibria with different market sizes in Table 6.2.

It is worth stressing the difference between tables 6.1 and 6.2: while the short-run equilibrium in Table 6.1 is computed for a *particular* draw of marginal costs for the seven firms, the long-run equilibria in Table 6.2 are computed for 500 draws of marginal cost for all entering firms. Then expected profits are computed as in (6.35), by averaging over firms and the draws of marginal cost. Of course, the number of surviving firms M can vary, depending on marginal costs, and that is why we report the minimum, maximum, mean, and median of the distribution of M in Table 6.2. Indeed, we don't take a stand on the question of which particular draw of marginal costs holds in the long-run equilibrium: if we extended our model by introducing dynamics with a death rate of firms, along with the entry of new firms, then the marginal costs would fluctuate over time due to entry and exit, and there would be no stationary, long-run equilibrium (in contrast to Melitz [2003]). We avoid these dynamic issues, however, and simply solve for a long-run equilibria by determining the (nonstochastic) number of entering firms, as in definition 6.2.

Table 6.2 shows that the long-run equilibrium number of entrants increases as the market size expands, and in fact, it increases in direct proportion. One reason for this result is that each surviving firm's profits, as shown in (6.34), is directly proportional to the market size. To ensure that the free-entry condition holds, the number of entrants must increase with the market size so that the expected net benefits from entry are close to zero. However, profits in (6.34) also depend on the market shares of firms, which differ with the marginal costs in each short-run equilibrium, so it is surprising that the increase in the number of entrants is in *direct proportion* to the market size. Interestingly, the equilibrium number of surviving firms in Table 6.2 is quite insensitive to the market size. This result is related to lemma 6.1, that the number of surviving firms in a short-run equilibrium does not depend on the size of the market, but we now find numerically that the same result holds when comparing the distribution of M across long-run equilibria.

With roughly the same distribution of the number of surviving firms M in markets of different size, but more entry in larger markets, it follows that less-efficient firms must exit in larger markets. Therefore, the surviving firms are expected to have higher productivity. This result in confirmed in Table 6.3. In the upper panel of Table 6.3, we give the descriptive statistics (maximum, minimum, mean, and median) of the highest marginal costs and highest prices for firms surviving in a long-run equilibrium. The lower panel of the same table gives the analogous descriptive statistics for the lowest marginal costs and lowest prices charged by firms surviving in a long-run equilibrium. It is clear from both panels that as market size expands, selection happens and the least efficient firms (with highest costs) drop out of the market. The distribution of marginal costs and also prices is shifted to the left as the market size expands.

With the selection effect shown in Table 6.3 operating, we expect that consumers are better off in larger countries. Reinforcing the selection effect is the impact of market size on the varieties produced and available to consumers. Table 6.4 gives statistics for the total number of varieties produced by all surviving firms and the aggregate market price index (as in (6.4′)) in a long-run equilibrium. From the left columns, we see that the total number of varieties available roughly doubles as the market size doubles. From Table 6.2 we show that the distribution of the number of surviving firms remains roughly the same when market size changes, so each surviving firm produces more varieties on average to accommodate the integrated market while the highest-cost firms exit. Consumers gain from larger markets: they

Table 6.3 Market size, marginal costs, and prices

Market size	Highest marginal cost				Highest prices			
R	ϕ_{min}	ϕ_{max}	ϕ_{mean}	ϕ_{median}	P_{min}	P_{max}	P_{mean}	P_{median}
4,000	1.30	3.44	2.45	2.58	1.65	4.17	3.11	3.14
2,000	1.42	3.94	2.80	2.82	1.89	4.74	3.49	3.50
1,000	1.84	4.65	3.30	3.33	2.51	5.60	4.12	4.17
500	1.62	4.94	3.79	3.86	2.21	5.94	4.71	4.77

Market size	Lowest marginal cost				Lowest prices			
R	ϕ_{min}	ϕ_{max}	ϕ_{mean}	ϕ_{median}	P_{min}	P_{max}	P_{mean}	P_{median}
4,000	0.70	3.02	1.96	1.99	1.55	4.04	2.98	3.01
2,000	0.69	3.40	2.22	2.23	1.85	4.62	3.36	3.36
1,000	0.92	4.24	2.62	2.64	2.48	5.49	3.96	4.01
500	1.02	4.43	3.00	3.07	2.18	5.83	4.52	4.60

Note: Parameters take the values $k_1 = 5$, $k_e = 10$, $\gamma = 5$, and $\eta = 6$, with 500 draws of marginal costs.

buy products at lower prices (Table 6.3), and they can also consume more varieties (Table 6.4, left columns). This leads to a drop in the aggregate price index, which is shown in the right-most columns of Table 6.4.

We can think of the increase in market size as due to the integration of two economies through trade. In contrast to Melitz (2003), we have not introduced iceberg trade costs between the economies and also do not have additional fixed costs of exporting. Without such costs, and assuming single-product firms with CES preferences, the integration of economies will have no impact on entry or exit in either country, even with heterogeneous firms (as shown by Bernard, Redding, and Schott [2007]). But in our multiproduct model, we have shown numerically that increasing the market size due to opening trade has several important impacts. These numerical results are summarized by the following proposition.

Proposition 6.2 *With a Pareto distribution of productivities and no fixed or iceberg costs of exporting, increasing the market size through international trade leads to*

1. *The world number of surviving firms roughly equal to the number of surviving firms in either country in autarky*

2. *Exit of the least efficient firms*

Table 6.4 Equilibrium varieties and aggregate price index

Market size	Total varieties				Aggregate price index			
R	min	max	mean	median	p_{min}	p_{max}	p_{mean}	p_{median}
4,000	57.3	127.0	110.7	113.5	0.63	1.57	1.18	1.19
2,000	28.2	63.6	55.7	56.8	0.83	2.05	1.52	1.53
1,000	15.2	32.3	27.8	28.5	1.28	2.78	2.06	2.09
500	6.0	15.9	14.0	14.3	1.29	3.38	2.70	2.74

Note: Parameters take the values $k_1 = 5$, $k_e = 10$, $\gamma = 5$, and $\eta = 6$, with 500 draws of marginal costs.

3. *An increase in the range of varieties produced by each firm on average*

4. *An increase in expected consumer welfare due to both (b) and (c)*

This proposition is proved by the numerical calculations of long-run equilibria we have just reviewed. We have shown in Table 6.2 that the distribution of M is quite insensitive to the market size, which is the basis for part (1) of proposition 6.2: each country will have roughly the same number of surviving firms in autarky, regardless of their respective market sizes, and likewise for the world economy after integration. Part (2) follows from our numerical finding that the number of entering firms M_e increases in proportion to the market size but that the distribution of surviving firms M is quite insensitive to the market size: the larger number of entering firms means that the surviving firms are more efficient than otherwise, as shown in Table 6.3. Part (3) follows that insensitivity of the distribution of M to market size together with Table 6.4: since the total number of varieties produced in a country (or the world) increases in proportion to the market size, while the distribution of M is roughly the same, we expect more varieties per firm on average. Consumers gain from the expansion of product varieties and the fall in prices due to having more-efficient firms.

We further demonstrate the numerical properties of our model by changing some of the key parameters. In each case, we will report results for two different market sizes, $R = 1,000$ and $R = 2,000$, to illustrate the effect of opening trade between two identical countries. This sensitivity analysis further confirms our numerical finding that the number of entering firms increased in direct proportion to the market size, and that the distribution of surviving firms is quite insensitive to the market size.

Table 6.5 Equilibrium number of entrants and the shape parameter

γ	$R = 1{,}000$ Long-run M_e	M_{min}	M_{max}	M_{ave}	M_{median}	$R = 2{,}000$ Long-run M_e	M_{min}	M_{max}	M_{ave}	M_{median}
		Number of surviving firms					Number of surviving firms			
1	44	2	4	2.11	2	88	2	4	2.10	2
2	30	2	5	2.30	2	56	2	6	2.30	2
4	18	2	7	2.80	3	37	2	6	2.87	3
5	16	2	7	2.97	3	32	2	6	2.90	3
10	10	2	9	4.17	4	20	2	10	4.14	4
15	7	2	7	5.12	5	14	2	11	5.35	5
20	6	2	6	5.45	6	11	3	11	6.30	6

Note: Parameters take the values $k_1 = 5$, $k_e = 10$, $\gamma = 5$, and $\eta = 6$, with 500 draws of marginal costs.

We begin with the shape parameter of the Pareto distribution, γ, as shown in Table 6.5. Larger γ implies more firms are concentrated in the left of the marginal cost distribution, or the density has a thinner right tail. When $\gamma = 1$, the cost parameter follows a uniform distribution. As γ rises, fewer firms enter the market, while the average number of surviving firms increases. When γ is quite large (for example, $\gamma = 20$), most of the firms have high marginal costs and most of the entrants will finally break even and stay in the market. When γ is large, potential firms face a larger probability of drawing high marginal costs, and so, realized entry falls; on the other hand, those who do enter the market are more likely similar to competitors in marginal cost, so more firms could survive in the end. Thus, the number of entering firms falls with γ in Table 6.5, but the median number of surviving firms rises.

Another important parameter, the elasticity of substitution, η, exerts its impact by affecting the intensity of competition and the price elasticity of demand. When η is low, varieties are less substitutable for each other, within a firm or across firms. Consequently, firms are able to charge higher markups and get higher profits. Larger η implies lower profits since it is easier for consumers to substitute among varieties, and so the median number of surviving firms is falling with η, as shown in Table 6.6. On the other hand, the movement of the number of entering firms is ambiguous. As η gets larger, the number of entrants first rises and then falls. One explanation for this is that when η is low, the turning point for the most productive firm to restrict its range of products, shown in (6.36), is relatively low. This gives low-productivity firms more chance to survive in equilibrium. While

Table 6.6 Number of entrants and the elasticity parameter

η	$R = 1{,}000$ Long-run M_e	M_{min}	M_{max}	M_{ave}	M_{median}	$R = 2{,}000$ Long-run M_e	M_{min}	M_{max}	M_{ave}	M_{median}
1.5	11	5	11	10.21	11	21	5	21	12.07	12
2.0	14	3	14	7.2	7	28	3	15	7.00	7
4.0	16	2	9	3.73	4	32	2	9	3.57	3
6.0	16	2	7	2.97	3	32	2	6	2.90	3
10	15	2	5	2.46	2	30	2	6	2.49	2
15	15	2	5	2.27	2	30	2	4	2.27	2
100	11	2	3	2.01	2	19	2	3	2.01	2

Note: Parameters take the values $k_1 = 5$, $k_e = 10$, and $\gamma = 5$, with 500 draws of marginal costs.

on the other hand, if η is getting relatively large, the inverted U-shape between varieties and market shares leans to the right. In this case, even the largest firm won't restrict its variety expansion since the cannibalization effect does not hurt as much. Therefore, little room is left for the high-cost firms to survive, so for high values of η, the number of entering firms falls as η grows further.

6.6   Conclusion

Recent literature has introduced multiproduct firms into the monopolistic competition model with international trade. When CES preferences have been used, there has been a reluctance to recognize that firms with a positive mass of products will command extra market power: their elasticity of demand with respect to the common price of their varieties is less than the elasticity of substitution. As a firm's range of varieties expands, the elasticity of demand falls further. The goal of this chapter has been to show that it is both tractable and interesting to take into account these demand effects. We show that the optimal markup for a firm is endogenous, and that it faces a cannibalization effect in demand as more product varieties are introduced. The optimal range of varieties is obtained by balancing the profits earned from each (using the optimal markups) with the cannibalization effect of shifting demand away from its own products.

We model international trade as an expansion of market size, as two formerly separate economies integrate frictionlessly into a larger, global economy. With multiproduct firms, we find interesting effects of trade even in the absence of trade costs.

We first take our benchmark model with firms with identical marginal costs. This corresponds to the model proposed by Krugman (1979, 1980). With identical costs and multiple varieties, firms respond to free trade by expanding their product range of varieties. This occurs because as the market size grows due to trade, each firm's market share decreases, which alleviates the cannibalization effect. Thus, firms tend to produce more varieties than they do in autarky. But not all firms can stay in the market, and there is exit in each country. Importantly, the expansion in varieties within the boundary of the firm dominates the fall in the number of local producing firms, so there are more varieties provided by (fewer) local producers. Consumers enjoy welfare gains because they not only have more domestic varieties, they also have more variety from imports, and because prices fall due to reduced market shares of each firm.

We then extend our benchmark model to incorporate heterogeneity in costs across firms. We show that in the short-run equilibrium, firms' market shares do not depend on the size of the market, while firms' variety ranges and profits are in direct proportion to the market size. Our numerical calculations confirm these predictions and also enable us to compute the long-run equilibrium. With heterogeneous costs, the number of firms surviving in equilibrium is quite insensitive to the market size. When trade is opened, more firms initially enter, but the larger market size reduces the cannibalization effect and expands the optimal scope of products. As a result, the less efficient firms exit, and the larger market is accommodated by more efficient firms that produce more varieties per firm on average.

Appendix

6A.1 Proof of Equation (6.20)

Using the fact that $R = \rho L$, (6.19) can be rewritten as

$$s_0(k_0/\rho L) = \frac{\sqrt{(\eta - 1)^2 \left(\frac{k_0}{\rho L}\right)^2 + 4\eta \frac{k_0}{\rho L}} - (\eta - 1)\frac{k_0}{\rho L}}{2}.$$

We take the derivative

$$\frac{\partial s_0(k_0/\rho L)}{\partial L} = \frac{1}{2}\left[\frac{(\eta - 1)^2 \left(\frac{k_0}{\rho L}\right) + 2\eta}{\sqrt{(\eta - 1)^2 \left(\frac{k_0}{\rho L}\right)^2 + 4\eta \left(\frac{k_0}{\rho L}\right)}} - (\eta - 1)\right].$$

We prove $\frac{\partial s_0}{\partial L} < 0$ by proving the term in the square bracket is positive, because

$$
\left[\frac{(\eta - 1)^2 \left(\frac{k_0}{\rho L}\right) + 2\eta}{\sqrt{(\eta - 1)^2 \left(\frac{k_0}{\rho L}\right)^2 + 4\eta \left(\frac{k_0}{\rho L}\right)}} - (\eta - 1) \right]
$$

$$
= (\eta - 1) \left[\frac{(\eta - 1)\left(\frac{k_0}{\rho L}\right) + 2\frac{\eta}{(\eta - 1)}}{\sqrt{(\eta - 1)^2 \left(\frac{k_0}{\rho L}\right)^2 + 4\eta \left(\frac{k_0}{\rho L}\right)}} - 1 \right]
$$

$$
= (\eta - 1) \left[\frac{\sqrt{(\eta - 1)^2 \left(\frac{k_0}{\rho L}\right)^2 + 4\eta \left(\frac{k_0}{\rho L}\right) + 4\frac{\eta^2}{(\eta - 1)^2}}}{\sqrt{(\eta - 1)^2 \left(\frac{k_0}{\rho L}\right)^2 + 4\eta \left(\frac{k_0}{\rho L}\right)}} - 1 \right] > 0.
$$

Then $\frac{\partial s_0}{\partial k_0} > 0$ (provided that L is fixed) follows directly from the above proof. □

ACKNOWLEDGMENTS

We thank Gene Grossman, Elhanan Helpman, Volker Nocke, and the CEPR Globalization and the Organization of Firms and Markets (February 2007) conference participants for very helpful comments.

NOTES

1. An economy with given parameters can permit a (1) strongly vertically integrated equilibrium, with a small number of very large groups, charging high prices for their sale of intermediate inputs or (2) a less-integrated equilibrium, with a large number of smaller groups, charging lower prices for their intermediate inputs. The former high-concentration equilibrium was compared to the large business groups known as *chaebol* in South Korea, while the latter low-concentration equilibrium was compared to the groups in Taiwan.

2. Aggregate demand is just the number of consumers L times the individual demand of each consumer.

3. See the Appendix for a proof.

4. Notice that the number of surviving firms is a random variable, depending on the draw of marginal costs, whereas the number of entering firms is a non-stochastic parameter for the short-run equilibrium.

REFERENCES

Allanson, Paul, and Catia Montagna. 2005. "Multiproduct Firms and Market Structure: An Explorative Application to the Product Life Cycle." *International Journal of Industrial Organization* 23: 587–97.

Bernard, Andrew B., J. Bradford Jensen, Stephen Redding, and Peter K. Schott. 2007. "Firms in International Trade." *Journal of Economic Perspectives* 21(3): 105–30.

Bernard, Andrew B., Stephen Redding, and Peter Schott. 2006a. "Multi-Product Firms and Product Switching." NBER working paper 12293.

———. 2006b. "Multi-Product Firms and Trade Liberalization." NBER working paper 12782.

———. 2007. "Comparative Advantage and Heterogeneous Firms." *Review of Economic Studies* 74:31–66.

Brambilla, Irene. 2006. "Multinationals, Technology, and the Introduction of Varieties of Goods." NBER working paper 12217.

Brander, James, and Jonathan Eaton. 1984. "Product Line Rivalry." *American Economic Review* 74(3):323–34.

Broda, Christian, and David Weinstein. 2006. "Globalization and the Gains from Variety." *Quarterly Journal of Economics* 121(2):541–85.

———. 2007. "Product Creation and Destruction: Evidence and Price Implications." NBER working paper 13041.

Eaton, Jonathan, Samuel Kortum, and Francis Kramarz. 2004. "Dissecting Trade: Firms, Industries, and Export Destination." *American Economic Review (Papers and Proceedings)* 94(2):150–54.

Eckel, Carsten, and Peter Neary. 2006. "Multi-Product Firms and Flexible Manufacturing in the Global Economy." CEPR discussion paper no. 5941.

Feenstra, Robert C., and Gary G. Hamilton. 2006. *Emergent Economics, Divergent Paths: Economic Organization and International Trade in South Korea and Taiwan.* Cambridge: Cambridge University Press.

Feenstra, Robert C., Deng-Shing Huang, and Gary G. Hamilton. 2003. "A Market-Power Based Model of Business Groups." *Journal of Economic Behavior and Organization* 51:459–85.

Helpman, Elhanan. 1985. "Multinational Corporations and Trade Structure." *Review of Economic Studies* 52:443–57.

Krugman, Paul. 1979. "Increasing Returns, Monopolistic Competition, and International Trade." *Journal of International Economics* 9:469–79.

———. 1980. "Scale Economies, Product Differentiation, and the Pattern of Trade." *American Economic Review* 70:950–59.

Melitz, Marc. 2003. "The Impact of Trade on Intra-Industry Reallocations and Aggregate Industry Productivity." *Econometrica* 71(6):1695–1725.

Melitz, Marc, and Gianmarco Ottaviano. 2005. "Market Size, Trade, and Productivity." *Review of Economic Studies* 75:295–316.

Nocke, Volker, and Stephen Yeaple. 2006. "Globalization and Endogenous Firm Scope." NBER working paper 12322.

— 7 —

Firm Heterogeneity, Intra-Firm Trade, and the Role of Central Locations

STEPHEN ROSS YEAPLE

7.1 Introduction

Multinational enterprises, those firms that produce in more than one country, play a key role in the conduct of international commerce. According to UNCTAD (2004) the volume of sales of the foreign affiliates of multinational enterprises are more than twice the volume of global exports. Further, multinational enterprises (MNE) account for much of international trade (Hanson, Mataloni, and Slaughter 2005). Although the empirical trade literature has accumulated a wealth of facts concerning the behavior of multinational enterprises, most empirical work has been motivated by two-country models that cannot capture the rich pattern of multinational investments across countries (Blonigen 2005).

A firm that has decided to invest abroad faces a wide array of complex problems. In which of the world's countries will a firm's good be sold? What configuration of production locations will minimize the cost of serving these markets? Since a good that is sold to final customers might require hundreds or even thousands of different types of intermediate inputs, the logistics of acquiring components represents a daunting problem.

Even without considering arm's-length transactions, the extent of vertical specialization within multinational production networks is substantial and is becoming increasingly important. Table 7.1 shows data for various aggregate measures of the level of the activity of the manufacturing affiliates of U.S. multinationals in 1989 and 1999 and their growth rate as reported in the benchmark surveys of the U.S. Bureau of Economic Analysis. The total values for the sales of these affiliates are shown in the first row, and the destinations of these sales are shown in the next three rows. The data show that while sales to local customers are still the largest component of total affiliate sales, the fast-growing components are exports to countries other than

200

Table 7.1 U.S. MNE activity in manufacturing industries, 1989–1999

	1989 $Billion	1999 $Billion	Growth, % 1989–1999
Sales	509	1,107	117
Local	334	652	89
Export to other, affiliated	79	180	128
Export to other, unaffiliated	43	110	159
Value added	207	316	54

Source: BEA Benchmark surveys.
Note: 1989–1999 change in U.S. CPI = 35%.
Total U.S. exports of goods in 1999 = $696 billion.
Numbers for 1989 slightly understate all values as they omit some petroleum refining.

the United States. Exports to affiliates in other countries (not including the United States) grew at a rate of 128% over the period, while sales to local customers grew by merely 89%, and the total sales of U.S. multinationals to all locations grew at a rate of only 117%. Although these data partially reflect changes in composition across firms, they are highly suggestive of an increasing importance of vertical specialization across countries within the multinationals' networks. Perhaps the most stark evidence of the increased vertical specialization of the foreign affiliates of U.S. multinationals can be seen in the final row: the value added of U.S. manufacturing grew by a paltry 54%, which is less than half the growth in total sales.

Further complicating our ability to understand the structure of international production is the substantial degree of heterogeneity across firms in terms of their international organization. To get an idea of the extent of this heterogeneity, consider the data for 1994 from the U.S. Bureau of Economic Analysis that is shown in Figure 7.1. This figure shows the number of countries in which each of approximately 1,500 U.S. MNEs in manufacturing industries owns a foreign affiliate. The height of each bar corresponds to the number of firms in the size categories (number of countries per firm) shown on the horizontal axis. Few multinationals own affiliates in more than a handful of foreign locations: more than a third of all U.S. multinationals produce in only one foreign country, and the median number of foreign locations is two.

Given the tradition in the international trade literature of analyzing the motives for and consequences of international commerce in a two-country

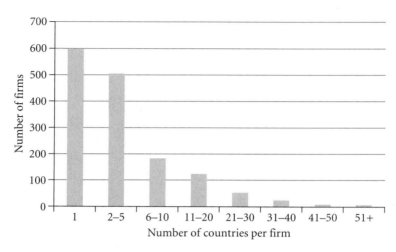

Figure 7.1 Number of countries in which manufacturing firms have affiliates.

framework in which all firms are identical, it is not surprising that existing work falls far short of explaining the structure of multinational production. This chapter presents a framework that makes the analysis of many of the complex logistical problems facing multinational enterprises tractable. The model has three key features. First, the world is composed of two regions, one of which is composed of many countries arrayed in a "hub and spokes" configuration. Geography matters in this framework because there are both interregional and intraregional transport costs. Transport costs within the region are lowest between the hub, which we refer to as the *central location,* and each of the spokes, which we refer to as the *peripheral countries.* Second, the model features a production technology in which final goods are assembled from a continuum of tradable intermediate inputs. There are fixed costs to opening each assembly plant and to opening a plant to produce a specific intermediate input. Third, firms are heterogeneous.

Firms maximize their profits by (1) choosing the set of countries in which they will assemble their final product, and (2) choosing from which countries they will source their intermediate inputs. Hence, the model endogenizes not only a firm's choice of which countries to own an affiliate but also the value-added at each location and the volume and direction of intrafirm trade. Since firms are heterogeneous, they each organize their international operations differently. Thus, the aggregate structure of foreign direct investment (FDI) across countries features both an *extensive* margin (the number of active firms) and an *intensive* margin (the volume of activity at the average firm).

We use the model to develop a rich set of predictions over the relationship between a firm's characteristics and the structure of its international operations. We show that small multinationals concentrate their foreign operations exclusively in central locations and source their intermediate inputs either from local plants or from their parent firms, while larger multinationals open assembly facilities in many foreign countries and source intermediates both from plants located in central locations and from their U.S. parents. For all but the largest multinationals, the central location plays a key role in the structure of a firm's international operations by acting either as an *export platform* for shipping final goods or as a primary location for producing intermediates that are in turn shipped to assembly plants elsewhere. These predictions are consistent with several empirical facts that we highlight below and are also consistent with recent empirical studies that explore the relationship between a country's *foreign market potential,* as measured by its geographic location, and its ability to attract multinational enterprises (see, for instance, Blonigen et al. 2005; Lai and Zhu 2006).

The comparative statics of the model highlight the importance of accounting for firm heterogeneity and regional geography. For instance, an increase in the distance between regions induces a larger set of firms to concentrate their foreign production in the single, central location. This result obtains because firms that centralize production optimally source a smaller percentage of their intermediates from their parent firm and so are less affected by the larger shipping costs associated with greater interregional distance. This mechanism provides a plausible explanation for why empirical studies typically find that greater distance between countries predicts smaller volumes of both exports and FDI between them.

Changes in regional characteristics, such as the level of intraregional transport costs or the number of countries within the region, are shown to have an effect on the structure of the international organization that operates through two channels. First, holding fixed the location of a firm's foreign assembly plants, a change in regional characteristics affects the manner in which that firm sources its intermediate inputs, thereby altering the local content of foreign production and the volume of interfirm trade in intermediates. Second, a change in regional characteristics induces some firms to alter the structure of their networks of foreign assembly plants. Since the optimal sourcing of intermediate inputs depends on this configuration, the volume of intrafirm trade is further altered.

This chapter is unique in endogenizing (1) the location of multinational affiliates, (2) the sourcing of intermediates from parent firms, and (3) the export of both final goods and intermediate inputs by foreign affiliates within a framework of firm heterogeneity. Nevertheless, it is related to several papers in the literature. Its closest relative is Helpman, Melitz, and Yeaple (2004), which analyzes the trade-off between exporting and FDI in serving any given foreign market. This chapter goes further than Helpman, Melitz, and Yeaple in incorporating key features of problems facing multinational enterprises. In particular, the analysis in this chapter considers a regional geography in which there are "central locations" and allows for a rich pattern of intrafirm trade.

Our analysis is also related to the work on export platform FDI by Ekholm, Forslid, and Markusen (2003) and models of "complex" FDI as presented in Yeaple (2003) and in Grossman, Helpman, and Szeidl (2006).[1] However, our focus differs in that it is on regional geography and not on factor prices as the motive for export platform and complex FDI strategies. Moreover, the production structure considered in our framework allows for a richer pattern of intermediate sourcing.

The remainder of the chapter is organized into six sections. In Section 7.2, we introduce a simple analytical framework in which central locations play a key role. In Section 7.3, we characterize the optimal structure of a firm's international operation as a function of its size. Comparative statics on the model's key variables are conducted in Section 7.4. Section 7.5 presents an extension of the model to a more complex regional geography and considers an application of the framework to a policy question: rules of origin in a regional trade agreement. Several of the model's key predictions are evaluated empirically in Section 7.6. In Section 7.7, we discuss the results and suggest extensions.

7.2   The Model

The analytical framework introduced in this section has three key components. First, to analyze the sourcing of intermediates, we specify a technology in which a final good is assembled from a continuum of inputs. Second, to analyze the role of regional geography, we consider a multiple-country, hub-and-spokes setting in which countries differ in their relative foreign-market access. Finally, to introduce an extensive margin of foreign direct investment, we allow for firm heterogeneity so that firms sort into mode of foreign-market access.

A final good is produced according to a Leontief technology with a continuum of inputs indexed by ω on the unit interval. If the marginal cost of producing intermediate ω is $c(\omega)$, then the cost of producing one unit of the final good is

$$C = \int_0^1 c(\omega)d\omega. \tag{7.1}$$

The advantage of a Leontief technology is that the marginal cost of supplying the final good is linear in the marginal cost of each intermediate input. Any number of alternative technologies would deliver similar results.

The production of intermediate inputs involves both fixed and variable costs. Intermediates vary in terms of the size of the fixed cost required to open a plant. The fixed cost to build a plant that is specific to intermediate ω is

$$f(\omega) = f\omega. \tag{7.2}$$

Once a plant has been built to assemble the final good from intermediates, assembly requires no additional inputs. To build an assembly plant requires a firm to incur a fixed cost F_A. To keep the analysis simple, we assume that a firm produces all the intermediates itself rather than outsource their production to outside contractors.

There are two regions. One region is composed of a country called Home. The other region is composed of $M + 1$ countries. M of these countries are identical and called peripheral. The other country is called Center. Factor prices are the same in all countries. To ship a final good internationally incurs per-unit (specific) transport costs. The cost of shipping an assembled final good between Home and any of the countries in the other region is τ. Within a region, final goods can be shipped between the central country and any of the M countries in the periphery but incur a specific transport cost t. For simplicity assume that shipping costs between countries in the periphery are sufficiently large that it does not occur.[2] Goods are more costly to ship between regions than within region so that $\tau > t$.

Intermediate inputs are also costly to ship between regions and countries within a region. The cost of shipping a unit of an intermediate input between regions is $\alpha\tau$ while the cost of shipping an intermediate input between the central country and a peripheral country is αt, where $\alpha \in [0, 1]$ measures differences in the transportability of intermediates relative to final goods. Note that these transport costs are independent of ω.

Firms differ in terms of the demand for their product. In each foreign country there are φ consumers each willing to pay no more than p for each unit of a firm of type-φ's output. This formulation of firm heterogeneity differs from other formulations found in the literature, such as Melitz (2003) or Helpman, Melitz, and Yeaple (2004), where firms vary in terms of their productivity. What induces sorting of firms into modes of foreign-market access in Helpman, Melitz, and Yeaple (2004) is not productivity differences per se, however, but the fact that more-productive firms sell a larger number of units in any given market. By assuming that firms differ in the number of customers rather than their productivity, we capture the key implications of firm heterogeneity in productivity in a simple and notationally clean way. Many of the results derived below would also obtain in a more complicated general equilibrium setting with monopolistically competitive firms and heterogeneity in terms of productivity.[3]

To serve the foreign market, a firm can either export the good from the home country or engage in FDI in the foreign region. Firms are assumed to be endowed with an assembly plant and a plant to produce each intermediate in the home country, so that there are no fixed costs associated with exporting to a foreign market. Once they have chosen in which of the $M + 1$ foreign countries they wish to assemble their final good, they organize their international production of intermediate inputs so as to minimize its total cost. Should intermediates be produced in the country of assembly, should they be imported from Home, or should their production be concentrated in the country called Center and exported to affiliates within the region?

7.3   Analysis

Firms can choose from three broad strategies for serving the foreign region that are defined by the location of assembly plants. First, they could assemble the final good exclusively in the home country and then export it to each foreign market. Second, they could open a single assembly plant in the central country and then serve the remaining M markets in the region by exporting the final good from the central country. This option corresponds to *export platform* FDI, which has received an increasing amount of attention in the literature. Since this mode involves complete centralization of foreign activity in one country, we refer to this option as *centralized* FDI. Third, they could open an assembly plant in each of the foreign markets and avoid shipping the final good across any borders. This type of firm may still concentrate the production of some of the intermediate inputs in the centralized country and so engage in intrafirm trade in intermediates within region. We refer to this strategy as *decentralized* FDI.

In our analysis, we characterize the optimal intermediate-input sourcing behavior of firms choosing each of these strategies and the profits associated with these strategies in turn. We then turn to sorting of firms into strategies on the basis of their type.

7.3.1 Exporting

Consider first the profits associated with exporting the final good from the home country to each of the $M + 1$ markets of the foreign region. Clearly, a firm that assembles the final good in its home country will also produce all of its intermediates there as well. Hence, such a firm incurs no fixed costs or shipping costs associated with the intermediate inputs. Since each final good shipped is subject to the interregional transport cost of τ, the profits associated with exporting for a firm of type φ are

$$\Pi_X(\varphi) = (M + 1)\varphi(p - \tau). \tag{7.3}$$

To make exporting a viable option, we assume that $p > \tau$.

7.3.2 Centralized FDI

Now consider the behavior and profits of a firm that engages in centralized FDI. A firm that has opened an assembly plant in the central country can then export the good to the M peripheral countries and incur a transport cost $t < \tau$ on final goods. The firm must then decide from where to obtain intermediates. A firm following a centralized FDI strategy will never produce the intermediates in a peripheral country because doing so will incur the fixed cost of building an additional plant and the transport cost of shipping the intermediate to Center. This transport cost could be avoided by simply producing the intermediate in Center.

There are two viable options for sourcing intermediate inputs. First, the firm may produce the intermediates in Home and then ship them to Center. This option avoids fixed costs but incurs interregional transport costs.

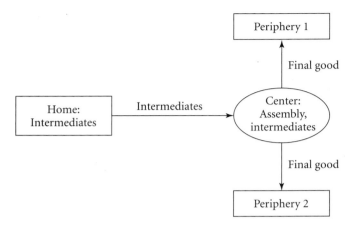

Figure 7.2 Centralized FDI strategy.

Second, a firm may produce the intermediate locally in Center, thereby avoiding transport costs but incurring the fixed cost of building local plants. Figure 7.2 provides a schematic of the location of production and implied trade patterns for a firm following a centralized FDI strategy. Since intermediates share the same transport cost between Home and Center ($\alpha\tau$) and since intermediates with a lower index of ω involve a lower fixed cost, the profitability of moving the production of an intermediate offshore is decreasing in ω. It follows that there is a threshold ω^* such that for $\omega < \omega^*$, intermediates are produced in Center while the remaining intermediates are imported from Home by the assembly affiliate in Center.

Since the final good must be shipped from the center to the periphery, incurring transport cost t while the measure $(1 - \omega^*)$ of intermediates incurs transport cost $\alpha\tau$, it follows from (7.1) that the marginal cost of serving a peripheral country for a firm that chooses cutoff intermediate ω^* is

$$t + (1 - \omega^*)\alpha\tau,$$

while the marginal cost of serving the central country is

$$(1 - \omega^*)\alpha\tau.$$

The total fixed cost for a firm that opens a single foreign assembly plant and an intermediate input plant for all $\omega < \omega^*$ is

$$F_A + f \int_0^{\omega^*} \omega\, d\omega = F_A + \frac{f}{2}(\omega^*)^2.$$

It follows that the profits of a firm of type φ with investment threshold ω^* are

$$\Pi_{CI}(\omega^*, \varphi) = (M + 1)\varphi p - \left\{ M\varphi t + F_A \right\}$$

$$- \left\{ (M + 1)\varphi(1 - \omega^*)\alpha\tau + \frac{f}{2}(\omega^*)^2 \right\}. \tag{7.4}$$

The profits of a firm following a centralized FDI strategy have three components. The first component is the revenue of the firm, which is given by the first term on the right-hand side of (7.4). The second term in (7.4) is the cost associated with assembly and moving the final good to foreign locations, which we refer to as the *downstream costs*. The last term is the cost associated with providing intermediates to assembly plants, which we refer to as the *upstream costs*.

A firm that has chosen a centralized FDI strategy minimizes its upstream costs by choosing ω^*. The first-order condition is

$$(M + 1)\varphi\alpha\tau - f\omega^* = 0,$$

which implies the following solution for the optimal cutoff between building an intermediate in Home and building it in the central location:

$$\omega^*(\varphi) = \begin{cases} \frac{(M+1)\alpha\tau}{f}\varphi & \text{if } \varphi \leq \varphi^* \\ 1 & \text{otherwise} \end{cases} \tag{7.5}$$

where

$$\varphi^* = \frac{f}{(M + 1)\alpha\tau}. \tag{7.6}$$

The sourcing of intermediate inputs by a centralized multinational across firms with different market sizes is depicted in Figure 7.3. As a firm's market size becomes larger, the goal of reducing total costs induces the firm to source an increasing share of its intermediates from plants within the central country. As such, the share of intrafirm imports of intermediate inputs from the home country in total value-added is decreasing in a firm's foreign output.

Note that as a firm's market size becomes larger, its marginal costs of serving a foreign market fall endogenously as the firm reorganizes production to avoid transport costs. The observation is interesting because the predictions of standard models of firm heterogeneity run from lower marginal costs to higher market size and not the reverse.

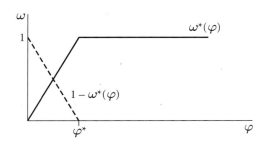

Figure 7.3 The sourcing of intermediate inputs by centralized multinationals.

Combining equations (7.4) and (7.5) yields the expression for the maximum profits that a firm of type φ can earn by engaging in centralized FDI:

$$\Pi_{CI}(\varphi) = \begin{cases} (M+1)\varphi p - \left(M\varphi t + F_A \right) \\ \quad - \left((M+1)\varphi\alpha\tau - \frac{((M+1)\alpha\tau\varphi)^2}{2f} \right) & \text{if } \varphi \leq \varphi^* \\ (M+1)\varphi p - \left(M\varphi t + F_A \right) - \frac{f}{2} & \text{otherwise.} \end{cases} \quad (7.7)$$

A few features of this profit function are notable. First, notice that while the function is continuous in φ, its first derivative is discontinuous at φ^* as a firm with this market share has moved the production of all its intermediate inputs offshore. Second, as a firm's market share φ rises, its upstream costs rise, but at a slower rate than if it could not adjust the sourcing of its intermediate inputs. This makes the profit function strictly convex for $\varphi \leq \varphi^*$.

7.3.3 Decentralized FDI

A firm that follows a decentralized FDI strategy opens an assembly plant in each foreign country. This firm incurs the fixed cost $(M+1)F_A$ and pays no shipping costs on the final good. The firm must then decide where to produce each intermediate input. There are three options for sourcing a given intermediate. If an intermediate ω is imported from Home, then no additional fixed costs are incurred and the marginal cost of serving any foreign plant is $c(\omega) = \alpha\tau$. If the production of intermediate ω is concentrated in Center, then the additional fixed cost $f\omega$ is incurred in Center and the marginal cost of serving an assembly plant in Center is zero and is $c(\omega) = \alpha t$ in a peripheral country. Finally, if a firm opens a plant to produce intermediate ω in each of the $M+1$ foreign markets, then the fixed cost associated

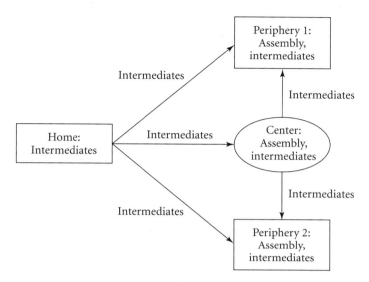

Figure 7.4 Decentralized FDI strategy.

with this intermediate is $(M + 1)f\omega$ and the marginal cost of serving an assembly plant in any foreign country is $c(\omega) = 0$. Figure 7.4 provides a schematic for the structure of production and implied trade patterns of a firm following a decentralized FDI strategy.

Since the fixed cost is increasing in ω, it follows that if any intermediates are produced exclusively in Home, then it is those with the largest ω, and the intermediates that are produced in each of the $(M + 1)$ countries will be those intermediates with the smallest ω. Therefore, two thresholds, ω_1 and ω_2, exist such that intermediates $\omega \geq \omega_2$ are produced in Home and imported by assembly plants, intermediates $\omega \in (\omega_1, \omega_2)$ are produced in Center and imported by assembly plants within the region, and intermediates $\omega \leq \omega_1$ are produced in each foreign country. Using (7.1), the marginal-cost equation for serving peripheral countries can be written

$$(\omega_2 - \omega_1)\alpha t + (1 - \omega_2)\alpha\tau.$$

The term on the left-hand side is the cost of procuring intermediates from Center, and the term on the right-hand side is the cost of procuring intermediates from Home. The marginal-cost equation for serving Center is

$$(1 - \omega_2)\alpha\tau.$$

Note that the local content of production is higher in Center than it is in the periphery. The total fixed cost is

$$(M+1)\left[F_A + f\int_0^{\omega_1}\omega d\omega\right] + f\int_{\omega_1}^{\omega_2}\omega d\omega$$

$$= (M+1)F_A + \frac{f}{2}\omega_2^2 + M\frac{f}{2}\omega_1^2.$$

It follows immediately that the profits of a firm of type φ with investment thresholds ω_2 and ω_1 are

$$\Pi_{DI}(\omega_1,\omega_2;\varphi) = (M+1)\varphi p - (M+1)F_A \tag{7.8}$$

$$- \Big\{\varphi\alpha\left[(M+1)\tau(1-\omega_2) - Mt(\omega_2-\omega_1)\right]$$

$$+ \frac{f}{2}\omega_2^2 + M\frac{f}{2}\omega_1^2\Big\}.$$

The three terms in (7.8) correspond to revenue, downstream costs, and upstream costs respectively.

Assuming an interior solution, the first-order condition for profit maximization with respect to ω_2 is

$$\varphi\alpha[\tau(M+1) - Mt] - f\omega_2 = 0,$$

which implies the following solution for the optimal cutoff ω_2 between building an intermediate in Home and building it in the central location:

$$\omega_2(\varphi) = \begin{cases} \frac{\alpha[\tau(M+1)-Mt]}{f}\varphi & \text{if } \varphi \leq \varphi' \\ 1 & \text{otherwise} \end{cases} \tag{7.9}$$

where

$$\varphi' = \frac{f}{\alpha\left[\tau(M+1) - Mt\right]}. \tag{7.10}$$

Assuming an interior solution, the first-order condition for profit maximization with respect to ω_1 is

$$\alpha\varphi t - f\omega_1 = 0,$$

which implies the following solution for the optimal cutoff ω_1 between building an intermediate in each country and building it exclusively in Center:

$$\omega_1(\varphi) = \begin{cases} \frac{\alpha t}{f}\varphi & \text{if } \varphi \leq \varphi'' \\ 1 & \text{otherwise} \end{cases} \tag{7.11}$$

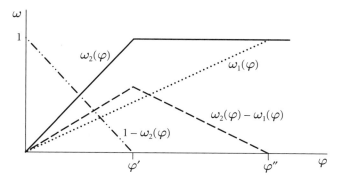

Figure 7.5 The sourcing of intermediate inputs by decentralized multinationals.

where

$$\varphi'' = \frac{f}{\alpha t}. \tag{7.12}$$

Note that the assumption that $\tau > t$ guarantees that $\omega_2 > \omega_1$ and that $\varphi'' > \varphi'$.

This simple framework predicts a rich pattern of intrafirm trade across firms following decentralized FDI strategies as shown in Figure 7.5. As a firm's market size φ increases, the share of intermediates that it sources from home is decreasing (the dotted and dashed line), the share of intermediates that it produces in each peripheral country is increasing (the small dotted line), and the share of intermediates that its affiliates in peripheral countries source from the central country is first increasing, as centrally produced intermediates substitute for imports from the home country, and then decreasing, as locally produced intermediates substitute for centrally produced intermediates. The solid line corresponds to the share of intermediates produced within the region.

Combining equations (7.8)–(7.12) yields the expression for the maximum profits that a firm of type φ can earn by engaging in decentralized foreign investment:

$$\Pi_{DI}(\varphi) \begin{cases} (M+1)\left(\varphi p - F_A\right) \\ \quad -\left\{(M+1)\varphi\alpha\tau - \frac{(\tau(M+1)-Mt)^2\alpha^2}{2f}\varphi^2\right. \\ \quad \left. -\frac{M(\alpha t)^2}{2f}\varphi^2\right\} & \text{if } \varphi \leq \varphi' \ (7.13) \\ (M+1)\left(\varphi p - F_A\right) - \left\{M\varphi\alpha t + \frac{f}{2} - M\frac{(\alpha t)^2}{2f}\varphi^2\right\} & \text{if } \varphi \in (\varphi', \varphi'') \\ (M+1)(\varphi p - F_A - \frac{f}{2}) & \text{otherwise.} \end{cases}$$

As was the case with centralized FDI, the profits of decentralized FDI are convex in a firm's market size as a firm adjusts its upstream costs. While upstream costs are strictly increasing in φ, they are bounded above by $(M + 1)f/2$—the cost of opening plants to produce each intermediate input in each country.

7.3.4 The Structure of International Commerce

The analysis of the selection of firms into modes of serving foreign markets involves comparing the profit functions (7.3), (7.7), and (7.13). Since firms' revenues are independent of their mode choice, the decision between modes depends solely on which mode offers the lowest cost of supplying the market. Further, modes differ in the relative magnitudes of their upstream and downstream costs. Our analysis of mode choice will depend on the relative importance of these two types of costs, which is governed at least in part by the cost of transporting intermediates relative to the cost of transporting final goods (α).

We begin our analysis with the case in which $\alpha = 0$ so that intermediates can be costlessly shipped and upstream costs are zero for all modes. When intermediates can be costlessly shipped, firms face a simple tradeoff between the marginal costs associated with shipping the final good and the fixed costs of building assembly plants. Since the fixed costs are greatest for decentralized FDI, lowest for exports, and

$$\frac{\partial \pi_{DI}(\varphi)}{\partial \varphi} > \frac{\partial \pi_{CI}(\varphi)}{\partial \varphi} > \frac{\partial \pi_X(\varphi)}{\partial \varphi}, \tag{7.14}$$

it follows that the firms with the largest market sizes will opt for decentralized FDI, firms with moderate market sizes will opt for centralized FDI, and the least-productive firms will export. This sorting is akin to the type found in Helpman, Melitz, and Yeaple (2004). The main difference is that the structure of FDI here features a geography that gives rise to centralized FDI.

Complications arise for the case in which $\alpha > 0$. To see why, note that the upstream costs associated with obtaining components are highest for firms following a decentralized FDI strategy and are zero for firms choosing to export the final good from the home country to the foreign region. Since upstream costs differ across modes in terms of their responsiveness to a

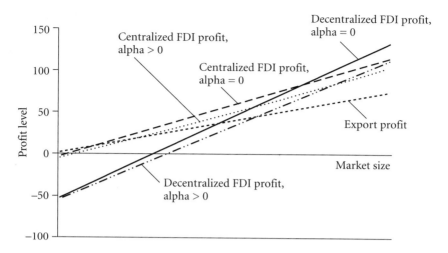

Figure 7.6 Profits as a function of market size and mode choice.

firm's market size, it is not generally possible to establish an ordering akin to (7.14) that holds for all values of φ.

To make progress, we consider the case in which α is so small that upstream costs are small relative to downstream costs. In particular, it can be shown that if

$$\alpha < \alpha^* \equiv \min \left\{ \frac{\tau - t\frac{M}{M+1}}{\tau}, \frac{\tau}{\tau + (\tau - t)} \right\},$$

then the ordering given by (7.14) is preserved. To see the implication of transport costs for intermediates on the mapping from a firm's market size to its mode choice, consider Figure 7.6.[4] The solid lines in this figure correspond to the case in which $\alpha = 0$ while the dashed lines correspond to the case in which $\alpha^* > \alpha > 0$. In both cases, the profit associated with decentralized FDI is highest for firms with the largest market shares, the profit associated with exports is highest for the smallest firms, while the profit for centralized FDI is highest for firms in between these extremes. Because exporters have the lowest upstream costs (they are zero) and because decentralized FDI has the highest upstream costs, an increase in α expands the range of market sizes for which export is the favored mode and shrinks the range of market sizes for which firms opt for decentralized FDI.

Let the cutoff market size between exporting and centralized FDI be given by φ_1 and let the cutoff market size between centralized FDI and decentralized FDI be given by φ_2. Choosing parameter values[5] such that these cutoffs fall below φ^* (that is, at these cutoffs, firms import some intermediates from their parent firms), the threshold φ_1 is implicitly defined by the function

$$\Psi(\varphi_1) = (M+1)\left[\frac{(M+1)(\alpha\tau\varphi_1)^2}{2f} - \tau\varphi_1(1-\alpha)\right] - M\varphi_1 t - F_A = 0,$$

(7.15)

and the threshold φ_2 is implicitly defined by the function

$$\Omega(\varphi_2) = M\left\{\varphi_2 t - \alpha^2\frac{(\varphi_2)^2}{2f}(M+1)(2\tau-t)t - F_A\right\} = 0. \quad (7.16)$$

Note that α^* can be derived from these expressions and the definition of an interior equilibrium. In summary, firms with size $\varphi < \varphi_1$ engage exclusively in export and own no foreign affiliates, firms with size $\varphi \in (\varphi_1, \varphi_2)$ invest exclusively in the central country, and firms with market size $\varphi > \varphi_2$ invest in all M markets in the foreign region.

Now consider the pattern of intrafirm trade between parent and affiliate as a function of a firm's type. The share of intermediates that are imported from the parent is given by $(1 - \widehat{\omega})$. For firms pursuing a centralized FDI strategy; $\widehat{\omega}$ is given by (7.5) while for firms pursuing a decentralized FDI strategy, $\widehat{\omega}$ is given by (7.9). Notice that the threshold intermediate cutoff given by (7.5) exceeds the threshold intermediate cutoff given by (7.9). For a given φ, the affiliates of firms pursuing a centralized FDI strategy import a smaller share of their intermediate inputs from the parent firm than the affiliates of firms that pursue a decentralized FDI strategy.

Firms that concentrate their assembly in one location can lower their cost of delivering a unit of intermediate input to the assembly plant by $\alpha\tau$. Firms that concentrate the marginal intermediate's production in Center must still export that intermediate to affiliates located in the periphery, and so, moving the production of an intermediate to Center reduces the cost by only $\alpha(\tau - t)$. Since, on the margin, firms face the same fixed cost of moving the production of an intermediate offshore, it follows that firms that concentrate assembly in Center have a stronger incentive to reduce their

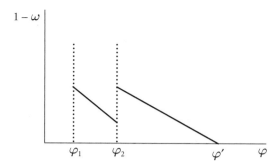

Figure 7.7 Imports from parent firms and firm size.

imports from their parent firm. Hence, local content tends to be higher for centralized firms. This has the implication that the relationship between the share of intermediates imported from the parent and a firm's size is non-monotonic and discontinuous at φ_2, the cutoff threshold firm size between those firms that pursue a centralized FDI strategy and those that pursue a decentralized FDI strategy, as shown in Figure 7.7.

Figure 7.7 has important implications for empirical work. Suppose that a researcher is interested in understanding the relationship between a firm's characteristics and the extent of intrafirm trade. A regression of the share of trade between a parent firm and an affiliate on firm size could yield a positive, negative, or zero coefficient depending on the distribution of firm sizes in the sample. Holding fixed a mode choice, however, the relationship between firm size and propensity to import intermediates is clearly negative.

7.4   Comparative Statics

We now consider the effect of changes in key exogenous variables on two components of the structure of FDI. First, a change in an exogenous variable will alter the mode choice of firms. These effects can be obtained by differentiating the threshold conditions (7.15) and (7.16). Second, holding fixed a firm's mode choice, a change in an exogenous variable will alter the structure of FDI within modes by inducing firms to change their intermediate-input sourcing policies. These effects can be obtained by differentiating equations (7.5), (7.11), and (7.9). Since the sourcing of intermediate inputs depends in part on mode choice, the total change in the location of intermediate-input production depends upon both effects.

First, consider an increase in the interregional transport cost. An increase in τ induces a decrease in φ_1 and an increase in φ_2. Higher interregional transport costs are therefore associated with a smaller share of firms engaged in exporting *and* a smaller share of firms engaged in decentralized FDI. The decrease in φ_1 is a straightforward result of the proximity-concentration trade-off built into the model.

The increase in φ_2 requires more explanation. This result obtains because the upstream costs of firms engaged in centralized FDI are more sensitive to interregional trade costs than the upstream costs of firms engaged in decentralized FDI (see Figure 7.7). The result has the interesting implication that for any peripheral country, higher interregional transport costs are associated with a smaller number of foreign investors entering the country. This might help explain why many studies find that FDI is actually decreasing on average in distance between the host and the source country. Moreover, it has the interesting implication that the effect of distance on the volume of FDI to a country interacts with that country's centrality: distance between a source and host country increases the volume of FDI in central locations and reduces it in peripheral locations.

Second, consider the effect of an increase in interregional trade costs on the sourcing of intermediates. Differentiating equations (7.5), (7.11), and (7.9) establishes that an increase in inter-regional trade costs induces a decrease in the share of intermediates sourced from the home country. This result is consistent with the finding in Hanson, Mataloni, and Slaughter (2005) who show that imports of intermediate inputs by the affiliates of U.S. multinational enterprises is decreasing in trade costs between the United States and the host country. Interaffiliate trade in the aggregate also falls because of the decrease in φ_2: firms engaged in centralized FDI demand fewer inputs from Home.

Third, consider the effect of an increase in intraregional trade costs. Total differentiation of (7.15) establishes that an increase in t results in an increase in the threshold φ_1. Hence, a reduction in intraregional trade costs, such as might occur with a preferential trade agreement, reduces the volume of final good imports from Home and increases the number of firms conducting FDI in the foreign region. An increase in t also leads to a decrease in the threshold φ_2 so that a reduction in intraregional trade costs is associated with a tendency for firms to centralize their foreign production. These results are consistent with recent empirical work presented in Chen (2006). She finds that the introduction of a preferential trade agreement within a region tends to increase U.S. FDI to that region but that FDI becomes more concentrated in particularly attractive countries within the region.

With respect to the effect of an increase in intraregional transport costs on the sourcing of intermediates, intermediate imports from Home increase for two reasons. First, as firms switch from a centralized to a decentralized FDI strategy, they increase their intermediates imports from Home because local content is higher among centralized multinationals. Second, holding fixed a firm's mode choice, an increase in intraregional trade costs induces firms to substitute the production of inputs away from Center toward Home.

Finally, an increase in the size of the foreign region, as measured by the number of markets in which there is demand M, has very similar implications to a reduction in intraregional transport costs. First, there is an increase in φ_1 and a decrease in φ_2: the number of firms engaged in centralized FDI expands at the expense of both exporters and firms engaged in decentralized FDI. Second, local content increases as centralized FDI expands at the expense of decentralized FDI and as a larger regional market induces firms to incur the additional fixed costs associated with moving production offshore.

7.5   An Extension and an Application

To illustrate the usefulness of this simple model, we consider an extension of the model to a more complex geography and an application of the model to the analysis of rules of origin in a regional trade agreement.[6]

7.5.1 Multiple Foreign Regions

Suppose that there are two identical foreign regions that firms from Home wish to serve. A firm that locates an assembly plant in the center country of one region can serve any market in the other foreign region at transport cost δ, where $\tau > \delta > t$. In this sense, an affiliate located in the central country of one region is "nearer" to another region than is Home and so can act as an export platform to that region. For simplicity, assume that $\alpha = 0$ so that the complications created by the cost-of-components effect do not arise.

This specification introduces a second kind of centralization strategy. In the first centralization strategy, a firm opens a single affiliate in one of the two foreign regions and then exports to all foreign countries from that region. In the second centralization strategy, the firm opens an affiliate in both central countries and ships its final good to each country within its region only.

The pattern of specialization is very similar to the one derived above. The larger a firm's market size φ, the more affiliates the firm has. The firms with the smallest φ export from home, while the firms with the highest φ own an affiliate in each foreign country. Among the intermediate ranges of φ, the firms with relatively smaller φ open a single affiliate in the center country of one region and that affiliate exports its final good both within and across foreign regions, while firms with relatively higher values of φ open an affiliate in each central country and each affiliate then exports final goods within its region.

This pattern of affiliate ownership across firms is intuitively sensible. As a firm's market size grows, its international production network first expands *across* regions. As it becomes even larger, it then begins to expand its affiliate network *within* regions.

The case in which intermediate inputs are costly to trade introduces additional complications, and there are many possible cases that can arise depending on the relative magnitudes of the parameters. For instance, it is possible that a firm opens an assembly affiliate in both central countries but continues to concentrate its production of some of its intermediates (those with relatively high fixed costs) in one of the two central locations and then ships those intermediates to the other foreign country.

7.5.2 Rules of Origin

To illustrate how the framework can be used for policy analysis, consider the following reinterpretation of the model. Suppose that the difference in trade costs $\tau - t$ reflects the size of the tariff on outside goods in a regional trade agreement. Once one has reinterpreted the difference in trade costs within a region relative to between regions in this way, there is no need to think of a central location. It is still true, however, that a firm choosing a "centralized" FDI strategy will assemble the final good in one location and any intermediates produced within that region will be produced in the country of assembly.

Suppose that for the intraregional exports of a multinational affiliate to enjoy this tariff reduction, the firm must have a minimum local content with region of $\underline{\omega}$. What impact does this policy have on the structure of FDI? Since only the final good uses intermediate inputs, rules of origin only directly affect the profits of firms choosing a centralized FDI strategy. Consider $\underline{\omega} = \omega^*(\varphi)$, where the function $\omega^*(\cdot)$ is given by equation (7.5) and $\underline{\varphi} \in (\varphi_1, \varphi_2)$, where φ_1 is the smallest market size of a firm that follows a centralized FDI strategy and φ_2 is the largest market size of a firm that follows a centralized FDI strategy when there are no rules of origin. For the firm with market size φ_1, the rules of origin lower the profit associated with centralized FDI relative to export and so induce that firm to export rather than engage in FDI within the region. For firms with higher market size φ_2, the rules of origin do not bind and so they do not affect the firm's choice of FDI strategy. This implies that there exists a new cutoff market-size threshold $\widetilde{\varphi}_1 \in (\varphi_1, \underline{\varphi})$ that is implicitly defined by

$$\Pi_{CI}(\widetilde{\varphi}_1 : \omega = \underline{\omega}) = \Pi_X(\widetilde{\varphi}_1),$$

where the profit of centralized FDI $\Pi_{CI}(\cdot)$ is given by (7.4) and the profit of exporting $\Pi_X(\cdot)$ is given by (7.3). Rules of origin have opposing effects on the size of local affiliate production. Firms with $\varphi \in (\varphi_1, \widetilde{\varphi}_1)$ cease to produce in the country at all, while firms $\varphi \in (\widetilde{\varphi}_1, \underline{\varphi})$ are induced to increase the share of intermediate inputs that they produce within the region.

The total effect of the rules of origin on the volume of local production is ambiguous. On the one hand, local production falls on the *extensive* margin as fewer firms produce in the region, while on the other hand, local production rises on the *intensive* margin as some firms are induced to open plants for the production of intermediates. The relative size of these two effects depends in part on the empirical distribution of φ, which is a variable that likely varies across industries (see Helpman, Melitz, and Yeaple 2004). For a high enough floor on local content, no firm would choose a strategy of centralized FDI, and the volume of within-region trade in final goods would collapse. Note that in this framework, rules of origin induce firms that stay in the market to lower their marginal costs.

7.6   Firm Heterogeneity and Central Locations: Empirics

In this section, we conduct two analyses of the data on U.S. multinational enterprises (MNE). First, we ask whether the assumptions of the model are consistent with the behavior of U.S. MNE. Do the multinationals that enter centrally located countries tend to export final goods and intermediates more than other countries? Second, we test the model's sorting prediction. Is the composition of multinationals that enter centrally located countries skewed toward those firms that produce in relatively few locations?

Our analysis relies on firm-level data from the 1999 Benchmark Survey of U.S. Direct Investment Abroad, conducted by the U.S. Bureau of Economic Analysis (BEA). In benchmark years, the BEA requires all U.S. firms with direct investment abroad to list all of the countries in which they own foreign affiliates. This requirement is independent of the affiliate's size so that the scope of this data is comprehensive. As an affiliate becomes larger, the BEA requires the U.S. parent to provide an increasingly larger set of information concerning the affiliate's operations, including the volume of its affiliate's exports to both related and unrelated customers in other foreign countries. From this database we consider all U.S. MNE, whose main line of business is in manufacturing, and their manufacturing affiliates.

7.6.1 Exports and Central Locations

We begin the analysis by asking whether there is in fact a tendency for affiliates located in centrally located countries to export heavily to third countries. We consider regressions of the form

$$EX_{ik} = \eta_i + \beta \cdot FMA_k + \alpha \cdot Z_k + e_{ik},$$

where EX_{ik} is a measure of the logarithm of affiliate i's exports from country k. There are two measures of exports. The first is the affiliate's exports to related affiliates located in other countries other than the United States. The second is the affiliate's exports to unrelated parties located in other countries other than the United States. Exports to related parties is a measure of cross-border vertical specialization, while exports to unrelated parties is a measure of the extent of export-platform FDI.

The other variables are defined as follows: η_i is a fixed effect by firm, FMA_k is a proxy for the centrality of country k, and Z_k is a vector of controls for other characteristics of country k. The key variable of interest is foreign market access (FMA). This variable is a proxy for the centrality of a country's location. We follow Redding and Venables (2004) in our construction of our measure of foreign-market access. The variable is defined as

$$FMA_k = \sum_{j \neq k} \exp(ptn_j)^{\widehat{\lambda}_j} dist_{kj}^{\widehat{\delta}_1} border_{kj}^{\widehat{\delta}_2} lang_{kj}^{\widehat{\delta}_3} RTA_{kj}^{\widehat{\delta}_4}, \qquad (7.17)$$

where j indexes other countries, ptn_j is an indicator variable for country j, $dist_{kj}$ is the distance between country j and country k, $border_{kj}$ is an indicator variable that is equal to one when countries j and k share a common border, $lang_{kj}$ is an indicator variable that is equal to one when countries j and k share a common language, RTA_{kj} is an indicator variable that is equal to one if countries k and j are partners in the same regional free trade agreement, and $\widehat{\lambda}_j$, $\widehat{\delta}_1$, $\widehat{\delta}_2$, $\widehat{\delta}_3$, and $\widehat{\delta}_4$ are coefficients estimated from a gravity equation.[7] Note that since our interest is on exports to third countries and not to the United States, FMA does not include the United States as a partner country.

The variables in Z_k are standard controls from gravity equations. The gravity variables include GDP_k, the logarithm of the host country's GDP; $ENGLISH_k$, which is the share of the population that speaks English; $DIST_k$, which is the logarithm of the distance between the United States and the country in question; ADJ_k, which is a dummy for Mexico and Canada; and $GDPPC_k$, which is the logarithm of a country's GDP per capita. Descriptive statistics for these variables are shown in Table 7.2.

Table 7.2 Descriptive statistics

	Mean	Std deviation
Number	1.21	1.15
Median locations	2.57	0.85
FMA	15.92	0.78
GDP	25.76	1.77
GDPPC	9.26	0.79
DIST	8.87	0.61
ENGFRAC	0.16	0.34
ADJ	0.05	0.22

Note: All variables except ENGFRAC and ADJ are in logarithms.

Table 7.3 Exports and central locations

	Logarithm of intrafirm exports (1)	Logarithm of other exports (2)
FMA	0.820	0.827
	(0.096)	(0.108)
GDP	−0.373	−0.529
	(0.089)	(0.099)
GDPPC	0.149	0.524
	(0.148)	(0.141)
DIST	−0.301	−0.077
	(0.234)	(0.185)
ENGLISH	0.211	0.151
	(0.190)	(0.141)
ADJ	−1.594	−1.142
	(0.602)	(0.542)
N	1,536	1,354
R-squared	0.174	0.222

Note: Both specifications include fixed effects by firm. All variables except *ENGLISH* and *ADJ* are in logarithms. Standard errors shown in parentheses are adjusted for heteroskedasticity and clustering by country.

The results of these regressions are shown in Table 7.3. The coefficient estimates corresponding to intrafirm trade are in column 1, and the results corresponding to unrelated-party exports are shown in column 2. Of particular interest is the result shown in the first row. Affiliates located in central locations export substantially more to both related and unrelated parties than to affiliates located elsewhere. Interestingly, the volume of both types of exports is decreasing in a country's GDP. The coefficient on *GDPPC* is positive for both types of exports but is statistically insignificant for related party exports while larger and statistically significant for unrelated party exports. Pure export-platform FDI is more common among developed countries while there is greater heterogeneity with respect to related party trade.

7.6.2 Central Locations and the Sorting of Multinationals

We now consider the tendency for multinationals to sort into countries based on their degree of centrality. We consider two measures of U.S. MNE activity to assess whether central locations attract a large number of U.S. multinationals with small international production networks. The first measure VOL_{jk} gauges the volume of activity of U.S. MNE in country k and industry j as captured by the number of U.S. multinationals that own an affiliate in the country k and industry j. The second measure $COMP_{jk}$ gauges the composition of U.S. MNE entrants into country k and industry j. This variable is the number of countries in which the median U.S. multinational entrant into country k owns affiliates. As this variable becomes smaller, the composition of investors is becoming skewed toward firms with smaller multinational networks.

We estimate the following specification:

$$y_{jk} = \eta_j + \beta \cdot FMA_k + \alpha \cdot Z'_k + e_{jk},$$

where $y_{jk} \in \{VOL_{jk}, COMP_{jk}\}$, FMA_k is the logarithm of the measure of country k's foreign-market access as calculated in (7.17), Z'_k is a vector of controls considered in the previous section, and η_j is a fixed effect for three-digit NAICs industry j. The variables in Z'_k are standard controls from gravity equations that were described in Section 7.6.1 plus a set of indicator variables for a country's region. These indicators have the effect of normalizing values of FMA_k for a country's neighborhood in order to better capture centrality. The model predicts that the coefficient on FMA_k should be positive when the dependent variable is VOL_{jk} and negative when the dependent variable is $COMP_{jk}$: central locations attract more firms than peripheral locations, and these additional firms are those that concentrate their production in a few offshore sites. The equation is estimated via ordinary least squares.

The results are shown in Table 7.4. Column 1 corresponds to coefficient estimates when the dependent variable is VOL_{ik}, and column 2 reports the coefficient estimates when the dependent variable is $COMP_{ik}$. Standard errors are heteroskedasticity consistent and allow for clustering by country and are shown in parentheses below their coefficient estimates.

Looking first at column 1, we see that all the coefficient estimates are positive and statistically different from zero at standard levels. U.S. multinationals are more likely to enter countries in central locations (FMA), that have large domestic demands (GDP), that have relatively high GDP per capital ($GDPPC$), that are relatively distant from the United States ($DIST$), and that speak English ($ENGLISH$). Canada and Mexico receive a

Table 7.4 Volume and composition as a function of country characteristics

	VOL (Number of entrants) (1)	COMP (Median locations) (2)
FMA	0.327	−0.213
	(0.084)	(0.057)
GDP	0.291	−0.092
	(0.026)	(0.023)
GDPPC	0.336	−0.108
	(0.074)	(0.047)
DIST	0.282	−0.025
	(0.144)	(0.113)
ENGLISH	0.565	−0.604
	(0.118)	(0.093)
ADJ	0.909	−0.493
	(0.112)	(0.102)
N	678	678
R-squared	0.739	0.654

Note: All variables except ENGFRAC and ADJ are in logarithms. Coefficients on three-digit industry dummies and regional dummies are suppressed. Standard errors are robust to heteroskedasticity and allow for clustering by country and are shown in parentheses below the coefficient estimates.

disproportionate amount of U.S. foreign direct investment as indicated by the positive coefficient on ADJ.

The positive coefficient on FMA confirms our hypothesis that geography is an important determinant of foreign direct investment patterns. This result is reminiscent of Blonigen et al. (2005). Interestingly, when FMA is dropped from the regression, the coefficient on DIST becomes zero (specification not shown), suggesting that it is important to control for regional geography to understand the impact of distance on FDI volumes.

Now consider the coefficient estimates in column 2. The first key observation is that the country characteristics that predict greater volume of U.S. multinational entry also predict a different composition of entrants into that country. Of key interest to our study is the negative and statistically significant coefficient estimate on FMA: countries with greater foreign-market potential tend to attract U.S. multinationals that are active in fewer locations than countries with lower foreign-market potential. This result is consistent with a key prediction of the model: firms whose international production is limited in scope concentrate their production in central locations.

7.7   Conclusion

This chapter makes the case that it is important to account for firm heterogeneity and the geography of regions to understand the structure of multinational enterprises. We analyzed a model that allows for both vertical and horizontally integrated multinationals in a multicountry setting. The model captures in the simplest possible way the complex logistical problems facing multinationals. Firms can choose between three broad strategies for assembling their final goods for foreign markets: home assembly followed by interregional trade, assembly in a central foreign region followed by intraregional trade, and assembly in each foreign location thereby avoiding all trade. Once a firm has chosen where to assemble its product, it must then decide where to produce intermediate inputs. Intermediates are costly to ship and since they vary in their transport costs, the optimal production location may vary over intermediates.

The analysis shows that firms with more popular products, and hence bigger market shares in any given foreign country, will organize their production within foreign regions in a very different fashion than firms with smaller market shares. Smaller multinationals centralize their production in central locations, while larger firms open assembly affiliates in many countries while centralizing the production of many components in central locations. These results are consistent with our empirical finding that countries with large market potential attract a disproportionate number of multinational firms and that these firms are on average less well represented in less centralized locations.

The model also has a number of interesting comparative statics. For instance, because centralized firms optimally concentrate a larger fraction of their intermediate-inputs production within a foreign region, an increase in interregional transport costs reduces the FDI in peripheral countries as firms substitute a centralized FDI strategy for a decentralized FDI strategy. This result may help us to understand why, as transport costs have fallen, the value of foreign sales of the affiliates of U.S. multinationals has been increasing faster than their value-added but more slowly than their volumes of trade to both affiliated and unaffiliated customers.

The key role played by central locations also suggests that regions that are not integrated attract fewer multinationals. This result may suggest why certain regions, such as Latin America, continue to attract relatively little FDI. The model has other empirical implications that would be worthwhile to test. For instance, as affiliates become larger, their local content should be increasing, while their participation in interaffiliate trade relative to value-added should exhibit an inverted U-shape in affiliate size.

Finally, the framework has been kept as simple as possible for the purpose of exposition but could be extended in many dimensions. For instance, it is conceptually straightforward to introduce product market competition and heterogeneity in productivity to generate heterogeneity in market shares. Doing so would introduce the types of complementarities that have been identified in the recent work of Yeaple (2003) and Grossman, Helpman, and Szeidl (2006). Allowing free entry by country would considerably complicate the model but would endogenize demand levels in each location, a possibly important extension. The assumptions that all intermediates use no inputs and are costlessly assembled into final output is also restrictive. Many intermediates require many stages of production in their own right, and a technology that captured the sequential nature of production might offer additional insights into the effect of geography on foreign direct investment. The current formulation abstracts from factor price differences across countries on vertical specialization in order to focus purely on the role of geography, but factor price differences are surely important determinants of FDI patterns in their own right and may also interact with geography. Finally, while we assumed away the possibility of outsourcing for simplicity, the framework could be applied to situations in which some intermediates are produced by the firm and others obtained arm's length on markets.

ACKNOWLEDGMENTS

The statistical analysis of firm-level data on U.S. multinational corporations reported in this chapter was conducted at the International Investment Division, U.S. Bureau of Economic Analysis, under arrangements that maintained legal confidentiality requirements. Views expressed are those of the author and do not necessarily reflect those of the U.S. Bureau of Economic Analysis. The author would like to thank the editors of this volume and Maurice Kugler for helpful comments and suggestions.

NOTES

1. Also see Neary (2007).

2. This formulation is consistent with the hub-and-spokes framework that occasionally appears in economic geography models.

3. In the case of monopolistic competition with CES preferences, a firm's revenues are monotonically decreasing in its marginal cost, which in turn is decreasing in a firm's productivity. What this specification rules out are certain types of "complementarities" that can arise when the reduction of a firm's marginal cost raises the volume of its sales. See, for instance, Grossman, Helpman, and Szeidl (2006).

4. Note that parameter values have been chosen so that the cutoff market sizes between the three modes occur for values of φ such that at these thresholds, firms engaged in FDI import at least some intermediates from their parent firms.

5. To obtain such an interior solution, one only need assume that F_A is sufficiently small.

6. The author would like to thank Elhanan Helpman and Thierry Verdier for inspiring this section.

7. The gravity data is from Andrew Rose's website (corrected in places using CEPII data), and the trade data is from Feenstra et al. (2005).

REFERENCES

Blonigen, Bruce. 2005. "A Review of the Empirical Literature on FDI Determinants." *Atlantic Economic Journal* 33:383–403.

Blonigen, Bruce, Ronald Davies, Glen Waddell, and Helen Naughton. 2005. "FDI in Space: Spatial Autoregressive Relationships in Foreign Direct Investment." Mimeo, University of Oregon.

Chen, Maggie. 2006. "Regional Economic Integration and Geographic Concentration of U.S. Multinational Firms." Mimeo, George Washington University.

Ekholm, Karolina, Rikard Forslid, and James Markusen. 2003. "Export Platform Foreign Direct Investment." NBER working paper 9517.

Feenstra, Robert, Robert Lipsey, Haiyan Deng, Alyson Ma, and Hengyon Mo. 2005. "World Trade Flows: 1962–2000." NBER working paper 11040 (January).

Grossman, Gene, Elhanan Helpman, and Adam Szeidl. 2006. "Optimal Integration Strategies for the Multinational Firm." *Journal of International Economics* 70:216–38.

Hanson, Gordon, Raymond Mataloni, and Matthew Slaughter. 2001. "Expansion Strategies of U.S. Multinational Firms," in *Brookings Trade Forum*, eds. Dani Rodrik and Susan Collins.

———. 2005. "Vertical Production Networks in Multinational Firms." *Review of Economics and Statistics* 87:664–78.

Helpman, Elhanan, Marc Melitz, and Stephen Yeaple. 2004. "Exports versus FDI with Heterogeneous Firms." *American Economic Review* 94(1):300–316.

Lai, Huiwen, and Susan Zhu. 2006. "U.S. Exports and Multinational Production." *Review of Economics and Statistics* 88(3):531–48.

Melitz, Marc. 2003. "The Impact of Trade on Intra-Industry Reallocations and Aggregate Industry Productivity." *Econometrica* 71:1695–1725.

Neary, Peter. 2007. "Trade Costs and Foreign Direct Investment." Mimeo, University of Oxford.

Redding, Stephen, and Anthony Venables. 2004. "Economic Geography and International Inequality." *Journal of International Economics* 62(1):53–82.

UNCTAD. 2004. *World Investment Report*. United Nations Publication, Geneva.

Yeaple, Stephen. 2003. "The Complex Integration Strategies of Multinationals and Cross Country Dependencies in the Structure of Foreign Direct Investment." *Journal of International Economics* 60(2):293–314.

— 8 —

Export Dynamics in Colombia

Firm-Level Evidence

JONATHAN EATON, MARCELA ESLAVA,
MAURICE KUGLER, AND JAMES R. TYBOUT

8.1   Introduction

Research in international trade, both theoretical and quantitative, is increasingly focused on the role of firm heterogeneity in shaping trade flows. One strand of the literature shows how firm-specific productivity shocks affect the mix of exporting firms and their foreign sales volumes (e.g., Clerides, Lach, and Tybout 1998; Bernard and Jensen 1999; Melitz 2003; Bernard et al. 2003; Das, Roberts, and Tybout 2007; Bernard et al. 2007). These studies provide insight into why some producers export and others do not, and into the role of market entry costs in shaping export dynamics. Another strand of the literature documents and interprets the relationship between firms' productivity levels and the collection of foreign markets that they serve (Eaton, Kortum, and Kramarz 2004, 2007). These papers report findings that most exporting firms sell only to one foreign market, with the frequency of firms' selling to multiple markets declining with the number of destinations. At the same time, firms selling only to a small number of markets tend to sell to the most popular ones. Less popular markets are served by firms that export very widely. These patterns are consistent with the notion that firms with relatively low marginal costs can profitably exploit relatively more foreign markets.

While both strands of the literature have furthered our understanding of the relationships between productivity distributions and trade flows, the necessary data have not been available to study both export dynamics and destination-specific flows for the same set of producers. Also, although several papers have examined the relationship between individual producer

231

decisions and aggregate export trajectories, they have done so only for selected manufacturing industries (Roberts and Tybout 1997b; Das, Roberts,
and Tybout 2007). This chapter exploits comprehensive transactions-level
trade data from Colombia to generate a new set of stylized facts on both
issues.

Our analysis proceeds in several steps. After reviewing, in Sections 8.2
and 8.3, patterns of aggregate exports across destination countries and over
time, in Section 8.4 we decompose export growth into two parts: changes
in sales volume among incumbent exporters ("the intensive margin") and
changes in the set of exporting firms ("the extensive margin"). Next, in
Section 8.5, we track the behavior of "cohorts" of exporters from their first
year in foreign markets onward. Finally, in Section 8.6, we characterize
firms' transition paths as they change the set of export markets that they
serve.

Several key patterns emerge. First, in any one year, almost all export expansion or contraction comes from changes in sales by firms that have been
exporting for at least one year. This dominance of existing firms is despite
the fact that one-third to one-half of all exporters are new entrants in a typical year. These new firms by and large do not add much to export growth
simply because (1) the majority do not last more than a year and (2) their
sales are very small. Second, however, the new exporters who *do* survive
their first year grow especially rapidly for several years thereafter and together account for about half of the total expansion in merchandise trade
over the course of a decade. An explanation for this pattern is that exporters
and importers frequently experiment with small-scale transactions, and
while most of these experiments fail, those that prove mutually profitable
quickly lead to larger shipments. Third, as exporters add or drop markets,
they appear to follow certain geographic patterns. For example, those that
begin by exporting to Latin American destinations are more likely to add
markets than those that begin by exporting to the United States. This pattern may partly reflect the nature of the goods being shipped, but it may
also mean that certain markets are well-suited to serve as "testing grounds"
for new exporters who wish to learn about their foreign-market potential.

8.2 Data

Our dataset includes all export transactions by Colombian firms between
1996 and 2005. Each transaction is recorded separately, and we aggre-

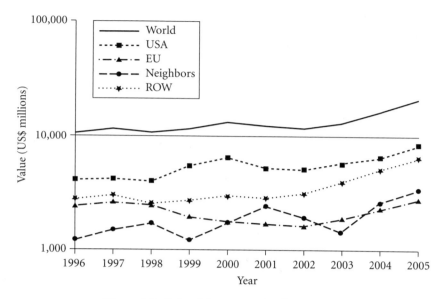

Figure 8.1 Colombian exports by destination.

gate transactions by a given firm to obtain total exports by that firm in each year. A transaction record includes the firm's tax ID (which serves as a time-invariant identifier), a product code, the value of the transaction in U.S. dollars, and the country of destination. Because we use the same data that are used for official statistics, the merchandise exports in our dataset aggregate to within 1% of total merchandise exports reported by the Colombian Bureau of Statistics (Departamento Administrativo Nacional de Estadística or DANE).[1]

Before turning to the firm-level data themselves, we set the stage by reviewing the aggregate movements in Colombian exports over the period we are considering. Figure 8.1 depicts annual Colombian merchandise exports from 1996 through 2005 (in current U.S. dollars) to external markets. It also breaks out exports to several significant destinations: (1) the United States, (2) the European Union, and (3) Venezuela and Ecuador, Colombia's contiguous neighbors with active cross-border trade.[2] Note that the first seven years exhibit alternating periods of modest growth and decline, with drops in 1998, 2001, and 2002. Growth picks up again in 2003 and then accelerates in the most recent two years. These patterns are reflected closely in exports to the United States, Colombia's largest destination in terms of overall value. Colombia's exports to the European Union, on the other hand, experience a much longer and more pronounced decline over the years 1999 through 2002, recovering to their 1997 level only at the end of the period.[3] Colombian exports to its neighbors have grown overall but have been much more volatile than exports to other destinations, with sharp declines in 1999, 2002, and 2003. These overall patterns should be kept in mind as we turn to the firm-level activity underlying them.

8.3   Total Exports and the Number of Firms: The Cross Section

With our firm-level data we can decompose aggregate exports into (1) the number of firms selling and (2) average sales per firm. Denoting by $X_n(t)$ aggregate Colombian exports to market n in year t, by $N_n(t)$ the number of firms selling there, and by $\bar{x}_n(t)$ average sales per firm we can write the identity:

$$\ln X_n(t) = \ln N_n(t) + \ln \bar{x}_n(t).$$

Figure 8.2 provides a quick sense of the contribution of the two terms on the right to the term on the left by plotting $N_n(t)$ against $X_n(t)$. Each data point represents a specific destination in a specific year. The relationship is clearly upward sloping, indicating that the extensive margin (more firms) plays an important role.

A regression of $\ln N_n(t)$ against $\ln X_n(t)$ provides a measure of the average contribution of entry to changes in the value of exports. The implied margin is 0.54, meaning that, in comparing two destination-years, a doubling of export volume reflects just over 50% more firms. An implication, of course, is that sales per firm rise by slightly less than 50%.

A similar exercise is conducted by Eaton, Kortum, and Kramarz (2004), who relate the total number of French exporters to the market size (rather than total exports, as we use here) of the destination for a 1986 cross section. They find a margin of entry of just under two-thirds. To the extent that total exports of a particular country are proportional to market size (as implied by the standard gravity formulation), the result then implies that the number of French exporters should rise with total French exports with the

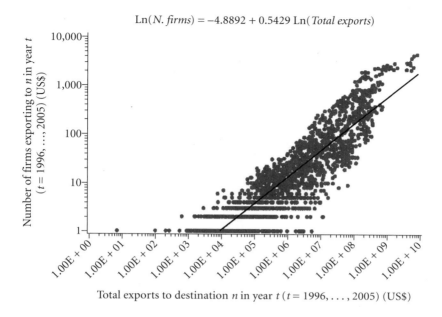

Figure 8.2 Number of firms and total exports to a given destination, 1996–2005.

same elasticity. The lower elasticity we find for Colombia seems to be related to the fact that many destinations are served by just a few, frequently just one or two, Colombian firms. Note in Figure 8.2 that the relationship between the two margins becomes much tighter for destinations served by ten or more firms. In the case of France, no market is served by fewer than sixty French exporters.

Note also in Figure 8.2 that many of the destinations with only one Colombian exporter purchased rather large volumes, suggesting that larger, probably more established, exporters tend to be those that explore new destinations. On the other hand, the destinations that attract the most Colombian exporters tend to purchase relatively little per exporter. These destinations may present Colombian exporters with relatively low entry-cost barriers and/or a diversified collection of potential buyers. Either characteristic would make them attractive to new exporters who wish to try out foreign markets on a small scale. We consider these possibilities further in Section 8.6.

8.4   Decomposing Growth: Continuing Firms, Entry, and Exit

Having seen the importance of the extensive margin in explaining cross-sectional variation, we now ask how much it contributes to changes over time. We first look at how growth in exports reflects the contributions of continuing firms, entrants, and exiters using the identity

$$\frac{X_{nCO}(t) - X_{nCO}(t-1)}{\left[X_{nCO}(t-1) + X_{nCO}(t)\right]/2} \tag{8.1}$$

$$= \left(\frac{\displaystyle\sum_{j \in CN_n^{t-1,t}} \left[x_n(j, t-1) + x_n(j, t)\right]/2}{\left[X_{nCO}(t-1) + X_{nCO}(t)\right]/2}\right)$$

$$\times \left(\frac{\displaystyle\sum_{j \in CN_n^{t-1,t}} \left[x_n(j, t) - x_n(j, t-1)\right]}{\displaystyle\sum_{j \in CN_n^{t-1,t}} \left[x_n(j, t-1) + x_n(j, t)\right]/2}\right)$$

$$+ \frac{NEN_n^{t-1,t}\overline{x}_n(t-1)}{\left[X_{nCO}(t-1) + X_{nCO}(t)\right]/2} + \frac{\displaystyle\sum_{j \in EN_n^{t-1,t}} \left[x_n(j, t) - \overline{x}_n(t-1)\right]}{\left[X_{nCO}(t-1) + X_{nCO}(t)\right]/2}$$

$$- \frac{NEX_n^{t-1,t}\overline{x}_n(t-1)}{\left[X_{nCO}(t-1) + X_{nCO}(t)\right]/2} - \frac{\displaystyle\sum_{j \in EX_n^{t-1,t}} \left[x_n(j, t-1) - \overline{x}_n(t-1)\right]}{\left[X_{nCO}(t-1) + X_{nCO}(t)\right]/2}.$$

Here $X_{nCO}(t)$ denotes total Colombian exports to destination n in year t, and $x_n(j, t)$ is exports by firm j to destination n in period t. The terms $CN_n^{t-1,t}$, $EN_n^{t-1,t}$, and $EX_n^{t-1,t}$ represent, respectively, the set of firms that exported to n in $t-1$ and t, that exported in t but not $t-1$, and that exported in $t-1$ and not t. We refer to these sets of firms as *pairwise continuing*, *pairwise entering*, and *pairwise exiting*. $NEN_n^{t-1,t}$ and $NEX_n^{t-1,t}$ represent the number of firms in the $EN_n^{t-1,t}$ and $EX_n^{t-1,t}$ sets, respectively. The term $\overline{x}_n(t-1)$ represents average exports of a firm to destination n in period $t-1$.[4]

The left-hand side of equation (8.1) measures the growth in exports between $t - 1$ and t. The expression on the first line of the right-hand side represents the contribution to growth of pairwise continuing firms, defined here as those that exported in both periods. It equals the share of continuing firms' exports over the two years multiplied by the growth in their sales.

The second and third lines measure the contributions of entry and exit, respectively, to export growth. The contribution of entry is expressed as the sum of two terms: (1) the growth in exports implied by the increase in the number of exporters *if new firms had the same average sales as those of the average firm in period $t - 1$*; and (2) the difference between exports of entrants and those of the average firm in $t - 1$. The first term is thus gross percentage entry in terms of numbers of firms, and the sum of the first and second is the total contribution of entry to growth. Similarly, the contribution of exit is expressed as the sum of the contraction that would have occurred *if each exiting firm had been as large as the average $t - 1$ exporter*, and a term that corrects for the fact that exiting firms are relatively small.

8.4.1 Aggregate Growth

Table 8.1 presents the results of applying equation (8.1) to decompose aggregate export growth, year by year. Cross-year averages of the growth components are presented in the last row. Also, to highlight the cumulative effects of entry and exit, the next-to-last row presents a cross-decade application of the decomposition. This latter set of figures treats all exporters observed in 2005 but not in 1996 as entering firms, all exporters observed in 1996 but not 2005 as exiting firms, and exporters observed in both years as continuers.[5]

The calculations in this table pool all the destinations. The main line for each component represents the contribution to growth itself by the corresponding term, and the expression in parentheses below is the percentage contribution to the total change. Similarly, Figure 8.3 shows year-to-year export growth disaggregated into the three basic components of equation (8.1) for all destinations. In addition to the contributions of continuing firms, entry, and exit, it also shows the *net* effect of entry and exit.

Table 8.1 and Figure 8.3 indicate that continuing firms drive most of the year-to-year fluctuations, although much less so after 2001. Note, for

Table 8.1 Contribution of pairwise entry and exit to the growth of total exports between $t - 1$ and t

	Left-hand side	Right-hand side	
		Contribution of pairwise continuers	
Year (t)	Growth of exports (1) $\dfrac{X_{CO}(t)-X_{CO}(t-1)}{\left(\frac{X_{CO}(t-1)+X_{CO}(t)}{2}\right)}$	Continuers' share in $t-1$ exports (2) $\dfrac{\sum\limits_{j\in CN^{t-1,t}}\frac{x(j,t-1)+x(j,t)}{2}}{\left(\frac{X_{CO}(t-1)+X_{CO}(t)}{2}\right)}$	Growth of exports by continuers (3) $\dfrac{\sum\limits_{j\in CN^{t-1,t}}[x(j,t)-x(j,t-1)]}{\sum\limits_{j\in CN^{t-1,t}}\frac{x(j,t-1)+x(j,t)}{2}}$
1997	8.1% (100%)	95.9% (119%)	10.1%
1998	−5.9% (100%)	95.9% (110%)	−6.8%
1999	6.0% (100%)	97.4% (105%)	6.5%
2000	12.6% (100%)	98.3% (96%)	12.3%
2001	−6.4% (100%)	98.1% (106%)	−6.9%
2002	−3.3% (100%)	98.4% (84%)	−2.9%
2003	9.8% (100%)	98.1% (89%)	8.9%
2004	24.1% (100%)	97.2% (91%)	22.6%
2005	23.5% (100%)	95.8% (81%)	19.8%
$t=2005$ $t-1=1996$	66.2% (100%)	77.4% (74%)	63.0%
Annual average	7.6% (100%)	97.2% (90%)	7.1%

	Right-hand side			
	Contribution of pairwise gross entry		Contribution of pairwise gross exit	
	Added number of firms (4)	Exports of entering firms relative to the average (5)	Dropped number of firms (6)	Exports of exiting firms relative to the average (7)
Year (t)	$\dfrac{NEN^{t-1,t}*\bar{x}(t-1)}{\left(\frac{X_{CO}(t-1)+X_{CO}(t)}{2}\right)}$	$\dfrac{\sum_{j\in EN^{t-1,t}}[x(j,t)-\bar{x}(t-1)]}{\left(\frac{X_{CO}(t-1)+X_{CO}(t)}{2}\right)}$	$-\dfrac{NEX^{t-1,t}*\bar{x}(t-1)}{\left(\frac{X_{CO}(t-1)+X_{CO}(t)}{2}\right)}$	$-\dfrac{\sum_{j\in EX^{t-1,t}}[x(j,t-1)-\bar{x}(t-1)]}{\left(\frac{X_{CO}(t-1)+X_{CO}(t)}{2}\right)}$
1997	55.2%	−51.9%	−55.7%	50.8%
		(41%)	(−60%)	
1998	36.8%	−32.3%	−64.0%	60.2%
		(−75%)	(65%)	
1999	35.9%	−33.5%	−47.7%	44.9%
		(41%)	(−46%)	
2000	46.3%	−44.4%	−34.3%	32.7%
		(16%)	(−12%)	
2001	52.8%	−50.7%	−36.6%	34.9%
		(−33%)	(27%)	
2002	42.6%	−41.3%	−39.6%	37.7%
		(−41%)	(57%)	
2003	46.9%	−44.5%	−36.4%	35.1%
		(24%)	(−14%)	
2004	45.3%	−41.4%	−34.6%	32.8%
		(16%)	(−7%)	
2005	46.6%	−40.1%	−43.6%	41.6%
		(28%)	(−8%)	
$t=2005$	61.5%	−30.2%	−53.9%	40.0%
$t-1=1996$		(47%)	(−21%)	
Annual average	45.4%	−42.2%	−43.6%	41.2%
		(42%)	(−32%)	

Note: This table reports the annual growth rate of total exports decomposed into the contribution of pairwise continuing, entering, and exiting firms. Pairwise continuing firms in t are those that exported in $t-1$ and t. Pairwise entering firms in t are those that exported in t but not in $t-1$. Pairwise exiting firms in t are those that did export in $t-1$ but not in t. The contribution of pairwise continuers is the product of columns 2 and 3. Percentage contribution of each term to growth of total exports is reported in parentheses.

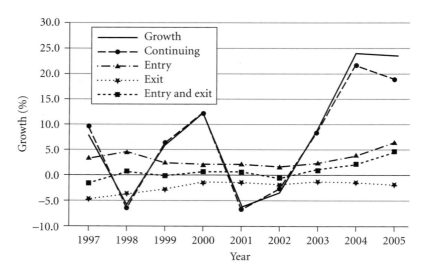

Figure 8.3 Decomposition of export growth.

instance, that in Figure 8.3, the lines for total growth and growth by continuers are almost identical up to 2001. For later years, total growth takes
off, reflecting an increase in net entry. Looking at the cross-decade decomposition, however, net entry contributed to over a quarter of the growth
in exports (26%, or 17.4 percentage points of growth, calculated from the
next-to-last line in Table 8.1).

Breaking the net entry effect for a typical year into its individual components, one finds that if entrants had exported as much per firm as pairwise
continuers, they would have generated about 46 percentage points of total
annual export growth, on average (last line of Table 8.1). But since their
exports per firm were smaller, the net export growth from gross entry averaged only 3.2 percentage points. Some algebra shows that behind these
figures is an average size of entrants, relative to those of firms selling the
previous year, equal to $1 - (42.2/45.4) = .066$ or 6.6%.[6] Similarly, exiting
firms would have reduced exports by 43.6 percentage points per year if they
had exported as much per firm as a typical firm the previous year. But since
their exports per firm were smaller by a factor of 5.5%, gross exit implied
only 2.3 percentage points of export contraction.

The cross-decade version of the decomposition (next-to-last line of Table 8.1) shows that the cumulative effects of entry and exit were nonetheless substantial. Gross entry contributed 47% (31.3 percentage points) of total growth, and would have implied 61.5 percentage points of growth if entrants exported as much as the average firm at the beginning of the period. (A calculation like the one above indicates that by the end of this period, these firms exported about half as much as the average firm at the beginning.) Similarly, the gross exit of firms would have implied a contraction of exports of 53.9 percentage points if those firms exported as much as the average firm at the beginning of the period. However, the average sales of exiting firms were about 25% of the beginning-of-period average, implying a net contraction of exports due to gross exit of 13.9 percentage points.

In sum, 8% of the average year-to-year growth in exports is explained by year-to-year net entry. This number is small despite vigorous turnover among exporters because firms that have just begun to export or are about to stop exporting typically sell relatively little. On the other hand, as we further discuss in Section 8.5, firms that enter foreign markets and survive more than a year are typically able to expand rapidly. Thus, net entry over the course of the sample period accounts for one-quarter of the cumulative total export expansion, while gross entry explains about half of total growth. In Section 8.5, we further explore and emphasize the importance of gross entry for long-run export growth.

8.4.2 Individual Destinations

Figure 8.4 shows annual averages of this decomposition for the ten most popular destination markets (on a transaction basis; see the notes to the figure for greater detail on the classification of destinations). Note that exports to some countries, particularly the Dominican Republic, grew phenomenally, while, as discussed above, exports to the European Union languished. Furthermore, with the exception of Panama, where there was little growth but much entry, high growth appears to be associated with more exporter turnover, as well as more net entry. And, with the exception of Europe, continuing firms explain a large part of the variation in growth rates across destinations. Thus, although markets are heterogeneous, some general patterns explain the behavior of exports to most destinations. In particular,

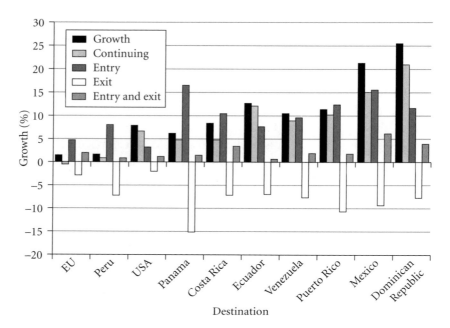

Figure 8.4 Decomposition of export growth across markets. Note: Results for the ten most popular destinations, classified according to the number of firms selling in that destination between 1996 and 2005, are being reported. The share of those destinations in total exports (annual average for 1996–2005) is as follows: United States (42.1%), European Union (17.0%), Venezuela (9.3%), Ecuador (5.1%), Peru (3.5%), Mexico (2.0%), Puerto Rico (1.5%), Panama (1.4%), Costa Rica (1.1%), and Dominican Republic (1.4%).

while net entry contributes positively to export growth, pairwise continuers explain most of it.

8.4.3 Differences in Size: Gibrat's Law Fails

Gibrat's Law holds that the growth rate of a firm is independent of its size. To what extent does Colombian export growth obey the law? To address this issue we next decompose the growth rate of continuing firms into quintile-specific components. More precisely, we decompose the contribution of continuing exporters in equation (8.1) as

$$\frac{\displaystyle\sum_{j\in CN_n^{t-1,t}} \left[x_n(j,t) - x_n(j,t-1)\right]}{\displaystyle\sum_{j\in CN_n^{t-1,t}} \left[x_n(j,t-1) + x_n(j,t)\right]/2}$$

$$= \sum_{q=1}^{5} \left(\frac{\displaystyle\sum_{j\in CN(q)_n^{t-1,t}} \left[x_n(j,t-1) + x_n(j,t)\right]/2}{\displaystyle\sum_{j\in CN_n^{t-1,t}} \left[x_n(j,t-1) + x_n(j,t)\right]/2} \right)$$

$$\times \left(\frac{\displaystyle\sum_{j\in CN(q)_n^{t-1,t}} \left[x_n(j,t) - x_n(j,t-1)\right]}{\displaystyle\sum_{j\in CN(q)_n^{t-1,t}} \left[x_n(j,t-1) + x_n(j,t)\right]/2} \right),$$

where $CN(q)_n^{t-1,t}$ denotes the set of firms that sold in both period $t-1$ and period t that were in the qth quintile according to their sales in market n in period $t-1$ (with the $t-1$ quintile defined regardless of whether firms went on to sell in period t or not). The first term in parentheses is the share of quintile q in total sales (obviously declining in q). The second is the growth rate of sales by that quintile.

Table 8.2 presents the quintile-specific growth rates that correspond to the right-hand side component in the product above. Quintile 1 includes those firms whose exports in year $t-1$ fell above the 80th percentile in that year, quintile 2 includes firms between the 60th and 80th percentile, and so on. For comparison purposes, Table 8.2 also reports quintile-specific growth rates inclusive of those firms that exited in the following year, and quintile-specific mean exports. Panel A does the analysis for total exports year by year, while Panel B presents annual averages taken over individual destinations.[7] Panel C presents the decompositions for the ten most popular destinations.

All three panels of Table 8.2 imply a major departure from Gibrat's Law: sales growth is systematically higher among firms in the low-sales quintiles, even when exit is taken into account. Remarkable is the huge growth in sales of continuing firms in the fifth quintile. This quintile is always the fastest growing. Nevertheless, because firms in this quintile initially sell so little, their contribution to overall growth is trivial. Sales of firms in the first

Table 8.2 Export growth by quintiles of value of exports in year $t - 1$, continuing and exiting firms

	Panel A: Total exports					
	Quintile 1			Quintile 2		
	Export growth continuing firms	Export growth continuing and exiting firms	Mean total exports between $t - 1$ and t (US$ million)	Export growth continuing firms	Export growth continuing and exiting firms	Mean total exports between $t - 1$ and t (US$ million)
	(1)	(2)	(3)	(1)	(2)	(3)
1997	8.9%	5.0%	10,883	31.1%	−15.4%	155
1998	−7.4%	−10.2%	10,977	21.4%	−21.8%	181
1999	5.7%	3.8%	10,955	16.4%	−11.4%	210
2000	10.9%	9.9%	12,061	47.4%	29.9%	217
2001	−10.4%	−11.7%	12,414	34.4%	18.6%	229
2002	−3.7%	−5.0%	11,815	20.6%	1.4%	220
2003	7.3%	6.4%	12,254	56.0%	38.1%	199
2004	20.9%	19.6%	14,664	55.0%	37.9%	206
2005	17.1%	15.6%	18,668	61.0%	35.0%	234
$t = 2005, t - 1 = 1996$	66.7%	48.0%	10,883	201.8%	124.8%	155
Annual average	5.5%	3.7%	12,743	38.1%	12.5%	206

	Quintile 3			Quintile 4		
	(1)	(2)	(3)	(1)	(2)	(3)
1997	60.4%	−4.3%	44	121.7%	48.7%	15
1998	47.9%	−23.4%	45	113.9%	27.4%	15
1999	40.8%	−12.2%	48	171.7%	108.1%	14
2000	93.4%	58.8%	49	137.3%	85.6%	14
2001	152.1%	119.1%	51	140.5%	92.4%	15
2002	36.0%	−3.8%	51	137.6%	77.8%	14
2003	84.8%	44.5%	46	147.4%	93.3%	13
2004	75.0%	37.7%	45	426.6%	370.7%	12
2005	160.7%	108.2%	45	131.7%	57.6%	11
$t = 2005, t - 1 = 1996$	193.3%	106.1%	44	400.1%	312.9%	15
Annual average	83.5%	36.1%	47	169.8%	106.8%	14

	Quintile 5		
	(1)	(2)	(3)
1997	244.2%	167.4%	4
1998	167.8%	72.7%	4
1999	218.6%	138.9%	3
2000	325.4%	261.7%	3
2001	8,052.0%	7,990.9%	3
2002	344.8%	268.9%	3
2003	1,320.2%	1,252.9%	3
2004	382.9%	311.9%	2
2005	8,004.7%	7,916.9%	2
$t = 2005, t - 1 = 1996$	1,155.3%	1,065.4%	4
Annual average	2,117.8%	2,042.5%	3

Panel B: Mean for destinations with 5 or more firms exporting every year

	Quintile 1			Quintile 2		
	Export growth continuing firms	Export growth continuing and exiting firms	Mean total exports between $t-1$ and t (US\$ million)	Export growth continuing firms	Export growth continuing and exiting firms	Mean total exports between $t-1$ and t (US\$ million)
	(1)	(2)	(3)	(1)	(2)	(3)
1997	8.2%	−16.1%	137.5	24.5%	−20.9%	4.0
1998	−8.9%	−37.6%	138.7	9.7%	−38.3%	4.4
1999	−14.1%	−32.3%	137.9	16.4%	−19.2%	4.9
2000	−0.2%	−16.5%	152.2	25.0%	−12.7%	4.9
2001	−4.5%	−24.1%	157.1	27.8%	−7.0%	5.2
2002	−1.1%	−20.7%	149.3	8.0%	−24.7%	5.1
2003	5.7%	−7.0%	155.0	20.7%	−5.1%	4.7
2004	9.3%	−9.8%	185.8	36.2%	5.7%	5.1
2005	6.5%	−11.6%	236.8	43.6%	11.0%	6.0
$t = 2005, t-1 = 1996$	27.3%	−31.5%	137.5	97.0%	18.7%	4.0
Annual average	0.1%	−19.5%	161.1	23.6%	−12.3%	4.9

	Quintile 3			Quintile 4		
	(1)	(2)	(3)	(1)	(2)	(3)
1997	43.7%	−13.4%	1.2	124.6%	59.1%	0.42
1998	63.3%	2.5%	1.2	98.3%	27.4%	0.42
1999	44.9%	−5.9%	1.3	100.0%	38.8%	0.41
2000	38.8%	−4.9%	1.3	101.0%	48.8%	0.43
2001	53.4%	13.9%	1.4	65.0%	6.4%	0.45
2002	36.7%	−6.8%	1.4	49.5%	−12.7%	0.45
2003	74.5%	37.2%	1.3	79.3%	27.7%	0.43
2004	71.1%	29.3%	1.4	97.9%	43.4%	0.44
2005	82.3%	36.2%	1.6	85.9%	23.8%	0.46
$t = 2005, t-1 = 1996$	120.5%	36.9%	1.2	234.6%	147.6%	0.42
Annual average	56.5%	9.8%	1.4	89.1%	29.2%	0.43

	Quintile 5		
	(1)	(2)	(3)
1997	164.6%	90.5%	0.11
1998	182.8%	109.8%	0.10
1999	207.4%	143.0%	0.10
2000	558.4%	494.7%	0.10
2001	231.6%	166.7%	0.10
2002	167.6%	99.8%	0.10
2003	225.3%	164.1%	0.10
2004	175.3%	109.8%	0.10
2005	1,095.8%	1,024.8%	0.10
$t = 2005, t-1 = 1996$	509.7%	419.4%	0.11
Annual average	334.3%	267.0%	0.10

(Continued on next page)

Table 8.2 *(continued across from previous page)*

	Panel C: Ten most popular destinations. Annual average 1997–2005					
	Quintile 1			Quintile 2		
	Export growth continuing firms	Export growth continuing and exiting firms	Mean total exports between $t-1$ and t (US$ million)	Export growth continuing firms	Export growth continuing and exiting firms	Mean total exports between $t-1$ and t (US$ million)
	(1)	(2)	(3)	(1)	(2)	(3)
United States	5.8%	4.5%	5,397.2	36.9%	12.0%	86.0
European Union	−1.5%	−3.8%	2,105.1	32.1%	4.2%	23.4
Venezuela	3.8%	−2.1%	1,122.9	47.4%	25.3%	69.3
Ecuador	8.3%	3.2%	625.0	28.6%	7.6%	35.9
Peru	−2.3%	−8.2%	403.9	34.7%	12.3%	18.9
Mexico	8.7%	1.7%	246.9	42.7%	18.8%	20.6
Puerto Rico	7.4%	−1.8%	189.4	25.4%	4.5%	7.6
Panama	0.8%	−12.5%	165.5	24.1%	−2.1%	10.9
Costa Rica	0.3%	−4.8%	137.0	27.7%	6.9%	9.3
Dominican Republic	18.4%	13.1%	176.2	28.2%	4.5%	8.3
	Quintile 3			Quintile 4		
	(1)	(2)	(3)	(1)	(2)	(3)
United States	68.4%	18.9%	16.8	126.5%	59.7%	4.5
European Union	60.8%	12.0%	6.1	148.7%	84.8%	1.7
Venezuela	72.3%	33.7%	19.2	160.5%	107.8%	6.0
Ecuador	58.7%	22.2%	11.0	185.4%	135.0%	4.0
Peru	37.2%	−3.1%	5.2	112.0%	59.9%	1.6
Mexico	95.8%	59.1%	5.8	134.6%	81.6%	1.7
Puerto Rico	34.2%	−1.8%	2.8	67.7%	14.9%	1.1
Panama	59.4%	19.2%	3.8	97.8%	43.2%	1.4
Costa Rica	61.4%	26.0%	3.2	104.6%	55.9%	1.2
Dominican Republic	67.9%	31.6%	2.9	79.0%	29.4%	1.1
	Quintile 5					
	(1)	(2)	(3)			
United States	839.9%	762.2%	0.9			
European Union	3,193.3%	3,117.4%	0.3			
Venezuela	376.5%	313.2%	1.5			
Ecuador	233.1%	170.4%	1.1			
Peru	567.0%	502.6%	0.4			
Mexico	475.0%	413.3%	0.3			
Puerto Rico	215.1%	149.5%	0.3			
Panama	227.4%	160.2%	0.4			
Costa Rica	347.6%	283.9%	0.3			
Dominican Republic	158.5%	95.1%	0.3			

Note: The table on the preceding three pages reports the average annual growth rate of exports by continuing and exiting firms, discriminated by quintiles of firm exports in $t - 1$. Panel A shows this figure for total exports, while panels B and C show the same figure by destinations, the former reporting averages across destinations with five or more firms exporting, and the latter reporting annual average for the ten most popular destinations. Pairwise continuing firms and pairwise exiting firms are defined as in Table 8.1 for panel A; panels B and C apply the same definition by destination. For each quintile q, column 1 in panel A reports the annual average of

$$\frac{\sum\limits_{j \in CN_n^{t-1,t}(q)} (x(j,t) - x(j,t-1))}{\frac{X(q,t-1)+X(q,t)}{2}},$$

where $CN^{t-1,t}(q)$ is the set of pairwise continuing firms that belonged to quintile q of the distribution of firm sales in $t - 1$. Column 2 in panel A reports the annual average of

$$\frac{\sum\limits_{j \in CN^{t-1,t}(q), EX^{t-1,t}(q)} (x(j,t) - x(j,t-1))}{\frac{X(q,t-1)+X(q,t)}{2}},$$

where $CN^{t-1,t}(q)$, $EX^{t-1,t}(q)$ is the set of all pairwise continuing and pairwise exiting firms that belonged to quintile q of the distribution of firm sales in $t - 1$. Column 3 reports the annual average of

$$\frac{X(q,t-1) + X(q,t)}{2},$$

the average value of exports to destination n by firms belonging to quintile q of the distribution of firm sales to destination n between $t - 1$ and t. In panels B and C, all statistics are calculated at the destination level, and quintiles are defined in terms of the distribution of firm sales to destination n in $t - 1$. The ten most popular destinations are characterized as described in Figure 8.4.

quintile for each destination grow by less than the overall growth rates of continuing firms. Even among these larger exporters, taking into account exit substantially lowers overall growth.

One explanation for this differential growth across quintiles is that firms face increasing resistance to foreign-market penetration as their exports grow. Sustaining growth may be difficult because exporters encounter capacity constraints, because their foreign demand elasticities fall as they expand, or because the return per dollar expenditure on advertising drops as their market penetration increases (as in Arkolakis 2008).

Alternatively, it may be that new exporters go through a learning period during which their buyers try them out on a very limited scale (Rauch and Watson 2003). Buyers may be learning about sellers' business practices and products, while sellers learn about the reliability of their potential partners and the scope for future sales. Once this exploration process has played out, firms either terminate their exporting relationship or experience a surge in orders.[8]

Panel C of Table 8.2 allows us to investigate the distribution of sales across the different destinations. We observe higher growth for firms in the low-sales quintiles, compared with the high-growth ones, for all destinations. However, there are some interesting differences across markets. The small growth of total exports to the European Union relative to other destinations is only replicated by the first quintile. Moreover, while the European Union exhibits no important differences with respect to the United States in quintiles 2–4, in quintile 5, exports to the EU actually show much larger growth than those to the United States.

Figure 8.5 plots (on a log scale) the ratio of each quintile's sales relative to the sales of the third quintile. For exports to the United States and Europe, sales by the first quintile are remarkably larger than those by the third quintile, much more so than for other destinations. This result contrasts with Eaton, Kortum, and Kramarz (2004), who find remarkable similarity in the sales distributions of French exporters across destinations.

We also explore how firms move from one quintile to another. Table 8.3 reports year-to-year transitions across quintiles, defined in terms of firms' total sales (across all destinations). Each element of the matrix reports the probability that a firm in the quintile corresponding to the column in year $t - 1$ transits into the quintile corresponding to the row in year t, with entry from not exporting and exit from exporting added possibilities. We define the population of firms as those that exported at least once during the 1996–2005 sample period. (There are, of course, many more firms selling in Colombia that never exported over our sample period while, at the same time, many of the firms in our population did not exist in all sample years.) Only firms in the top two quintiles face more than half a chance of staying in their quintile or higher. Only those in the top three quintiles face more than half a chance of surviving. At the same time, of those firms that didn't export in period $t - 1$ but did export in period t, one in three start in the fifth percentile, but a surprising one in six start in the second percentile.

Table 8.4 fleshes out the potential link between size on entry and longevity of the firm in exporting. The bottom row reports the fraction of entrants in each quintile in year of entry. A third of entrants start in the smallest (fifth quintile) while 4% begin in the top one. The elements in the matrix

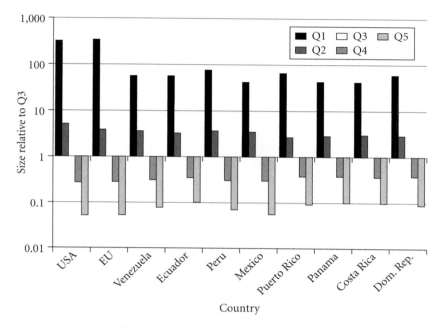

Figure 8.5 Size distribution by quintiles.

Table 8.3 Transition matrix for the quintile of exports to which a firm belongs; conditional probability of transiting from quintile of exports x in $t-1$ to quintile y in t

Final quintile (y)	Initial quintile (x)					
	1	2	3	4	5	None
1	0.77	0.12	0.02	0.01	0.00	0.00
2	0.11	0.39	0.15	0.05	0.02	0.02
3	0.02	0.12	0.20	0.11	0.04	0.03
4	0.01	0.04	0.09	0.13	0.08	0.03
5	0.00	0.02	0.04	0.06	0.10	0.04
None	0.10	0.31	0.50	0.64	0.76	0.88
P(start exporting in quintile x)	0.04	0.04	0.04	0.04	0.04	0.80

Note: This table reports number of firms that transited from quintile of exports x in $t-1$ to quintile y in t, divided by the number of firms in quintile x in $t-1$. Sample consists of all firms that reported at least one year exporting.

Table 8.4 Transition matrix between $t - 1$ and subsequent year for the quintile of exports to which a firm in entry cohort $t - 1$ belongs; conditional probability of a firm in entry cohort $t - 1$ transiting from exporting in quintile of exports x in $t - 1$ to quintile y in t

Quintile in t (y)	Quintile in $t - 1$ (x)				
	1	2	3	4	5
1	0.46	0.10	0.02	0.00	0.00
2	0.11	0.20	0.10	0.04	0.01
3	0.03	0.09	0.12	0.08	0.03
4	0.01	0.03	0.06	0.09	0.06
5	0.01	0.02	0.03	0.05	0.08
None	0.38	0.56	0.67	0.74	0.82
P(firm in entry cohort $t - 1$ starts exporting in quintile x)	0.04	0.12	0.22	0.28	0.34

Note: This table reports number of firms in entry cohort $t - 1$ that transited from quintile of exports x in $t - 1$ to quintile y in t, divided by the number of firms in entry cohort $t - 1$ and in quintile x in $t - 1$. Sample consists of all firms in entry cohort $t - 1$ for $t - 1 = 1997, \ldots, 2004$. A firm belongs to entry cohort $t - 1$ if it exported in $t - 1$ but not in previous years.

report the probability that a firm that entered in the quintile in the column transits into the quintile in the row the following year. Only sellers in the top quintile face a higher probability of continuing than of exiting. Hence initial first-year sales are an excellent indicator of survival. Nevertheless, about 10% of firms that enter in the fifth quintile transit into quintiles with more sales by the following year.

8.4.4 Interaction across Markets

Table 8.5 provides a decomposition similar to that shown in Table 8.1 for the ten most popular destinations. Going beyond Table 8.1, however, it distinguishes continuing exporters, entrants, and exiters according to their participation in other markets in the same year (t) or previous year ($t - 1$). Specifically, for continuing firms, we separate firms that sell only in market n from those that sell in other markets as well in year t. We separate firms that enter market n into "old" entrants, who exported to some other country in $t - 1$, and "new" entrants, who exported nowhere in $t - 1$.

Similarly, we classify firms that exit from exporting to n into firms that continue exporting in t to some other destination, and those that drop exporting altogether. See the table notes for the precise definitions. Since we report averages across years, the figures don't obey exactly the identity equivalent to (8.1).

Among continuing firms, those selling in multiple markets represent a much larger share of total sales, especially in less popular markets. This pattern is consistent with Eaton, Kortum, and Kramarz's (2007) model, in which firms with low marginal costs or highly appealing products reach more export markets, and sell relatively large volumes in those markets where less efficient exporters are also present. There does not appear to be any systematic difference between the growth of sales of firms selling to multiple markets and just that particular market; in some markets the former grow much more rapidly, while in others the opposite is the case.

New entrants are particularly important, relative to entrants that were already selling in other markets, in those countries that represent the largest shares of exports: the United States, the European Union, Venezuela, Ecuador, and Panama.[9] For other destinations, such as the Dominican Republic, this pattern is reversed. Because they tend to export much more, however, entry by experienced exporters tends to contribute much more to growth in all destinations.

It is also the case that, for popular destinations, firms that cease exporting altogether are more numerous than firms that exit that market but continue exporting elsewhere, while the opposite is true for the average destination. Taken together, these patterns suggest that countries are attractive as proving grounds for new exporters either if they offer a relatively large and diversified consumer base (the United States and the European Union), or they are relatively easy to access (Venezuela, Ecuador, and Panama). Other destinations seem to be visited mostly by firms that export elsewhere.

8.4.5 Numbers, Revenues, and Size

We saw in the growth decompositions that large numbers of firms enter or exit each destination market every year. We now examine these entering and exiting firms in more detail, distinguishing those that are present for only one year from those that remain for longer periods. Table 8.6 reports, for each year in our sample that is not an endpoint, data on firms that: (1) enter exporting, (2) continue exporting, (3) exit from exporting, and (4) export

Table 8.5 Contribution of pairwise entry and exit to the growth of total exports between $t - 1$ and t, by destination; firms classified according to where else they sell (ten most popular destinations; annual average 1997–2005)

	Left-hand side	Right-hand side			
		Contribution of pairwise continuers			
		Single-market continuer		Multiple-market continuer	
Destination	Growth of exports (1)	Share in $t - 1$ exports (2)	Growth of exports (3)	Share in $t - 1$ exports (4)	Growth of exports (5)
United States	7.9%	7.6%	6.0%	89.8%	7.0%
European Union	1.5%	1.0%	7.0%	95.2%	−0.6%
Venezuela	10.5%	5.6%	1.9%	85.7%	10.3%
Ecuador	12.7%	3.2%	17.1%	89.5%	13.0%
Peru	1.7%	0.6%	18.5%	91.8%	0.6%
Mexico	21.2%	0.6%	37.3%	86.9%	17.2%
Puerto Rico	11.4%	1.7%	14.9%	86.8%	11.4%
Panama	6.2%	2.0%	−1.1%	82.1%	5.6%
Costa Rica	8.3%	1.1%	−2.3%	90.1%	5.4%
Dominican Republic	25.4%	0.5%	9.5%	89.8%	23.2%

Note: The table on these two pages decomposes the contribution of pairwise continuing, exiting, and entering firms to exports growth in a given destination, classifying firms according to whether they sell to other destinations in t or $t - 1$. A pairwise continuing firm in t is one that exported to market n in $t - 1$ and t. It is defined as single-market continuer if it exported to a single market in $t - 1$ and t, and as multiple-market continuer if it exported to multiple markets in $t - 1$ or t. A pairwise entering firm in t is one that exported to market n in t but not in $t - 1$. It is defined as new entrant if it did not export in year $t - 1$ to other markets, and as old entrant otherwise. A pairwise exiting firm in t is one that exported to market n in $t - 1$ but did not export to n in t. It is defined as exiting-dying in every market if it does not export to any market in t and as exiting-continuing in some other market if it continues to export to at least one other market in t. The ten most popular destinations are characterized as described in Figure 8.4. For other relevant definitions see Table 8.1.

	Right-hand side			
	Contribution of gross pairwise entry			
	New-entrant firms		Old-entrant firms	
Destination	Added number of firms (6)	Exports relative to the average (7)	Added number of firms (8)	Exports relative to the average (9)
United States	37.5%	−35.1%	11.2%	−10.4%
European Union	29.5%	−27.0%	18.9%	−16.7%
Venezuela	24.8%	−17.3%	11.8%	−9.7%
Ecuador	22.9%	−18.8%	13.5%	−10.1%
Peru	17.1%	−14.7%	21.6%	−15.9%
Mexico	20.6%	−17.3%	27.2%	−14.9%
Puerto Rico	20.8%	−18.4%	22.5%	−12.4%
Panama	26.4%	−20.8%	19.2%	−8.2%
Costa Rica	21.9%	−18.5%	21.3%	−14.1%
Dominican Republic	15.3%	−12.8%	25.0%	−15.8%

	Contribution of gross pairwise exit			
	Exiting-dying in every market		Exiting-continuing in some other market	
Destination	Added number of firms (10)	Exports relative to the average (11)	Added number of firms (12)	Exports relative to the average (13)
United States	−34.1%	32.7%	−9.5%	9.0%
European Union	−29.0%	26.8%	−16.5%	15.9%
Venezuela	−25.1%	20.0%	−12.7%	10.1%
Ecuador	−23.8%	19.6%	−12.0%	9.3%
Peru	−19.9%	17.2%	−19.5%	14.9%
Mexico	−17.1%	13.7%	−19.2%	13.3%
Puerto Rico	−19.0%	17.0%	−19.0%	10.2%
Panama	−24.2%	18.8%	−17.1%	7.3%
Costa Rica	−18.9%	16.2%	−17.5%	13.0%
Dominican Republic	−13.7%	12.0%	−20.1%	14.1%

for just one year. Entry and exit are defined differently from Table 8.1, where we were just referring to pairwise entry and exit (i.e., entry and exit defined over $t - 1$ and t). With the pairwise definitions above, a firm that exports only in year t is considered to have entered in that year and to have exited in the following year, and it is not treated differently from other firms that export for longer periods. In Table 8.6 we differentiate single-year exporters from firms that start exporting and keep doing so for at least an additional year, and from firms that exit after having exported for at least two consecutive years. More specifically, entrants in year t are now firms that not only (1) did not export in $t - 1$ and (2) exported in t, but (3) must export in $t + 1$ as well. Exiters in t must (a) export in $t - 1$, (b) export in t, and (c) not export in $t + 1$. Continuers must not only (i) export in $t - 1$ and (ii) export in t, as above, but (iii) export in $t + 1$ as well. The remaining firms, those that exported in t but not in $t - 1$ or $t + 1$ are what we call *single-year* exporters. As mentioned, they would have been included with both entering and exiting firms in our pairwise definitions in Table 8.1.

The top panel of Table 8.6, looking across exporters to any destination, presents the numbers of such firms for each year. The middle panel presents the total value of their exports, while the bottom panel reports mean exports per firm, which is the ratio of the corresponding number in the middle panel to the corresponding number on the top panel.

Starting with the counts, Table 8.6 confirms that single-year exporters are very common.[10] It further shows that the total number of exporting firms varies over the period substantially, dropping from 10,517 in 1996 to a trough of 6,765 firms in 1999 (a year of deep recession), rising back to 11,720 by the end of the period. This volatility is due to single-year exporters and, to a lesser extent, exiting firms. The number of entering and continuing firms exhibits smaller fluctuations around trend growth. The second panel shows, as was suggested by Table 8.1, that continuing firms provide the bulk of exports for all the years.

As shown in the third panel, continuing firms export the most per firm by a huge amount. Note that exports per continuing firm have not grown, but have fluctuated around US$3 million. The growth in total exports of continuing firms, and therefore most aggregate growth, has been overwhelmingly at the intensive margin of continuing firms although, as documented earlier, net entry contributed several percentage points to growth during 2003–2005. Both the number of continuing exporter firms

Table 8.6 Entering, exiting, continuing, and single-year exporters, 1996–2005

Year	Number of firms				
	Entering	Continuing	Exiting	Single year	Total
1996	—	—	—	—	10,517
1997	1,002	2,957	1,457	5,047	10,463
1998	1,073	2,841	1,118	2,665	7,697
1999	1,101	3,191	723	1,750	6,765
2000	1,358	3,569	723	1,987	7,637
2001	1,420	3,975	952	2,490	8,837
2002	1,310	4,304	1,091	2,397	9,102
2003	1,519	4,609	1,005	2,966	10,099
2004	1,326	4,412	1,716	3,880	11,334
2005	—	—	—	—	11,720

Year	Total value of exports (US$ millions)				
	Entering	Continuing	Exiting	Single year	Total
1996	—	—	—	—	10,651
1997	189	10,933	249	181	11,552
1998	338	10,244	149	160	10,890
1999	204	11,177	116	71	11,569
2000	165	12,735	140	77	13,118
2001	187	11,887	148	82	12,305
2002	104	11,629	105	63	11,901
2003	230	12,638	191	69	13,127
2004	480	15,876	272	104	16,731
2005	—	—	—	—	21,190

Year	Exports per firm (US$ thousands)				
	Entering	Continuing	Exiting	Single year	Total
1996	—	—	—	—	1,013
1997	188	3,697	171	36	1,104
1998	315	3,606	133	60	1,415
1999	186	3,503	160	41	1,710
2000	122	3,568	194	39	1,718
2001	132	2,990	155	33	1,392
2002	79	2,702	96	26	1,307
2003	152	2,742	190	23	1,300
2004	362	3,598	158	27	1,476
2005	—	—	—	—	1,808

Note: The table reports numbers of continuing, exiting, entering, and single-year exporting firms, as well as value of exports in each category, using three-year definitions of entry and exit. Continuing firms in t are those that exported in $t-1$, t, and $t+1$. Entering firms in t are those that did not export in $t-1$, and did export in t and $t+1$. Exiting firms in t are those that exported in $t-1$ and t, but not in $t+1$. Single-year exporters in t are those that exported in t, but not in $t-1$ nor in $t+1$.

and the total amount they exported rose about 50% over the period, while exports per continuing firm remained stable.

Entering and exiting firms have been similar in size to each other, small, and volatile year to year. Single-year exporters have been much smaller still. Several interpretations are available for the fact that so many firms are jumping into and out of foreign markets, earning little revenue while they are in. One is that sunk entry costs are quite modest for a large fraction of producers. Given that other studies have found significant entry costs for many firms (Roberts and Tybout 1997a; Das, Roberts, and Tybout 2007), this interpretation further suggests that the costs of "testing the waters" may be substantially less than the cost of locking in major exporting contracts. Such a two-tiered entry-cost structure is implied by Rauch and Watson's (2003) model of international matching between buyers and sellers. An alternative (and not necessarily competing) interpretation is that firms undergo serially correlated productivity or product-quality shocks. Those that experience a sequence of very favorable draws find that exporting is very profitable, and they persistently do so on a large scale. In contrast, those with draws just sufficient to induce them to export, do so on a small scale and frequently experience shocks negative enough to bump them out of foreign markets altogether. This is the mechanism used by Das, Roberts, and Tybout (2007) to explain patterns of exporter turnover and sales heterogeneity.[11]

Table 8.7 presents the results for individual destinations, averaging across the ten most popular. While the numbers are scaled down, the overall picture is very similar.

Table 8.7 Entering, exiting, continuing, and single-year exporters to individual destinations, 1996–2005; mean for the ten most popular destinations (table opposite)

Note: The table on the facing page reports numbers of continuing, exiting, entering, and single-year exporting firms in a given destination, as well as value of exports in each category, using three-year definitions of entry and exit. For a given destination n, continuing firms in t are those that exported to market n in $t-1$, t, and $t+1$. Entering firms in t are those that did not export to market n in $t-1$, and exported to market n in t and $t+1$. Exiting firms in t are those that exported to market n in $t-1$ and t, but not in $t+1$. Single-year exporters in t are those that exported to market n in t, but not in $t-1$ nor in $t+1$. The average for the ten most popular destinations is reported. The ten most popular markets are characterized as in Figure 8.4.

Table 8.7 (continued)

Year	Entering	Number of firms Continuing	Exiting	Single year	Total
1996	—	—	—	—	1,446
1997	175	506	185	570	1,436
1998	181	520	161	353	1,215
1999	200	562	139	265	1,165
2000	253	621	141	321	1,335
2001	273	697	177	389	1,536
2002	248	750	220	398	1,616
2003	277	801	197	455	1,730
2004	270	808	271	574	1,922
2005	—	—	—	—	1,953

Year	Entering	Value of exports (US$ millions) Continuing	Exiting	Single year	Total
1996	—	—	—	—	896
1997	22	887	25	21	956
1998	40	840	19	20	919
1999	31	920	24	14	990
2000	24	1,065	18	12	1,119
2001	47	977	19	14	1,058
2002	23	953	21	13	1,009
2003	43	1,025	19	13	1,100
2004	49	1,294	38	17	1,397
2005	—	—	—	—	1,748

Year	Entering	Exports per firm (US$ thousands) Continuing	Exiting	Single year	Total
1996	—	—	—	—	620
1997	125	1,753	137	38	666
1998	219	1,616	120	55	756
1999	157	1,639	171	53	849
2000	93	1,716	128	38	838
2001	174	1,402	105	37	688
2002	91	1,270	97	32	625
2003	155	1,280	94	29	636
2004	181	1,602	141	29	727
2005	—	—	—	—	895

8.5   Analysis by Cohort

From Table 8.1 we saw that entering firms made only a very small contribution to export growth in the year of entry, although gross entry explained almost half of growth over the full eight-year period. To examine the connection between the small year-to-year effect and the large long-term effect, we investigate the role that entrants play as their cohort ages, as surviving members acquire experience in foreign markets.[12] In doing so, we come closer to characterizing the "life cycle" of an exporting episode, getting a better sense of what would happen to export sales if new firms faced higher barriers to initiating foreign operations.

Table 8.8 presents data on the activity of firms that enter in a particular year t over the remaining years of our sample. A firm is assigned to cohort t if the first report of an export transaction by that firm over our whole period of study occurs in year t. We don't know what firms did before 1996 but, for comparison purposes, we report firms present in 1996 as if they belonged to a "1996" cohort. Hence figures for this "cohort" should be interpreted very differently, as they group firms starting to export in 1996 with survivors from previous cohorts.

In parallel with Tables 8.6 and 8.7 the top panel reports the number of firms, the middle panel, the total exports of these firms, and the bottom panel, the consequent average exports per firm. Note first that the survival rate among first-year exporters is typically around one-third, and in some cases is much lower. Thus an enormous "weeding out" occurs in the year of entry.[13]

Interestingly, however, the survival rate typically rises substantially after the first year to 0.8 or 0.9, except in the last year in the sample, when it is much lower across all cohorts. Thus, firms that make it through the first year are much more likely to survive to the end of the period. This finding is consistent with learning on both sides of the market, as discussed above.

Turning to total sales, those of firms that were present in 1996 remain quite stable at about US$10 billion until the last two years, when they grew substantially, in parallel with total exports. At the end of the period, their exports still accounted for 76% of total foreign sales. On the other hand, post-1996 entrants gained market share relative to the 1996 cohort in most years, and accounted for 47% of the expansion in total exports

Table 8.8 Firms by initial-export-year cohorts, 1996–2005

Number of firms
First year of report between 1996 and 2005

Year	1996	1997	1998	1999	2000	2001	2002	2003	2004	2005	Total number of firms
1996	10,517	0	0	0	0	0	0	0	0	0	10,517
1997	4,414	6,049	0	0	0	0	0	0	0	0	10,463
1998	3,306	1,002	3,389	0	0	0	0	0	0	0	7,697
1999	2,718	617	938	2,492	0	0	0	0	0	0	6,765
2000	2,539	552	761	938	2,847	0	0	0	0	0	7,637
2001	2,418	523	700	735	1,113	3,348	0	0	0	0	8,837
2002	2,260	484	632	621	833	1,156	3,116	0	0	0	9,102
2003	2,200	465	578	553	697	903	1,048	3,655	0	0	10,099
2004	2,089	435	528	519	637	759	859	1,131	4,377	0	11,334
2005	2,051	420	362	407	505	568	578	769	1,000	5,060	11,720

Value of exports (US$ millions)
First year of report between 1996 and 2005

Year	1996	1997	1998	1999	2000	2001	2002	2003	2004	2005	Total value of exports
1996	10,651	0	0	0	0	0	0	0	0	0	10,651
1997	11,182	369	0	0	0	0	0	0	0	0	11,552
1998	10,053	361	477	0	0	0	0	0	0	0	10,890
1999	10,514	421	392	241	0	0	0	0	0	0	11,569
2000	11,723	475	335	377	207	0	0	0	0	0	13,118
2001	10,373	483	296	395	525	233	0	0	0	0	12,305
2002	10,049	422	286	362	406	240	136	0	0	0	11,901
2003	10,651	490	358	381	546	228	222	251	0	0	13,127
2004	13,547	442	409	342	600	366	269	329	427	0	16,731
2005	16,207	725	451	588	891	435	295	349	585	665	21,190

Exports per firm (US$ thousands)
First year of report between 1996 and 2005

Year	1996	1997	1998	1999	2000	2001	2002	2003	2004	2005	Total exports per firm
1996	1,013	0	0	0	0	0	0	0	0	0	1,013
1997	2,533	61	0	0	0	0	0	0	0	0	1,104
1998	3,041	360	141	0	0	0	0	0	0	0	1,415
1999	3,868	683	418	97	0	0	0	0	0	0	1,710
2000	4,617	861	440	402	73	0	0	0	0	0	1,718
2001	4,290	923	423	537	471	70	0	0	0	0	1,392
2002	4,446	872	452	584	487	208	44	0	0	0	1,307
2003	4,841	1,053	620	689	783	252	212	69	0	0	1,300
2004	6,485	1,016	776	658	942	482	313	291	98	0	1,476
2005	7,902	1,725	1,247	1,444	1,764	766	510	454	585	131	1,808

Note: This table classifies firms exporting each year according to the first year in which they reported exporting in our sample period (1996–2005). Total number of firms and value of exports represented by these firms are reported for each entry cohort.

between 1996 and 2005, as was also seen in Table 8.1.[14] Different cohorts grow at different rates, however. Some (such as the 1998 cohort) are slow to blossom, while others (such as the 2000 cohort) establish themselves quickly.

In terms of exports per firm, size jumps substantially after the first year. Hence, even though many firms drop out after the first year, total exports by the cohort do not fall accordingly. As of 2005, firms that exported in 1996 remained over four times larger than those in any entering cohort. But older cohorts are not always larger than younger ones. The 2000 cohort has the most exports per firm among cohorts that entered after 1996.

Table 8.9 reports results of a similar exercise for the ten most popular destinations; results for the average destination (among the ten most popular ones) are reported. The overall patterns are similar, although, across these individual destinations, the 2001 rather than the 2000 cohort stands out as the most successful among entrants, while the 1998 cohort looks closer to average. Also, post-1996 entrants play a more important role in the most popular destinations, accounting for 70% of the export expansion by 2005.

To summarize, in the aggregate or within individual markets, firms that exported in the first sample year (1996) remain more numerous ten years later than any but the most recent cohort. These long-time exporters continue to be the largest, both in total export sales and in exports per firm. Nonetheless, post-1996 entrants account for roughly half of the total expansion in exports over the sample period. Although each wave of entering firms exhibits very high attrition rates within a year of their appearance, those new exporters that survive this initial shakedown are very likely to thrive. Cohorts differ in their performance over the years, with leapfrogging in size occurring. The heterogeneity in export growth conditional on survival suggests that, among firms attaining the threshold profitability of operating in a new destination, there is a wide variety in export performance thereafter.[15]

Table 8.9 Firms by initial-export-year cohorts to individual destinations, 1996–2005; mean for the ten most popular destinations (table opposite)

Note: The table on the facing page classifies firms exporting to market *n* each year according to the first year in which they reported exporting to market *n* in our sample period (1996–2005). Total number of firms and value of exports to market *n* represented by these firms are reported for each entry cohort. Simple averages for the ten most popular destinations, shown in Figure 8.4, are reported.

Table 8.9 (continued)

Number of firms
First year exporting to destination n

Year	1996	1997	1998	1999	2000	2001	2002	2003	2004	2005	Total number of firms
1996	1,446	0	0	0	0	0	0	0	0	0	1,446
1997	691	745	0	0	0	0	0	0	0	0	1,436
1998	559	175	481	0	0	0	0	0	0	0	1,215
1999	484	127	159	395	0	0	0	0	0	0	1,165
2000	454	114	127	162	479	0	0	0	0	0	1,335
2001	432	106	118	131	198	552	0	0	0	0	1,536
2002	410	97	101	113	153	216	526	0	0	0	1,616
2003	391	92	88	97	132	161	186	585	0	0	1,730
2004	383	91	85	91	122	141	147	201	661	0	1,922
2005	372	86	70	78	100	118	112	136	180	702	1,953

Value of exports (US$ millions)
First year exporting to destination n

Year	1996	1997	1998	1999	2000	2001	2002	2003	2004	2005	Total value of exports
1996	896	0	0	0	0	0	0	0	0	0	896
1997	913	43	0	0	0	0	0	0	0	0	956
1998	824	39	55	0	0	0	0	0	0	0	919
1999	868	47	42	32	0	0	0	0	0	0	990
2000	966	44	32	48	29	0	0	0	0	0	1,119
2001	848	42	31	47	41	48	0	0	0	0	1,058
2002	811	31	26	35	33	43	29	0	0	0	1,009
2003	813	47	34	30	35	70	33	38	0	0	1,100
2004	999	56	42	37	44	88	42	45	45	0	1,397
2005	1,163	55	50	42	58	116	43	44	53	123	1,748

Exports per firm (US$ thousands)
First year exporting to destination n

Year	1996	1997	1998	1999	2000	2001	2002	2003	2004	2005	Total exports per firm
1996	620	0	0	0	0	0	0	0	0	0	620
1997	1,321	58	0	0	0	0	0	0	0	0	666
1998	1,476	225	115	0	0	0	0	0	0	0	756
1999	1,792	371	267	81	0	0	0	0	0	0	849
2000	2,127	387	249	299	60	0	0	0	0	0	838
2001	1,965	398	266	358	207	88	0	0	0	0	688
2002	1,979	324	255	310	217	201	56	0	0	0	625
2003	2,080	513	386	306	269	434	177	66	0	0	636
2004	2,608	621	492	404	358	624	284	225	68	0	727
2005	3,125	646	714	540	575	984	386	327	298	175	895

8.6   Cross-Market Dynamics

We now use transition matrices to characterize cross-market patterns of entry and exit in more detail. Table 8.10 breaks our sample into firms that sell to different numbers of destination markets: none, one, two, three to five, and so on, and then documents year-to-year transition frequencies between the categories. Again, we define the population of firms to be those that exported at least once during the 1996–2005 sample period. The bottom row of Table 8.10 reports the fraction of firms in each cell at the beginning of the period. Note that the modal number of destination markets is zero, with the frequency of firms selling to multiple markets declining in the number of markets.[16]

The main part of Table 8.10 reports the frequency with which firms assigned to the column categories in year $t - 1$ transited to the various row categories in year t. The columns thus sum to 100. As expected, non-exporters almost always enter a single market when they initiate foreign sales, and when firms add or subtract markets, they are more likely to do so gradually than in large clumps. This pattern is consistent with the model developed in Eaton, Kortum, and Kramarz (2007), augmented to allow for serially correlated productivity shocks.

While transition matrices are typically diagonal dominant, note that firms selling to one destination are more likely to drop out of exporting than to continue exporting. Here again, we are picking up the high failure rates among first-year exporters. A similar, albeit more muted, pattern appears among firms selling to two destinations. A member of this group is more likely to drop down to one, or to drop out of exporting altogether, than to continue selling to two or more. Only firms selling to three or more destinations are more likely to stay where they are or move up. The most stable firm types are the non-exporters and those selling to ten or more destinations.

Applying the transition matrix over and over again to an arbitrary initial allocation of firms across the cells gives the ergodic distribution implied by the transition matrix. Doing so 1,000 times (by which point the distribution of cells has converged) yields an ergodic distribution very close to the initial one given in the bottom row.

We can also look at transitions across various groups of destinations. We first assign destinations to three groups: the United States, neighbors

Table 8.10 Transition matrix for number of destinations a firm sells to; conditional probability of transiting from exporting to x destinations in $t-1$ to y destinations in t

Final number of destinations (y)	Initial number of destinations (x)					
	0	1	2	3–5	6–10	10+
0	0.88	0.65	0.27	0.10	0.04	0.01
1	0.11	0.26	0.27	0.10	0.02	0.01
2	0.01	0.06	0.25	0.16	0.02	0.00
3–5	0.00	0.03	0.20	0.49	0.22	0.02
6–10	0.00	0.00	0.02	0.14	0.57	0.16
10+	0.00	0.00	0.00	0.01	0.13	0.80
P(start exporting to x number of destinations)	0.80	0.13	0.03	0.03	0.01	0.01

Note: This table reports number of firms that transited from exporting to x destinations in $t-1$ to y destinations in t, divided by the number of firms exporting to x destinations in $t-1$. Sample consists of all firms that reported at least one exporting transaction between 1996 and 2005.

(Venezuela and Ecuador), and others. We then look at the various combinations of these groups. We create cells of these different combinations and, as above, include a cell for not exporting in year $t-1$, conditional on exporting in some year of our sample period. Table 8.11 reports the groups and the transitions between them.

The bottom row of Table 8.11 reports the initial frequency of firms in the different cells. "No destinations" is most common, followed by "Others," "Neighbors," and the United States. Notable is the lack of overlap between firms selling to the United States and firms selling to neighbors. The transition matrix is highlighted to show transitions between cells involving the same number and different numbers of destination categories.

The fact that the numbers in any row are quite different across columns implies that a firm's probabilities of moving into different markets depend upon its current market position. For example, firms in the "Neighbors" group are much more likely to move into "Neighbors, others" than firms in the "Others" market are. More generally, the "Neighbors" cell offers the greatest promise of launching into a larger number of destination groups (with frequency 0.1, compared with 0.08 for others and the United States).

Table 8.11 Transition matrix for groups of destinations a firm sells to: USA, neighbors, and others; conditional probability of transiting from exporting to group of destinations x in $t-1$ to group of destinations y in t

	Initial group of destinations (x)							
Final group of destinations (y)	None	Others	Neighbors	USA	Neighbors, others	USA, others	Neighbors, USA	Neighbors, USA, others
None	**0.88**	0.63	0.56	0.64	0.12	0.15	0.19	0.04
Others	0.06	**0.27**	0.03	**0.02**	0.10	0.10	0.04	0.03
Neighbors	0.03	**0.02**	**0.31**	**0.01**	0.09	0.00	0.16	0.02
USA	0.03	**0.01**	**0.01**	**0.26**	0.00	0.09	0.13	0.01
Neighbors, others	0.00	0.04	0.08	0.00	**0.56**	**0.02**	**0.08**	0.16
USA, other	0.00	0.03	0.00	0.06	**0.01**	**0.57**	**0.05**	0.08
Neighbors, USA	0.00	0.00	0.01	0.01	**0.01**	**0.01**	**0.18**	0.02
Neighbors, USA, others	0.00	0.01	0.01	0.01	0.11	0.07	0.17	**0.65**
P (start exporting to group of destinations x)	0.80	0.07	0.04	0.03	0.03	0.02	0.00	0.01

Note: This table reports the number of firms that transited from exporting to the group of destinations y in t, divided by the number of firms exporting to the group of destinations x in $t-1$. Destinations are classified into USA, neighbors, and others, where "neighbors" refers to Venezuela and Ecuador. Combinations where x and y represent the same number of destinations are highlighted. Sample consists of all firms that reported at least one exporting transaction between 1996 and 2005.

On the other hand, the first row indicates that firms are most likely to drop out of exporting from the U.S. cell, followed closely by the "Others" cell. A nontrivial fraction of firms selling to more than one destination also drop out from exporting by the following period. The cell containing neighbors and the United States is the least stable, offering the greatest chance of launching into the cell with all three groups but also the greatest chance of dropping down to zero or one destination. This path dependence may reflect differences in the types of products that are exported to different destinations, destination-specific threshold costs for exporters breaking into new markets (which create incentives to stay put), or some combination of both factors.

The "others" category in Table 8.11 pools some very heterogeneous countries. To give a more detailed picture of trade with countries in this residual group, Table 8.12 breaks countries falling under this "Others" heading into two subgroups: (1) nonneighbor Latin American countries and (2) the European Union and the rest of the world (ROW). Organization for Economic Cooperation and Development (OECD) countries dominate the second category. We had seen in Table 8.11 that the "Neighbors" category showed the greatest probability of diversifying into more markets; Table 8.12 shows that this expansion occurs mainly by entering other countries in Latin America. Moreover, while it is as likely that, in $t - 1$, a firm exports solely to the neighbors category as it is that it exports to other destinations in Latin America, the two categories differ in that the "Neighbors" column shows higher probability of both continuing exporting and diversifying into new markets. Firms that sell only to other Latin American destinations in $t - 1$ stop exporting in t with probability 0.64, compared to 0.56 for firms that export only to the neighboring destinations. Also, moving to the rows of "Neighbors, LA" or "Neighbors, USA, LA" occurs with probability 0.07 for firms that start selling only to neighbors, compared to 0.04 for those that start in the "LA" only column.

Once a firm exports to both neighbors and other Latin American destinations, it enjoys a 19% chance to expand further to reach an OECD destination, while firms that sell only to neighbors or only to other countries in Latin America are very unlikely to move on to sell to an OECD country. Thus, while neither neighbors nor Latin America stand alone as "stepping stones," jointly they often constitute the first two rungs to climb in the ascent to reach either the United States or other OECD countries.

Table 8.12 Transition matrix for groups of destinations a firm sells to: USA, neighbors, Latin America, EU, and ROW; conditional probability of transiting from exporting to group of destinations x in $t-1$ to group of destinations y in t

Final group of destinations (y)	Initial group of destinations (x)				
	None	EU and ROW	Neighbors	USA	LA
None	**0.88**	0.67	0.56	0.64	0.64
EU and ROW	0.02	**0.23**	**0.01**	**0.01**	**0.01**
Neighbors	0.03	**0.01**	**0.31**	**0.01**	**0.02**
USA	0.03	**0.01**	**0.01**	**0.26**	**0.01**
LA	0.03	**0.01**	**0.02**	**0.01**	**0.23**
Neighbors, EU, and ROW	0.00	0.01	0.01	0.00	0.00
USA, EU, and ROW	0.00	0.02	0.00	0.04	0.00
USA, LA	0.00	0.00	0.00	0.02	0.01
Neighbors, LA	0.00	0.00	0.06	0.00	0.04
LA, EU, and ROW	0.00	0.02	0.00	0.00	0.02
Neighbors, USA	0.00	0.00	0.01	0.01	0.00
Neighbors, USA, EU, and ROW	0.00	0.00	0.00	0.00	0.00
USA, LA, EU, and ROW	0.00	0.01	0.00	0.01	0.00
Neighbors, LA, EU, and ROW	0.00	0.00	0.01	0.00	0.01
Neighbors, USA, LA	0.00	0.00	0.01	0.00	0.00
Neighbors, USA, LA, EU, and ROW	0.00	0.00	0.00	0.00	0.00
P(start exporting to group of destinations x)	0.80	0.03	0.04	0.03	0.04
Share in total exports	0.00	0.01	0.02	0.05	0.01

Note: The table on these three pages reports the number of firms that transited from exporting to the group of destinations x in $t-1$ to the group of destinations y in t, divided by the number of firms exporting to the group of destinations x in $t-1$. Destinations classified into USA, neighbors, Latin America and Caribe (LA) excluding neighbors and others, where "neighbors" refers to Venezuela and Ecuador and "ROW" refers to rest of world. Combinations where x and y represent the same number of destinations are highlighted. Sample consists of all firms that reported at least one exporting transaction between 1996 and 2005. Last row represents exports to column group of destinations in year t ($t = 1996, \ldots , 2004$) as a percentage of total exports in year t ($t = 1996, \ldots , 2004$).

Final group of destinations (y)	Initial group of destinations (x)					
	Neighbors, EU, and ROW	USA, EU, and ROW	USA, LA	Neighbors, LA	LA, EU, and ROW	Neighbors, USA
None	0.23	0.15	0.24	0.13	0.26	0.19
EU and ROW	0.11	0.07	0.01	0.00	0.11	0.01
Neighbors	0.16	0.00	0.01	0.11	0.01	0.16
USA	0.01	0.12	0.13	0.00	0.01	0.13
LA	0.02	0.00	0.13	0.09	0.14	0.03
Neighbors, EU, and ROW	**0.20**	**0.00**	**0.00**	0.01	0.01	0.02
USA, EU, and ROW	**0.01**	**0.50**	**0.03**	0.00	0.03	0.02
USA, LA	**0.00**	**0.01**	**0.20**	0.01	0.02	0.02
Neighbors, LA	**0.07**	**0.00**	**0.03**	0.46	0.04	0.05
LA, EU, and ROW	**0.02**	**0.01**	**0.02**	0.01	0.21	0.01
Neighbors, USA	**0.01**	**0.00**	**0.01**	0.01	0.00	0.18
Neighbors, USA, EU, and ROW	0.02	0.02	0.01	0.00	0.00	0.04
USA, LA, EU, and ROW	0.01	0.09	0.09	0.00	0.06	0.01
Neighbors, LA, EU, and ROW	0.10	0.00	0.01	0.10	0.07	0.01
Neighbors, USA, LA	0.01	0.00	0.05	0.06	0.00	0.10
Neighbors, USA, LA, EU, and ROW	0.02	0.01	0.03	0.03	0.03	0.04
P(start exporting to group of destinations x)	0.00	0.01	0.00	0.02	0.00	0.00
Share in total exports	0.01	0.07	0.04	0.03	0.01	0.01

(Continued on next page)

A similar exercise (not reported) was conducted separating the European Union rather than Latin America from others. The results show that very few Colombian firms sell to the European Union, and that it is an unlikely destination for an initiate. At the same time, the few firms that sell only to the European Union are less likely to increase their groups of destinations and are most likely, among single group exporters, to drop out of exporting. These patterns trace at least partly to the fact that the European Union has remained a stagnant market from the perspective of Colombian firms.

Table 8.12 *(continued across from previous page)*

Final group of destinations (y)	Neighbors, USA, EU, and ROW	USA, EU, and ROW	Neighbors, LA, EU, and ROW	Neighbors, USA, LA	Neighbors, USA, LA, EU, and ROW
	Initial group of destinations (x)				
None	0.08	0.08	0.05	0.05	0.02
EU and ROW	0.03	0.03	0.01	0.00	0.00
Neighbors	0.03	0.00	0.03	0.04	0.00
USA	0.03	0.03	0.00	0.02	0.00
LA	0.00	0.02	0.02	0.04	0.01
Neighbors, EU, and ROW	0.05	0.00	0.03	0.01	0.01
USA, EU, and ROW	0.18	0.16	0.00	0.01	0.01
USA, LA	0.00	0.03	0.00	0.04	0.01
Neighbors, LA	0.01	0.00	0.17	0.19	0.02
LA, EU, and ROW	0.02	0.04	0.05	0.00	0.01
Neighbors, USA	0.05	0.00	0.00	0.03	0.01
Neighbors, USA, EU, and ROW	**0.22**	**0.02**	**0.01**	**0.01**	0.02
USA, LA, EU, and ROW	**0.07**	**0.47**	**0.01**	**0.02**	0.05
Neighbors, LA, EU, and ROW	**0.03**	**0.01**	**0.42**	**0.07**	0.10
Neighbors, USA, LA	**0.03**	**0.01**	**0.03**	**0.29**	0.05
Neighbors, USA, LA, EU, and ROW	0.15	0.09	0.17	0.18	**0.68**
P(start exporting to group of destinations x)	0.00	0.01	0.01	0.00	0.01
Share in total exports	0.01	0.21	0.06	0.02	0.45

8.7 Summary

Each year, large numbers of new Colombian exporters appear in foreign markets. Most drop out by the following year, but a small fraction survive and grow very rapidly. Thus, while the entering cohort in any given year makes a trivial contribution to total export sales, its contribution over a longer period is significant. Indeed, over the course of a decade, almost half of the total growth in Colombian merchandise exports was attributable to firms that were not initially exporters. One interpretation of this pattern is that new exporters and their potential buyers undergo a period of learning about one another. As the uncertainty is resolved, exporters either expand their sales substantially or abandon the particular market.

While aggregate export levels are primarily accounted for by big established firms, there is an apparently important role of experimentation and selection. As explained above, entry is important to export growth. In fact, the panel data shed light on the life cycle of exporters by showing that new exporters, upon survival of the first year, are crucial to growth. While other studies have found significant entry costs into export markets by individual firms, our finding of substantial short-lived entry suggests that the costs of shipping small volumes to new destinations are relatively small for many firms. Those costs may be viewed as part of the larger cost of establishing lucrative long-term export contracts. This two-tiered entry cost structure is consistent with learning in export markets by both buyers and sellers.

There appear to be dominant geographic expansion and contraction paths that firms follow as they add or subtract foreign destinations. Neighboring markets appear to act as stepping stones for other Latin American markets. Once firms have successfully penetrated both neighboring and other Latin American destinations, they are more likely to reach larger OECD markets (including the United States and European Union), but not vice versa. These patterns may well reflect demand mix effects, or market sizes and distances, as formalized in Eaton, Kortum, and Kramarz (2007). But they may also reflect learning processes at work and regional differences in the mix of products demanded. That is, success in smaller markets may provide a signal that the expected payoff of testing the waters in larger markets exceeds the sunk costs.

ACKNOWLEDGMENTS

We gratefully acknowledge Banco de la República de Colombia for its support of this project, both financially and in terms of data access. We also thank Pietro Bonaldi, Monica Hernández, and Miguel Rueda for excellent research assistance, as well as Enrique Montes for expert data advice. Finally we are grateful to Costas Arkolakis, Sascha Becker, Gene Grossman, Ricardo Hausmann, Elhanan Helpman, Dalia Marin, Marc Melitz, and participants in the Centre for Economic Policy Research (CEPR) conference on "Globalization and the Organization of Firms," as well as members of the Board of Governors of Banco de la República de Colombia, for valuable comments.

NOTES

1. The deviation is due to mistakes in the records of tax identifiers. Since following firms over time is central to our analysis, our database includes only records of transactions in which the tax identifier has the appropriate format. Not satisfying this requirement is a clear indication that the firm is not correctly identified in the record.

2. Colombia also shares borders with Brazil, Panama, and Peru, but the borders lie mostly in unpopulated jungle areas, so that cross-border trade is much less intense. Moreover, most economic activity in Colombia takes place in the valleys between the various Andean mountain ranges and on the Caribbean coast. These areas are contiguous with Venezuela and Ecuador but not with the other neighbors.

3. European integration and the emergence of former Soviet states as new sources of imports probably contributed to the sluggish growth of European demand for Colombian goods.

4. Note that we follow the convention of treating growth as the change between two dates divided by the average level in the two dates rather than the change divided by the level in the earlier date. Benefits are that (1) $x\%$ growth followed by $-x\%$ growth returns us to the same level and (2) values close to zero in the first year have a less extreme effect on the growth rate. See Eslava et al. (2004) for a related decomposition.

5. The bottom row of the table reports annual averages. Unlike the other rows, the overall growth rate in the first column does not relate exactly to the remaining components according to the identity above since some of the individual terms enter nonadditively.

6. The average size of entrants relative to incumbents is

$$\frac{\dfrac{\sum\limits_{j\in EN^{t-1,t}} x(j,t)}{NEN^{t-1,t}}}{\overline{x}(t-1)}$$

$$= \frac{\overline{x}(t-1)*NEN^{t-1,t} + \sum\limits_{j\in EN^{t-1,t}}(x(j,t)-\overline{x}(t-1))}{\overline{x}(t-1)*NEN^{t-1,t}} = 1 + \frac{(5)}{(4)},$$

where in the last equality, "(4)" and "(5)" refer to numbers of columns in Table 8.1.

7. In order to calculate quintiles, we limited ourselves to destinations with at least five exporters.

8. This process is analogous to models of passive learning where, at the start of operations, there is resolution upon entry of ex ante uncertainty about profitability (see, e.g., Jovanovic 1982).

9. Jointly, these countries capture over 70% of Colombian merchandise exports.

10. This high exit rate among first-year exporters is consistent with Besedes's (2006) findings using 10-digit product level data on U.S. exports.

11. Another dimension underlying the pattern of export entry, which may be relevant (and is left for future research), is whether the firm is linked with a multinational corporation that may have partially sunk some of the costs associated with distribution and product placement associated with penetration of new markets. The evidence in Kugler (2006) shows that in other important dimensions (such as productivity, scale, skill intensity, and capital intensity), multinational affiliate manufacturing plants display higher averages than domestically owned ones.

12. Brooks (2006) performs a similar analysis using Colombian plant-level data.

13. This result was of course implied by the large number of one-year exporters discussed above.

14. They account for 100% of the expansion between 1996 and 2003.

15. Irarrazabal and Opromolla (2006) provide a dynamic model of entry into export markets, based on Luttmer (2006), which captures some of these elements qualitatively.

16. This result parallels what Eaton, Kortum, and Kramarz (2004) found in a cross-section of French firms.

References

Arkolakis, Konstantinos. 2008. "Market Penetration Costs and Trade Dynamics." Working paper, Yale University, Department of Economics.

Bernard, Andrew, and J. Bradford Jensen. 1999. "Exceptional Exporter Performance: Cause, Effect, or Both?" *Journal of International Economics* 47:1–25.

Bernard, Andrew, Jonathan Eaton, J. Bradford Jensen, and Samuel Kortum. 2003. "Plants and Productivity in International Trade." *American Economic Review* 93(4):1268–90.

Bernard, Andrew, J. Bradford Jensen, Stephen J. Redding, and Peter K. Schott. 2007. "Firms in International Trade." *Journal of Economic Perspectives* 21(3):105–30.

Besedes, Tibor. 2006. "A Search Cost Perspective on Duration of Trade." Working paper, Louisiana State University.

Brooks, Eileen. 2006. "Why Don't Firms Export More? Product Quality and Colombian Plants." *Journal of Development Economics* 80:160–78.

Clerides, Sofronis, Saul Lach, and James Tybout. 1998. "Is Learning-by-Exporting Important? Micro-dynamic Evidence from Colombia, Mexico and Morocco." *Quarterly Journal of Economics* 113:903–47.

Das, Mita, Mark Roberts, and James Tybout. 2007. "Market Entry Costs, Producer Heterogeneity and Export Dynamics." *Econometrica* 75(3):837–74.

Eaton, Jonathan, Samuel Kortum, and Francis Kramarz. 2004. "Dissecting Trade: Firms, Industries, and Export Destinations." *American Economic Review Papers and Proceedings* 94:150–54.

———. 2007. "An Anatomy of International Trade: Evidence from French Firms." Working paper, Department of Economics, New York University.

Eslava, Marcela, John Haltiwanger, Adriana Kugler, and Maurice Kugler. 2004. "The Effects of Structural Reforms on Productivity and Profitability Enhancing Reallocation: Evidence from Colombia." *Journal of Development Economics* 75:333–71.

Irarrazabal, Alfonso A., and Luca David Opromolla. 2006. "Hysteresis in Export Markets." Working paper, New York University.

Jovanovic, Boyan. 1982. "Selection and the Evolution of Industry." *Econometrica* 50:649–70.

Kugler, Maurice. 2006. "Spillovers from Foreign Direct Investment: Within or Between Industries?" *Journal of Development Economics* 80(2):444–77.

Luttmer, Erzo. 2007. "Selection, Growth, and the Size Distribution of Firms." *Quarterly Journal of Economics* 122:1103–44.

Melitz, Marc. 2003. "The Impact of Trade on Intra-Industry Reallocations and Aggregate Industry Productivity." *Econometrica* 71:1695–1725.

Rauch, James, and Joel Watson. 2003. "Starting Small in an Unfamiliar Environment." *International Journal of Industrial Organization* 21:1021–42.

Roberts, Mark, and James Tybout. 1997a. "The Decision to Export in Colombia: An Empirical Model of Entry with Sunk Costs." *American Economic Review* 87(4):545–63.

———. 1997b. *What Makes Exports Boom?* Directions in Development Monograph Series, Washington, DC: the World Bank.

— 9 —

Fair Wages and Foreign Sourcing

GENE M. GROSSMAN AND ELHANAN HELPMAN

9.1 Introduction

Most social scientists agree that humans care not only about their own absolute well-being but also about their standing *compared to others*. Relative position affects individuals' self-reporting of their happiness (Easterlin 2001; Frey and Stutzer 2002; Luttmer 2005) and job satisfaction (Clark and Oswald 1996; Hammermesh 2001). It features prominently in psychologists' theories of internal equity and relative deprivation, in sociologists' theories of social exchange and in economists' theories of reciprocity and internal labor markets. It is accepted wisdom among personnel managers and authors of compensation texts (Bergmann and Scarpello 2000; Milkovich and Newman 2005). Based on a wealth of evidence of various sorts, it is more than reasonable to take the utility function of "economic man" as having relational variables among its several arguments.

Wage comparisons play an increasingly important role in labor economics. Akerlof (1982) described the work relationship as a "gift exchange" in which workers voluntarily provide effort (in the absence of enforceable contracts) in exchange for "fair" compensation. When a worker perceives his pay to be insufficient, his morale may suffer and his anger flare. Then the worker may withhold his effort, to the detriment of his productivity on the job. In this theory, workers gauge fairness at least in part by what others are being paid. Akerlof and Yellen (1990) and others have applied this notion of "fair wages" to develop an explanation for wage rigidity and unemployment.[1] Firms may be reluctant to alter relative wages in the face of shocks, or to reduce nominal wages when demand falls, for fear that employees would regard these actions as unjust and would work less hard in response. If wages fail to adjust when demand declines, excess supply and involuntary unemployment may result.

273

The theorizing by Akerlof and others spawned empirical research to investigate its behavioral underpinnings. Researchers have surveyed business managers to question their tendency to preserve pay structure in response to increases in the minimum wage (Grossman 1983) and their reluctance to pare wages in the face of flagging demand (Blinder and Choi 1990; Campbell and Kamiani 1997; Bewley 1999). They find that managers regard morale to be an important consideration in setting wages. Experimentalists have established a role for reciprocity in a variety of laboratory games (see the survey by Gächter and Fehr [2002]). Field studies too find a link between relative wages and perceptions of fairness. For example, in a recent case study of the freight-handling industry, Verhoogen, Burks, and Carpenter (2007) find a positive correlation between workers' views on the fairness of their pay and the gap between their wage and the (predicted) outside wage they would earn based on their demographics and labor market conditions (see also Martin 1981; Lincoln and Kalleberg 1990; and Levine 1993).

If workers' job satisfaction depends upon comparison to others, an immediate question that arises is, who are the "others" in the relevant reference group? Workers might compare themselves to others elsewhere in the economy who have similar backgrounds and perform relatively similar jobs. Or they may compare themselves to others in the same office, plant, or firm within a somewhat broader occupational grouping. Psychologists emphasize the frequency of interaction and the ease of comparison as crucial in defining reference groups (Patchen 1961; Goodman 1977). Their arguments suggest that comparisons within the workplace may be especially important. The available survey evidence supports this view. For example, the managers interviewed by Bewley (1999) point to internal wage structure as an important determinant of company morale, whereas external pay differentials rarely are mentioned, except in highly unionized industries. The managers indicated that employees often know little about pay rates at other firms, even for those in similar occupations and jobs. Levine (1993) reports similarly that internal equity concerns take precedence over external considerations in determining the compensation of corporate executives.

When internal wage comparisons are important to job satisfaction and employee morale, they might affect firms' organizational choices. Baron and Kreps (1999) have suggested that considerations of internal pay structure could motivate firms to outsource certain low-skill activities to independent contractors, in order to avoid the dissatisfaction and jealousy that can develop among these workers when they are permanent employees of the firm. In this chapter we explore a related idea: firms may choose to *offshore* certain activities in order to separate the workers who perform them from those in the firm who have higher pay. This strategy might improve morale if individuals have better information about coworkers employed in the same (or nearby) office or plant than they do about those toiling in a different country, and use only the more salient coworkers in forming their views of the fair wage.

Why might a firm profit by segmenting its labor force geographically, above and beyond any gains that may come from cross-country wage differentials? The fair wage-effort hypothesis offers one possible answer. When workers feel they are being treated unjustly, they may express their displeasure by shaving effort. So separating those who receive below-average pay from the targets of their potential envy may raise labor productivity. We do not deny the plausibility of this mechanism, but note that variable effort is not necessary for our argument. Relative-wage considerations can play a role in organizational choices even if they do not affect worker performance, so long as they influence job satisfaction. After all, firms must offer a competitive level of utility in order to attract and hold workers. The survey findings suggest that personnel managers are aware of this channel; Blinder and Choi (1990), Campbell and Kamiani (1997), and Bewley (1999) all report that firms preserve internal wage equity, among other reasons, in order to alleviate labor turnover and enhance prospects for recruitment of new workers.

This is an exploratory chapter in which we begin to examine how fair-wage considerations affect organizational choices and offshoring decisions in general equilibrium. We assume that a worker's job satisfaction (or, equivalently, his utility from employment) depends upon his real income and his pay rate relative to a reference wage. We take the reference wage to be the average pay in the office or plant in which the worker is employed. By assumption, the worker does not compare himself to others who may be located in an offshore facility, because it is difficult for him to obtain information about the pay of these foreign workers and perhaps difficult to interpret what the pay rates mean in real terms. In other words, the foreign labor force of a multinational firm is less salient to an employee than those who work nearby. Note too our assumption that the *average* wage matters. In much of the literature on fair wages, the worker is assumed to suffer when he is relatively poorly paid compared to some other class of workers, and suffer equally no matter how many workers are members of that class. We find this assumption to be implausible. But our alternative implies that firms must take account of fair-wage concerns in deciding the *composition* of their workforce inasmuch as the proportions of employees of different types affect the firm's average wage.

In Section 9.2 we develop a very simple model with relative-wage concerns. The model has one good and two types of labor. Each worker derives utility from real income, but suffers a loss in utility if his wage is lower than the average in his firm. Firms behave competitively. The only departure from the standard competitive model is in the utility function of the worker. Firms must take workers' jealousies into account in setting wages and choosing the composition of employment, in order that they can attract and retain the workers they demand.

In Section 9.3 we illustrate how relative-wage concerns can affect the organization of production, with a simple example akin to that in Akerlof and Yellen (1990). We posit a linearly separable production function that relates output to the inputs of the two types of labor. High-skill workers are assumed to be more productive than their low-skill counterparts. But this generates a wage gap and incipient jealousies on the part of the lower-paid employees. In a competitive equilibrium, the two types of workers are separated in different firms. In this setting, there is no efficiency cost to such separation and all firms avoid employee dissatisfaction by hiring homogeneous labor forces.

Section 9.4 introduces a nonlinear production function in which the two types of labor are complementary. Firms choose the wage for low-skill workers and the composition of employment in their company to minimize unit cost, taking the wage of the high-skill workers and the utility level for low-skill workers as given by the market. In making their choices, firms are constrained by the requirement that their work environment be sufficiently attractive to allow them to hire low-skill workers. We show that the closed-economy general equilibrium has full employment, and characterize the equilibrium choices by firms. Interestingly, when workers' relative-wage concerns are intense, the equilibrium may be characterized by heterogeneity in the behavior of otherwise identical firms. Some will choose to pay a relatively low wage to low-skill workers and employ relatively many of them, while others will pay a higher wage and employ relatively fewer of them.

In Section 9.5, we introduce the possibility of offshoring. A firm can conduct some of its production activities offshore and thereby isolate a subset of workers from others in the firm. The isolated workers do not compare themselves to higher-paid coworkers in a distant, foreign plant. A key finding is that firms will either employ all of their low-skill workers in a foreign subsidiary, or else all such workers are employed in the domestic plant. In equilibrium, although all firms are ex ante identical, some offshore the production of one intermediate input, while others do not. Offshoring occurs even when the foreign production cost for the activities performed abroad exceeds what it would cost to perform those activities domestically at the equilibrium wage. Moreover, for any given cost of foreign production, more offshoring takes place when relative-wage concerns are present than when they are absent. We show as well that the domestic industrial structure can be very sensitive to changes in foreign production costs when relative-wage concerns are intense.

A final section addresses the efficiency properties of our model. We show that the market equilibrium with offshoring does not maximize the net output of the domestic economy. Nonetheless, a social planner who can choose the wage rates for the two types of workers, the allocation of resources to domestic firms, and the volume of inputs imported from foreign subsidiaries could not achieve a Pareto improvement over the free-market outcome.

9.2 A Simple Model with Relative-Wage Concerns

We study an economy with one sector and two types of labor. The single final good serves as numeraire. The model is "standard" in every respect except for the manner in which individuals assess their own well-being. We assume, as usual, that individuals derive additional utility from higher real incomes, but add that a substandard wage causes dissatisfaction, the more so the lower is the worker's wage relative to the reference wage w_r. We take the reference wage to be the average wage among employees in the individual's place of employment.[2]

Let $u\left(w, w/w_r\right)$ be the utility function of every individual, where w is the individual's real wage and w_r is the reference wage, equal to the average wage in the individual's workplace. We make the following assumption about the properties of this utility function.

Assumption 9.1   *u (x, y) is continuous, differentiable at all (x, y) except, perhaps, at y = 1 (i.e., at w = w_r), and satisfies (i) ∂u (x, y) /∂x > 0, (ii) ∂u (x, y) /∂y > 0 for y < 1, and (iii) ∂u (x, y) /∂y = 0 for y ≥ 1.*

That is, an individual's utility rises with his own real income and rises with his relative pay when his wage is below average. We take utility to be independent of the relative wage when a worker receives more than the average, to capture our sense that the unhappiness caused by a perceived slight is not matched by symmetric delight from receiving one's "just dessert."[3]

An unemployed individual receives no pay, but suffers no disutility from unflattering comparisons. We normalize the utility of such an individual to equal zero and adopt the following.

Assumption 9.2   *u(0, y) = 0 and u(x, y) > 0 for all x > 0.*

In other words, every individual prefers employment at a positive wage to unemployment, regardless of the structure of his employer's wages.

It will prove useful in what follows to define the reduced-form utility function,

$$v \left(w, w_r \right) \equiv u \left(w, \frac{w}{w_r} \right). \tag{9.1}$$

The properties of $v \left(w, w_r \right)$ are characterized in the following.

Lemma 9.1   *Assumptions 9.1 and 9.2 imply that $v \left(w, w_r \right)$ is continuous; differentiable at all $\left(w, w_r \right)$ except, perhaps, at $w = w_r$; $v \left(0, w_r \right) = 0$; $\partial v \left(w, w_r \right)/\partial w > 0$; $\partial v \left(w, w_r \right)/\partial w_r < 0$ for $0 < w \leq w_r$; $\partial v \left(w, w_r \right)/\partial w_r = 0$ for $w > w_r$; and $v \left(\lambda w, \lambda w_r \right) > v \left(w, w_r \right)$ for $w > 0$ and $\lambda > 1$.*

The economy is populated by two types of individuals, high-skill workers with human capital of h_H per capita and low-skill workers with human capital h_L per capita, $h_H > h_L$. There are fixed numbers N_H and N_L (respectively) of each type. All workers, regardless of type, hold the preferences represented by (9.1). Perfect competition prevails in the product market and both labor markets. In the latter, firms take as given the utility levels they must offer in order to attract employees. A firm sets its own pay rates w_H and w_L, and hires ℓ_H and ℓ_L high-skill and low-skill workers, respectively, subject to the constraint that the employees must be willing to accept the jobs with the prescribed wage and employment conditions. Each worker opts for employment at the firm that offers the highest utility, or at any one of such firms in the event of ties. In equilibrium, firms provide competitive levels of utility and workers are indifferent as to the identity of their employers.

9.3   An Illustration of Effects on Organization

Our goal is to understand how jealousies within the workplace can influence the organization of production, especially when firms have opportunities to move some production processes offshore. Before turning to this problem, we will show with a simple and somewhat obvious example how relative-wage concerns can affect organizational choices.

Consider a closed economy in which the two types of labor produce final output according to the linear production function

$$q = h_H \ell_H + h_L \ell_L. \tag{9.2}$$

With this technology, high-skill and low-skill workers substitute perfectly for one another albeit with different levels of productivity. A competitive firm that produces with constant returns to scale seeks to minimize its per-unit cost. It takes as given the utility levels v_i that workers of type $i \in \{H, L\}$ can obtain from their best alternative employment opportunities. The problem facing a typical firm is to find

$$\min_{\ell_H, \ell_L, w_H, w_L} \frac{w_H \ell_H + w_L \ell_L}{q}$$

subject to

$$h_H \ell_H + h_L \ell_L \geq q$$

and

$$v\left(w_i, w_r\right) \geq v_i \text{ for } i = H, L,$$

where

$$w_r \equiv \frac{w_H \ell_H + w_L \ell_L}{\ell_H + \ell_L}.$$

The minimand in this problem is the firm's per-unit cost. The first constraint dictates that the composition of employment suffices to generate q

units of output. The remaining conditions describe the participation constraints for workers of each type and define the average wage w_r. The firm
must pay sufficiently given the composition of its employment to attract the
workers that it wishes to hire. Of course, a firm can choose not to produce
at all or to employ workers of only one type.

In every solution to this problem, the first constraint is satisfied with
equality. Therefore we can simplify the statement of the problem by defining the fraction of low-skill workers,

$$\mu \equiv \frac{\ell_L}{\ell_L + \ell_H},$$

and imposing the first constraint as an equality, to rewrite the minimand as

$$\min_{\mu, w_H, w_L} \frac{\mu w_L + (1 - \mu)\, w_H}{\mu h_L + (1 - \mu)\, h_H} \tag{9.3}$$

and the remaining constraints as

$$v\left[w_i, \mu w_L + (1 - \mu)\, w_H\right] \geq v_i \text{, for } i = H, L,$$

and

$$0 \leq \mu \leq 1.$$

In this formulation, the average wage is $w_r = \mu w_L + (1 - \mu)\, w_H$. As the
problem is now stated, the firm minimizes unit cost subject to the participation constraints for workers of each type and the feasibility constraint on
the fraction μ.

The effect of fair-wage concerns on the organization of production can
be seen here.

Lemma 9.2   *In an economy with the linear technology described by (9.2),
every active firm employs only one type of worker. Firms that employ workers
of type i pay wages of $w_i = h_i$ for $i = H$ or $i = L$.*

In the equilibrium, every worker receives the average wage of the firm.
Therefore, no worker suffers from unpleasant comparisons, and all workers
regard their wages as "fair."

To prove this result, suppose to the contrary that there exists an equilibrium in which some firm f employs positive numbers of both types of
workers. Let the fraction of low-skill workers in this firm be μ, which lies

strictly between zero and one. The firm must satisfy the participation constraint for each type of worker, of course. Assumption 9.1 implies that

$$v\left(w_i, w_i\right) \geq v\left[w_i, \mu w_L + (1 - \mu)\, w_H\right] \geq v_i,$$

and that the first inequality is strict for workers of type i if $w_i < w_j$ for $i \in \{L, H\}$ and $i \neq j$. That is, if an actual or hypothetical firm were to hire only workers of type i, it could meet the participation constraint by paying its workforce the same as what the similarly skilled workers are paid by firm f, and it could do so with slack if workers of type i are the (strictly) lowest paid workers in firm f.

Now note that the unit cost of production for firm f satisfies

$$\frac{\mu w_L + (1 - \mu)\, w_H}{\mu h_L + (1 - \mu)\, h_H} \geq \min \left\{ \frac{w_H}{h_H}, \frac{w_L}{h_L} \right\},$$

whereas the unit cost in an actual or hypothetical firm that employs only workers of type i and pays them the same as does firm f is w_i / h_i. It follows that the latter firm can achieve a strictly lower unit cost than firm f. It can do so by employing only workers with the lowest w_i / h_i ratio, if $w_L / h_L \neq w_H / h_H$. And if $w_L / h_L = w_H / h_H$, it can do so by employing only low-skill workers and paying them slightly less than what firm f pays its low-skill workers. In the latter case, the competing firm can attract workers despite the slightly lower wage due to the slack in its participation constraint that would be present if it paid the same wage as firm f. It follows that either firm f suffers losses or a potential entrant could make positive profits. This contradicts the supposition that firm f produces positive output in the competitive equilibrium.

In an economy with linear technologies, a firm can avoid internal jealousies by hiring a homogeneous workforce. But the firm is bound to confront such jealousies if it mixes workers of different types. The absence of any technological benefit from mixing workers dictates the equilibrium organizational structure.

Our example shows that relative-wage concerns can affect organizational choices even when workers cannot vary their exertion of effort. In what follows, we enrich the firms' employment problem by introducing a technology that provides incentive for each firm to diversify its workforce. In such an environment, firms face a nontrivial choice of employment composition and wage structure.

9.4 Closed Economy with Complementary Labor

A firm can always avoid invidious wage comparisons by hiring a homogeneous workforce and paying all of its employees the same wage. When the technology is such that all potential employees are perfect substitutes, such homogeneity comes at no cost to the firm. But when workers bring potentially complementary skills, homogeneity may not be the best option even if diversity begets jealousy. To introduce a trade-off in a firm's choice of workforce composition, we henceforth assume imperfect substitutability between low-skill and high-skill labor.

More specifically, we assume that production requires two intermediate inputs, X_1 and X_2. The two inputs combine to produce final output according to the concave and linearly homogeneous production function,

$$q = F\left(X_1, X_2\right).$$

The maintained properties of $F\left(\cdot\right)$ are summarized in the following.

Assumption 9.3 *(i) $F\left(0, X_2\right) = F\left(X_1, 0\right) = 0$ and (ii) $\partial F\left(X_1, X_2\right)/ \partial X_i > 0$ and $\partial^2 F\left(X_1, X_2\right)/\partial X_i^2 < 0$ when $X_j > 0$ for $j = 1, 2$.*

We think of the production of X_1 as a manual activity that can be performed with equal productivity by either type of labor.[4] By choice of units, we suppose that $1/h_L$ workers of any skill level are needed to produce one unit of X_1. In contrast, the production of X_2 is a cognitive activity in which the high-skill workers enjoy a comparative advantage. For simplicity (and to avoid a taxonomy), we take this to the extreme by assuming that only high-skill workers can perform this activity. Units are such that $1/h_H$ high-skill workers generate one unit of input X_2.

In this chapter, we shall not address decisions about internalization, but rather will simply assume that firms must provide for themselves both of the inputs needed for production of the final output. Later, we will allow the firm to move the production of X_1 offshore and thereby separate the workers engaged in this activity from those who produce input X_2. But for now we assume that both inputs must be produced in the same place. This means that every firm either produces entirely with high-skill labor or else it hires a mix of workers and deploys low-skill workers to perform the manual activities and high-skill workers to perform the cognitive tasks.

The option that a firm has to produce input X_1 with high-skill labor implies that the equilibrium wage paid to these workers must be at least as high as what any firm pays to low-skill workers. Moreover, all firms pay high-skill workers the same wage. To see this, consider a firm that pays $w_H < w_L$ and that successfully hires both types of labor. Such a firm could replace all of its low-skill workers with high-skill workers, pay the latter the same wage as before, and meet the participation constraint for high-skill workers with slack. Since the high-skill workers are as productive as low-skill workers in producing X_1, this would reduce the firm's cost. Now, if all firms pay high-skill workers at least as much as low-skill workers, the former suffer no disutility from internal wage comparisons. It follows that no firm can attract a high-skill worker unless it offers at least what other firms are paying to these workers. In equilibrium, all firms pay $w_H \geq w_L$ and $v_H = v(w_H, w_H)$.

The productivity of high-skill labor in producing input X_1 also puts a lower bound on the equilibrium wage of these workers. A firm could hire only high-skill workers and devote a fraction λ of them to producing X_1 and the remaining fraction $1 - \lambda$ to producing X_2. Let $\lambda^* = \arg\max_\lambda F\left[\lambda h_L, (1 - \lambda) h_H\right]$ be the fraction that maximizes output per worker under this employment strategy. Were a firm to follow this strategy, it would achieve a unit cost of $w_H / F\left[\lambda^* h_L, (1 - \lambda^*) h_H\right]$, which can be no less than the price (of unity) of the final good in equilibrium. It follows that high-skill labor must earn at least $w_{\min} = F\left[\lambda^* h_L, (1 - \lambda^*) h_H\right]$ in equilibrium, which proves the following.

Lemma 9.3 *All firms pay high-skill workers the same wage w_H in equilibrium, with $w_H \geq \max\{w_{\min}, w_L\}$. These workers attain utility of $v_H = v(w_H, w_H) > 0$.*

The last part of lemma 9.3 implies that high-skill workers are fully employed.

Next we show that low-skill workers also are fully employed in equilibrium.[5] Suppose to the contrary that there are unemployed low-skill workers in equilibrium and that some firm f employs low-skill workers at a positive wage w_L. Firm f earns zero profits in a competitive equilibrium. But then a potential entrant f' could offer w_H to high-skill workers and w'_L to low-skill workers, where $w_L > w'_L > 0$, and hire the two types in the same proportions as firm f. Firm f' meets the participation constraint for high-skill workers, because it offers these workers the same utility as firm f (which, by supposition, operates in equilibrium). And firm f' offers a better option to the low-skill workers than unemployment (by assumption 9.2). It follows that firm f' can attract workers and that it can achieve a lower unit cost than does firm f. The potential entrant earns positive profits, which contradicts the supposition of an equilibrium in which firm f is active and low-skill workers are unemployed. Finally, we consider the possibility that all low-skilled workers are unemployed because active firms hire only high-skill workers to produce both inputs. In such a situation, a potential entrant could earn positive profits by producing the two inputs in the same proportions as an active firm, but using low-skill workers paid $w_L < w_H$ in place of high-skill workers for the production of X_1.

We proceed now to characterize several different wage structures that can prevail in equilibrium, and discuss when each arises. We begin with the case in which all workers receive the same pay. To this end, suppose that all firms pay their workers a common wage of $w_H = w_L = w$. In the event, every firm is indifferent between using high-skill workers or low-skill workers (or a mix of the two) for the production of X_1. A firm that chooses to use only high-skill workers to produce X_1 (and, of course, X_2) minimizes cost by inputting X_1 and X_2 in the proportions λ^* and $1 - \lambda^*$, where $\lambda^* = \arg\max_\lambda F\left[\lambda h_L, (1-\lambda) h_H\right]$ as before, thereby achieving a minimal unit cost of $w_H / F\left[\lambda^* h_L, (1-\lambda^*) h_H\right]$. Other firms must achieve the same unit cost, which means that they use the two inputs in the same proportions. These firms employ the same number of total workers to produce a unit of X_1 as the firm that hires only high-skill workers for this purpose, and also the same number of high-skill workers to produce a unit of X_2 as this firm. It follows that, in every firm, at most a fraction λ^* of employees are low-skill workers. An equilibrium with equal wages exists if the fraction of low-skill workers in the economy is no greater than λ^*, that is, if $N_L / \left(N_L + N_H\right) \leq \lambda^*$. In such an equilibrium, all firms break even, which means that all have a unit cost of one. Then the common wage must be $w = w_{\min}$ inasmuch as $w_{\min}$ is the wage for high-skill workers that generates a unit cost of one for a firm that employs only high-skill workers.

To verify that an equilibrium like this exists when $N_L / \left(N_L + N_H\right) \leq \lambda^*$, note that no firm could attract workers of a type i if it were to offer these workers a wage $w_i < w_{\min}$. And no firm has an incentive to offer workers of type i a higher wage then $w_{\min}$, because doing so can only raise its unit cost.

Finally, no firm has an incentive to use the inputs in a different proportion than $\lambda^*/(1 - \lambda^*)$, no firm can use low-skill workers to produce X_2, and all firms are indifferent as to how they produce X_1. We note as well that when $N_L/(N_L + N_H) \leq \lambda^*$, there exists no equilibrium with unequal wages, because if firms pay low-skill workers $w_L < w_H$, they prefer to hire only these workers to produce X_1 and to use a greater share of X_1 in total inputs than the fraction λ^*. This means that low-skill workers will comprise more than the fraction λ^* of the workforce in every firm, which is not possible when they comprise at most the fraction λ^* in the population of workers.[6]

We summarize the arguments to this point in the following.

Proposition 9.1   *Let assumptions 9.1–9.3 be satisfied and let $N_L/(N_L + N_H) \leq \lambda^*$. Then, in all firms, $w_L = w_H = w_{\min}$ and $X_1/X_2 = \lambda^*/(1 - \lambda^*)$. Each firm is indifferent as to the employment mix used to produce X_1, but, in the aggregate, firms fully employ both types of workers.*

We next consider environments in which low-skill workers are in relatively abundant supply; that is, $N_L/(N_L + N_H) > \lambda^*$. As should be clear from the previous discussion, the two types of workers cannot be paid the same wages in such circumstances, and, in fact, the high-skill workers will enjoy greater utility than their lesser-skilled counterparts. A typical firm seeks to minimize its unit cost by choosing the employment mix μ and the wage of low-skill workers w_L to solve

$$\min_{\mu, w_L} \frac{\mu w_L + (1 - \mu)\, w_H}{F\left[\mu h_L, (1 - \mu)\, h_H\right]} \tag{9.4}$$

subject to the participation constraint for low-skill workers,

$$v\left[w_L, \mu w_L + (1 - \mu)\, w_H\right] \geq v_L,$$

and the feasibility constraint

$$0 \leq \mu \leq 1.$$

In solving this problem, each firm takes the market wage for high-skill workers w_H and the reservation utility level for low-skill workers v_L as given. It employs only low-skill workers to produce X_1, inasmuch as these workers are as productive as their high-skilled counterparts in this activity and they command a lower wage.

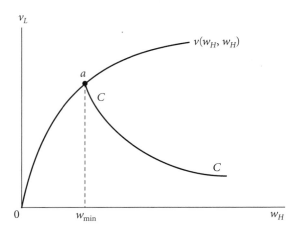

Figure 9.1   Unit cost.

Every firm chooses a combination of μ and w_L such that it meets the participation constraint for low-skill workers as an equality. Failure to do so would mean that the firm could reduce the wage paid to low-skill workers while maintaining the same composition of its workforce, still attract its desired employees, and thereby reduce its unit cost.[7] It follows that the minimum unit cost, which we denote by $c_n\left(w_H, v_L\right)$, is continuous and increasing in both arguments for all $v_L < v_H = v(w_H, w_H)$.[8]

The downward sloping curve CC in Figure 9.1 depicts the combinations of w_H and v_L that satisfy

$$c_n\left(w_H, v_L\right) = 1, \tag{9.5}$$

that is, combinations that yield a minimum unit cost equal to the price of the final good. The curve emanates from the $v(w_H, w_H)$ curve at the point a at which $w_H = w_{\min}$. The location of the equilibrium along CC depends on the relative abundance of low-skill workers. Two types of equilibria are possible, as we shall now illustrate by means of an example.

To this end, consider an economy with a Cobb-Douglas production function

$$F\left(X_1, X_2\right) = X_1^\alpha X_2^{1-\alpha}, \quad 0 < \alpha < 1,$$

and the utility function

$$u\left(w, \frac{w}{w_r}\right) = \begin{cases} w\left(\frac{w}{w_r}\right)^{1/\eta} & \text{for } w < w_r \\ w & \text{for } w \geq w_r \end{cases}, \quad \eta > 0.$$

The parameter η measures (inversely) a worker's concern about his relative wage. The standard setting in which workers care only about their own pay is represented by the limiting case in which $\eta \to \infty$. This utility function yields an associated indirect utility function of the form

$$v\left(w, w_r\right) = w^{1+1/\eta} w_r^{-1/\eta},$$

which implies that the $v(w_H, w_H)$ curve in Figure 9.1 is a ray through the origin.

With these functional forms, a firm's cost-minimization problem for $w_L < w_H$ can be written as

$$\min_{\mu, w_L} \frac{\mu w_L + (1-\mu) w_H}{h_L^{\alpha} h_H^{1-\alpha} \mu^{\alpha} (1-\mu)^{1-\alpha}}$$

subject to

$$\frac{w_L^{1+\eta}}{\mu w_L + (1-\mu) w_H} \geq v_L^{\eta},$$

and

$$0 \leq \mu \leq 1.$$

To characterize the solution to this problem, recall that for equilibrium values of w_H and v_L, the participation constraint is satisfied with equality. We can therefore solve from this constraint the fraction μ as a function of the other variables to obtain

$$\mu = \frac{1 - w_\ell^{1+\eta}/v_\ell^{\eta}}{1 - w_\ell}, \tag{9.6}$$

where $w_\ell = w_L/w_H$ is the relative wage of the unskilled and $v_\ell = v_L/w_H$ is their relative utility, and both must lie between zero and one. The constraint that μ fall between zero and one implies that

$$v_\ell \leq w_\ell \leq v_\ell^{\eta/(1+\eta)}.$$

Next, substitute the solution for μ into the firm's objective function to obtain an equivalent cost-minimization problem,

$$\min_{w_\ell \in \left[v_\ell, v_\ell^{\eta/(1+\eta)}\right]} \frac{k w_\ell^{\eta+\alpha}\left(1-w_\ell\right)}{\left(1-\dfrac{w_\ell^{1+\eta}}{v_\ell^\eta}\right)^\alpha \left(\dfrac{w_\ell^\eta}{v_\ell^\eta}-1\right)^{1-\alpha}}, \tag{9.7}$$

where

$$k = \frac{w_H}{v_\ell^\eta h_L^\alpha h_H^{1-\alpha}}.$$

The firm takes k as given in solving this problem.

The minimand in (9.7) is continuous for permissible values of w_ℓ and all $v_\ell < 1$. Therefore, there exists a solution to the minimization problem for every value of $v_\ell < 1$. Moreover, the solution does not depend on k, but only on v_ℓ and the parameters α and η. As w_ℓ approaches v_ℓ from above or $v_\ell^{\eta/(1+\eta)}$ from below, the unit cost tends to infinity. It follows that the cost-minimizing choice of w_ℓ lies strictly in the interior of the permissible range. This implies from (9.6) that the fraction of low-skill employees lies strictly between zero and one. The remaining question is whether the solution to the firm's cost-minimization problem is unique.

To answer this question, we resorted to numerical simulation. We found a unique solution to the minimization problem for all values of v_ℓ when η is large. Moreover, in these cases, we found w_ℓ to be increasing in v_ℓ and to covary inversely with μ. In other words, when workers are mostly concerned about their own real wages and less worried about their relative standing within the firm, an increase in the reservation level of utility for low-skill workers causes firms to pay these workers higher wages and to employ relatively fewer of them as a share of total employment.

In Figure 9.2 we show the relationship between μ and w_ℓ implied by (9.6) and the solution to (9.7), when η is large. Each point on the curve corresponds to a different value of v_ℓ; the higher is v_ℓ, the higher is w_ℓ and the smaller is μ. In the limit, as the utility of the low-skill workers approaches that of the high-skill workers, the wage rates converge (i.e., $w_\ell \to 1$) and the fraction of low-skill workers in every firm approaches λ^*.

When the solution to the firm's problem is unique and can be depicted as in Figure 9.2, the general equilibrium also is unique. In the equilibrium, all firms choose the same composition of employment, which must of course match the economy's relative supplies of the two types of workers. There-

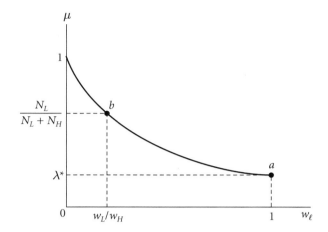

Figure 9.2 Relative wages and composition of employment for large η.

fore, $\mu = N_L/\left(N_L + N_H\right)$. Using this value of μ, we can find the corresponding relative wage at point b in the figure. There is a unique value v_ℓ associated with point b, which we can take to Figure 9.1 to find the corresponding point on the CC curve. This, finally, yields the equilibrium values of v_L and w_H.

The unique equilibrium that emerges when $N_L/\left(N_L + N_H\right) > \lambda^*$ and η is large has standard properties. For example, an increase in the relative supply of low-skill workers generates a shift in the composition of employment in all firms toward these workers, an increase in the wage and utility of high-skill workers, and a fall in the wage and utility of those with lesser skills.

A different type of equilibrium can emerge when low-skill workers are in relatively abundant supply and workers place great weight on their relative pay (i.e., η is small). In such circumstances, there may exist values of v_ℓ for which the solution to the cost minimization problem (9.7) is not unique. Consider Figure 9.3, which plots a firm's unit cost against its choice of relative wage for a particular set of parameter values that includes a small value of η. As is clear, the function relating unit cost to w_ℓ has two local minima. For the parameters that underlie this figure, the global minimum is attained at the right-most critical point. However, a similar diagram drawn for the same parameter values but a lower value of v_ℓ would show the global minimum at the left-most critical point. And for a particular,

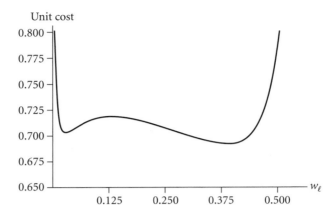

Figure 9.3 Unit cost with two local minima: $k = 1$, $\alpha = 0.2$, $\eta = 0.1$, $v_\ell = 0.001$.

intermediate value of v_ℓ that we denote by v_b, the same unit cost is achieved at both local minima; that is, a firm's optimization problem has multiple solutions.

When $v_\ell = v_b$, a given firm can minimize costs by choosing either of two alternative strategies. It can pay low-skilled workers a low wage and employ relatively many of them, by using a great input of X_1 and a smaller input of X_2, or it can pay the low-skill workers a higher wage but employ relatively fewer of them, substituting more of X_2 for less of X_1. Under the former strategy, the firm attracts low-skill workers despite paying a relatively unattractive wage by providing a work environment with relatively little jealousy. The heavy use of low-skill workers means that the average wage is low, and the typical low-skill worker does not suffer too much from unflattering comparisons. Under the latter strategy with a higher w_L, the low-skill workers derive greater utility from their own pay, but suffer greater disutility when comparing themselves to the average employee in the workplace. In other words, the different compositions of employment imply different comparator groups and therefore different perceptions of fairness.

For low values of η that imply a nonmonotonic relationship between a firm's unit cost and the relative wage it offers, the equilibrium relationship between μ and w_ℓ is as depicted in Figure 9.4. Again, the points along the (discontinuous) downward sloping curve correspond to different values of v_ℓ, which each firm takes as given. For high values of $v_\ell > v_b$, each firm perceives a unique cost-minimizing choice of w_ℓ, which is a relatively

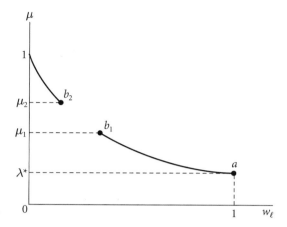

Figure 9.4 Relative wages and composition of employment for small η.

high value that achieves the right-most local minimum in a figure like Figure 9.3.[9] For $v_\ell > v_b$, the relationship between μ and w_ℓ is continuous, and variations in v_ℓ in this range trace out the continuous curve between points b_1 and a in Figure 9.4. Similarly for low values of $v_\ell < v_b$, each firm perceives a unique cost-minimizing choice of w_ℓ, but now it is a relatively low value that achieves the left-most local minimum in a figure like Figure 9.3. Again, the relationship between μ and w_ℓ is continuous and downward sloping, and variation in v_ℓ in the range $v_\ell < v_b$ generates the curve between points b_2 and 1 in Figure 9.4. Finally, for $v_\ell = v_b$, each firm is indifferent between choosing a relatively high value of w_ℓ and the corresponding composition of employment μ_1 or a lower value of w_ℓ and the fraction of low-skill workers μ_2. The alternative solutions to a firm's cost-minimization problem for $v_\ell = v_b$ are represented by points b_1 and b_2 in the figure.

We are now ready to describe the equilibrium, the nature of which depends upon the relative supplies of the two types of workers. In equilibrium, the (average) composition of employment within firms must match the relative supplies of the two types of workers in the population. Suppose $\lambda^* < N_L/(N_L + N_H) < \mu_1$. Then the factor markets can clear only if all firms hire a fraction $\mu = N_L/(N_L + N_H)$ of low-skill workers. In the event, the equilibrium relative wage can be read off Figure 9.4 at the corresponding point along the curve between b_1 and a. The equilibrium relative utility of low-skill workers is the value of v_ℓ associated with the equilibrium μ and w_ℓ. Similarly, if $N_L/\left(N_L + N_H\right) > \mu_2$, all firms choose the same cost-minimizing mix of workers, and the equilibrium falls along the curve between b_2 and 1 in Figure 9.4. But consider how markets can clear when $\mu_1 < N_L/\left(N_L + N_H\right) < \mu_2$. On the one hand, there is no single firm that minimizes cost by hiring workers in the precise proportions that they are represented in the labor force, no matter what the value of v_ℓ. On the other hand, if $v_\ell = v_b$, all firms are indifferent between hiring a fraction μ_1 of low-skill workers and paying the relative wage associated with point b_1 and hiring a fraction μ_2 of low-skill workers and paying the relative wage associated with point b_2. The labor markets can clear only if in equilibrium $v_\ell = v_b$ and if some firms use the employment mix μ_1 and others use the employment mix μ_2 such that on average the two types of workers are employed in the proportions that they populate the labor force.[10]

To summarize, we have the following.[11]

Proposition 9.2   *Let assumptions 9.1–9.3 be satisfied and let $N_L/\left(N_L + N_H\right) > \lambda^*$. Then $w_H > w_L$. For some parameter values, firms that are ex ante identical will differ in their employment mixes. An equilibrium with heterogeneous hiring behavior can arise only when $\partial u\left(w, y\right)/\partial y$ is large relative to $\partial u\left(w, y\right)/\partial w$, where $y = w/w_r$.*

We see that fair-wage concerns can change the nature of equilibrium when workers are sufficiently sensitive to their relative position in the pay structure. In such circumstances, there may be no equilibrium in which otherwise similar firms pay the same wages and make the same hiring decisions. The explanation for this lies in a positive feedback mechanism: paying a high wage to low-skill workers induces a firm to substitute away from these workers, which changes the composition of employment and necessitates an even higher wage so that workers are attracted to the firm despite the jealousies that are aroused.

9.5   Foreign Sourcing

In our model of fair wages, firms have an incentive to separate employees in order to reduce or eliminate jealousies among those who are lower paid. We have seen in Section 9.3 that when firms can hire a homogeneous workforce without any adverse effects on productivity, the profit incentive will drive them to do so. By separating workers, a firm can avoid compensating low-paid workers for the disutility they suffer from unflattering comparisons with notable coworkers.

Firms may attempt to manage jealousies in the workplace via their decisions about internal organization. For example, the mitigation of internal wage comparisons has been suggested as a reason for firms to outsource certain low-skill activities, such as janitorial services, to specialized suppliers (see Baron and Kreps 1999). Here we are interested in a similar motivation for offshoring. If individuals assess the fairness of their wages by comparing themselves to others who work with them in close proximity, then firms might consider moving certain activities offshore to alleviate wage jealousies. In this section we study how the decision to offshore is affected by relative-wage concerns.

To keep matters simple, we assume that firms can produce input X_1 in a foreign plant at a constant cost p_1. Implicitly, we are assuming that by producing the input X_1 offshore, the firm creates a foreign facility with a homogeneous workforce and that foreign low-skill workers are paid a wage that is independent of the equilibrium in the home country. Domestic workers have the utility function $u\left(w, \, w/w_r\right)$, where the comparator group, in assessing the average wage w_r, comprises all workers and only workers in the home facility. We focus henceforth on the case in which low-skill workers are relatively abundant; that is, we impose the following.

Assumption 9.4 $N_L/\left(N_L + N_H\right) > \lambda^*.$

With this assumption, the wage of high-skill workers would be strictly greater than that of low-skill workers in the absence of any offshoring. We denote by w_H^n and v_L^n the (unique) equilibrium values of the wage of high-skill workers and the utility of the low-skill workers in the equilibrium without offshoring, which we described in Section 9.4.

The problem now facing the typical firm is to choose the wage of low-skill workers, the composition of domestic employment, and the sourcing of input X_1 so as to minimize unit cost. We let m_1 denote the ratio of the firm's foreign production of X_1 to the size of its domestic labor force. Then the new problem facing the firm can be written as

$$\min_{\mu, w_L, m_1} \frac{p_1 m_1 + \mu w_L + (1 - \mu)\, w_H}{F\left[m_1 + \mu h_L, \, (1 - \mu)\, h_H\right]} \tag{9.8}$$

subject to

$$v\left[w_L, \mu w_L + (1 - \mu) w_H\right] \geq v_L,$$

and

$$0 \leq \mu \leq 1.$$

To characterize the equilibrium, we will first argue that no firm produces the input X_1 both at home and abroad. To see that this is so, suppose to the contrary that there exists an equilibrium in which some firm f has $m_1 > 0$ and $\mu > 0$. First note that a firm that chooses to manufacture some of input X_1 in a foreign country chooses the quantity m_1 that maximizes the objective function in (9.8) without constraints, because the imports of this input do not directly affect the participation constraint for low-skill workers. The first-order condition for the choice of m_1 by firm f, together with the equilibrium requirement that its unit cost equals one, implies

$$F_1\left[m_1 + \mu h_L, (1 - \mu) h_H\right] = p_1 \tag{9.9}$$

and

$$F\left[m_1 + \mu h_L, (1 - \mu) h_H\right] = p_1 m_1 + \mu w_L + (1 - \mu) w_H, \tag{9.10}$$

where $F_1 = \partial F / \partial X_1$. That is, the value-marginal product of the imported inputs equals their marginal cost p_1 and the unit cost of the final good equals one. It also follows that if $\{m_1, \mu\}$ minimizes the firm's unit cost with $\mu > 0$, then the firm would realize a unit cost at least as great were it to offshore all of its production of X_1. In particular, consider the alternative strategy available to firm f to set $\mu = 0$ and choose imports of X_1 per domestic employee so as to minimize $(p_1 m_1 + w_H) / F (m_1, h_H)$. Let $\tilde{m}_1$ be the cost-minimizing imports per employee with μ constrained to be zero. It is defined implicitly by the first-order condition,

$$F_1\left(\tilde{m}_1, h_H\right) = p_1. \tag{9.11}$$

Since this strategy must yield a per-unit cost of producing the final good at least as high as the optimal choice $\{m_1, \mu\}$, and since the latter achieves a minimal cost of one in the hypothesized equilibrium, it follows that

$$w_H + p_1 \tilde{m}_1 \geq F (\tilde{m}_1, h_H).$$

The linear homogeneity of the production function $F(\cdot)$ then implies that

$$w_H \geq F_2\left(\tilde{m}_1, h_H\right) h_H.$$

Also note that (9.9) and (9.11), together with the linear homogeneity of the production function, imply that the marginal products F_1 and $F_2 = \partial F/\partial X_2$ are the same under the alternative strategies open to firm f, because $\tilde{m}_1 = \left(m_1 + \mu h_L\right) / (1 - \mu)$. Therefore

$$F_1 \mu h_L + F_2 (1 - \mu) h_H = \mu w_L + (1 - \mu) w_H \qquad (9.12)$$

and

$$w_H \geq F_2 h_H, \qquad (9.13)$$

where F_1 and F_2 are the common marginal products.

Next, consider a firm f' that chooses to produce all of X_1 at home and employs $\left(\mu + m_1/h_L\right) / (1 - \mu)$ low-skill workers for every high-skill worker. In this firm the fraction of low-skill workers is μ', which satisfies $\mu'/\left(1 - \mu'\right) = \left(\mu + m_1/h_L\right) / (1 - \mu)$. Suppose that firm f' were to set the same wage w_L as that paid by firm f. By doing so, it would offer strictly higher utility to low-skill workers than firm f, because the fraction of low-skill workers in firm f' would exceed that in firm f, that is, $\mu' > \mu$.[12] Therefore, firm f' could attract low-skill workers with $w_L' < w_L$. Then firm f' would achieve a unit cost of

$$
\begin{aligned}
c' &= \frac{\mu' w_L' + \left(1 - \mu'\right) w_H}{F\left[\mu' h_L, \left(1 - \mu'\right) h_H\right]} < \frac{\mu' w_L + \left(1 - \mu'\right) w_H}{F\left[\mu' h_L, \left(1 - \mu'\right) h_H\right]} \\
&= \frac{\left(\mu + m_1/h_L\right) w_L + (1 - \mu) w_H}{F\left[\mu h_L + m_1, (1 - \mu) h_H\right]} \\
&= 1 + \frac{m_1\left(w_L/h_L - p_1\right)}{F\left[\mu h_L + m_1, (1 - \mu) h_H\right]}.
\end{aligned}
$$

The last equality follows from (9.10). Note that $p_1 \geq w_L/h_L$ because $p_1 = F_1$, F is linearly homogeneous, and $w_H \geq F_2 h_H$ by (9.13). But this implies that $c' < 1$ or that firm f' could make a positive profit. Evidently, the assumption that firm f is active in equilibrium leads to a contradiction.

Why is offshoring attractive only as an all-or-nothing proposition? Again, the answer reflects a positive feedback mechanism that operates in the presence of relative-wage concerns. A firm that finds it profitable to produce a unit of X_1 abroad at a cost p_1 will find that by doing so, it alters the mix of employment at home in such a way as to reduce the attractiveness of employment for low-skill workers. To retain its remaining low-skill workers in its home operation, it must pay these workers more. But this increases the attractiveness of moving offshore the production of the next unit of X_1, and so on.

To further characterize the equilibrium that arises when offshoring is possible, consider the unit cost function defined by

$$c_m\left(p_1, w_H\right) \equiv \min_{m_1} \frac{p_1 m_1 + w_H}{F\left(m_1, h_H\right)}. \tag{9.14}$$

This is the minimum unit cost that can be achieved by a firm that imports all of its input of X_1 at a cost of p_1 per unit, and that faces a market wage for high-skill workers of w_H. If $c_m\left(p_1, w_H^n\right) > 1$, then no firm takes up the opportunity to offshore and the equilibrium with potential offshoring is the same as in Section 9.4. Not surprisingly, offshoring is unattractive when the cost of manufacturing X_1 abroad is sufficiently high. But when the cost of manufacturing X_1 abroad is less than the critical value p_1^n defined implicitly by $c_m\left(p_1^n, w_H^n\right) = 1$, then some firms will offshore their production of X_1 in equilibrium. Since these firms will produce all of their input of X_1 abroad, and since they must break even, the equilibrium wage of high-skill workers must satisfy

$$c_m\left(p_1, w_H\right) = 1. \tag{9.15}$$

Firms that produce their input X_1 at home also must break even, which means that their unit cost equals one, or that

$$c_n\left(w_H, v_L\right) = 1. \tag{9.16}$$

In Figure 9.5 we plot the two equilibrium conditions, (9.15) and (9.16), for the case in which $p_1 = p_1^n$. These conditions jointly determined w_H and v_L, which of course turn out to be the same as in the equilibrium without an offshoring option when, as here, the cost of foreign inputs is equal to the critical value. For a lower foreign manufacturing cost, the $c_m = 1$ curve is further to the right. Then the wage of high-skill workers exceeds that in the equilibrium without offshoring, and the low-skill workers fare worse in utility terms than they do when offshoring is not a possibility. We summarize as follows.

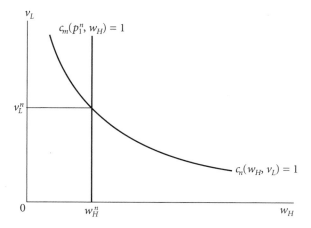

Figure 9.5 Equilibrium wage and welfare with foreign sourcing.

Proposition 9.3 *Let assumptions 9.1–9.4 be satisfied. If $p_1 \geq p_1^n$, all firms produce X_1 at home and the equilibrium is the same as that described in Section 9.4. If $p_1 < p_1^n$, then some firms produce X_1 entirely at home while others produce the input entirely abroad. In such an equilibrium, $w_H > w_H^n$ and $v_L < v_L^n$.*

Note that relative-wage concerns strengthen the incentive to offshore in the following sense. When a firm elects to produce X_1 abroad, it pays more to do so than it would pay to manufacture the same quantity of the input at home. To see this, consider an equilibrium in which some firms produce X_1 offshore and others produce it at home. The former pay p_1 per unit of the input. The latter pay a wage w_L and require $1/h_L$ workers per unit of output, so their cost per unit is w_L/h_L. Suppose it were the case that $p_1 = w_L/h_L$. Then a firm that produces X_1 at home could earn the same profits by importing X_1 and maintaining its original composition of inputs X_1 and X_2 in producing the final good. But then it could increase profits by reoptimizing its choice of X_1/X_2. The firm would strictly benefit from reoptimization, because it would no longer face a binding participation constraint for low-skill workers. So, equality between the per-unit cost of manufacturing the input X_1 at home and abroad would mean that all firms have an incentive to shift production abroad. In equilibrium, no such incentive can exist, so it must be the case that $p_1 > w_L/h_L$.

We can see that relative-wage concerns strengthen the incentive to offshore in another way. Suppose we compare two economies that are otherwise identical, but job satisfaction depends on relative pay in one economy but not the other. Let a superscript A denote an economy in which workers care only about their own incomes; that is, $v(w, w_r) = v^A(w)$. A superscript B denotes an economy in which workers care about their relative standing, as described by assumption 9.1. Then there exists a range of foreign production costs (p_1^{nA}, p_1^{nB}) such that for p_1 in this range, offshore production takes place if relative-wage concerns are present but not if they are absent. And, for $p_1 < p_1^{nA}$, the volume of offshore production is greater when such concerns are present than when they are absent.

To prove this assertion, let's start with a comparison of the critical cost p_1^n at which firms are indifferent between producing X_1 at home and producing it abroad. The critical cost p_1^{nJ} in economy J is defined by $c_m\left(p_1^{nJ}, w_H^{nJ}\right) = 1$, where w_H^{nJ} is the equilibrium wage of a high-skill worker in setting J when offshoring is not an option. The unit cost function $c_m\left(\cdot\right)$ is the same in both settings, because the technologies are the same and firms that offshore minimize their unit cost without constraints. But the closed-economy wage of high-skill workers is higher when relative-wage concerns are absent; that is, $w_H^{nA} > w_H^{nB}$.[13] It follows that $p_1^{nB} > p_1^{nA}$.

Now suppose that $p_1 < p_1^{nA}$ so that offshoring takes place whether workers care about their relative standing or not. In both settings, the equilibrium wage of high-skill workers is determined by the zero-profit condition for firms that offshore production of input X_1, namely $c_m(p_1, w_H) = 1$. Therefore, the wage of high-skill workers is the same in either setting. In the economy without relative-wage concerns, the wage equals the marginal product of high-skill labor in firms that produce entirely at home, so $w_H = F_2^A\left[\mu^A h_L, \left(1 - \mu^A\right)\right] h_H$, where μ^A is the fraction of low-skill workers employed by a firm that produces X_1 at home. For simplicity, assume that a firm either produces all of X_1 domestically or it produces all of it abroad.[14] Then $\mu^A > \bar{\mu}$, and the extent of offshoring increases with μ^A.

In the economy with relative-wage concerns, by contrast, the marginal product of high-skill workers exceeds their wage in firms that produce X_1 domestically, because they hire extra low-skill workers to alleviate the participation constraint. In any firm j that produces X_1 at home, $w_H < F_2^{Bj}\left[\mu^{Bj} h_L, \left(1 - \mu^{Bj}\right) h_H\right]$, where μ^{Bj} is the fraction of low-skill workers employed by firm j.[15] Since the wage of the high-skill workers is the same in the two economies, $F_2^{Bj} > F_2^A$ for all j and therefore $\mu^{Bj} > \mu^A$ for all j. In other words, every firm that manufactures X_1 domestically uses a larger fraction of low-skill workers when relative-wage concerns are present than when these concerns are absent. It follows that more high-skill workers are employed by firms that offshore production of X_1 in the economy with relative-wage concerns. The quantity of X_1 produced abroad must be larger as well. We have thus established the central result in this section.

Proposition 9.4   *Suppose firms can produce X_1 abroad at a constant and common unit cost, $p_1 < p_1^n$. Let assumptions 9.1–9.4 be satisfied. Then the quantity of offshore production is greater than it would be in an otherwise similar economy in which workers' utility does not depend on w_r.*

When workers are quite sensitive to relative-wage concerns, there can be a sharp and dramatic response of industrial structure to small changes in the opportunities for offshoring. Consider, for example, an economy with p_1 slightly above p_1^n. Suppose $N_L/(N_L + N_H)$ lies between the values μ_1 and μ_2 depicted in Figure 9.4, and other parameter values are the same as those that underlie this figure. As we have seen, the initial equilibrium is characterized by heterogeneity in firm hiring strategies, with some firms offering the low-skill wage associated with point b_1 and hiring the mix of workers represented by μ_1, and others paying the low-skill wage associated with b_2 and hiring a fraction μ_2 of low-skill workers. Both types of firms pay high-skill workers the market wage w_H^n, and both offer low-skill workers a common utility level v_L^n.

Now let the cost of offshoring fall slightly to a level just below p_1^n, so that offshore production becomes marginally profitable. Then, as can be seen from Figure 9.5, the wage of high-skill labor will rise to a new equilibrium rate $w_H^o > w_H^n$, and the equilibrium utility level for low-skill workers will fall to $v_L^o < v_L^n$ (where the superscript ^{o} denotes the equilibrium with offshoring). These changes are small, since the c_n curve in Figure 9.5 is continuous. However, the implied changes in industrial structure are large. With $v_L^o < v_b$ and $w_H^o > w_H^n$, the firms that produce X_1 domestically are no longer indifferent between the alternative employment mixes and pay structures represented by points b_1 and b_2 in Figure 9.4. Rather, they strictly prefer to employ a fraction of low-skill workers μ^o that is greater than μ_2

and to pay a relative wage w_ℓ^o that is smaller than w_ℓ^n. Note that for p_1 close to p_1^n, μ^o will be close to μ_2. Nonetheless, the implications for industrial structure are dramatic. With p_1 slightly above p_1^n, a share s_1 of the domestic population works for firms in which low-skill workers comprise a fraction μ_1 of the workforce, while the remaining fraction of the population works for firms in which low-skill workers comprise a fraction μ_2 of the workforce, $s_1\mu_1 + (1 - s_1)\mu_2 = N_L/(N_L + N_H)$. After offshoring becomes just marginally viable, a strictly positive share s^o of domestic workers is employed by firms that produce the input X_1 abroad. This fraction is determined by the requirement that the employment mix among firms that produce both inputs locally must match the residual supplies of the two types of workers after accounting for the high-skill types that work for firms that source X_1 abroad. That is, if $s^o(N_L + N_H)$ workers are employed by firms that source X_1 abroad, and all are high-skill types, there are $N_H - s^o(N_L + N_H)$ high-skill workers left to be hired by firms that produce X_1 at home. In equilibrium, each such firm hires a fraction μ^o of low-skill workers, so s^o is given implicitly by

$$\mu^o = \frac{N_L}{N_L + N_H - s^o(N_L + N_H)}.$$

It bears emphasizing that the discontinuous change in industrial structure is not an endemic feature of our model, inasmuch as it cannot happen when fair-wage concerns are absent or small. Take, for example, the case where η is very large, so that with p_1 slightly above p_1^n, the equilibrium relationship between μ and w_ℓ is as depicted in Figure 9.2. When offshoring becomes marginally viable due to a small decline in p_1, the wage of the high-skill workers rises slightly and the utility of the low-skill workers falls slightly, due to the small rightward shift of c_m in Figure 9.5. These changes are associated with a small reduction in v_ℓ, and therefore a small increase in the cost-minimizing fraction of low-skill workers employed by the firms that produce their inputs X_1 locally. With μ^o now slightly above $N_L/(N_L + N_H)$ in these firms, there is a small residual supply of high-skill workers who are employed instead by firms that offshore production of input X_1. In short, a small reduction in p_1 from just above to just below p_1^n induces a small and continuous change in industrial structure, with a few domestic high-skill workers taking employment with firms that engage in offshoring, and the remainder working for firms that continue to produce their inputs locally, albeit with a slightly increased ratio of X_1 to X_2.

9.6   Efficiency Properties of the Equilibrium with Offshoring

In this section, we explore the efficiency properties of the equilibrium with offshoring. To this end, we consider further the equilibrium in which some firms offshore all of their production of X_1 and others produce the input entirely at home. The firms that produce X_1 abroad import m_1^o units of the input per domestic employee. In firms that produce the input at home, low-skill workers comprise a fraction μ^o of the workforce.

We observe first that the equilibrium outcome does *not* maximize net output. To establish this point, we will show that the marginal product of high-skill workers is greater in firms that produce X_1 domestically than in firms that import the input from abroad. In a firm that produces the input domestically,

$$
F_2[\mu^o h_L, (1 - \mu^o) h_H] h_H - F_1[\mu^o h_L, (1 - \mu^o) h_H] h_L
$$
$$
= (w_H^o - w_L^o) \left(1 - \frac{\mu^o v_2}{v_1 + \mu v_2}\right), \tag{9.17}
$$

where $v_1 = \partial v(w_L, w_r)/\partial w_L$ and $v_2 = \partial v(w_L, w_r)/\partial w_r$, with both evaluated at $w_L = w_L^o$, $w_H = w_H^o$ and $\mu = \mu^o$.[16] The fact that $v_2 < 0$ and $v_1 + \mu v_2 > 0$ implies $F_2[\mu^o h_L, (1 - \mu^o) h_H] h_H - F_1[\mu^o h_L, (1 - \mu^o) h_H] h_L > (w_H^o - w_L^o)$. But $F[\mu^o h_L, (1 - \mu^o) h_H]$ is homogeneous of degree one, and firms make zero profits, which together imply that $F_2[\mu^o h_L, (1 - \mu^o) h_H] h_H > w_H^o$. In contrast, firms that produce X_1 offshore minimize cost by setting

$$
F_2 (m_1^o, h_H) h_H = w_H^o.
$$

So, value added can be increased by shifting the marginal high-skill worker from a firm that produces X_1 offshore to one that does not. The reason is simple: firms that produce domestically use "extra" low-skill workers in order to mitigate the jealousy factor, which leaves the marginal product of skilled workers higher there than in firms that separate their employees.

However, the fact that the equilibrium allocation fails to maximize the economy's net output is not proof of market inefficiency. Allocations that yield greater value-added may leave low-skill workers with less utility, if they cause these individuals to suffer greater wage jealousy. We therefore pose a different question: could a social planner choose a wage for low-skill workers and a wage for high-skill workers, and assign workers to firms, so as to achieve a Pareto improvement relative to the equilibrium outcome? We consider the following planner's problem:

$$\max_{w_L, w_H, m_1, \mu, s} w_H$$

subject to

$$v\left[w_L, \mu w_L + (1 - \mu) w_H\right] \geq v_L^o,$$

$$\left[F\left(m_1, h_H\right) - p_1 m_1\right] s + F\left[\mu h_L, (1 - \mu) h_H\right] (1 - s) \geq \frac{w_L N_L + w_H N_H}{N_L + N_H},$$

$$\mu = \frac{N_L}{(1 - s)\left(N_L + N_H\right)},$$

and

$$0 \leq \mu \leq 1,$$

where s again is the share of the domestic workforce employed by firms that engage in offshoring. In this problem, the planner seeks to maximize the wage paid to high-skill workers subject to the constraint that the low-skill workers fare at least as well as in the equilibrium with offshoring, that per capita net output suffices to pay the average wage in the economy, and that the employment mix of employees in firms that produce X_1 domestically matches the residual supplies, after accounting for the high-skill workers employed by firms that produce X_1 abroad. Implicit in this formulation is the assumption that the planner cannot make side-payments to workers independent of their "wages" in a manner that avoids comparison and jealousy.

The planner's optimal choice of m_1 is given implicitly by

$$F_1(m_1, h_H) = p_1. \tag{9.18}$$

A similar condition characterizes a firm's choice of imports in the market equilibrium, so $m_1 = m_1^o$. Now we solve $s = (\mu - \bar{\mu}) / \mu$ from the third constraint, where $\bar{\mu} \equiv N_L / (N_L + N_H)$, and substitute for s in the second constraint. Then the remaining first-order conditions imply[17]

$$F_2\left[\mu h_L,\,(1-\mu)\,h_H\right]h_H - F_1\left[\mu h_L,\,(1-\mu)\,h_H\right]h_L$$

$$= (w_H - w_L)\left(1 - \frac{\mu v_2}{v_1 + \mu v_2}\right) + \left(w_H^o - w_H\right)\frac{1}{\mu},\qquad(9.19)$$

$$F\left[\mu h_L,\,(1-\mu)\,h_H\right]$$

$$= \mu w_L + (1-\mu)\,w_H + \left(w_H - w_H^o\right)\left(\frac{\mu - \bar{\mu}}{\bar{\mu}}\right),\qquad(9.20)$$

and

$$v\left[w_L,\,\mu w_L + (1-\mu)\,w_H\right] = v_L^o,\qquad(9.21)$$

where v_1 and v_2 are evaluated at $w = w_L$ and $w_r = \mu w_L + (1-\mu)\,w_H$.

Observe that $\mu = \mu^o$, $w_H = w_H^o$, and $w_L = w_L^o$ satisfy these first-order conditions.[18] Moreover, we can show that there exists no other solution to (9.19)–(9.21) with $w_H > w_H^o$ and $\mu \in [0, 1]$. It follows that the planner cannot improve on the market outcome.

To see that there is no solution to (9.19)–(9.21) with $w_H > w_H^o$, suppose to the contrary that such a solution exists with $\mu = \mu^*$, $w_L = w_L^*$, and $w_H = w_H^* > w_H^o$. Then (9.20) implies that $F\left[\mu^* h_L,\,(1-\mu^*)\,h_H\right] > \mu^* w_L^* + (1-\mu^*)\,w_H^o$. But then, in the equilibrium setting of Section 9.4, a firm f' could offer low-skill workers a wage w_L^* and seek to hire a fraction μ^* of low-skill employees to produce the input X_1. Firm f' could attract workers on these terms, because[19]

$$v\left[w_L^*,\,\mu^* w_L^* + \left(1 - \mu^*\right) w_H^*\right] > v\left[w_L^*,\,\mu^* w_L^* + \left(1 - \mu^*\right) w_H^o\right] = v_L^o.$$

And, by doing so, it would earn positive profits, because[20]

$$F\left[\mu^* h_L,\,\left(1 - \mu^*\right) h_H\right] - \mu^* w_L^* - \left(1 - \mu^*\right) w_H^o >$$
$$F\left[\mu^* h_L,\,\left(1 - \mu^*\right) h_H\right] - \mu^* w_L^* - \left(1 - \mu^*\right) w_H^* \geq 0.$$

Of course, the fact that a firm f' could make positive profits when facing the market opportunities contradicts the assumption that $\{w_H^o, v_L^o\}$ characterizes a competitive equilibrium. Thus, no solution to (9.19)–(9.21) with $w_H > w_H^o$ exists.

We conclude that the social planner cannot improve on the market equilibrium with offshoring. Although firms' incentives to separate employees induce offshoring beyond the level that maximizes net output, the psychological gain to domestic workers who suffer less from unfavorable wage comparisons justifies the loss of material well-being.

9.7 Conclusion

When low-paid workers suffer disutility from earning less than the average in their office or plant, they will be attracted to firms that offer more equitable pay structures. In such an environment, firms face a trade-off between the wages they pay to low-skill workers and the mix of workers they employ. This trade-off, which exists even if job satisfaction has no effect on effort or productivity, has implications for resource allocation and the organization of firms.

In this chapter, we have developed a simple general equilibrium model of an economy in which individuals compare their own wage to the average pay of their fellow workers. The concerns over relative wage impact firms' decisions about pay structure, employment mix, and the organization of production. We study these links for a closed economy and for an open economy in which firms can produce an intermediate input abroad. General equilibrium interactions play an important role in our analysis, because firms must structure jobs so that they can hire workers, which means that the optimal organization of production depends on workers' outside options. In our model, the outside options are endogenous and vary with the opportunities firms have to move part of their operation abroad. If workers compare themselves only to coworkers in the same location, then relative-wage concerns enhance the incentives for offshoring.

Our analysis has focused on economies that produce a single final good. It would be desirable to extend the model to include additional sectors. Such an extension is essential, for example, if one wishes to understand the links between relative-wage concerns and comparative advantage. We have not conducted such an analysis as yet, but offer some tentative observations.

Consider an economy similar to the one described here but with two industries that produce different final goods. Each sector uses two intermediate inputs, one produced primarily by high-skill labor, the other produced primarily by low-skill labor. Let the industries differ in their relative use of the two inputs. Suppose there are two countries that share identical technologies, identical homothetic preferences over the two final goods, and identical labor endowments. The countries differ, however, in their workers' sensitivity to below-average wages. We might ask, "Does the country with individuals who care more about their relative wage have a comparative advantage in producing skill-intensive products?" The answer appears to be "Not necessarily."

The source of ambiguity lies in the fact that relative-wage concerns cause relatively severe problems for firms that use an even mix of employees, but less severe problems for those that employ a relatively homogeneous work force. Wage jealousies have relatively little adverse effect on cost in firms that hire mostly low-skill workers, but also in firms that hire mostly high-skill workers. So a country whose workers are more sensitive to wage comparisons may gain a comparative advantage in either sector, if the factor intensity in that sector is extreme. The trade pattern will depend on structural features, such as the nature of the technologies, and on the general equilibrium interactions between sectors. In such an environment, the opportunities for offshoring affect the industrial structure in a complex way that we do not yet fully understand. The complexity of these interactions raises interesting questions for future research.

We have focused on offshoring as a way to reduce labor costs in the face of fair wage comparisons. There obviously exist additional options for mitigating these types of cost concerns, whose potency depends on how workers view their comparison groups. One possibility is to domestically outsource activities—such as janitorial services—that are intensive in low-skill workers. In the United States this has been a major trend in recent years. Another possibility is to have separate plants with largely segregated groups of workers. But this may not entirely eliminate jealousy across workers of different types, and it may be less effective than offshoring. A proper analysis of these choices requires a richer model that contains explicit preferences over wider forms of wage comparisons and costs of alternative organizational forms. Modelling these features would be quite interesting, and it can also be useful for analyzing technology adoption and technological change. In other words, if firms choose technologies to minimize cost, they may as well factor in the impact on cost of the required composition of labor. Under these circumstances technological change will be directed toward employment structures that save such costs. Evidently, these are interesting questions for future research.

ACKNOWLEDGMENTS

We thank Volker Nocke and Thierry Verdier for useful comments, and the National Science Foundation and the U.S.–Israel Binational Science Foundation for financial support.

NOTES

1. See also, for example, Agell and Lundberg (1992, 1995), Kreickemeier and Nelson (2006), and Kreickemeier and Schoenwald (2006).

2. Our specification of relative-wage concerns differs from status concerns in economic models. As an example consider Fershtman and Weiss (1993), who model utility as a function of consumption (income) and occupational status, but in their specification, the occupational status depends on the average wage of the occupation and the fraction of skilled workers employed in the occupation. In their case, a worker is not concerned with the mix and compensation of workers in the firm that employs him, as in our specification, but rather with the broad features of his occupation across the economy.

3. Akerlof and Yellen (1990) note the ambiguous results that have been found in psychological experiments that look for *increased* effort on the part of those who are *overpaid*. They assume in their modeling that effort does not respond to relative wage once a worker's pay exceeds the reference wage. This is in the same spirit as our assumption that workers do not derive extra utility from an above-average wage. An alternative formulation, in which workers who were paid above the average derive utility from their high relative compensation, could also be entertained. The justification for this would be a form of "social status" attached to the high relative income. We do not consider this possibility in the chapter. As will become clear from the analysis, this type of status concern would introduce a tension between the cost of hiring low-skill and high-skill workers, which conflicts with the tension which is the main focus of this chapter.

4. Alternatively, we could allow the high-skill workers to have an absolute advantage but a comparative disadvantage in producing X_1. Then, for a range of productivities of the high-skill workers in this activity, it would not be profitable for firms to use these workers for this purpose, as in the equilibria we study below.

5. This property of the model contrasts with results that are commonly found in the literature on fair wages; see, for example, Akerlof and Yellen (1990), Agell and Lundberg (1995), and Kreickemeier and Nelson (2006). It might seem that the different finding reflects the different assumptions about the

observability of effort. In the earlier papers, workers' efforts are variable and firms pay efficiency wages to promote high productivity. The optimal wage is above the market-clearing wage, which results in unemployment. However, our model would yield an equilibrium with full employment even if workers' efforts were variable. The key difference instead is that we take the reference wage to be the *average* in the firm, whereas previous authors either take the reference wage to be w_H no matter how many employees are hired at that rate or else they take the reference wage to be determined outside the firm. When the reference wage is the average wage, firms can hire many low-skill workers when their wage is sufficiently low without losing their ability to attract workers or to induce positive effort. Firms' willingness to hire many low-skill workers at a sufficiently low wage, together with our assumption that workers always prefer to be employed at a positive wage than to be unemployed, is what eliminates the possibility of unemployment in our model.

6. Note that if $w_L < w_H$ in some firm, then $w_H > w_{\min}$, because if w_H were to equal $w_{\min}$, then the firm with $w_L < w_H$ would have a unit cost below one, which is not possible in equilibrium. It therefore follows that if a firm pays $w_L < w_H$ in equilibrium, then all firms pay the low-skill workers less then the high-skill workers and $w_H > w_{\min}$. Under the circumstance every firm seeks to employ a fraction of the unskilled in excess of λ^*, which is not possible when $N_L / \left(N_L + N_H \right) \leq \lambda^*$.

7. To see this formally, note that the first-order condition with respect to w_L is

$$\frac{\mu}{F} - \zeta \left(v_1 + v_2 \mu \right) = 0,$$

where $\zeta \geq 0$ is the Lagrangian multiplier of the participation constraint, v_1 is the partial derivative of $v \left(\cdot \right)$ with respect to its first argument, and v_2 is the partial derivative with respect to its second argument. The last part of Lemma 9.1, that is, $v \left(\lambda w, \lambda w_r \right) > v \left(w, w_r \right)$ for $w > 0$ and $\lambda > 1$, implies that $v_1 w_L + v_2 \left[\mu w_L + (1 - \mu) w_H \right] > 0$, which implies in turn that $v_1 + v_2 \mu > 0$, because $v_2 < 0$. As a result, the first-order condition for $w_L > 0$ can be satisfied only if $\zeta > 0$, or the participation constraint is satisfied with equality.

8. Using the envelope theorem we obtain

$$c_{n1} = \left(\frac{1}{F} - \zeta v_2 \right) (1 - \mu) > 0,$$

$$c_{n2} = \zeta > 0,$$

where c_{n1} is the partial derivative of $c_n \left(\cdot \right)$ with respect to its first argument and c_{n2} is the partial derivative with respect to its second argument. The inequalities result from the fact that the multiplier ζ is strictly positive, as explained in note 7, and the fact that $v_2 < 0$.

9. For v_ℓ large enough, the left-most local minimum in a figure like 9.3 may disappear entirely, leaving the higher value of w_ℓ as the unique critical point.

10. More formally, let a fraction s_1 of final producers employ low-skill workers as a fraction μ_1 of their workforce, and let the remaining fraction $s_2 = 1 - s_1$ of firms employ low-skill workers as a fraction μ_2 of the their workforce. Then, in equilibrium, the proportions of each type of firm are determined by $s_1\mu_1 + s_2\mu_2 = N_L / (N_L + N_H)$.

11. The last part of the proposition follows from the fact that for $\partial u\,(w,y)\,/\partial y \equiv 0$ there is a unique standard equilibrium with one type of firm.

12. In firm f', the ratio of low-skill to high-skill workers is $(\mu + m_1/h_L)\,/\,(1 - \mu)$, while in firm f this ratio is $\mu/(1 - \mu)$. With a greater fraction of low-skill workers and similar wages, firm f' offers low-skill workers a higher relative wage than firm f.

13. In the economy with no relative-wage concerns, every firm employs a proportion $\bar{\mu}$ of low-skill workers and $w_L^{nA} = F_1^A h_L$ and $w_H^{nA} = F_2^A h_H$, where F_i^A is F_i evaluated at $X_1 = \bar{\mu} h_L$ and $X_2 = (1 - \bar{\mu})\,h_H$ for $i = L, H$. In the economy with relative-wage concerns, the first-order conditions of the cost-minimization problem (9.4) for a firm of type j imply $F_2^{Bj} h_H - F_1^{Bj} h_L > w_H^{nB} - w_L^{nBj}$ and $w_H^{nB} < F_2^{Bj} h_H$, as we show in Section 9.6, where F_i^{Bj} is F_i evaluated at $X_1 = \mu^{Bj} h_L$ and $X_2 = (1 - \mu^{Bj})\,h_H$ for $i = L, H$, and μ^{Bj} is the proportion of low-skill workers employed by a firm of type j. If all firms are symmetric, then $\mu^{Bj} = \bar{\mu}$, but we have seen that the equilibrium may have heterogeneous firm behavior such that different firms employ different fractions of low-skill workers. In such circumstances, full employment ensures that a weighted average of the μ^{Bj}s equals $\bar{\mu}$. Note that in both types of equilibrium, the wage of the high-skill workers, w_H^{nB}, is the same in all firms. Since F_2^{Bj} is homogeneous of degree zero in $\mu^{Bj} h_L$ and $(1 - \mu^{Bj})\,h_H$ and the production function is concave, F_2^{Bj} is increasing in μ^{Bj}. Therefore, $F_2^{Bj} h_H \leq F_2^A h_H$ for some j, because a weighted average of the μ^{Bj}s must equal $\bar{\mu}$. It follows that $w_H^{nB} < F_2^A h_H = w_H^{nA}$.

14. In the absence of relative-wage concerns, every firm is indifferent in equilibrium between producing X_1 at home or abroad. Firms also are indifferent between producing all of X_1 in one location, or producing some in both locations. The discussion in the text assumes that no firm mixes the two forms of acquisition of X_1, but this is done for expositional purposes only; the result does not depend on this assumption.

15. The argument is the same as in note 13.

16. Equation (9.17) is implied by the first-order conditions for maximizing profits subject to the participation constraint $v[w_L, w_r] \geq v_L$ and the feasibility constraint $\mu \in [0, 1]$.

17. In writing (9.19) and (9.20), we make use of the fact that $m_1 = m_1^o$ and $F\left(m_1^o, h_H\right) - p_1 m_1^o = w_H^o$.

18. With $\mu = \mu^o$, $w_H = w_H^o$, and $w_L = w_L^o$, (9.19) is satisfied by (9.17), (9.20) is satisfied because firms in the market equilibrium make zero profits, and (9.21) is satisfied because firms in the market equilibrium satisfy the participation constraint for low-skill workers.

19. The first inequality follows from the hypothesis that $w_H^* > w_H^o$. The second inequality follows from (9.21).

20. Again, the first inequality follows from the hypothesis that $w_H^* > w_H^o$. The second inequality follows from (9.20), $w_H^* > w_H^o$, and $\mu^* \geq \bar{\mu}$.

REFERENCES

Agell, Jonas, and Per Lundberg. 1992. "Fair Wages, Involuntary Unemployment and Tax Policies in the Simple General Equilibrium Model." *Journal of Public Economics* 47:299–320.

———. 1995. "Fair Wages in the Open Economy." *Economica* 62:335–51.

Akerlof, George A. 1982. "Labor Contracts as Partial Gift Exchange." *Quarterly Journal of Economics* 97:543–69.

Akerlof, George A., and Janet L. Yellen. 1990. "The Fair Wage-Effort Hypothesis and Unemployment." *Quarterly Journal of Economics* 105:255–83.

Baron, James N., and David M. Kreps. 1999. *Strategic Human Resources: Frameworks for General Managers.* New York: John Wiley & Sons.

Bergmann, Thomas, and Vida Scarpello. 2000. *Compensation Decision Making*, 4th ed. Fort Worth, TX: The Dryden Press.

Bewley, Truman F. 1999. *Why Wages Don't Fall During a Recession.* Cambridge, MA: The MIT Press.

Blinder, Alan S., and Don H. Choi. 1990. "A Shred of Evidence on Theories of Wage Stickiness." *Quarterly Journal of Economics* 105:1003–15.

Campbell, Carl, and Kunal Kamiani. 1997. "The Reasons for Wage Rigidity: Evidence from a Survey of Firms." *Quarterly Journal of Economics* 112:759–89.

Clark, Andrew E., and Andrew J. Oswald. 1996. "Satisfaction and Comparison Income." *Journal of Public Economics* 61:359–81.

Easterlin, Richard A. 2001. "Income and Happiness: Towards a Unified Theory." *The Economic Journal* 111:465–84.

Fershtman, Chaim, and Yoram Weiss. 1993. "Social Status, Culture and Economic Performance." *The Economic Journal* 103:946–59.

Frey, Bruno S., and Alois Stutzer. 2002. *Happiness and Economics.* Princeton, NJ: Princeton University Press.

Gächter, Simon, and Ernest Fehr. 2002. "Fairness in the Labour Market: A Survey of Experimental Results." In *Surveys in Experimental Economics: Bargaining, Cooperation and Election Stock Markets*, eds. F. Bolle and M. Lehmann-Waffenschmidt, Heidelberg: Physica Verlag.

Goodman, Paul. 1977. "Social Comparison Processes in Organizations." In *New Directions in Organizational Behavior*, eds. B. Staw and G. Salancik, Chicago: St. Clair.

Grossman, Jean B. 1983. "The Impact of the Minimum Wage on Other Wages." *Journal of Human Resources* 18:359–78.

Hammermesh, Daniel A. 2001. "The Changing Distribution of Job Satisfaction." *Journal of Human Resources* 36:1–30.

Kreickemeier, Udo, and Douglas Nelson. 2006. "Fair Wages, Unemployment and Technological Change in the Global Economy." *Journal of International Economics* 70:451–69.

Kreickemeier, Udo, and Steffi Schoenwald. 2006. "Fair Wages and Unemployment in a Small Open Economy." GEP research paper series no. 2006/13, University of Nottingham.

Levine, David I. 1993. "Fairness, Markets, and Ability to Pay: Evidence from Compensation Executives." *American Economic Review* 83:1241–59.

Lincoln, James L., and Arne Kalleberg. 1990. *Culture, Control and Commitment.* New York: Cambridge University Press.

Luttmer, Ezro F. P. 2005. "Neighbors as Negatives: Relative Earnings and Well-Being." *Quarterly Journal of Economics* 120:963–1002.

Martin, Joanna. 1981. "Relative Deprivation: A Theory of Distributive Injustice for an Era of Shrinking Resources." In *Research in Organizational Behavior*, eds. B. Staw and L. Cummings. Greenwich, CT: JAI Press.

Milkovich, George T., and Jerry M. Newman. 2005. *Compensation*, 8th ed. New York: McGraw Hill.

Patchen, Martin. 1961. *The Choice of Wage Comparisons.* Englewood Cliffs, NJ: Prentice Hall.

Verhoogen, Eric, Stephen V. Burks, and Jeffrey P. Carpenter. 2007. "Fairness and Freight-Handlers: A Test of Fair-Wage Theory in a Trucking Firm." *The Industrial and Labor Relations Review* 60:477–98.

— 10 —

Organizing Offshoring

Middle Managers and Communication Costs

POL ANTRÀS, LUIS GARICANO,

AND ESTEBAN ROSSI-HANSBERG

10.1 Introduction

Recent developments in the world economy have led to a staggering disintegration of the production process across borders.[1] Why do firms decide to offshore certain parts of their production process to foreign locations? What qualifies certain countries as particularly attractive locations to offshore? In this chapter we address these questions with a theory of production hierarchies in which cross-country differences in the distribution of skills, as well as differences in the cost of transmitting knowledge internationally versus locally, determine the decision of whether or not to offshore to a particular country.

Our model illustrates how the decision to offshore parts of the production process to foreign countries may be associated with changes in the organizational structure of firms, as firms may introduce intermediate layers of managers to minimize the costs of transmitting knowledge across borders. More specifically, our theory describes situations in which international offshoring to a particular host country is only profitable if the production facility in the host country is composed of two layers rather than one: a set of workers specialized in production and a set of middle managers in charge of supervision. By shielding the top management in the home country from having to deal with routine problems faced by workers in the host country, the presence of middle managers allows a more efficient (time-saving) transmission of knowledge across countries.

As in Antràs, Garicano, and Rossi-Hansberg (2006), we develop these ideas in a general equilibrium framework with two countries, the North

311

and the South. We model a world economy in which production requires time and knowledge, and where agents with heterogeneous abilities sort into teams competitively. The distribution of skills in the host country (the South) plays a central role in the analysis. In particular, in situations in which the efficient organization of production demands the presence of middle managers in the host country, the availability of "middle skills" in the host country becomes crucial for attracting offshoring.

We show however that the availability of middle skills is *not* always conducive to offshoring into a particular country. When the communication technologies available to Southern teams are sufficiently developed, the presence of middle skills may actually hinder the emergence of offshoring. The intuition for this result is that advanced Southern communication technologies foster the formation of domestic teams in the host country, thus increasing the opportunity cost and equilibrium remuneration of local agents hired by multinational firms.[2] We show that this increase in the opportunity cost of host-country agents may be large enough to altogether deter offshoring to that particular country.

Our analysis thus shows that the distribution of skills in host countries, together with local production possibilities, are crucial in determining the desirability of a country as a target of offshoring. We examine the empirical validity of one of the main predictions of the model using data on average FDI inflows and educational attainment measures in a large cross-section of countries in the period 1993–2002. After constructing an index of the availability of communication technologies in different countries, we show that, consistent with the model, a higher availability of middle skills (as measured by secondary school enrollment) is associated with higher FDI inflows (as a percentage of GDP) into countries with poor communication technologies, but with lower FDI inflows into countries with advanced communication technologies.[3]

This chapter is most closely related to our previous work in Antràs, Garicano, and Rossi-Hansberg (2006), where we developed the notion of international offshoring as being the outcome of the assignment of heterogeneous agents into international hierarchical teams. In that paper we studied the consequences of international team formation for the matching between managers and workers and for the implied structure of wages. For that purpose, we simplified our analysis by focusing on two-layer teams and by drawing no distinction between international and local communication costs within multinational and in Southern teams. As a consequence of these features, the model ruled out any active role of host-country middle managers and always generated international offshoring in equilibrium, being thus unable to shed light on the extensive margin of offshoring.[4]

In a related paper, Burstein and Monge-Naranjo (2009) use an extension of Lucas' (1978) span-of-control model to analyze FDI flows across countries. Their analysis distinguishes between firm-specific and host-country embedded productivity and shows how the lack of high-productivity firms in the host country, combined with high country-wide embedded productivity, fosters offshoring. In contrast with Burstein and Monge-Naranjo (2005), our analysis here incorporates endogenous organizational structures with potentially more than two layers. We therefore underscore the role of middle managers in increasing firm productivity and the role of local communication costs in determining a country's embedded productivity.

The remainder of the chapter contains six sections. In Section 10.2, we describe the general setup. In Section 10.3, we analyze the emergence of offshoring in a model where a host country (the South) has very limited opportunities of production, and we illustrate the positive role of middle managers in bringing about offshoring. In Section 10.4, we look at the other polar case in which the North and the South share access to the same communication technologies, while in Section 10.5 we consider intermediate cases. Section 10.6 summarizes one of the key empirical implications of the theory and contrasts it with the data. The last section concludes.

10.2 General Setup

The model builds on Antràs, Garicano, and Rossi-Hansberg (2006)—AGR hereafter—which in turn builds on Garicano and Rossi-Hansberg (2006a). The framework here is simpler in that we assume a discrete number of skill levels (rather than a continuum). The model is however more general than AGR in that (1) we allow for the formation of teams with more than two layers (which is a prerequisite for studying the role of middle management); and (2) we introduce differences between the costs of transmitting knowledge locally and internationally.

The world economy is inhabited by a unit measure of agents, each endowed with a skill level $z \in [0, 1]$ and a unit of time. The distribution of skills in the world population is given by the distribution function

$$
s(z) = \begin{cases} s_h & \text{if } z = z_h \\ s_m & \text{if } z = z_m , \\ s_l & \text{if } z = z_l \end{cases}
$$

with $z_h > z_m > z_l$ and $s_h + s_m + s_l = 1$.[5]

The world consists of two countries: the North and the South. As in AGR, we assume that the North and the South are endowed with different distributions of skills, with the North being endowed with relatively higher skill levels. We capture this feature in a stark way: all agents in the North are endowed with a skill level equal to z_h, while agents in the South are endowed with a skill level equal to z_m or z_l.[6] Our assumptions on the distribution of skills lead to a stylized model of the decision of high-skilled Northern agents of whether to offshore to the South or remain self-employed.[7]

Agents derive linear utility from consuming the only good in the economy, whose price is normalized to one. Production of this good combines labor and knowledge. As in Garicano (2000) and Garicano and Rossi-Hansberg (2006a), production requires solving the problems that arise in production. An agent with skill z can solve all problems indexed between 0 and z, so an agent with skill $z' > z$ can solve all the problems that z can solve plus some extra ones. That is, knowledge is cumulative. We normalize the set of problems so that the skill level z is also the proportion of problems an agent can solve. Agents have one unit of time that they can use in production or communicating with other agents. Agents face a unit measure of problems per unit of production time, and we normalize output so that a unit measure of solved problems yields one unit of output.

Agents can choose to produce together in teams or work on their own (self-employment). A self-employed agent with knowledge z spends all his time in production and solves a fraction z of the problems that he confronts. Hence, his expected output and income is given by $y = z$. Agents producing in teams can communicate their knowledge to others, and thus help them solve problems. This possibility allows them to form organizations in which several individuals combine their time and knowledge to produce together. Such organizations are composed of production workers, who draw problems, and problem solvers (managers), who can answer questions and thus help workers solve the problems they cannot solve on their own. Agents are income maximizers and so choose the occupation that pays them the highest wage given their ability.

Workers draw problems and try to solve them. If they can, they produce; if they cannot, they ask for help from the managers right above them, in which case these managers incur a communication cost $h_i \in (0, 1)$, where i denotes the identity and location of the parties communicating (which we will specify below). If the manager knows the solution to the problem, the team produces output. If the manager does not know the solution but has a manager above him, he asks this manager for help, and this upper-level manager incurs a communication cost h_j (more on this below). In such a case, production occurs only if the upper-level manager knows the solution to the problem. The skill distribution we assume above, with only three levels of skill, implies that three organizational forms can potentially arise in equilibrium, namely, three-layer teams, two-layer teams, and self-employed agents.[8] Hence, the above discussion suffices to cover the workings of all possible production teams.

To summarize, production is organized in knowledge hierarchies, with some agents specialized in production and some in management. This production structure also gives rise to "management by exception," whereby production workers deal with the most common problems and problem solvers deal with the exceptions. These characteristics are optimal under the assumption that agents do not know who may know the solution to problems they cannot solve, as Garicano (2000) showed in a model with homogeneous workers. The purpose of the hierarchy is to protect the knowledge of those who are more knowledgeable from easy questions others can solve.

Communication costs depend on the circumstance in which communication occurs. We denote communication costs within Southern teams that are not part of a multinational by h_S. Communication costs between Southern agents within a multinational are denoted by h_L, and international communication costs by h_I. We assume throughout that international communication costs are higher than local communication costs within multinational teams, and so $h_I > h_L$. We also assume that local communication technology within multinational teams is at least as good as Southern communication technology available to agents belonging to Southern teams, and so $h_L \leq h_S$.

Hence, multinationals will provide two different inputs to agents in the South: first, the ability to benefit from the knowledge of high-skilled agents in the North; and second, access to a (weakly) better technology for local communication. We interpret the latter feature as a form of technology transfer from multinationals to the South.[9] Throughout the chapter we assume that there is no international market for the better local communication technology of multinationals. On top of local telecomunications, this technology can be thought of as processes and a common culture that together are designed to facilitate information flows within the team. Such processes are not codified or systematized and, therefore, cannot be sold or transferred in the market across borders and firm boundaries (e.g., Arrow 1974).[10] As we will see below, the relative quality of the local multinational and Southern technologies will be crucial in the analysis.

Let us illustrate how production in a two-layer team is carried out. Suppose a top manager with knowledge z_2 leads a one-layer team of n_0 production workers. These workers draw a unit measure of problems each, and solve a fraction z_0 of them. Hence they pass on a fraction $(1 - z_0)$ of all problems. Managers are thus asked to solve $n_0 (1 - z_0)$ problems, which they can address in $n_0 (1 - z_0) h_i$ units of time. Optimally, managers join teams with precisely the right number of production workers so that they use all their time. Since all agents have one unit of time available, the team size n_0 is implicitly given by

$$n_0 h_i (1 - z_0) = 1,\qquad(10.1)$$

where $i \in \{I, L, S\}$. The time constraint implies that the span of the managers is limited by the knowledge of their subordinates.

Output is produced whenever either workers or manager know the solution to the problems, so

$$y = z_2 n_0.$$

Note the source of complementarity between skills in our model: an able top manager increases the productivity of all workers in the team. At the same time, the more knowledgeable are the subordinates, the larger the team and the more can managers leverage their own knowledge.

Denote the earnings of workers by w_0. Then zero profits implies that the wage of managers is given by

$$w_2 = n_0(z_2 - w_0) = \frac{z_2 - w_0}{h_i(1 - z_0)}.$$

Production in three-layer teams is similar but it includes a measure n_1 of middle managers. Let their skill level be given by z_1. Then if the skill of workers is given by z_0, the top manager is only asked to solve $n_0 \left(1 - z_1\right)$ problems, while the layer of middle managers are asked to solve $n_0 \left(1 - z_0\right)$ problems. The time constraints of these two layers of managers are thus

$$n_0 h_i \left(1 - z_1\right) = 1 \tag{10.2}$$

and

$$n_0 h_j \left(1 - z_0\right) = n_1, \tag{10.3}$$

where h_j for $j \in \{I, L, S\}$ denotes the cost of communicating knowledge from top to middle managers. These two equations pin down the size of each of the two lower layers in the team.

Denoting the earnings of middle managers by w_1, we have that

$$w_2 = n_0(z_2 - w_0) - n_1 w_1 = \frac{z_2 - w_0 - h_j \left(1 - z_0\right) w_1}{h_i(1 - z_1)}.$$

In the next three sections, we turn to analyze the equilibrium of our two-country world economy, where all agents maximize utility, and labor markets clear in both countries. We denote by w_i the earnings of an agent with skill z_i. Note that if the equilibrium is such that a fraction of agents with skill level z_i remain self-employed, then the equilibrium wage of all agents with that skill level necessarily equals $w_i = z_i$.

As mentioned above, the simple skill distribution we have assumed implies that we can focus on studying three-layer teams, two-layer teams, and self-employment. This is because it is never optimal to assign two agents with the same skill level to different layers of an organization. Similarly, a team will never have a manager who is less skilled than his subordinates. In terms of the specifics of our two-country model, this implies that Northern agents with skill z_h will either be self-employed or top managers, while Southern agents with skill z_l will either be self-employed or workers. Southern agents with skill z_m may be top managers of two-layer teams, middle managers, workers, or self-employed.

We shall assume throughout that s_h is sufficiently low relative to s_m and s_l, which ensures that high-skilled Northern agents are self-employed only in situations in which *all* other agents in the world economy are also self-employed.[11]

10.3   Equilibrium with Inefficient Southern Communication

We start by analyzing a situation in which the local communication costs h_S faced by Southern agents in domestic teams are so high that domestic Southern teams never form. Namely, h_S is such that

$$\frac{z_m}{h_S(1-z_l)} < z_m + \frac{z_l}{h_S(1-z_l)}$$

or

$$h_S \geq \widehat{h}_S \equiv \frac{z_m - z_l}{z_m\left(1-z_l\right)}.$$

That is to say, total production in a local Southern team is smaller than what its members can get if they work as self-employed. This leads to a world economy that will be in one of four possible equilibria:[12]

1. No offshoring. This corresponds to a situation in which agents in the North do not find it profitable to form two- or three-layer teams with agents in the South. In such a case, all agents are necessarily self-employed (since middle- and low-skilled agents do not form teams in the South). This implies that all agents earn their self-employment wages:

$$w_i = z_i \text{ for } i = h, m, l.$$

2. Two-layer middle-skill offshoring ($z_0 = z_m$). In this case, Northern agents decide to form international teams, but only with Southern middle-skilled agents (who become workers). Northern agents thus earn a wage equal to

$$w_h = \frac{z_h - w_m}{h_I(1-z_m)},$$

where w_m refers to the wage of Southern middle-skilled agents. It is clear that agents with skill z_l will in this case be self-employed and thus $w_l = z_l$. Furthermore, notice that equation (10.1) with $h_i = h_I$ pins down the relative share of agents of each type in a two-layer team as a function of parameters. It will thus be the case that, for sufficiently low s_h (our assumption above), a fraction of medium-skilled agents will also remain unemployed in equilibrium, and thus $w_m = z_m$.[13]

3. Two-layer low-skill offshoring ($z_0 = z_l$). This case is similar to the one above, but now Northern agents form teams with low-skilled Southern agents. The wages of the Northern agents are in this case given by

$$w_h = \frac{z_h - w_l}{h_l(1 - z_l)}.$$

In addition, it is clearly the case that $w_m = z_m$ (all medium-skilled Southern agents are self-employed), and for sufficiently low s_h, a fraction of the low-skilled Southern agents will also be self-employed, implying that $w_l = z_l$.

4. Three-layer offshoring. In this case, agents in the North form three-layer teams and obtain a wage given by

$$w_h = \frac{z_h - w_l - w_m h_L(1 - z_l)}{h_I(1 - z_m)}. \tag{10.4}$$

Notice from equations (10.2) and (10.3) that the relative shares of agents of each type in these teams are fixed, in the sense that they are pinned down by parameters. It will thus (generically) be the case that a fraction of agents of at least two types will end up being self-employed in equilibrium, and the wages of these two types will then be determined by their self-employment wages. For low enough s_h, it will necessarily be the case that all agents in the South will earn their self-employment wages: $w_m = z_m$ and $w_l = z_l$.

10.3.1 Communication Costs, Middle Skills, and Offshoring

Having described these four potential types of equilibria, let us study when they emerge in equilibrium. First note that high-skilled agents in the North always prefer to form two-layer teams with low-skilled agents than two-layer teams with medium-skilled agents. That is,

$$\frac{z_h - z_l}{h_I\left(1 - z_l\right)} > \frac{z_h - z_m}{h_I(1 - z_m)}$$

for all $z_m > z_l$. This implies that given our assumptions on the supply of skills, equilibria of type 2 never arise.[14]

Next note that an equilibrium with three-layer offshoring requires

$$\frac{z_h - z_l - z_m h_L(1 - z_l)}{h_I(1 - z_m)} > \max\left\{z_h, \frac{z_h - z_l}{h_I\left(1 - z_l\right)}\right\}. \tag{10.5}$$

Straightforward differentiation implies that the left-hand side of this inequality is increasing in middle skills z_m if and only if

$$h_L < \widehat{h}_L \equiv \frac{z_h - z_l}{1 - z_l}. \tag{10.6}$$

In that case, when z_m is close to z_l, (10.5) will not hold, while when z_m is sufficiently large, (10.5) will necessarily hold. Hence, there exists a unique threshold skill level $\widehat{z}_m \in (z_l, 1)$ over which three-layer offshoring is an equilibrium and under which it is not. The threshold $\widehat{z}_m$ is obtained by setting (10.5) to equality.

In the converse case in which $h_L > \widehat{h}_L$, one can easily verify that condition (10.5) cannot possibly hold for any $z_m \in (z_l, 1)$, and thus three-layer offshoring cannot be an equilibrium.[15] In such a case, the equilibrium will entail no offshoring or two-layer offshoring. In particular, no offshoring is preferred to two-layer offshoring if international communication costs are high, $z_h > (z_h - z_l) / [h_I (1 - z_l)]$, or

$$z_h h_I > \widehat{h}_L, \tag{10.7}$$

while two-layer offshoring is preferred to no offshoring when the converse of condition (10.7) holds.[16]

Formally stated, if we define offshoring as the volume of production in multinational teams, we have shown the following.

Proposition 10.1   *If $h_S \geq \widehat{h}_S$, there exist two thresholds $\widehat{h}_L \in (0, 1)$ and $\widehat{z}_m \in (z_l, 1)$ such that*

1. *Three-layer offshoring is an equilibrium if and only if $h_L < \widehat{h}_L$ and $z_m > \widehat{z}_m$.*

2. *Otherwise, offshoring is independent of z_m. If $z_h h_I > \widehat{h}_L$, there is no offshoring in equilibrium, while if $z_h h_I < \widehat{h}_L$, two-layer offshoring is an equilibrium.*

Because the choice between no offshoring and two-layer offshoring is independent of z_m, we can thus conclude that a larger z_m tends to (weakly) favor the emergence of an equilibrium with offshoring.[17] In addition, the output of offshoring teams is (weakly) increasing in the skill level of middle managers. Therefore, we can conclude the following.

Corollary 10.1   *If $h_S \geq \widehat{h}_S$, in equilibrium, offshoring is (weakly) increasing in the skill level z_m of middle-skilled agents.*

Our analysis therefore highlights the role of middle-skilled agents in fostering offshoring. Intuitively, higher-ability, middle-skilled agents are better able to protect top managers in the North from "expensive" routine problems, thus making offshoring more attractive.

10.4   Equilibrium with Efficient Southern Communication

In the previous section we have shown that the existence of middle skills in the South fosters international offshoring. This section briefly illustrates that this result heavily relies on our assumption that domestic team formation is limited by high local Southern communication costs.

To see this, consider the case in which $h_S = h_L$, and so, local communication costs are the same no matter if local communication happens within multinational teams or within Southern domestic teams. Relative to the previous section, the only new feature is that an equilibrium may now include two-layer teams between agents with skills z_m and z_l. The ability to form local teams imposes the following restriction on Southern wages:

$$w_m \geq \frac{z_m - w_l}{h_L \left(1 - z_l\right)}. \tag{10.8}$$

If this condition was not satisfied in equilibrium, Southern agents would have incentives to deviate from that equilibrium and form two-layer teams among themselves. Using condition (10.8), one can show that the rents that Northern agents with skill z_h obtain from three-layer offshoring must satisfy

$$w_h = \frac{z_h - w_l - w_m h_L (1 - z_l)}{h_I (1 - z_m)} \leq \frac{z_h - z_m}{h_I (1 - z_m)} < \frac{z_h - z_l}{h_I (1 - z_l)}. \tag{10.9}$$

With the possibility of the formation of two-layer Southern teams, there is an additional instrument to clear factor markets, and (generically) the equilibrium will now feature only one type of agent being (partially) self-employed. Condition (10.9) above implies that whenever some agents with skills z_m or z_l are self-employed (which will be the case whenever s_h is low, as we have been assuming throughout), then three-layer offshoring will be dominated by two-layer international offshoring.[18]

The intuition behind this result is that when agents in the South have the option of forming teams between themselves, the opportunity cost of forming three-layer international teams increases to the point where these become unprofitable.[19]

How do medium skills affect the extensive margin of offshoring in this case? It is straightforward to see that whenever low-skilled Southern agents are partially self-employed, then $w_l = z_l$. And since $w_m \geq z_m$, two-layer offshoring will only emerge if it involves low-skilled workers. The analysis of this case is as in the previous section, with offshoring emerging only if $z_h h_I < \widehat{h}_L$, which is independent of z_m. If, alternatively, middle-skilled Southern agents are partially self-employed, then it is no longer clear which type of two-layer offshoring will emerge in equilibrium. This depends on a relative comparison of $(z_h - z_m) / [h_I(1 - z_m)]$ and $[z_h - z_m (1 - h_L (1 - z_l))] / [h_I(1 - z_l)]$. Regardless of the form of two-layer offshoring, it is clear however that a larger z_m will *reduce* the attractiveness of offshoring versus no offshoring.

This section has therefore shown that the emergence of offshoring, and in particular that of three-layer offshoring, depends crucially on inefficient local communication technology in the South. If this technology is as good as the one used by multinationals, better medium-skilled agents imply better local teams, *not* more offshoring! On the contrary, with good local communication, the model is actually consistent with better middle skills in the South reducing the attractiveness of offshoring.

10.5   The Intermediate Case

Let us finally consider intermediate cases. In particular, consider the case in which the technology to communicate in the South is less efficient than the local communication technology of multinationals ($h_S > h_L$). The formation of Southern teams now imposes the constraint

$$w_m \geq \frac{z_m - w_l}{h_S (1 - z_l)}. \tag{10.10}$$

When h_S is high enough ($h_S \geq \widehat{h}_S$), two-layer Southern teams will not be formed in equilibrium and the analysis is as in Section 10.3. For lower h_S ($h_S < \widehat{h}_S$), these teams will be formed and will ensure that only one type of agent is self-employed in equilibrium. Let us focus on these situations hereafter.

We next consider the four cases discussed in Section 10.3, but now taking into account that the wages of Southern agents will satisfy (10.10) with equality. To simplify the exposition, we will focus on the case in which s_l is high enough to ensure that low-skilled Southern agents are partially self-employed, and thus $w_l = z_l$ and $w_m = (z_m - z_l) / [h_S (1 - z_l)]$. We briefly consider an alternative scenario at the end of this section.

As in Section 10.3, we begin by noting that since $w_m > z_m$ whenever $h_S < \widehat{h}_S$, two-layer offshoring with middle-skilled Southern agents will again be dominated by two-layer offshoring with low-skilled Southern agents. Furthermore, since $w_l = z_l$, the comparison between this latter option and no offshoring is identical to that discussed in Section 10.3, and no offshoring will dominate two-layer offshoring whenever $z_h h_I > \widehat{h}_L$ (where, remember, $\widehat{h}_L \equiv (z_h - z_l) / (1 - z_l)$) and vice versa when $z_h h_I < \widehat{h}_L$.

Next note that an equilibrium with three-layer offshoring requires

$$\frac{z_h - z_m \frac{h_L}{h_S} - z_l \left(1 - \frac{h_L}{h_S}\right)}{h_I (1 - z_m)} > \max\left\{z_h, \frac{z_h - z_l}{h_I \left(1 - z_l\right)}\right\}. \tag{10.11}$$

Straightforward differentiation implies that the left-hand side of this inequality is increasing in middle skills z_m if and only if

$$h_L / h_S < \widehat{h}_L. \tag{10.12}$$

This condition is analogous to (10.6) in Section 10.3, but it also applies to cases in which h_S is not prohibitively high (i.e., $h_S < 1$). Moreover, it is again the case that, provided that (10.12) holds, when z_m is close to z_l, (10.11) will not hold, while when z_m is sufficiently large, (10.11) will necessarily hold. Hence, there again exists a unique threshold skill level $\bar{z}_m \in (z_l, 1)$—obtained by setting (10.11) to equality—over which three-layer offshoring is an equilibrium and under which it is not.

Following the same logic as in Section 10.3, one can show that in the converse case in which $h_L / h_S > \widehat{h}_L$, condition (10.11) cannot possibly hold for any $z_m \in (z_l, 1)$, and thus three-layer offshoring cannot be an equilibrium. In such a case, the equilibrium will entail no offshoring or two-layer offshoring, with the choice determined by the relative size of $z_h h_I$ and $\widehat{h}_L$.

Formally stated we have shown the following.

Proposition 10.2   *If $h_S < \widehat{h}_S$, there exist two thresholds $\widehat{h}_L \in (0, 1)$ and $\bar{z}_m \in (z_l, 1)$ such that*

1. *Three-layer offshoring is an equilibrium if and only if $h_L / h_S < \widehat{h}_L$ and $z_m > \bar{z}_m$.*
2. *Otherwise, offshoring is independent of z_m. If $z_h h_I > \widehat{h}_L$, there is no offshoring in equilibrium, while if $z_h h_I < \widehat{h}_L$, two-layer offshoring is an equilibrium.*

Relative to proposition 10.1, the main new result is the effect of the domestic communication cost h_S. Consistent with the results in Section 10.4, if h_S is sufficiently low, then three-layer offshoring may cease to emerge in equilibrium, and the condition that determines the emergence of offshoring is independent of z_m. In particular, notice that whenever $h_S \rightarrow h_L$, as in Section 10.4, the condition $h_L / h_S < \widehat{h}_L$ cannot possibly hold (because $\widehat{h}_L < 1$), which explains why we did not observe three-layer teams emerging in equilibrium in that case.

In addition, straightforward differentiation also indicates that the positive effect of z_m on the left-hand side of equation (10.11) is increasing in h_S.[20] This implies that the positive effect of z_m on the attractiveness of an equilibrium with three-layer offshoring is not only discretely higher in the case with inefficient Southern communication costs, but it is also the case that this marginal effect of z_m smoothly increases as communication costs in the South become worse.

Moreover, because the choice between no offshoring and two-layer offshoring is independent of z_m and h_S, we can conclude the following.

Corollary 10.2   *If $h_S < \widehat{h}_S$ in equilibrium, offshoring is (weakly) increasing in the skill level z_m of middle-skilled agents. Furthermore, the positive effect of z_m is (weakly) increasing in domestic communication costs h_S in the South.*

To sum up, this section has generalized the results in Section 10.3 and 10.4 to the case in which local communication costs in the South are high but not prohibitive. Consistent with the results above, we have found that middle skills can play a crucial role in bringing out the emergence of offshoring but only when communication technologies in the South are sufficiently inefficient.

10.5.1 Overall Effect of Middle Skills

So far, we have divided the analysis into two regions: $h_S \geq \widehat{h}_S$ (Section 10.3) and $h_S < \widehat{h}_S$ (Sections 10.4 and 10.5). Because the threshold $\widehat{h}_S$ depends, itself, on z_m, one might worry that by increasing z_m we could jump from one region to another discontinuously. This is not the case. In particular, when we substitute the expression for $\widehat{h}_S$ in the left-hand side of (10.11) (the profits from three-layer offshoring when $h_S < \widehat{h}_S$), we obtain exactly the left-hand side of condition (10.5) (the profits from three-layer offshoring when $h_S \geq \widehat{h}_S$). In other words, the profits from three-layer offshoring are continuous in z_m when we cross $\widehat{h}_S$. Since the right-hand side of these conditions is identical in both cases, the positive effect of z_m on three-layer offshoring (or simply offshoring) holds globally.

Figure 10.1 shows the different thresholds that determine the values of z_m and h_S for which there is offshoring in equilibrium and for which there is no offshoring. In the graph, we fixed all other parameters and look at the thresholds as functions of z_m and h_S. We chose parameter values such that international communication costs are high, $z_h h_I > \widehat{h}_L$, and so either there is offshoring via three-layer teams or there is no offshoring. That is, for these parameter values, offshoring is never organized in two-layer teams. The graph illustrates that the North offshores to the South only if middle-skilled agents are able enough (high z_m) and if communication technology is inefficient (h_S high). This is also illustrated in Figure 10.2, where we present the case in which international communication costs are low and so there is always offshoring. However, offshoring with three layers, and therefore middle-skilled agents, only occurs for high z_m and high h_S.

The following corollary sums up our main result.

Corollary 10.3 *In equilibrium, offshoring is (weakly) increasing in the skill level z_m of middle-skilled agents. Furthermore, the positive effect of z_m is (weakly) increasing in domestic communication costs h_S in the South.*

For most of the chapter, we have assumed that s_l is high relative to s_m and s_h, which ensures that some low-skilled agents are self-employed in equilibrium. The case in which some middle-skilled agents are self-employed in

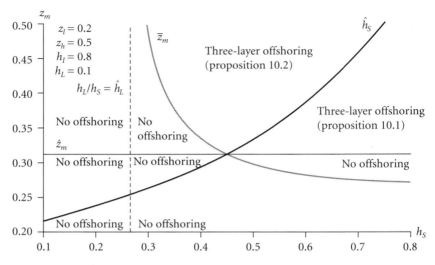

Figure 10.1 Offshoring, middle skills, and Southern communication costs (High h_I).

equilibrium delivers very similar results. In particular, the model continues to predict that the partial effect of z_m on offshoring is (weakly) increasing in h_S.[21] The main difference is that, consistent with the results at the end of Section 10.4, the effect of z_m on offshoring may now be negative for sufficiently low h_S.

10.6   Evidence

The simple model above was useful to understand the target country characteristics that lead to international offshoring. In this section we underscore the main empirical implication of the model and present evidence that suggests that it is supported by the data. In our theory, when Southern communication costs are high, offshoring increases with the ability of middle-skilled agents (corollary 10.3). The intuition is that, in some cases, in order for high-skilled agents in the North to benefit from offshoring, they need to add a layer of local managers that allows them to economize on international communication costs. In order for middle-skilled agents to serve this role, they need to be sufficiently skilled and their opportunity cost must be sufficiently low. Hence, the main implication of the model is that

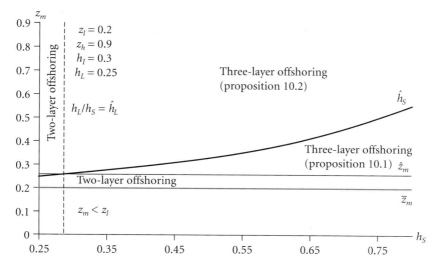

Figure 10.2 Offshoring, middle skills, and Southern communication costs (Low h_I).

in countries where local communication technology is relatively bad (so middle managers can only lead small and inefficient Southern teams), offshoring increases with the ability of middle-skilled managers. In contrast, in countries where communication technology is good, these middle managers will organize local teams and so more-talented middle-skilled agents may not result in more offshoring, but only in more-productive local teams.

The main empirical prediction of the theory can then be expressed as:

The volume of offshoring increases more with intermediate skills in countries where communication technology is relatively bad than in countries where communication technology is relatively good.

Note that this implication of our theory takes as given the level of international communication technology h_I, as well as the level of within-multinational local communication technology h_L, and focuses on the level of local communication technology, h_S, as the source of cross-sectional variation in the data. To illustrate this, consider a Northern firm that is deciding where to offshore, as in our theory. Then our empirical strategy assumes that this firm faces the same h_I and h_L in any host country but can choose where to offshore depending on the host country's h_S.

To contrast this prediction with the data, we use data from the World Bank's World Development Indicators (WDI). We use data on FDI inflows as a fraction of GDP as a measure of offshoring.[22] As a measure of intermediate skills we use the percentage of agents in the relevant age range enrolled in secondary school (*SSE*). Finally, our measure of Southern communication costs is an index of the availability of communication technologies constructed using data on telephone, computer, and Internet usage. The Appendix includes a description of the factor analysis that leads to this index as well as more details on the raw series. Using the index, we divide countries into two sets. Countries with bad communication technology (*BCI* = 1, for bad communication index) and countries with good communication technology (*BCI* = 0). The Appendix lists both sets of countries. We use a dummy variable for communication costs instead of the continuous index.[23] This is because offshoring is independent of h_S whenever $h_S \geq \widehat{h}_S$, so the model does *not* predict a strictly monotonic effect of communication technology. Throughout the analysis we use averages of these variables for the decade 1993–2002. We use the set of 122 countries for which we have complete data for all the variables of interest.

The raw data is presented in Figure 10.3. The figure also presents the corresponding regression lines, using a quantile regression with medians. All results presented in this section use quantile regressions to diminish the influence of outliers. The Appendix includes a discussion of quantile regressions and all results using OLS. In the graph, and in all OLS results in the Appendix, we eliminate two countries from the sample: Luxembourg and Equatorial Guinea. Both of these countries have extraordinarily high FDI over GDP ratios. This is probably the result of their small size and the predominance of particular industries, characteristics that our model is not designed to address. All quantile regressions do include these two observations. Figure 10.3 shows that at first glance the prediction of the theory does well. The regression line for countries with bad communication has a larger slope than for countries with good communication. In countries with good communication technology the slope is in fact negative, which is consistent with the prediction of the theory described at the end of sections 10.4 and 10.5.

The coefficients of both regression lines are presented in columns 1 and 2 of Table 10.1. One may think that the result is due to the fact that the countries with good communication all have SSE values higher than 70%,

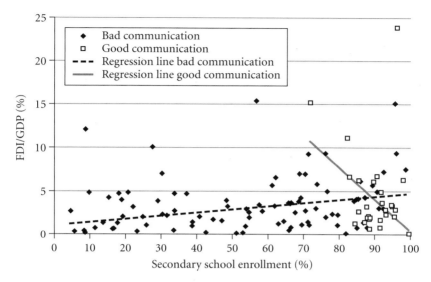

Figure 10.3 FDI and secondary education (1993–2002 averages). *Source*: World Bank Development Indicators. All data points are averages for the decade 1993–2002. For visibility we left out Luxembourg and Equatorial Guinea with FDI/GDP equal to 459.47 and 43.84 respectively. The regression-line coefficients and estimation procedure are reported in the text.

while the larger sample of countries with low communication have values of SSE throughout the [0%, 100%] range. This does not seem to be the case. If we restrict the sample of countries with poor communication to the ones that have $SSE > 70$ (which results in a set of 31 countries), we obtain similar qualitative results. The coefficient on SSE then becomes 0.1665 with a standard error of 0.0646 which is significant at a 5% level. Hence, for the rest of the empirical study we use the whole sample of countries.

We next seek to estimate more efficiently the interaction effect between the BCI dummy and secondary school enrollment by running a specification that incorporates the whole set of countries and includes an interaction term, together with the BCI dummy and the level of SSE in the regression. Column 3 of Table 10.1 presents these results. The prediction of our theory is that the interaction term should be positive and significant, and this is what we find in Table 10.1. This result does not depend on the particular construction of our index, as the coefficient on the interaction term is

Table 10.1 Median regression results

	(1)	(2)	(3)	(4)	(5)	(6)
	Dependent variable: $\frac{FDI}{GDP}$					
	Years: 1993–2002 averages					
Constant	1.06*	36.74**	36.74***	36.74***	−3.35	19.87
	(.64)	(12.87)	(8.72)	(8.45)	(12.43)	(11.15)
SSE	.036***	−.363**	−.363***	−.352***		−.379***
	(.011)	(.143)	(.0971)	(.097)		(.085)
SSE*BCI			.398***	.390***		.413***
			(.098)	(.097)		(.086)
BCI			−35.68***	−35.11***	4.01	−19.21
			(8.75)	(8.76)	(12.26)	(10.96)
PSE*BCI					−.043	−.183*
					(.126)	(.108)
PSE					.087	.203
					(.123)	(.105)
$\frac{GDP}{Pop}$				−.095	−.206	−.177
				(.371)	(.329)	(.313)
Countries	$BCI = 1$	$BCI = 0$	All	All	All	All
Number of observations	93	29	122	122	122	122

Note: Standard errors are in parentheses. The symbols ***, **, and * denote significant coefficients at 1%, 5%, and 10% levels.

positive and significant at the 5% level using each of the components of the index separately.

A potential problem with these results is that secondary school enrollment may be highly correlated with other factors that, one may reasonably argue, influence the level of FDI/GDP, although they are not part of our theory. One of these factors is GDP per capita. In particular, our data on FDI inflows includes horizontal FDI, that is, FDI aimed at producing and selling products in these countries. Because GDP per capita is a proxy for market potential, it could have an independent effect on the ratio FDI/GDP. Column 4 of Table 10.1 presents the results if we add GDP per capita to our empirical specification. It is clear that this hardly changes our results. The coefficient of the interaction term remains positive and significant. The coefficient of GDP per capita is not significant at the 10% level. Another concern is that our BCI index might be capturing some general level of development in these countries. To address this, we have also incorporated

GDP as a dummy variable (that is, we divide the sample into high- and low-income countries) as well as an interaction of SSE and GDP (both directly and as a dummy variable). Our results are robust to these empirical exercises and in all cases the variables related to GDP are not significant as long as we incorporate the BCI index as well.

Our theory makes a clear distinction between agents with different skill levels. These agents perform different roles in the economy and have different occupations in equilibrium. It is important, therefore, that these results are not just driven by some average level of education, but by secondary or intermediate levels of education. In particular, the prediction of our theory for the effect of the skill level of medium-skilled agents on FDI/GDP does not hold for low-skilled agents. Thus, to study whether the results presented reflect the forces in our theory, we repeat the regression presented in column 4 of Table 10.1 but using, instead, *primary* school enrollment (PSE). The results are presented in column 5 of Table 10.1. We find reassuring that the interaction term involving primary school enrollment and communication technology appears statistically insignificant. To emphasize this conclusion we also run the regression using both levels of schooling. In column 6, the interaction term of secondary schooling remains positive and significant, while the one for primary schooling is insignificant. Overall, we interpret our results as strongly suggestive of the existence of a disproportionately positive effect of middle skills on offshoring in countries with bad communication technology.

In linking the main prediction of the theory with this empirical exercise in Table 10.1, we have equated secondary school enrollment to intermediate skills. In our setup, however, these intermediate skills are the highest skill levels in developing countries. Therefore, a reasonable concern is that the actual empirical counterpart of our intermediate skills is probably some measure of tertiary education—which leaves post-graduate education as the counterpart of high skills in the North—or a combination of tertiary and secondary education. Of course, secondary education is a requirement for tertiary education, and so the union of tertiary education and secondary educations is equivalent to using SSE. We repeated the exercise in Table 10.1 and obtain the same qualitative results using tertiary education. Given that many managers in less-developed countries are agents without college, we prefer to call intermediate skills the union of secondary and tertiary school enrollment and so, to save on space, we do not present the results using only tertiary education.

A potential concern with the results above is that our index of local communication costs is constructed using data on telephone, computer, and internet *usage*, which may lead to endogeneity of our communication cost index. FDI can determine how much agents use these technologies, which would lead to biased coefficients. Following this logic, a natural conjecture is that FDI decreases the index of bad communication technology, and it does so more the higher is secondary school enrollment. However, this mechanism would tend to bias the interaction term toward zero. Hence, this type of endogeneity would tend to reinforce our finding that the true coefficient is positive and significant. Of course, endogeneity may take other forms, and so this argument does not definitely solve the endogeneity problem. We would need better data on the state of communication technology, not the use of technology, in order to rule out other potential sources of endogeneity.

Table 10.A1 in the Appendix presents the same six regressions using OLS instead of quantile regressions. The results are qualitatively similar. We obtain all the right signs and all the relevant coefficients are significant, although only at the 10% level. Admittedly, this body of evidence, although consistent with the theory, is more suggestive than conclusive. Bilateral data (and preferably at the industry level) seems to be needed to develop a much more complete taxonomy of the characteristics that make some countries good targets of offshoring.[24] We leave this for future research.

A final caveat of our empirical analysis is that we have used FDI flows as a proxy for offshoring in our theory. Of course, while in our theory, offshoring is a measure of real activity, in the data, FDI is a measure of financial activity. As such, FDI flows could well be affected by the characteristics of the financial system in the host country. For instance, Desai, Foley, and Hines (2004) and Antràs, Desai, and Foley (2007) show that foreign affiliates of U.S. multinational firms tend to rely relatively more on local financing (and less on FDI flows) when they operate in countries with more developed financial markets. To address this potential omitted-variable problem, we have experimented with including measures of credit-market deepness (namely domestic credit extended to the private sector and domestic credit provided by banking sector, both as a percentage of GDP) into the regression in the last column of Table 10.1. Both financial variables enter the regression with a coefficient that is not significantly different from zero, while our main interaction term remains significant and the value of the coefficient remains, essentially, unchanged.

10.7 Conclusion

The theory we develop in this chapter makes two main points. The first is that the ability of multinationals to change their organizational form and make use of agents with different talents is important to understand the decision of organizations to offshore part of their production. In our theory, this organizational change takes the form of an extra intermediate layer of management, and so the ability of these managers becomes a crucial determinant of the extensive margin of offshoring. The second is that the local communication technology of a country determines the opportunity costs of workers—since it determines the characteristics of local teams—and therefore the desirability of such a country as a target for offshoring. In order to understand this second argument, and the interaction between both arguments, it is necessary to have a general equilibrium theory where these opportunity costs and offshoring decisions are both determined in equilibrium.

These two main arguments lead to several empirical implications from among which we have highlighted one that can be readily contrasted with the data, namely, that the ability of middle-skilled agents increases offshoring by relatively more in countries where communication technology is bad than in countries where communication technology is relatively good. The empirical results we present are encouraging in that the data suggests that this is in fact the case, and that this relationship is not driven by the level of development or the availability of agents with lower skills. The model has other predictions that we have not studied empirically, most importantly, that offshoring will happen in larger teams (and with more layers) in countries where middle-skilled agents are relatively able. Since large teams are also more efficient (output per worker is higher), this also provides an implication for the productivity of the firms that offshore to these countries. An empirical investigation of this prediction requires, of course, data on firm characteristics, and so we leave it for future work.

Appendix: Data and Empirical Analysis

10A.1 Communication Index

The raw data used to construct our index of the state of communication technology in each country is taken from the online version of the World

Bank's World Development Indicators (WDI). The index is constructed using data on telephone, computer, and Internet usage. The three series are, respectively, (i) fixed-line and mobile phone subscribers per 1,000 inhabitants; (ii) personal computers per 1,000 inhabitants; and (iii) Internet users per 1,000 inhabitants. To build the communication index, we first average the three indicators for the 1993–2002 period, and then we perform a factor analysis of the correlation matrix. We used the first factor as the basis for the country-by-country communication index, which has mean 0 and standard deviation equal to 1.

A 0.5 cutoff in this index yields a division of countries into 93 countries with "bad" communication technologies ($BCI = 1$) and 29 countries with "good" communication technologies ($BCI = 0$). We list the countries in each group below.

10A.1.1 Countries with Low Communication Costs ($BCI = 0$)

Australia, Austria, Belgium, Canada, Cyprus, Germany, Denmark, Estonia, Finland, France, Hong Kong, Iceland, Ireland, Israel, Italy, Japan, Korea, Luxembourg, Malta, Netherlands, New Zealand, Norway, Portugal, Slovenia, Spain, Sweden, Switzerland, United Kingdom, United States.

10A.1.2 Countries with High Communications Costs ($BCI = 1$)

Albania, Algeria, Armenia, Bahrain, Bangladesh, Barbados, Belize, Benin, Bolivia, Botswana, Brazil, Bulgaria, Burkina Faso, Burundi, Cambodia, Cape Verde, Chad, Chile, Colombia, Costa Rica, Cote d'Ivoire, Croatia, Czech Republic, Djibouti, Dominica, Ecuador, Egypt, El Salvador, Equatorial Guinea, Eritrea, Ethiopia, Fiji, Gambia, Georgia, Ghana, Greece, Grenada, Guatemala, Guinea, Guyana, Hungary, Indonesia, Jamaica, Jordan, Kenya, Kuwait, Lao, Latvia, Lithuania, Madagascar, Malaysia, Maldives, Mauritania, Mauritius, Mexico, Moldova, Mongolia, Morocco, Mozambique, Nicaragua, Niger, Nigeria, Oman, Panama, Papua New Guinea, Paraguay, Peru, Philippines, Poland, Romania, Samoa, Saudi Arabia, Seychelles, Slovakia, South Africa, St. Kitts and Nevis, St. Lucia, St. Vincent and the Grenadines, Swaziland, Syria, Tanzania, Togo, Tonga, Trinidad and Tobago, Tunisia, Ukraine, Uruguay, Vanuatu, Venezuela, Vietnam, Yemen, Zambia, Zimbabwe.

Table 10.A1 OLS regression results

	(1)	(2)	(3)	(4)	(5)	(6)
	Dependent variable: $\frac{FDI}{GDP}$					
	Years: 1993–2002 averages					
Constant	2.08***	21.91	21.91**	22.86**	−10.15	1.65
	(.70)	(15.19)	(10.79)	(11.39)	(19.41)	(19.81)
SSE	.026**	−.192	−.193	−.190		−.240*
	(.011)	(.168)	(.120)	(.120)		(.126)
SSE*BCI			.219*	.221*		.261**
			(.120)	(.121)		(.127)
BCI			−19.83*	−20.14*	10.31	−.035
			(10.82)	(10.93)	(19.13)	(19.65)
PSE*BCI					−.110	−.244
					(.196)	(.203)
PSE					.151	.268
					(.194)	(.201)
$\frac{GDP}{Pop}$				−.119	−.0001	−.168
				(.441)	(.378)	(.445)
Countries	$BCI = 1$	$BCI = 0$	All	All	All	All
Number of observations	92	28	120	120	120	120
R^2	0.04	0.05	0.07	0.07	0.05	0.08

Note: Standard deviations are in parentheses. The symbols ***, **, and * denote significant coefficients at 1%, 5%, and 10% levels.

10A.2 Empirical Analysis

The empirical analysis in Table 10.1 (Section 10.6) presents a quantile (median) regression, or least absolute value model; the model chooses, by maximum likelihood, the vector of regressors b to minimize $\sum_i |y - xb|$ (rather than, as in OLS, $\sum_i (y - xb)^2$). Such an estimator is preferred whenever there are substantial outliers in the dependent variable, which are given excessive weight in the calculation of the regression by OLS.

Our results remain, however, unchanged if we proceed by OLS and restrict our attention to a sample of countries with $FDI/GDP < 40\%$. Such restriction excludes from the analysis two extreme outliers: Luxembourg, with an average FDI/GDP for the sample period of 459.5% and Equatorial Guinea with an average of 43.84%. These should be compared to a sample distribution with quantiles 1.44%, 2.93%, and 4.86%. For completeness, in Table 10.A1, we present OLS results in exactly the same order as in Table 10.1 in the body of the chapter.

ACKNOWLEDGMENTS

We are thankful to Daron Acemoglu for a very helpful discussion at the AEA meetings and for encouraging us to explore the issues studied in this chapter. We thank seminar participants at the AEA meetings, Brown University, the NBER ITI meetings, and the Globalisation and the Organisation of Firms conference, as well as Doireann Fitzgerald, Elhanan Helpman, and Steve Redding for useful comments.

NOTES

1. See Feenstra (1998) or the more recent but less formal account in Friedman (2005).
2. In the model, whether host-country domestic teams are formed or not depends on the level of Southern communication costs. We stick to this interpretation in the empirical section of the chapter, but it should be clear that, in the real world, other technological and institutional factors play an important role in fostering or hindering the formation of such teams.
3. Our results also seem to accord well with casual discussions of particular offshoring decisions. For instance, Spar (1998) and Larraín, López-Calva, and Rodríguez-Clare (2001) describe the decision of Intel to locate a microprocessor plant in Costa Rica in 1996. Intel was considering four alternative locations in Latin America: Argentina, Brazil, Chile, and Mexico. Both these studies describe the main factors that made Intel finally decide to locate the plant in Costa Rica despite frequent bottlenecks in telecommunication and electricity services in the country. The authors emphasize the availability of highly trained graduates in Costa Rica as being one of the decisive factors. Further evidence of the importance that Intel gave to middle skills comes from the active involvement of the company in redefining the curricula of the country's technical high schools and advanced-training programs (Spar 1998).
4. Our model is also related to models of vertical FDI and outsourcing, where the incentive to fragment the production process is driven by factor-price differentials (see Helpman 1984; Yeaple 2003; and Antràs 2003).
5. Garicano and Rossi-Hansberg (2006b) use a similar framework, with a discrete number of skill levels, to study the emergence of large U.S. corporations at the turn of the twentieth century.
6. This implies that the relative size of the North is given by $s_h/(s_m + s_l)$.

7. It would be straightforward to extend the analysis and allow domestic team formation in the North. This would, however, substantially increase the taxonomy of cases to consider without providing many insights into the role of Southern skills in fostering offshoring.

8. More specifically, it is never optimal to assign two agents with the same skill level to different layers of an organization (or to have subordinates with higher talent than managers). The reason is that then managers would not increase the output of subordinates but the cost of production would increase by their wage (see Garicano and Rossi-Hansberg 2006a).

9. This feature is also consistent with widely available data suggesting that foreign affiliates of multinational firms appear to be more productive than comparable domestic firms in the same host country (see, for instance, Aitken and Harrison 1999).

10. Note also that if one could systematize these processes in manuals, we would expect markets for this technology not to form. The breakdown of this market would result from low marginal costs of reproducing this technology combined with the imperfect enforcement of patent laws.

11. Without this assumption, high-skilled Northern agents would not appropriate the profits of the team and would thus be indifferent to the organizational form and the decision to offshore.

12. We ignore the possibility of "mixed equilibria," with some of the four situations below coexisting. The discussion below should make clear that, for a sufficiently low fraction s_h of high-skilled agents (our maintained assumption), these mixed equilibria can only happen in knife-edge cases.

13. What do we mean by a "sufficiently low s_h"? For this particular case, the condition for medium-skilled agents to be in excess supply at a wage higher than z_m is given by $s_h < s_m h_l(1 - z_m)$. Analogous conditions can be derived for the other cases.

14. Note that this is not inconsistent with skill stratification and positive sorting (see Garicano and Rossi-Hansberg 2006a).

15. This is because, when $h_L > (z_h - z_l) / (1 - z_l)$, the left-hand side of (10.5) is decreasing in z_m, and the condition is not satisfied for $z_m = z_l$.

16. Note that in order for three-layer teams to be *necessary* for the emergence of offshoring, we need that both $z_m > \widehat{z}_m$ and $z_h h_l > \widehat{h}_L > h_L$. This is to say, we need middle-skilled agents in the South to be relatively able and the cost of communicating knowledge *across* borders to be large relative to the cost of communicating knowledge *within* borders.

17. Since $\widehat{h}_S$ depends on z_m, increases in z_m may move the equilibrium away from the set in which the proposition applies, namely, $h_S \geq \widehat{h}_S$. However, we show in proposition 10.2 that when $h_S < \widehat{h}_S$, the equilibrium has the same properties.

18. Note also that when high-skilled Northern agents are (partially) self-employed, then they will earn the same wage regardless of the equilibrium organization. They are thus indifferent between different organizational modes.

19. This is not the case in Garicano and Rossi-Hansberg (2006a) where the incentives for top managers to acquire knowledge increase with the size of their teams, making teams of three (or more) layers profitable even though agents in lower layers can organize by themselves.

20. This follows from

$$\frac{\partial^2 \left(\frac{z_h - z_m \frac{h_L}{h_S} - z_l \left(1 - \frac{h_L}{h_S} \right)}{h_I (1 - z_m)} \right)}{\partial z_m \partial h_S} = \frac{h_L \left(1 - z_l \right)}{h_S^2 h_I \left(1 - z_m \right)^2} > 0.$$

21. In this case $w_l = \left[1 - h_S \left(1 - z_l \right) \right] z_m$ and $w_m = z_m$. This can be used to show that in the case of three-layer offshoring or two-layer offshoring with low types, $\partial^2 w_h / \partial z_m \partial h_S > 0$, while in the case of two-layer offshoring with medium types, $\partial^2 w_h / \partial z_m \partial h_S = 0$.

22. We divide by GDP since the absolute level of offshoring in the model can be arbitrarily determined by choice of productivity and population size. We are aware that FDI is an imperfect measure of the volume of offshoring (see Lipsey 2003). Unfortunately, data on the operations of offshoring facilities is not available for a large cross section of host countries.

23. The cutoff used to build the dummy variable *BCI* is 0.5, which corresponds to one-half standard deviation above the mean communication index. All our results are robust to increasing or decreasing this cutoff by one-quarter standard deviation. Consistent with the model, if we lower the threshold even more (say, to the mean communication index, that is, 0) the results become insignificant although they have the predicted sign. The reason is that we are mixing countries for which the effect of middle skills should be positive with countries (such as Kuwait) for which the effect should be negative, which leads to insignificant coefficients.

24. See Ramondo (2005) for an attempt along these lines.

REFERENCES

Aitken, B., and A. Harrison. 1999. "Do Domestic Firms Benefit from Foreign Direct Investment? Evidence from Panel Data." *American Economic Review* 89(3): 605–18.

Antràs, Pol. 2003. "Firms, Contracts, and Trade Structure." *Quarterly Journal of Economics* 118(4):1375–1418.

Antràs, Pol, Mihir A. Desai, and C. Fritz Foley. 2007. "Multinational Firms, FDI Flows and Imperfect Capital Markets." Mimeo, Harvard University.

Antràs, Pol, Luis Garicano, and Esteban Rossi-Hansberg. 2006. "Offshoring in a Knowledge Economy." *Quarterly Journal of Economics* 121(1):31–77.

Arrow, Kenneth J. 1974. *The Limits of Organization*. New York: Norton.

Burstein, Ariel, and Alexander Monge-Naranjo. 2009. "Aggregate Consequences of Foreign Firms in Developing Countries." *Quarterly Journal of Economics* 124(1).

Desai, Mihir A., C. Fritz Foley, and James R. Hines Jr. 2004. "A Multinational Perspective on Capital Structure Choice and Internal Capital Markets." *Journal of Finance* 59(6):2451–88.

Feenstra, Robert C. 1998. "Integration of Trade and Disintegration of Production in the Global Economy." *Journal of Economic Perspectives* 12(4):31–50.

Friedman, Thomas L. 2005. *The World Is Flat: A Brief History of the Twenty-First Century*. New York: Farrar, Straus and Giroux.

Garicano, Luis. 2000. "Hierarchies and the Organization of Knowledge in Production." *Journal of Political Economy* 108(5):874–904.

Garicano, Luis, and Esteban Rossi-Hansberg. 2006a. "Organization and Inequality in a Knowledge Economy." *Quarterly Journal of Economics* 121(4): 1383–1435.

———. 2006b. "The Knowledge Economy at the Turn of the Twentieth Century: The Emergence of Hierarchies." *Journal of the European Economic Association* 4(2–3):396–403.

Helpman, Elhanan. 1984. "A Simple Theory of International Trade with Multinational Corporations." *Journal of Political Economy* 92(3):451–71.

Larraín, Felipe, Luis F. López-Calva, and Andrés Rodríguez-Clare. 2001. "Intel: A Case Study of Foreign Direct Investment in Central America." In *Economic Development in Central America, vol. 1: Growth and Internationalization*, ch. 6, ed. Felipe Larraín. Cambridge, MA: Harvard University Press.

Lipsey, Robert E. 2003. "Foreign Direct Investment and the Operations of Multinational Firms: Concepts, History, and Data." In *Handbook of International Trade*, eds. E. Kwan Choi and James Harrigan. Oxford, UK: Blackwell.

Lucas, Robert E. Jr. 1978. "On the Size Distribution of Business Firms." *Bell Journal of Economics* 9:508–23.

Ramondo, Natalia. 2005. "Size, Geography, and Multinational Production." Mimeo, University of Chicago.

Spar, Debora. 1998. "Attracting High Technology Investment: Intel's Costa Rican Plant." FIAS occasional paper 11. Washington, D.C.: World Bank.

Yeaple, Stephen. 2003. "The Role of Skill Endowments in the Structure of U.S. Outward FDI." *Review of Economics and Statistics* 85(3):726–34.

List of Contributors

POL ANTRÀS, Professor of Economics, Department of Economics, Harvard University; CEPR and NBER

JAMES A. COSTANTINI, Assistant Professor of Strategy, INSEAD, Singapore

JONATHAN EATON, Professor of Economics, New York University; and NBER

MARCELA ESLAVA, Assistant Professor, Department of Economics, Universidad de Los Andes, Bogotá

ROBERT C. FEENSTRA, Professor of Economics, and C. Bryan Cameron Distinguished Chair in International Economics, Department of Economics, University of California at Davis; and NBER

LUIS GARICANO, Professor of Economics and Strategy, University of Chicago, Graduate School of Business; and CEPR

GENE M. GROSSMAN, Jacob Viner Professor of International Economics, Department of Economics and Woodrow Wilson School of Public and International Affairs, Princeton University; CEPR and NBER

ELHANAN HELPMAN, Galen L. Stone Professor of International Trade, Department of Economics, Harvard University; CEPR, CIFAR, and NBER

MAURICE KUGLER, CIGI Chair in International Public Policy and Professor of Economics, Wilfrid Laurier University

HONG MA, PhD candidate, Department of Economics, University of California at Davis

DALIA MARIN, Professor of Economics, Department of Economics, University of Munich; CEPR and NBER

MARC J. MELITZ, Professor of Economics and International Affairs, Department of Economics and Woodrow Wilson School of Public and International Affairs, Princeton University; CEPR and NBER

NATHAN NUNN, Assistant Professor of Economics, Department of Economics, Harvard University; and NBER

GIANMARCO I. P. OTTAVIANO, Professor of Economics, Department of Economics, University of Bologna; CEPR and FEEM

ESTEBAN ROSSI-HANSBERG, Professor of Economics and International Affairs, Department of Economics and Woodrow Wilson School of Public and International Affairs, Princeton University; and NBER

DANIEL TREFLER, J. Douglas and Ruth Grant Canada Research Chair in Competitiveness and Prosperity, Joseph L. Rotman School of Management and Department of Economics, University of Toronto; CIFAR and NBER

JAMES R. TYBOUT, Professor of Economics, Department of Economics, Pennsylvania State University; and NBER

THIERRY VERDIER, Scientific Director, Paris School of Economics; Professor of Economics, School of Social Sciences, University of Southampton; and CEPR

STEPHEN ROSS YEAPLE, Associate Professor, Department of Economics, Pennsylvania State University; and NBER

Author Index

Page numbers with an "n" indicate citations in notes; page numbers with an "r" indicate citations in references.